THE RISE OF
SOUTHERN REPUBLICANS

EARL BLACK

MERLE BLACK

THE RISE OF
SOUTHERN REPUBLICANS

THE BELKNAP PRESS OF
HARVARD UNIVERSITY PRESS
Cambridge, Massachusetts, & London, England
2002

Library of Congress Cataloging-in-Publication Data
Black, Earl, 1942–
The rise of southern Republicans / Earl Black and Merle Black.
p. cm.
Includes index.
ISBN 0-674-00728-X
1. Republican Party (U.S. : 1854–) 2. Southern States–Politics
and government—1951– I. Black, Merle. II. Title.
JK2356 .B55 2002
324.2734′0975—dc21   2001051531

AGAIN FOR OUR FAMILIES
SENA AND SHAMEEM
DEBRA, CLAIRE, AND JULIA

ACKNOWLEDGMENTS

We are grateful to many individuals who have helped us make this book a reality. It was our good fortune to have the advice of Richard F. Fenno Jr. and Charles S. Bullock III. Readers so knowledgeable and so generous are rare. We thank them for their friendship, encouragement, and constructive criticism.

At Harvard University Press we especially wish to thank Aida Donald, who has long encouraged our efforts to write books about southern politics and who, before her retirement, got this project squared away. Joyce Seltzer then guided us swiftly and expertly through the editorial process; and Ann Hawthorne improved the book with skilled and meticulous editing.

Excellent research assistance came from Jonathan Williamson, Adam Cooper, and Paul Fabrizio at Emory and from Brian Posler, Carl Rhodes, Nancy Martorano, Martin Johnson, and Jason Yuan at Rice. Jonathan processed most of the survey data used in the book and is due special thanks. Our colleagues Randy Strahan and Alan Abramowitz generously shared their expert knowledge of congressional politics, and Alan graciously provided results from the 2000 Voter News Service Exit Poll. Paige Schneider expanded our understanding of the importance of religious conservatives in the southern Republican party.

In this book we have made frequent use of the exit polls conducted in each presidential election from 1976 to 1988 by CBS News and the *New York Times,* as well as exit polls of selected Senate and House campaigns conducted by these news organizations in the 1980s. In the elections from 1992 to 2000, we have used the Voter News Service General Election exit polls. We have also made use of National Election Studies of presidential elections from 1952 to 1996 conducted by the Center for Political Studies of the Institute for Social Research at the University of Michigan. The National Election Studies surveys, the CBS News/New York Times exit polls, and the Voter News Service exit polls were made available through the Inter-University Consortium for Political and Social Research. We are grateful to the consortium for the use of these data collections; neither the collector of the original data nor the consortium bears any responsibility for the analysis or interpretations presented here.

We wish to thank the *Journal of Politics* for permission to incorporate material from Earl Black, "The Newest Southern Politics," *Journal of Politics* 60 (August 1998).

Our greatest debts, impossible to repay, are to our wives, Sena Black and Debra Larson, and to our daughters, Shameem, Claire, and Julia. It is a joy to dedicate this book to them. Shameem prepared the index.

All errors of fact and interpretation are our responsibility.

CONTENTS

1. The Southern Transformation   1

2. Confronting the Democratic Juggernaut   40

3. The Promising Peripheral South   72

4. The Impenetrable Deep South   114

5. The Democratic Smother   138

6. The Democratic Domination   174

7. Reagan's Realignment of White Southerners   205

8. A New Party System in the South   241

9. The Peripheral South Breakthrough   268

10. The Deep South Challenge   294

11. The Republican Surge   328

12. Competitive South, Competitive America   369

Notes   407

Index   433

THE RISE OF
SOUTHERN REPUBLICANS

1

THE SOUTHERN TRANSFORMATION

In 1964 Strom Thurmond of South Carolina, a tenacious champion of unreconstructed southern conservatism, abandoned the Democratic party to become the first Republican senator from the Deep South in the twentieth century. Three decades later Thurmond was bound and determined to make history again, this time by serving longer than any other U.S. senator. To satisfy his remarkable personal ambition he needed to win an unprecedented eighth term. Ignoring some pleas and many hints that he should retire gracefully, in 1996 the aged Thurmond asked friendly crowds to support him "just one mo' time."[1]

Late on election night, when his victory was at last assured, a dazed and plainly exhausted Thurmond was carefully shuffled to a podium for the customary televised victory speech. Looking not a day older than ninety-three, Thurmond mumbled a few words to the people of South Carolina. The senator made no reference to issues, ideology, or political principles, nor did he venture any coherent interpretation of his achievement. He said absolutely nothing of substance. Instead he slowly read, page by page, prepared thank-you messages directed to the men who had masterminded his final campaign. It was a thoroughly perfunctory and lifeless performance. That necessary duty completed, Thurmond was then ushered away a few steps, whereupon a young television reporter stuck a microphone in his face, described the campaign as extremely "hard-fought," and inquired whether the senator might harbor any "hard feelings" toward his Democratic opponent. Instantly

Thurmond perked up. "No haard feelins' on mah paart," he shouted, *"Ah won!"*[2]

Republicans from the South have transformed American politics. The collapse of the solid Democratic South and the emergence of southern Republicanism, first in presidential politics and later in elections for Congress, have established a new reality for America: two permanently competitive national political parties. Not since Democrats battled Whigs before the Civil War has there been such a thoroughly nationalized two-party system. The Democratic party has always been a national enterprise, commanding durable strength in both the South and the North. Traditionally, the Republican party's geographic reach was quite different. A broadly based *northern* party, Republicans maintained active wings in the Northeast, Midwest, West, and Border states but secured only a nominal presence in the South. Apart from the short-lived Reconstruction era, for many generations southern Republicanism "scarcely deserve[d] the name of party. It waver[ed] somewhat between an esoteric cult on the order of a lodge and a conspiracy for plunder in accord with the accepted customs of our politics."[3]

When the Republicans recaptured both houses of Congress in 1994 for the first time since 1952, they did not construct their Senate and House majorities in the old-fashioned way. Republican control of Congress traditionally involved a purely sectional strategy in which enormous Republican surpluses in the North trumped huge Republican deficits in the South. The novel feature of the Republicans' 1994 breakthrough was its national character. Republicans won majorities of House and Senate seats in both the North *and* the South, a feat they had not achieved since 1872, and their new southern majorities were vital to the Republicans' national victories. Across the nation Republicans as well as Democrats now realistically believe they have fighting chances to win both the White House and Congress in any particular election. Focusing on elections to both the Senate and the House of Representatives, this book examines the regional causes and national consequences of rising southern Republicanism.

It is easy to forget just how thoroughly the Democratic party once dominated southern congressional elections. In 1950 there were no Republican senators from the South and only 2 Republican representatives out of 105 in the southern House delegation. Nowhere else in the

United States had a major political party been so feeble for so many decades. A half-century later Republicans constituted *majorities* of the South's congressional delegations—13 of 22 southern senators and 71 of 125 representatives. This immense partisan conversion is our subject. Just as the emergence of southern Republicanism restored competition to America's presidential politics, so has the rise of Republican senators and representatives from the South revitalized congressional politics.

The old southern politics was transparently undemocratic and thoroughly racist. "Southern political institutions," as V. O. Key Jr. demonstrated, were deliberately constructed to subordinate "the Negro population and, externally, to block threatened interferences from the outside with these local arrangements."[4] By protecting white supremacy, southern Democrats in Congress institutionalized massive racial injustice for generations. Eventually the civil rights movement challenged the South's racial status quo and inspired a national political climate in which southern Democratic senators could no longer kill civil rights legislation. Led by President Lyndon B. Johnson of Texas, overwhelming majorities of northern Democrats and northern Republicans united to enact the Civil Rights Act of 1964 and the Voting Rights Act of 1965. Landmark federal intervention reformed southern race relations and helped destabilize the traditional one-party system. In the fullness of time the Democratic party's supremacy gave way to genuinely competitive two-party politics.[5]

But if the old solid Democratic South has vanished, a comparably solid Republican South has not developed. Nor is one likely to emerge. Republican politicians hold majorities of the region's House and Senate seats, but their majorities are much smaller than those traditionally maintained by southern Democrats. Even more important, neither Republicans nor Democrats enjoy majority status among the southern electorate. In the old southern politics, whites overwhelmingly considered themselves Democrats and voted accordingly. Political battles in the contemporary South feature two competitive minority parties rather than the unmistakable domination of a single party. "Republicans know we are a minority party," observed former Republican senator Howard H. Baker of Tennessee even as his party enjoyed huge victories in 1994, "but the Democrats have had a terrible time facing [the fact] that they are, too."[6] For Republicans the new competitive situation represents a vast improvement over their past standing, while for Democrats the transition from an assured majority party to a competitive minority party has been experienced as a marked deterioration in their grassroots base.

Modern competitive two-party politics is grounded in the region's rapidly growing and immensely diverse population. The central political cleavage, as ancient as the South itself, involves race. When the Republican party nominated Arizona Senator Barry Goldwater—one of the few northern senators who had opposed the Civil Rights Act—as their presidential candidate in 1964, the party attracted many racist southern whites but permanently alienated African-American voters. Beginning with the Goldwater-versus-Johnson campaign more southern whites voted Republican than Democratic, a pattern that has recurred in every subsequent presidential election. Two decades later, in the middle of Ronald Reagan's presidency, more southern whites began to call themselves Republicans than Democrats, a development that has also persisted. These two Great White Switches, first in presidential voting and then almost a generation later in partisan identification, laid the foundations for highly competitive two-party politics in the South. Gradually a new southern politics emerged in which blacks and liberal to moderate whites anchored the Democratic party while many conservative and some moderate whites formed a growing Republican party that owed little to Abraham Lincoln but much to Goldwater and even more to Reagan. Elections in the contemporary South ordinarily separate extraordinarily large Democratic majorities of blacks from smaller Republican majorities of whites.[7]

Yet modern southern politics involves more than its obvious racial divisions. The South, an increasingly complex society, is the largest region in the United States. More than 84 million people, three of every ten Americans according to the 2000 Census, now reside in the eleven states of the old Confederacy. During the 1990s the region's population grew by 19 percent, much faster than the increase (11 percent) that occurred in the rest of the nation, and its congressional delegation expanded from 125 to 131 seats in the 2002 apportionment.[8] The South's population growth was rooted in the liberating effects of civil rights legislation and the tremendous expansion of the economy. As Dan Balz and Ronald Brownstein have concluded, "The decline of the agrarian South and the rise of a modern economy grounded in manufacturing, defense, tourism, services, and technology has been, by anyone's measure, one of the great success stories of the late twentieth century–but in creating a more diversified society, the South's transformation made it difficult for Democrats to speak for the interests of all, as they once claimed to do."[9] Whites and blacks born and raised in the region no longer had to leave in search of better opportunities in the North. Many individuals reared elsewhere in the nation and world–whites, blacks, Hispanics, Asians, and others–now found the South an acceptable, even desirable, place in which to work and retire.

The rise of a middle and upper-middle class has produced millions of voters with substantial incomes subject to substantial federal and state taxation. Many of these upwardly mobile individuals, wanting to keep the lion's share of their earnings, view the Republicans as far more sympathetic than the Democrats to their economic interests and aspirations. Another major fault line divides white southerners who are part of the religious right political movement (strongly pro-Republican) from the much larger group who are not (slightly pro-Republican). And among whites who are not attracted to conservative religious groups, men are strongly pro-Republican while women are more evenly divided in their partisanship. Thus economic class, religion, and gender also structure the social foundations of southern two-party politics.

THE SOUTHERN REPUBLICAN SURGE

In January 1995, at the beginning of the 104th Congress, the power and visibility of the southern Republicans transcended their sheer numbers. Never before in American history had southerners, much less aggressively conservative southerners, dominated the Republican leadership in the House of Representatives. All three of the most influential leaders of the new Republican majority in the House of Representatives–Speaker of the House Newt Gingrich, of Atlanta, Georgia; Majority Leader Dick Armey, of Dallas, Texas; and Whip Tom DeLay, of Houston, Texas–represented overwhelmingly white, suburban, middle-class districts in key southern metropolitan areas. Southern Republicanism especially thrived in the region's new suburbs. "In concert with the economic changes, in-migration from the North and the swell of refugees from the farms to the cities and the imposition of court-ordered busing gave rise to a suburban South where one had never existed," observe Balz and Brownstein. "Around cities like Dallas and Houston, Atlanta, Birmingham, Orlando, Raleigh, Richmond, Charlotte, and Greenville, suburbs sprouted relentlessly . . . Almost every new housing development rising in the suburban and exurban counties of the South represented another potential Republican enclave and a further nail in the Democrats' coffin."[10]

Operating from their safely Republican districts, Gingrich, Armey, and DeLay epitomized the interests, beliefs, values, and priorities of the South's rising white middle class. Gingrich's political base, "Newtland," located in the northwestern Atlanta suburb of Cobb County, symbolized the worldview of much of modern southern Republicanism. According to *New York Times* reporter Peter Applebome, "Gingrich likes to cite Cobb County as an entrepreneurial, technologically savvy model for a Republican America of economic prosperity and conservative values."

As Gingrich casually explained the lay of the land in 1994:

"What they [his constituents] find here is a sort of Norman Rockwell world with fiberoptic computers and jet airplanes. But the values that would have been the *Saturday Evening Post* of the mid-fifties are the values of most of these people now." Soon he was on a roll, contrasting the pristine work ethic of Cobb versus the "welfare state" values of Atlanta, a pitch as old as the South. Fifteen years ago even a Strom Thurmond or Jesse Helms would have been leery of using the most transparent of codes to stigmatize a whole race. But the South they grew up in was one where blacks and whites always, on some level, had to confront one another. Cobb's past was full of the starkest issues of race, but in Cobb now blacks were largely symbolic rather than real—representing the unseen menace, horror, and decay of Atlanta, 70 percent black, just across the Chattahoochee [River]—so Gingrich's words flew out in his usual, breezy, unfiltered flow.

"People in Cobb don't object to upper-middle class neighbors who keep their lawn cut and move to the area to avoid crime," he [Gingrich] went on. "What people worry about is the bus line gradually destroying one apartment complex after another, bringing people out for public housing who have no middle-class values and whose kids as they become teenagers often are centers of robbery and where the schools collapse because the parents who live in the apartment complexes don't care that the kids don't do well in school and the whole school collapses."

Gingrich concluded this remarkable interview "with a ringing endorsement of his constituents. 'It's the places like Cobb that are entrepreneurial, that have weak unions, that have a strong work ethic, that are going to do well,' he said." In the suburbs of "Newtland," as well as in scores of small towns and rural areas across the South, the dominant beliefs summed to "Low tax, low union, strong work ethic, strong commitment to family and community."[11]

Southerners were also conspicuous among Republican leaders in the Senate, although they were initially less prominent than in the House of Representatives. While Robert Dole of Kansas was unopposed as he shifted from minority leader to majority leader, Trent Lott of Mississippi successfully challenged Dole's veteran deputy, Alan Simpson of Wyoming, for the position of Republican whip. Mississippi's Thad Cochran continued in the third leadership position as the Republican conference chairman, and Connie Mack of Florida filled Lott's vacancy as conference secretary. Southerners thus held three of the four elected Republican leadership positions at the beginning of the 104th Congress, and Lott later defeated Cochran for majority leader when Dole resigned his Senate seat to run for president in 1996.

Within the Democratic party different regional realities prevailed. Throughout most of the twentieth century a southern Democrat had usually held at least one of the House Democrats' top leadership positions (Speaker, majority leader, or whip when the Democrats were the majority party and minority leader or minority whip when they were not). After Texas Democrat Jim Wright resigned as House Speaker in 1989, however, the new leadership chosen by the House Democratic caucus consisted of Washington's Tom Foley as Speaker, Missouri's Richard Gephardt as majority leader, and, for the first time, an African American, Philadelphia's William Gray, as whip.[12] Since then not a single southerner has appeared in the upper ranks of Democratic leadership in the House of Representatives, a telling indicator of the region's declining influence in the congressional party. Indeed, when Charlie Rose of North Carolina rashly challenged Gephardt of Missouri for the position of minority leader after the 1994 election, he was resoundingly defeated in the Democratic caucus.

In the Senate Jim Sasser of Tennessee, the influential chair of the Budget Committee, expected to succeed the retiring George Mitchell of Maine in 1995 as Democratic majority leader. Only reelection to a fourth term stood between Sasser and the leadership of the Senate Democrats. Yet despite his excellent prospects, a political unknown drove Sasser out of the Senate in 1994. After David Pryor of Arkansas subsequently decided not to seek reelection as conference secretary, the nine remaining southern Democrats entered the 104th Congress without formal representation in their party's leadership. Times had indeed changed radically when southerners could achieve major leadership positions in the Republican party while failing to do so in the Democratic party.

Overrepresenting southerners in the Republican House leadership, and especially overrepresenting southerners with utterly safe suburban districts, placed a national media spotlight on combative conservatives drawn from the most conservative region in the country. Gingrich, Armey, and DeLay assuredly knew how to challenge and confront House Democratic leaders, but they were completely inexperienced in the practicalities of governance. Their economic conservatism translated into an ambitious attempt to shrink the size of the national government that threatened (or could easily be attacked as so doing) long-established New Deal and Great Society entitlements, ranging from Social Security, Medicare, and welfare to a wide array of domestic programs with established beneficiaries.

Beyond threatening economic benefits, the southern Republicans' dependence on the religious right meant that public policies involving such social and cultural flashpoints as abortion, gun control, school prayer, and the treatment of gays and lesbians appeared to be up for grabs. The incessant moralizing of the new Republican leaders quickly raised fears and anxieties among many Americans, North and South, who did not share the southern Republicans' cultural values, economic conservatism, and policy objectives generally. Particularly under Gingrich's mercurial leadership, the defining image of the congressional Republicans was one of a southern-led Republican party not only bent on telling millions of Americans precisely how they should and should not live their lives but even willing to shut down the federal government in order to get their way. Republican actions, particularly as communicated to the nation by news media generally unsympathetic to the Grand Old Party, resulted in a devastating portrait of the House Republicans as irresponsible political extremists.

By winning an unexpected victory, the House Republicans assumed the duties of a majority party without any previous experience in that role.[13] Because of their thin majority, House Republicans could pass their conservative program for reform—Gingrich's Contract with America—only by establishing unprecedented party unity between northern Republicans and southern Republicans. Although the southern Republican leaders and many rank-and-file southern Republicans did not have to face the discipline or accountability of running in highly competitive districts, fewer northern Republicans enjoyed the luxury of similarly safe districts. Many northern Republicans were forced to vote more conservatively than they wished, and the result was precarious Republican national majorities during the 1990s (see Table 1.1). While the southern Republicans increased their lead over southern Democrats from three seats in 1994 to seventeen in 1996, in the North the Republican surplus fell from twenty-three in 1994 to three in 1996 and dropped to a five-seat deficit two years later. After 1998 southern surpluses alone accounted for the Republicans' tiny majorities in the House of Representatives. In the Senate Republicans maintained small southern and northern surpluses from 1994 through 1998. However, the 2000 Senate elections resulted in a partisan standoff in which the Republicans' southern surplus of four seats equaled the party's deficit in the rest of the nation, and only the vote of Republican vice president Richard Cheney allowed the GOP to organize the Senate. This unusual pattern of Republican control was exceedingly short-lived in the Senate. In May 2001 Vermont senator James Jeffords abandoned the Republican party,

Table 1.1 Precarious Republican majorities: sectionalism and the congressional party battle, 1992–2000

Seats	1992			1994			1996			1998			2000		
	R	D	R-D	R	D	R-D	R	D	R-D	R	D	R-D	R	D	R-D
House of Representatives															
North	128	181	-53	166	143	+23	156	153	+3	152	157	-5	151	158	-7
South	48	77	-29	64	61	+3	71	54	+17	71	54	+17	71	53	+18
Nation	176	258	-82	230	204	+26	227	207	+20	223	211	+12	222	211	+11
Senate															
North	34	44	-10	40	38	+2	40	38	+2	41	37	+4	37	41	-4
South	9	13	-4	13	9	+4	15	7	+8	14	8	+6	13	9	+4
Nation	43	57	-14	53	47	+6	55	45	+10	55	45	+10	50	50	0

Sources: Calculated from *Congressional Quarterly Weekly Report*, various issues.

declared himself an independent, and voted to reorganize the Senate under Democratic leadership. Republican strength in the South clearly did not guarantee GOP control of Congress.

THE SHAPE OF THE SOUTHERN CONGRESSIONAL DELEGATION

The unique characteristics of the South's modern House delegation can best be appreciated when set against historical patterns of representation. Figure 1.1 tracks the percentage distribution of southern House seats among white Democrats, white Republicans, black Republicans, and black Democrats in each congressional election from 1866 through 2000. During Reconstruction the Union Army occupied much of the South and oversaw the establishment of Republican state governments. Enfranchising former slaves while disqualifying many ex-Confederates temporarily produced a political order in which Republican electorates could send mostly Republicans to the House of Representatives. Reconstruction could not withstand the intense hostility of white southerners, and the contrasting trajectories of white Republicans (swiftly descending) and white Democrats (rapidly ascending) capture its destruction. This big "X" symbolizes the annihilation of southern Republicanism.

White supremacy was the undisguised political theory and standard practice of the racist white Democrats who ended Reconstruction. Violence, intimidation, and extensive ballot-box fraud converted a congressional delegation that was nine-tenths white Republican in 1866 into one that was almost four-fifths white Democratic by 1874. An artificially Democratic electorate replaced an artificially Republican electorate. There was nothing remotely "normal" or "constitutional" about the relentlessly undemocratic and morally corrosive mechanisms that restored white Democrats to their preeminence in the southern House delegation.

Although white Republicans (unlike black Republicans) could never be stamped out completely, the term "Solid South" accurately described the white Democrats' prominence in Congress. As the protracted agrarian upheavals of the late nineteenth century subsided and the remaining black voters were driven out of the political system, the southern delegation settled down to almost perfect white Democratic domination. Having eliminated their racial and partisan opponents from the electorate,

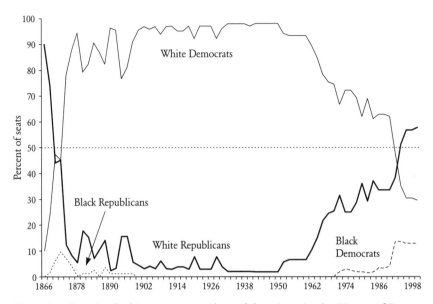

Figure 1.1 Sustained white power: southern delegations in the House of Representatives, 1866–2000. *Sources: Congressional Quarterly's Guide to U.S. Elections,* 3d ed. (Washington, D.C., 1994); *Congressional Quarterly Weekly Report,* various issues; and Raymond W. Smock, "Black Members: Nineteenth Century," in *The Encyclopedia of the United States Congress,* ed. Donald C. Bacon, Roger H. Davidson, and Morton Keller, vol. 1 (New York: Simon & Schuster, 1995), pp. 170–173.

racially conservative white Democrats chosen by racially conservative white voters easily monopolized the region's congressional delegation.

The Great Depression and New Deal maintained the lopsided partisan division of the southern House delegation. Outside the South the greatest economic catastrophe of the twentieth century revived the Democratic party and discredited the Republican party in many congressional districts. Because southern Republicans already hovered close to zero, in the South the Great Depression simply gave most whites additional reasons to hate Republicans and powerfully reinforced Democratic supremacy. Before federal intervention into southern race relations, congressional representation in the region amounted to a simple story of sustained white Democratic power.

Most of the white Democrats who served through the mid-1960s defended racial segregation and worked hard to prevent civil rights legislation. Gradually, however, as the older Democratic segregationists departed, they were replaced by younger white Democratic politicians who understood that cultivating biracial coalitions was essential to their survival. Many of the white Republicans who began to win congressional elections positioned themselves as far more conservative on racial issues than their Democratic opponents. Yet with widespread acceptance of the finality of racial change, little remains of the overt racial rhetoric that often characterized the first generation of southern Republican congressmen. By and large, Republican House members from the South emphasize their economic and social conservatism. After federal intervention the gap between white Democrats and white Republicans began to narrow, but as late as 1990 white Democrats still outnumbered white Republicans by better than three to two.

Striking partisan changes in southern representation occurred during the 1990s. In 1991, following the last election based on districts established after the 1980 Census, the South's delegation consisted of 72 white Democrats, 39 white Republicans, and 5 black Democrats. Ten years later, after the creation of many new majority black districts, it included 71 white Republicans, 1 white independent (Virginia's Virgil Goode) who caucused with the Republicans, 37 white Democrats, and 16 black Democrats. The emergence of the newest southern politics is captured by a little "X" at the end of Figure 1.1, in which white Republicans have displaced white Democrats as the new majority in the southern congressional delegation.

THE NORTHERN REPUBLICANS' SOUTHERN PROBLEM

The northern politicians who organized the Republican party in the 1850s were ambitious risk-takers. Republican leaders gambled that it was possible to win the presidency and both houses of Congress—over the long haul and not just for a few election cycles—by aligning the more numerous free states of the North against the slave states of the South. According to this audacious Lincoln Strategy, if the North could be sufficiently unified, the Republican party could write off the South entirely and still control the national government. And the most promising way to unite the North was to attack the South in presidential and congressional elections. Abraham Lincoln's 1860 campaign put Republican theory into practice. His northern triumph demonstrated that Republicans could win the presidency without the electoral votes of any slave state, and the ensuing Civil War both reflected and intensified sectional hatreds between the victorious North and the defeated South.

Preserving the Union by winning the Civil War institutionalized the Lincoln Strategy of the Republican party. The war and its aftermath produced indelible personal experiences that made sectional thinking second nature for the Civil War and Reconstruction generation and its successors. Clearly more than standard disagreements about public policy separated northerners and southerners. At stake was not ordinary sectional conflict but *battlefield sectionalism.* There was no mystery about sectional winners and losers. Sectional political cultures formed or reinforced on the battlefield became the starting point for sorting most voters into the two-party system. As a result the intense struggle between Republicans and Democrats that emerged from the Civil War and Reconstruction generally paralleled the traditional geographic division between free states and slave states. For many decades Rebels and Yankees (and their descendants) would continue to fight the political equivalent of the Civil War through the nation's two major political parties. Battlefield sectionalism funneled most victorious northerners as well as most defeated southerners toward enduring "standing decision[s]"[14] regarding their political friends and certainly their political enemies.

The revolutionary insight of the politicians who invented the Republican party–that a major political party deliberately founded on sectional rather than national interests could dominate national politics– was generally borne out by subsequent events. For seven decades the Lincoln Strategy was the Lincoln Solution (see Figure 1.2). From 1860 through 1930 the Republican party controlled the Senate in thirty-one of thirty-six Congresses.[15] In twenty-three Congresses–almost two-thirds–it won national majorities in the House of Representatives. Battlefield sectionalism explains how the Republicans achieved their remarkable success. Each dot in the figure represents a key political unit. In this book the South is defined as the eleven ex-Confederate states, the slave states that attempted to leave the Union. The North consists of the rest of the nation. It may be usefully subdivided into the Border states (the slave states that did not secede), the Northeast, the Midwest, and the West. For each political unit (including the nation) we have calculated the percentage of House seats (on the horizontal axis) and Senate seats (on the vertical axis) controlled by the Republican Party from 1860 through 1930.

From the Civil War to the Great Depression a stark sectional cleavage structured elections to Congress. All the northern regions except the Border states are clustered in the upper right quadrant, the area that identifies Republican majorities in both the Senate and the House. Republicans were especially strong in the Northeast and the Midwest, the largest northern regions. Republican strength in the North frequently produced the national majorities required by the Lincoln Strategy. The lower left quadrant contains the South and the Border states, states that the Republicans could afford to lose.

The Great Depression was the turning point in post–Civil War party politics. When Republican president Herbert Hoover proved unable to respond effectively to the calamity of mass unemployment, the nation turned to the Democratic party. President Franklin Roosevelt's inspirational, agile, and ultimately "reconstructive" leadership[16] then established a national Democratic party whose congressional victories rested on the Democratic Solid South and northern majorities or near-majorities. The Lincoln Solution quickly deteriorated into the Lincoln Dissolution (see Figure 1.2).

For the next six decades the same sectional strategy that had enabled the Republican party to win most Congresses now condemned it to permanent minority status. From 1932 through 1992 the Republicans controlled the Senate in only five and the House in merely two of thirty-one Congresses. Although the Republican party could absorb southern and Border state defeats and still control Congress, it could not lose the South, the Border states, and many northern states and still produce national majorities. In election after election the Republicans began with the same huge southern deficits as before, but they now faced a northern Democratic party identified with Roosevelt and the New Deal rather than rebellion and white supremacy.[17] During the same period the Republicans controlled majorities of Senate and House seats (57 percent in both institutions) only in the Midwest. Northeastern Republicans secured 55 percent of their Senate opportunities but only 48 percent of House contests. In the West, the entire North, and the nation as a whole

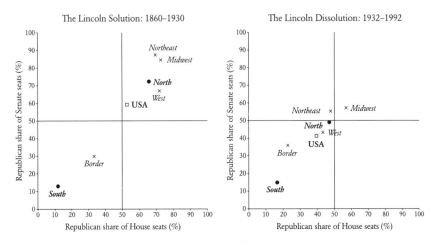

Figure 1.2 The Lincoln Strategy and Congress: durable success followed by durable failure. *Source: Congressional Quarterly's Guide to U.S. Elections,* 3d ed. (Washington, D.C., 1994).

Republicans lost more Senate and House races than they won. Clearly, without regaining lost ground in the North and reducing their enormous southern deficits, Republicans could not realistically challenge Democrats for control of Congress. The Lincoln Dissolution left the Republican party without any extensive geographic base, North or South, capable of generating sustained Republican surpluses in Senate or House elections comparable to those frequently achieved before the Great Depression in the Midwest and Northeast.

THE CHANGING ANATOMY OF BATTLEFIELD SECTIONALISM

Southern white Democratic solidarity flowed from demography as well as from politics. The North and the South were extraordinarily different societies. In addition to disagreements over the morality and future of slavery, battlefield sectionalism rested on stark differences in racial concentrations. Nothing distinguished slave states more dramatically from free states, and nothing had more obvious political implications, than the relative size of the black population. Urban-rural disparities also characterized the sections. Before and after the Civil War, the South was far more rural than the North. Demography powerfully reinforced history and thereby intensified rather than moderated sectional cleavages in the party system.

The demographic anatomy of battlefield sectionalism helps explain why Republicans have only recently become competitive in the South. Figure 1.3 presents results for 1880, 1930, 1950, and 1990. Within the South it is important to distinguish the Peripheral South states (those with relatively lower black populations) of Texas, Florida, Tennessee, Arkansas, Virginia, and North Carolina from the more traditional Deep South states (those with the highest black populations) of Mississippi, South Carolina, Louisiana, Alabama, and Georgia. As Key argued at midcentury, the southern "states . . . with fewest Negroes seem most disposed toward deviation from the popular supposition of how the [white] South behaves politically." Peripheral South states "manifest a considerably higher degree of freedom from preoccupation with the race question than do the states of the Deep South."[18] The higher the black population, the stronger the attachment of southern whites to the traditional Democratic party.

Lines drawn at 15 percent black on the horizontal axis and at 50 percent urban on the vertical axis create a demographic framework containing four cells. By highlighting the immense distance between the North and the South, this grid reveals the demographic underpinnings of battlefield sectionalism. By far the most significant demographic contrasts involve rural societies with black populations greater than 15 percent (the lower right-hand cells) versus urban societies with black populations of less than 15 percent (the upper left-hand cells). The former represents demographic traditionalism; the latter contains far more dynamic environments. Rural societies with very low black populations (the lower left cells) occupy an intermediate position, as do urban societies with higher black populations (the upper right cells).

In this framework southern distinctiveness appears as the intersection of race and ruralism. According to the 1880 Census blacks were 41 percent of the southern population but only 3 percent in the North, a difference of almost thirteen to one. When the Border states are set aside, blacks accounted for less than 2 percent of the population in the rest of the North, a difference of better than twenty to one. Moreover, nine-tenths of all southerners (compared to less than two-thirds of all northerners) lived on farms and plantations or in hamlets and small towns.

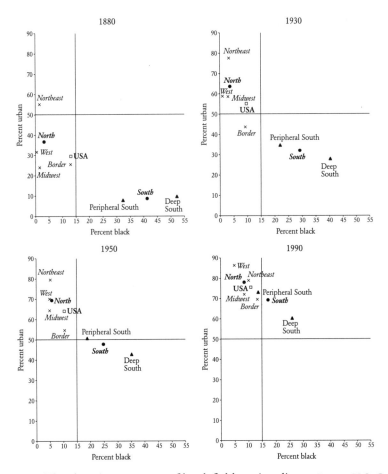

Figure 1.3 The changing anatomy of battlefield sectionalism. *Sources:* U.S. Census, 1880, 1930, 1950, and 1990.

The South was truly different from the rest of the nation. Because most white southerners did not accept blacks as their equals, racial conflict was endemic in the southern states. Such an immense demographic cleavage between the South and the North generated and sustained extraordinarily different worldviews and political imperatives. An especially stark historical contrast involves the Northeast, the only northern region combining a tiny black population and an urban majority, versus the Deep South, where whites were the racial minority in a heavily rural landscape. Battlefield sectionalism was firmly rooted in the contrasting societies and economies of the North and South as well as in the profound firsthand experiences generated by the Civil War and Reconstruction.

Richard Franklin Bensel, characterizing American industrialization at the end of the nineteenth century, has emphasized "the broad division of the United States into what was then an advanced northeastern and midwestern industrial core and a comparatively stagnating southern periphery . . . In the manufacturing belt of the Northeast and Midwest, a rapid industrial expansion, accompanied by an equally rapid urbanization, dominated the pattern of economic growth. In the Plains and West, growth was driven by frontier settlement and expanding commodity grain cultivation." Outside the North there was little economic development. "The South, however, was an entirely different world where only isolated areas were able to climb out of the deepest dungeons of the American economy: the Piedmont where expanding textile production underpinned light industrialization, the Birmingham district of Alabama with the construction of iron and steel plants, and the western frontier in Texas with the extension of cotton production."[19]

In 1930, at a time when the Great Depression was redefining the Republicans as the "party of Depression," all three southern units were still situated in "Confederate" or–to use bumper-sticker terminology–"Forget, Hell!" environments. By contrast, in 1930 all northern groups except the Border states featured very low black populations and urban majorities. The Great Depression made the South even more Democratic and revived the Democratic party in the urban-industrial North. Even without the Great Depression, the growing complexity of many northern states made one-party Republican politics harder to sustain. Compared to the rest of the nation, the South remained considerably more receptive to one-party Democratic domination.

By 1950, however, even the Jim Crow South was on the verge of major demographic change. Though considerably less traditional than before, its demography continued to advantage the Democratic party. Black populations were proportionately four times greater in the South than in the North. Within the region the Peripheral South had (just barely) moved into the space defined by higher black populations with urban majorities.

Between 1950 and 1990 the South rejoined the nation demographically. Net white in-migration and net black out-migration fused with the rapid growth of cities and suburbs to transform the southern landscape. These forces uprooted millions of southerners and attracted many northerners to the South. In their totality, demographic changes represented a socioeconomic complexity that further destabilized southern one-party politics. By 1990 the South was far more similar to the rest of the nation than ever before. All northern units and the Peripheral South had very low black populations and substantial urban majorities. No single political party, Democratic or Republican, could possibly represent the diverse interests, multiple conflicts, and alternative aspirations found in the modern South.

THE DEMOGRAPHIC ANATOMY OF THE SOUTHERN STATES

In 1880 every one of the eleven southern states possessed highly traditional demographic foundations (see Figure 1.4). "Confederate" conditions especially prevailed in the Deep South states. Whites were the racial minority in South Carolina, Mississippi, and Louisiana, and they were only narrowly in the majority in Alabama and Georgia. Aside from Florida (most of its 1880 population was concentrated in the northern panhandle), the Peripheral South states contained relatively smaller black populations. Yet even in Texas, Tennessee, and Arkansas, blacks were around a quarter of the total population. Ruralism pervaded every southern state.

By 1930, as a result of modest demographic changes, Texas emerged as the first southern state with a comparatively small black population, and Florida became the first southern state with an urban majority. Nine states, including all five Deep South states, continued to combine higher black populations with substantial rural majorities. With the Great Depression further discrediting the Republican party and reinforcing the pro-Democratic heritage of most white southerners, the Solid Democratic South remained unchallenged.

In 1950 the South's demography continued to advantage the Democratic party. Populated mainly by native southerners with limited formal education, the region remained a racially segregated society with a one-party political system. It was still generally characterized by relatively

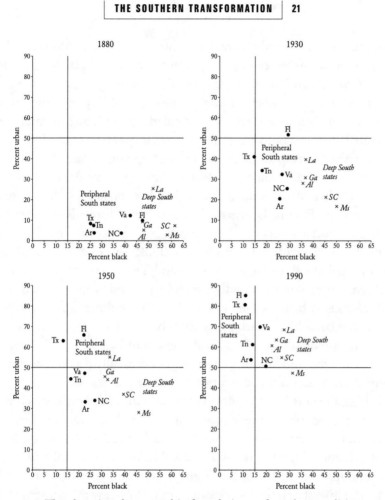

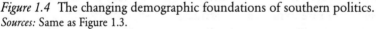

Figure 1.4 The changing demographic foundations of southern politics.
Sources: Same as Figure 1.3.

large black populations and by extensive ruralism. Whatever the Constitution and the Supreme Court might say about black voting rights,
whites born and raised in the South dominated the region's small electorates. The political expression of this highly traditional society remained the Solid Democratic South.

Old South environments—substantial black populations united with
rural majorities—still defined the region's center of gravity in 1950.
"Confederate" settings prevailed in eight states. Mississippi, South

Carolina, Alabama, and Georgia, the four rural Deep South states, had black populations exceeding 30 percent. The Peripheral South states with "Confederate" settings were North Carolina, Arkansas, Virginia, and Tennessee. Everywhere racism prevailed as public policy and private practice. Few black southerners, particularly those living in rural areas and small towns, could freely participate in politics; and white racial conservatism was especially pervasive in Deep South states.

Three states had somewhat less traditional demographic environments. Higher black populations with urban majorities characterized Louisiana and Florida. Louisiana, however, was a distinctly unpromising setting for racial change or Republican growth. Its big city, New Orleans, was thoroughly Old South in outlook, and its black population was the region's third largest. Florida and Texas were different. Steady northern migration was rapidly expanding Florida's urban population and diluting its black population. In 1950 Texas alone exhibited a New South demography: a black population of less than 15 percent in conjunction with urban majorities. Only Texas and Florida were developing large urbanized middle classes that might eventually produce socioeconomic foundations for competitive two-party politics.

During the next four decades every southern state experienced fundamental demographic upheavals as well as federal intervention designed to attack the racial status quo (see 1990 in Figure 1.4). Many southerners, black and white, left farms and small towns in search of better jobs and an improved quality of life. Some moved to bigger towns and cities in their native states, others relocated from slow-growth southern states to those with more dynamic economies, and still others abandoned the region altogether. The South's leading metropolitan areas also began to attract migrants from the North and (selectively) the rest of the world.

In the repressive racial conditions of 1950 the size of the black population served as an indicator of racial traditionalism among white Democrats. The larger the black population, the more "southern Democratic" the behavior of native whites. In 1990, long after federal intervention, the percentage of black voters in the total population signified the political strength of black Democrats. The greater the black population, the larger the white majority required by Republican politicians to win statewide elections. In every state blacks accounted for smaller shares of the total population than they did in 1950. The mobilization of blacks as committed Democrats and the Republicans' permanent need to secure sizable white majorities lie at the heart of the two-party battle in southern politics.

The development of biracial electorates, however, is only part of the story of increased Republican competitiveness. Equally dramatic changes in the urban-rural balance also occurred. The rise of a much larger urbanized middle class has stimulated party competition. Rapid urbanization and later suburbanization disrupted the Solid Democratic South for millions of native whites as surely as the enfranchisement of blacks revolutionized the traditional southern Democratic party. As we have argued elsewhere, "the cumulative impact of these vast transformations has been to undermine the complete supremacy of the traditionalist political culture. The emergence of entrepreneurial individualists promoting modernization, and the diffusion of a philosophy sanctioning unrestrained rather than controlled growth, have produced a region energetically committed to economic development."[20]

As of 1990 only Mississippi retained an "Old South" demography. The other seven states with Confederate settings in 1950 had moved in two directions. Virginia, Georgia, Alabama, South Carolina, and (just barely) North Carolina joined Louisiana in the upper right-hand cell of higher black populations and urban majorities. All these states contained extensive suburbs and affluent urban neighborhoods, environments where being a Republican or an independent might be considered a social advantage. Tennessee and Arkansas shifted into the New South cell of very low black populations and urban majorities. And Florida joined Texas as the South's second "megastate," the two states where at least four-fifths of the population resided in urban areas and where blacks were only slightly more than a tenth of the total population.[21]

Texas serves as a leading indicator of southern development. "For years, out-of-state elites and liberals in Texas have called on the state to become more like New York or California or Michigan," Michael Barone and Grant Ujifusa have written. "But most Texans prefer their own model. Indeed, in important respects New York and California and Michigan are choosing to become more like Texas; so is Mexico: the last 25 years can be seen as—at least the beginnings of—the Texafication of North America. Low taxes and high tech, few barriers to opportunity but a less elaborate safety net, moving away from reliance on agriculture and oil, bypassing the era of big factories and big unions of the Great Lakes and eschewing the liberal cultural values of the two coasts: this is Texas's way, and increasingly North America's."[22] With appropriate hedges and qualifications, the same analysis would hold for most of the other southern states. The combined impact of federal intervention on racial practices and rapid urbanization fundamentally disrupted the Democratic Solid South. Massive demographic transformations provide a partial explanation for the spread of competitive two-party politics in statewide elections.

REAGAN'S REALIGNMENT OF CONSERVATIVE SOUTHERN WHITES

Demographic changes alone, however, did not automatically make the Republicans competitive. In state after state, new demographic foundations had to be converted into new presidential foundations and, even more important, into new partisan foundations. Presidential politics is the great engine of the American political system. Repeated success in presidential elections, reinforced by White House performances that persuaded many conservative whites and a sizable minority of moderate whites that their interests, values, and aspirations would be better served by the Republican party, also worked to destabilize the once solidly Democratic electorate. As more and more whites came to identify with the Republican party and support its candidates with votes, money, and organization, the Republicans finally became a competitive political party in the South.

The partisan realignment of white southerners was not quickly realized. For almost thirty years after General Dwight Eisenhower pioneered Republican presidential politics in the South, the Republican party failed to string together successful presidential administrations in ways that genuinely transformed southern partisanship. Eisenhower's pathbreaking candidacy in 1952 was directed primarily toward the more dynamic Peripheral South states, where urbanization and industrialization were creating large white middle classes sympathetic to the economic conservatism of the Republican party. However, the Republican presidential candidate wasted no energy persuading southern whites to become Republicans or encouraging southern Republicans to run for Congress.

A decade later Goldwater's aggressive and pugnacious Republicanism was disastrous. Goldwater Republicanism placed the southern Republicans squarely on the wrong side of the civil rights issue. Moreover, it was aimed primarily at white voters in the Deep South, where segregationist Democratic senators and representatives were especially entrenched. When the Republicans turned against the newly emerging black electorate, they anchored their future success to winning levels of white support that were frequently unrealistic, particularly against experienced Democratic politicians. Many more southern white voters would need to abandon the Democratic party and become Republicans or independents before Republican candidates could achieve landslide white majorities. Richard Nixon's "Southern Strategy" targeted conservative whites. Against liberal Democrat George McGovern in 1972, Nixon achieved landslide victories in every southern state. Yet Nixon's attempt to realign conservative white southerners evaporated in the Watergate scandal that squandered his political capital and forced his resignation.

When Ronald Reagan defeated President Jimmy Carter in 1980, Republicans once again had an opportunity to use the White House to reshape southern partisan affiliations. Reagan's presidency was the turning point in the evolution of a competitive, two-party electorate in the South. The Reagan realignment of the 1980s dramatically expanded the number of Republicans and conservative independents in the region's electorate. These developments, in turn, encouraged Republican candidates and strategists to target more and more Senate and House seats. The California Republican's initial victories in ten southern states did not produce landslide majorities, nor was his presidency an immediate success. "Reaganomics," as Reagan's opponents derisively called his economic policies, put the Republicans on the defensive through the 1982 elections. Exit polls taken in six southern states (Alabama, Arkansas, Mississippi, Tennessee, Texas, and Virginia) in 1982 illustrate the GOP's weakness among white voters: on average, 45 percent of southern white voters were Democrats and only 23 percent were Republicans, a two-to-one Democratic advantage. However, as the economy recovered, Reagan's optimistic conservatism began to resonate with many conservative white southerners. In 1984 the president who had dramatically cut marginal tax rates had the good fortune to run against a Democratic challenger, former vice president Walter Mondale, who used his acceptance speech at the Democratic National Convention to guarantee voters that he would raise their taxes. Against an authentic northern liberal, Reagan won the landslide southern support that had eluded him in 1980. Only in Tennessee, where he was held to 58 percent, did Reagan fail to win at least three-fifths of the total vote.

Republicans faced a more formidable challenge in 1988. Because Vice President George Bush ran to perpetuate Reagan's philosophy and because he was universally considered Reagan's inferior as a campaigner, the 1988 Bush vote provides a fairly hard test of Reagan's southern legacy. Bush achieved landslide victories (60 percent or greater) in South Carolina, Florida, Mississippi, Georgia, and Virginia; near-landslide victories (58–59 percent) in Alabama, North Carolina, and Tennessee; and comfortable victories (54–56 percent) in Texas, Arkansas, and Louisiana. (No doubt Texas senator Lloyd Bentsen's presence on the Democratic ticket prevented a landslide Bush victory in the Lone Star State.) In every southern state Bush's vote in 1988 exceeded Reagan's vote in 1980. Never before had the Republicans carried the southern states in three consecutive presidential elections. Bush's landslide and near-landslide victories in 1988 encouraged Republican strategists and candidates to conclude that no southern state should be conceded to the Democrats in Senate elections.

Reagan's presidency built the firmest grassroots base of Republican partisans ever to appear in the region. Presidential Republicanism set the stage for competitive party politics. According to the 1988 exit polls in the eleven southern states, on average 45 percent of southern white voters now identified themselves as Republicans, nearly double the Republican average in 1982. Only 34 percent of southern white voters still called themselves Democrats in 1988. Reagan's performance in office had allowed the Republicans to displace the Democrats as the new plurality party among southern white voters. According to the exit polls, white Republicans outnumbered white Democrats in nine southern states: Alabama, Florida, Georgia, Mississippi, North Carolina, South Carolina, Tennessee, Texas, and Virginia. Only in Arkansas and Louisiana did white Democrats still exceed white Republicans. Throughout most of the South, the Republican party had finally become a highly competitive minority party.

In 1988 Vice President George Bush defined the central theme of his candidacy in his acceptance speech at the Republican National Convention. "The Congress will push me to raise taxes, and I'll say no, they'll push, and I'll say no, and they'll push again," candidate Bush declared. "And all I can say to them is: Read my lips: no new taxes."[23] His bold declaration thrilled and energized Republicans. Two years later, in a defining gesture, President Bush reneged on that campaign promise in order to reach a budget agreement with Democratic leaders in Congress. By breaking his promise Bush severely damaged his standing within his own party. "No new taxes!" was implicitly reconceived and repromised as "No *more* new taxes!"

By disrupting and acutely disappointing his political base, Bush threw away the advantage of his presidential incumbency even as the Democratic party was turning to Governor Bill Clinton of Arkansas as its presidential nominee in 1992. Like most southern Democrats holding statewide office, Clinton had spent his entire political career learning how to bob and weave liberal and conservative themes in order to create and maintain a successful biracial coalition. Liberal on civil rights issues but conservative on budgetary matters and on selected cultural matters such as the death penalty, Clinton was a far shrewder opponent for Bush than Massachusetts governor Michael Dukakis had been in 1988. Running as "New Democrats" with an all-southern national ticket of Clinton and Tennessee senator Al Gore, as well as benefiting from Ross Perot's third-party candidacy, the Democrats took back the White House in 1992. White southerners had averaged 70 percent for Bush in 1988 but dropped to 52 percent in 1992.

Despite substantial weakness at the top of the presidential ticket for both major parties, only minor ripples appeared in the partisan identifications of southern whites in the eleven states. On average, 43 percent of southern whites called themselves Republicans in 1992, only two points lower than in 1988, while 34 percent of southern white voters identified themselves as Democrats–the same as in 1988. Republicans continued to outnumber Democrats among the white voters in the same nine states as in 1988. President Bush's collapsing popularity had not undermined Republican grassroots strength. Republican party identification had become institutionalized in the modern South. Substantial numbers of southern whites identified themselves as Republicans, sufficiently large to support GOP candidacies for the Senate and House of Representatives.

Moreover, during the first two years of his presidency, Clinton launched his ill-fated plan for national health insurance. The president's proposal reawakened fears among Republicans and many independents of a much bigger and more expensive national government. Opposition to Clinton's health-care proposal ultimately energized southern Republicans and created the proximate political dynamic that triggered the Republicans' Senate and congressional breakthroughs in the 1994 elections.

SOUTHERN REPUBLICAN IMPERATIVES

At the time of federal intervention in southern race relations most Republican candidates followed the lead of Arizona senator Barry Goldwater, the 1964 presidential nominee of the Republican party, in disregarding potential black support and attempting to unify whites behind a program of racial and economic conservatism. Goldwater's strategy of concentrating almost totally on winning white support gave the southern Democrats—traditionally the party of southern segregation par excellence—an opportunity to redeem themselves in the eyes of black southerners and to offset defections among racially conservative whites. The 1964 presidential election, after all, dramatized clearly the choice between the Democratic president from Texas who had just led the fight to pass the Civil Rights Act versus one of the few Republican senators who had tried hard to defeat it.

Whereas disgust with southern slavery and fear of its spread into northern territories had helped establish the Republican party in the North, the southern activists who were inspired by Goldwater made plain their opposition to federal intervention on civil rights as well as their opposition to "big government" generally. President Reagan later reinforced Goldwater Republicanism, though in a more subtle way. Like that of his hero Goldwater, Reagan's conservatism resonated with many white southerners as forcefully as it angered most black Americans.

The theoretical and practical consequences of Goldwater and Reagan Republicanism appear in Table 1.2, which specifies the percentage of the white vote Republican candidates need for victory given the size of the black vote (as a percentage of the total vote cast) and the percentage of the black vote won by Republicans. The table can be applied to any congressional district, any state, or indeed any general election in which the electorate is composed of whites and blacks.[24] Since the mid-1960s the partisan division of the black vote has been the principal constant in southern politics. A rough rule of thumb would be that white Democratic nominees typically enjoy an advantage over white Republican candidates of at least nine to one among black voters. Sometimes the advantage rises to nineteen to one or even higher.

As a consequence, white Republicans always need to win sizable majorities of the white vote, and their white necessities increase as blacks constitute bigger percentages of the total electorate. Only substantial white majorities can compensate for the Republicans' poor showing among black voters. Conversely, the certainty of black support relieves all white Democrats of the need to secure a majority of the white vote in order to launch or to sustain their political careers. The larger the white Democrats' black vote, the smaller their white necessities.

Southern Republicans were originally constrained by the difficulty of winning white majorities when running against conservative Democrats. Later, as moderate Democratic candidates emerged who appealed to black Democrats as well as white Democrats, many Republican candidates failed because they could not assemble landslide white majorities. Biracial coalitions consisting of most blacks and a sufficiently big minority of whites can always produce Democratic victories.

The regional imperatives for southern Republicans are straightforward. If blacks are a fifth of the southern electorate and Republicans attract only a tenth of the black vote, Republicans must win three-fifths of the white vote in order to carry the South. Reagan's presidency made the Republican party seem respectable, reasonable, and quite useful to many white southerners who had been taught from birth to revere Democrats and despise Republicans. More than any other Republican politi-

Table 1.2 Republican white vote needed for bare majority of total vote (%)

Size of black vote	Percent of black vote won by Republicans						Size of white vote
	0	5	10	15	20	25	
0	50	50	50	50	50	50	100
5	53	52	52	52	52	51	95
10	56	55	54	54	53	53	90
15	59	58	57	56	55	54	85
20	63	61	60	59	58	56	80
25	67	65	63	62	60	58	75
30	71	69	67	65	63	61	70
35	77	74	72	69	66	63	65
40	83	80	77	73	70	67	60
45	91	87	83	79	75	70	55
50	100	95	90	85	80	75	50
55	111	105	99	93	87	81	45
60	125	118	110	103	95	88	40
65	143	134	124	115	106	96	35
D:R ratio	100:1	19:1	9:1	6:1	4:1	3:1	

cian in the second half of the twentieth century, Reagan's optimistic persona and political boldness gave him—and his party—an appeal that went far beyond conservative Republicans (see Figure 1.5). At the end of his presidency, Reagan's approval rates among white voters exceeded the Republicans' regional white target of 60 percent among conservative Republicans (98 percent), liberal and moderate Republicans (90), conservative independents (89), moderate independents (67), and conservative Democrats (62). Among white southerners only liberal Democrats (20 percent) and moderate Democrats and liberal independents (40) resisted Reagan's appeal.

Although Reagan showed attentive Republicans how to assemble the landslide white majorities they needed for southern victories, the nature of his success was, ironically, lost on Gingrich, the architect of the Republicans' congressional breakthrough in 1994. Resettled in an utterly safe suburban white district on the perimeter of Atlanta, Gingrich seemed to believe his atypical district was the nation writ large. Gingrich acted as though he was Goldwater's reincarnation, and in 1995 he led

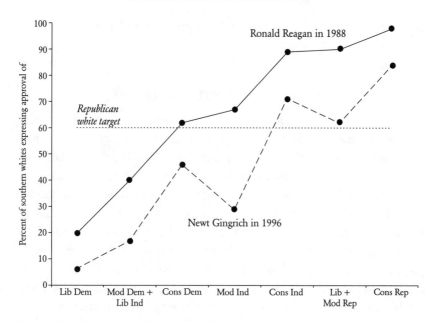

Figure 1.5 Reagan advantage, Gingrich gap. *Sources:* Voter News Service General Election exit polls, 1988 and 1996.

his House Republicans into a disastrous government shutdown over a budget fight with President Clinton. It was a political showdown that the Republican Speaker could not possibly win. Against a Democratic president armed with the veto, how could a Speaker presiding over a tiny Republican majority assemble the two-thirds House majority (to say nothing of a two-thirds Senate majority) needed to override presidential vetoes?

Gingrich's harsh, argumentative, and relentlessly confrontational style gave fellow Republicans a hard lesson in how not to govern. Gingrich scared and disgusted many white southerners, and he especially frightened the moderate independents and conservative Democrats whom Reagan had attracted. The "Gingrich gap" stands out vividly in every comparison of his 1996 approval ratings with those of Reagan in 1988 (see Figure 1.5). Even among conservative Republicans, his strongest supporters, Gingrich trailed Reagan by eighteen points. Only among conservative Republicans, liberal and moderate Republicans, and conservative independents did Gingrich exceed the Republicans' white target.

THE REVIVAL OF PARTY COMPETITION

For decades southern Democrats in Congress had warned northern Democrats that they would desert the Democratic party if northerners failed to help them hold the line against civil rights legislation. During a 1938 filibuster of an antilynching bill, Democratic senator Josiah W. Bailey of North Carolina bluntly addressed his Democratic colleagues from the North: "in the hour that you come down to North Carolina and try to impose your will upon us about the Negro, so help me God, you are going to learn a lesson which no political party will ever again forget," he threatened. "That is the truth. Some may not like me for saying it now, but one of these days those who do not like it will say, 'Would to God we had listened to the warning.' The civilization in the South is going to be a white civilization; its government is going to be a white man's government." Bailey spoke as an unreconstructed veteran of the Democrats' violent white-supremacy campaigns of the 1890s. Northern Democrats, Bailey thought, should ponder carefully the fate of the Republican party in the South, because "just as when the Republicans in the [1860s] undertook to impose the national will upon us with respect to the Negro, we resented it and hated that party with a hatred that has outlasted generations; we hated it beyond measure; we hated it more than was right for us and more than was just; we hated it with an intolerance that nobody could probably approve, but we hated it because of what it had done to us, because of the wrong it undertook to put upon us; and just as that same policy destroyed the hope of the Republican party in the South, that same policy adopted by the Democratic party will destroy the Democratic party in the South."[25]

And yet there was no stampede to the Republican party when the South's Democratic senators lost their filibuster in 1964 against the Civil Rights Act. Following Goldwater's presidential nomination later that summer, however, Senator Thurmond, at age sixty-one, "broke through the political wall that had surrounded the South since Reconstruction, cut his Democratic ties, and joined the GOP." Abandoning the Democratic party was in character for Thurmond. Born in 1902 in

Edgefield County, a rural black-belt setting in which the Democratic party was thoroughly synonymous with white supremacy, Thurmond was elected governor of South Carolina in 1946. He first left the Democratic party when President Truman changed the party platform to support civil rights. "Thurmond's political legacy is found not in the annals of legislative achievement," Jack Bass and Marilyn W. Thompson have argued, "but in redefining America's political culture. As the segregationist Dixiecrat candidate for president in 1948, he won four Deep South states and shook the foundations of the Democratic 'solid South.' This psychological break opened the path for two-party development in the region."[26]

Returning to the party to finish his governorship, Thurmond was elected to the Senate in 1954 as an independent Democrat. He soon developed a reputation as an earnest and long-winded segregationist. His senior South Carolina colleague, Senator Olin D. Johnston, an experienced professional segregationist himself, once sized up Thurmond's attitude toward racial segregation. "Listen to ol' Strom," Johnston remarked to a Democratic staffer as they watched Thurmond defend southern racial practices on the Senate floor. "He really *believes* all that shit."[27]

Thurmond's second blow to southern Democracy came when he switched to the Republicans and "campaign[ed] across the South for presidential candidate Barry Goldwater. This symbolic act, after Goldwater had voted against the landmark Civil Rights Act of 1964, for the first time helped attract large numbers of the most racially conscious white Southerners into the GOP. It helped lay the foundations for a race-flavored 'Southern strategy' that altered the character of the party of Abraham Lincoln."[28] Thurmond did not expect many of his rank-and-file supporters to become Republicans immediately, and he was therefore careful to maintain his close ties to conservative Democrats. As a pioneer Republican he was much less interested in building a Republican party than in perpetuating his own career. The maverick Democrat became a loyalist Republican, but Thurmond's conservatism rather than his party label was the common denominator of his political style.

Eventually Thurmond came to terms with the irreversibility of racial desegregation and black participation. In 1982 he finally voted for a civil rights bill. Despite reservations about some provisions of the Voting Rights Act, he voted to extend the law for twenty-five years. "I must take into account," he told the Senate, "the common perception that a vote against the bill indicates opposition to the right to vote, and, indeed, opposition to the group of citizens who are protected under the Voting Rights Act."[29] By blending conservative ideology with practical politics (excellent constituency service was a hallmark of Thurmond's Senate office), Thurmond leveraged his personal popularity among whites into a Senate career of almost five decades, ultimately achieving in South Carolina the same sort of legendary status associated with such commanding politicians as Huey Long in Louisiana and Edward Kennedy in Massachusetts.

Although Thurmond's party switching was exceptional rather than representative, in a grand symbolic sense his political journey personified the crisscrossing streams of southern congressional conservatism (see Figure 1.6).[30] The partisan transformation of southern conservatism is a development of profound significance in regional and national politics. Details and timing varied somewhat between the Senate and the House of Representatives, but the big picture was roughly similar in both branches of Congress. For decades conservative Democratic incumbents prevented the rise of southern Republicans in Congress. Not until the 1980s did the lines cross and Republicans begin to outnumber conservative Democrats. And as the long-term impact of federal intervention took hold, conservatism ceased to be a Democratic asset and became instead a major liability in Democratic primaries or general elections.

Individual white voters began to draw conclusions similar to Senator Thurmond's. For example, in 1978 Mississippi Democratic senator Jim Eastland, an unreconstructed champion of the Old South, decided to retire. His departure ignited fights in both the Republican and Democratic primaries, and a *Washington Post* reporter discovered some lifelong Mississippi Democrats preparing themselves psychologically for the daunting experience of voting in a Republican primary. As a white farmer explained the situation to Republican candidate Thad Cochran, "I was telling her [his wife] about you, and I said, 'I know this sounds silly, but I decided I'm going to vote Republican this time.'" An elderly white woman likewise advised Cochran of her startling political conver-

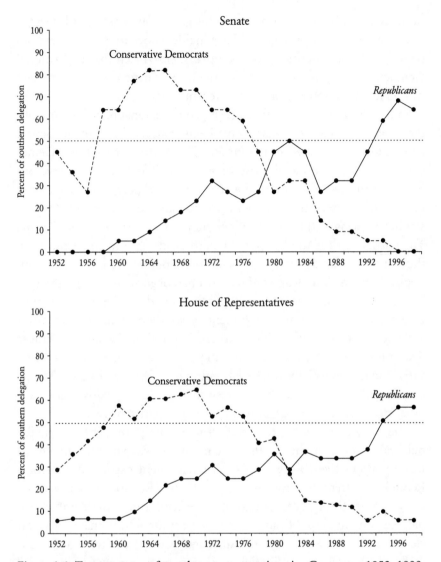

Figure 1.6 Two streams of southern conservatism in Congress, 1952–1998. *Sources: Congressional Quarterly's Guide to U.S. Elections,* 3d ed. (Washington, D.C., 1994); and *Congressional Quarterly Weekly Report,* various issues.

sion: "My daddy would turn over in his grave if he knew, but I decided I'm going to vote Republican." These incidents occurred, T. R. Reid observed, as "more and more Mississippians, convinced that the national Democratic party is too liberal for their taste, have shown themselves willing to cast a Republican vote in recent years."[31]

In the 1990s, as the Republicans surged to regional majorities in both the Senate and House, conservative Democrats vanished in the Senate and almost disappeared in the House. The decline of southern Democratic conservatism and the rise of southern Republican conservatism have contributed mightily to the clarification of party and ideology in Congress. Conservative southern Democrats no longer constitute a significant wing within the Democratic party in the House or Senate. Their absence frees the Democratic party leadership to speak more authoritatively as an aggressively liberal force. Before the rise of southern Republicanism, American conservatism had been weakened by the split between northern conservative Republicans and southern conservative Democrats. The partisan realignment of southern white conservatives and the emergence of sizable southern Republican Senate and House delegations have given the Republican party its own aggressively conservative image, especially on social, cultural, and fiscal issues. The national upshot is that both congressional parties regularly fight each other over the entire range of ideological and partisan issues.

The party battle within the South is now highly competitive. The Republicans' surge in the 1990s built upon the Reagan realignment of white conservatives. Reagan's partial realignment expanded grassroots Republican strength sufficiently to make the Republican party genuinely competitive in every southern state. Yet because it was only a partial realignment, Republicans were in no position to dominate open-seat elections in any southern state. Although both parties have numerous "safe" districts where domination is assured, neither party has any "safe" states. Hence while competition represents a major gain for southern Republicans, the term "competitive South" assuredly refers to southern Democrats as well as to southern Republicans. Across the South the Democratic party has characteristically responded to Republican surges by making significant adjustments to keep itself competitive. As religious-right whites have emerged as a substantial wing of southern Republicanism, southern Democrats have quickly countered by emphasizing to moderates and independents that the Democratic party resolutely opposes the social and cultural agenda of the religious right. At the beginning of the twenty-first century neither southern Democrats nor southern Republicans can win elections simply by uniting their bases—blacks and liberal whites for the Democrats versus white economic conservatives and religious-right conservatives for the Republicans—and turning them out on election day. Moderate independents remain the main swing voters in the competitive South.

A competitive South has produced a competitive nation. Beginning with the New Deal, the Democrats' unshaken megamajorities in the eleven states of the former Confederacy—by our reckoning the most important sustained "given" in the history of American party politics—became the key to winning Congress. Provided that Democrats controlled the South's House districts and Senate seats, the party needed to hold no more than a third of the seats in the rest of the country in order to create national majorities. As long as the Republicans failed to live down their excruciating new image as the party of Depression, the Solid Democratic South normally guaranteed Democratic Congresses.

The rise of southern Republicans in Congress gradually reduced but did not eliminate the Democrats' southern surplus until—in the 1994 elections—the Republicans finally overcame the formidable barrier of Democratic incumbency and won small majorities of Senate and House seats in the South. The disappearance of the southern Democrats' surpluses of House and Senate seats has made the partisan fight for control of Congress much more competitive than it has been for decades. Democrats are now adjusting to the loss of their southern surpluses, surpluses that have functioned since the New Deal as Democratic insurance policies against the possibility of northern losses. For the Republican party the establishment of southern and northern surpluses in 1994 was a major achievement, but the size of their surpluses was quite modest. Because of the rise of southern Republicans, both national parties are positioned to win—or lose—control of the Senate and the House of Representatives. As the extraordinary 2000 elections made plain, the national stakes of the events unfolding in the South are truly immense.

If their southern gains have restored the national competitiveness of the Republican party in Congress, the prominence of new southern leaders like Gingrich, Armey, DeLay, and Lott has nonetheless been a very mixed development for voters in many northern states and congressional districts. Especially in the Northeast, Republican politicians have often combined economic conservatism with moderate to liberal positions on many social issues. An overtly southern congressional leadership inevitably placed many northern Republicans in the defensive position of having to "explain" the worldview of the southern Republicans to their constituents.

And just as segregationist southern Democrats once profoundly embarrassed northern Democrats and forced them to explain to their constituents that the southerners did, after all, ensure that the Democratic party controlled Congress, so moderate northern Republicans might have to explain to their constituents the reality that the southern congressional realignment was largely responsible for the Republicans' small national majorities. The southern Republicans' broad-ranging conservatism on economics, race, culture, and defense, particularly when communicated in crusading and absolute terms, may well have weakened the appeal of the party in the old strongholds of moderate to liberal Republicanism in the North. Just as the changing social bases of the Democratic party in the 1930s in time created tremendous strains and culminated in the exodus of conservative white southerners from the party, so, too, widespread perceptions of southern conservatives as proselytizing extremists, unless reversed by new and more inclusive Republican leadership styles, may well erode its appeal in parts of the North.

Our book on southern congressional politics tells the story of an entrenched one-party system gradually morphing into a competitive two-party system. Why did it take decades for southern Republicans to become a competitive force in House and Senate elections? The Republicans' exceedingly slow rise cannot be understood without appreciating the tenacity, resilience, and profound transformations of their Democratic opponents. In the aftermath of federal intervention southern Democrats first exploited their overwhelming advantages in grassroots white Democracy, congressional incumbency, and conservative ideology to suffocate most electoral challenges from southern Republicans. Later, a generation of New South Democrats emerged to contain southern Republicans through the creation of majority biracial coalitions.

Not until President Reagan significantly expanded grassroots southern Republicanism by realigning the white conservatives and neutralizing the white moderates did the GOP become capable of competing seriously in most Senate elections and a majority of House elections. Skillful Democratic adaptations and counterattacks thus long delayed the rise of southern Republicans in Congress. When the Republicans' southern breakthrough finally came in 1994, however, it intensified and nationalized the two-party battle for control of Congress.

2

CONFRONTING THE DEMOCRATIC JUGGERNAUT

After white Democrats systematically drove most black men and many impoverished white men from the electorate, the South became a thoroughgoing Democratic juggernaut. At the midpoint of the twentieth century the principal obstacle facing potential Republican candidates was the staggering preponderance of Democratic voters in every state and almost all congressional districts. In 1952 nearly four-fifths of white southerners identified themselves as Democrats. Only one in eleven were Republicans, and many of them lived in the isolated highlands of East Tennessee, southwestern Virginia, and western North Carolina. Trent Lott, growing up in Mississippi during the 1940s and 1950s, had "never met a live Republican." The future majority leader of the Senate Republicans was typical of his generation. From 1902 through 1950 all southern Senators and almost all southern Representatives were Democrats. Most Republicans who ran for federal office quickly learned, often through unpleasant and humiliating experiences, that taking on a southern Democrat meant encountering a "massive inexorable force or object that crushes whatever is in its path."[1]

Experienced Democratic officeholders reinforced their party's lopsided advantage in the South. Politicians wearing the Democratic label monopolized thousands of local and state offices, thereby generating a huge pool of experienced Democratic candidates for seats in the House of Representatives and Senate. In time, many of these career politicians rose to positions of leadership in Congress. The policies they pursued in Washington–protecting white supremacy, minimizing the influence of organized labor, keeping taxes as low as possible, and delivering services and benefits paid for mainly by affluent northerners—reflected the interests, values, and prejudices of the most influential white southerners. The few southern Republicans who ventured to run for the House and Senate in the 1950s did not possess a marketable product.[2]

Most southern whites actively loathed the Republican party. It was still seen as the political instrument of the mysterious and hated North. In the eyes of southern whites, the Republican party's most prominent leaders, Abraham Lincoln and Herbert Hoover, had brought calamity upon calamity to the region. Lincoln's party had destroyed the Old South. After provoking a war, Republicans had freed blacks from slavery, occupied the defeated South, and awarded the vote to black men. Only after they ruthlessly disfranchised black men and sent northern Republicans packing did native southern whites regain mastery of "their" society. Racist white Democrats sanctified the process as "Redemption."

Casting Democrats as the chosen instrument of white supremacy and portraying Republicans as relentless sectional enemies, these "interpretations" of southern history gave Democratic politicians powerful rhetorical ammunition well into the twentieth century. "As long as I honor the memory of the Confederate dead, respect and revere the gallant devotion of my Confederate father to our Southland and wear his name," shouted Texas Democrat and future Speaker of the House Sam Rayburn to an audience in Bonham's First Baptist Church during the 1928 election campaign, "I will never vote for the electors of a Party which sent the carpetbagger and the scalawag to the prostrate South with saber and sword to crush the white civilization to the earth." So fiercely did Rayburn attack Republican presidential candidate Herbert Hoover "for trying to abolish segregation and promote a 'deal with Negroes' that one astonished listener thought flames of fire were coming out of the congressman's nose."[3]

As if Lincoln's legacy were not a sufficient handicap in a region where white racism saturated private and public life, the onset of the Great Depression compounded the Republicans' southern problem. Economic catastrophe, occurring in the late 1920s when the Republican party controlled every elective institution of the national government, further discredited the GOP. "What is it so bad about the Republicans?"

a seven-year-old boy asked his Alabama grandfather in the 1940s. Much later, journalist Wayne Greenhaw still recalled the old man's response: "He rared back, clicked his false teeth together, and focused his eyes on me. 'Son, the Republicans brought on the Great Depression. They don't care one whit about the workingman. They let us rot without jobs before the Democrats came along and Mr. Roosevelt created job programs, the CCC, WPA, and made it worthwhile for a farmer to live out on his land. The last Republican president, Mr. Herbert Hoover, just turned his back on the little people like us,' he said with the utmost of surety." An influential uncle concurred: "Old Herbert Hoover just sat on his fat ass up there in the White House and didn't do one thing for anybody as far as I could tell," only to be reminded by the grandfather that the Republican president did "take care of the rich birds with the big oil companies and the automobile manufacturers and such."[4]

After an especially irritating encounter in 1933 with New York City lawyers led by future Republican secretary of state John Foster Dulles, who sought relief for brokerage houses from proposed securities legislation, Rayburn returned to his office and privately appraised these Wall Street Republicans: "I've never seen such shitasses in my life." His caustic assessment would have gone down well among the good-ole-boys in the rural and small-town South. Negative views of the Republican party persisted long after recovery from the Great Depression. When Donald R. Matthews and James W. Prothro surveyed southerners in 1961, the main grievance they discovered against the Republican Party was the lingering perception that it was "favorable to big business and opposed to the 'common man.'"[5] As a rule most southern whites had scant interest in—and no real use for—the party of Lincoln and Hoover.

THE SOLID SOUTH

Defending white supremacy and frustrating any northern attempts to control southern race relations—these common objectives defined the grand strategic imperatives of the South's Democratic senators and representatives for many decades after the Civil War. Southern Democrats of the old school aggressively defended the South's racial traditions against the faintest sign of northern criticism. The egregious Ellison D. "Cotton Ed" Smith of South Carolina, for example, defiantly refused to "be a party to the recognition of the 14th and 15th amendments." As a senator his guiding "precepts . . . [were] agrarianism and white supremacy. 'Cotton is king and white is supreme' was Cotton Ed Smith's constant campaign slogan, and it served him well enough in South Carolina to have provided him with reelection five times to the Senate by 1936." Smith's notoriety as a straightforward southern racist peaked at the 1936 Democratic national convention in Philadelphia, where he was flabbergasted to discover a black minister delivering the invocation. "'By God, he's as black as melted midnight,' Smith loudly exclaimed, and without waiting for the prayer to end, he immediately left his seat" and departed the convention.[6] During the heyday of unreconstructed southern Democrats, the adjective "southern" was frequently used to assert, justify, or defend specific political positions. On racial matters traditional southern Democrats did not hesitate to assert "the South wants this" or "the South won't stand for that." Regional identity was proudly burnished, worn like a badge of honor, and exhibited freely whenever the patterns and practices of white southerners were criticized.

"Southern one-party politics originated in the resolve of white southerners to hold Negroes to a well-defined economic, social, and political place," Alexander Heard concluded. "Whites joined in the Democratic party and made it their weapon in state politics and in national politics. Sensitiveness about the Negro was such, and could be so manipulated, that white southerners never disagreed among themselves sufficiently on nonracial matters to destroy their Democratic unity in state politics." The paramount Democratic advantage was the widespread and deeply felt belief of most southern whites that the Democratic party had wholeheartedly championed and defended white supremacy. "Unity on the national scene was essential," as V. O. Key Jr. explained, "in order that the largest possible bloc could be mobilized to resist any national move toward interference with southern authority to deal with the race question as was desired locally."[7]

For the white men who overthrew Reconstruction the first order of business involved restoring white supremacy as the taproot of the southern way of life. "Whatever it takes" might well have been their watchword. The application of physical violence, threats, and intimidation, as well as massive ballot-box fraud, eventually resulted in the "legal" disfranchisement of most blacks and many low-income whites through poll taxes, secret ballots, and literacy tests. This artificial electorate produced, as its architects intended, a Solid Democratic South that structured political life for generations.[8]

In their old age some white Democrats reflected on their bloody deeds with immense satisfaction. Senator Benjamin Ryan "Pitchfork Ben" Tillman of South Carolina took the floor of the Senate in 1907 to memorialize the terrorist tactics that he and other white Democrats had devised to eradicate "negro rule" and thus guarantee white supremacy. Tillman spoke with signature bluntness. In 1876, he recalled, "We felt the very foundations of our civilization crumbling beneath our feet, that we were sure to be engulfed by the black flood of barbarians who were surrounding us and had been put over us by the Army under the reconstruction acts." Deliverance from this outrageous and utterly intolerable state of affairs, an arrangement that Tillman asserted had "never been the lot of white men at any time in the history of the world to endure," finally arrived in the shape of the revived Democratic party. "We organized the Democratic party with one plank, and only one plank, namely, that 'this is a white man's country and white men must govern it,'" Tillman said. "Under that banner we went to battle." He was not speaking metaphorically. Violent, sometimes murderous confrontations soon commenced, and in fairly short order the white Democrats of South Carolina, many of whom were experienced ex-Confederate soldiers with an appetite for combat, emerged in absolute command and control of the political process. The stakes were enormous. "It was a fight," Tillman explained, "between barbarism and civilization, between the African and the Caucasian, for mastery."[9]

The senator continued to reminisce: "It was then that 'we shot them'; it was then that 'we killed them'; it was then that 'we stuffed ballot boxes.' After the troops came and told us, 'You must stop this rioting,' we had decided to take the government away from men so debased as were the negroes . . . We saw the evil of giving the ballot to creatures of this kind, and saying that one vote shall count regardless of the man behind the vote and whether that vote would kill mine. So we thought we would let you see that it took something else besides having the shape of a man to make a man." The Democrats' violence against blacks generated a new political climate in which both blacks and whites clearly understood who was in charge. "I want to say now that we have not shot any negroes in South Carolina on account of politics since 1876," Tillman reassured the Senate. "We have not found it necessary. [Laughter.]"[10] Tillman's fanatical racism, his shameless glorification of evil deeds, indeed his obvious satisfaction in running "creatures of this kind" with only "the shape of a man" completely out of the political system—all related with unembarrassed enthusiasm three decades after the events themselves—testify powerfully to the brutal origins and cultural mainsprings of traditional white Democratic rule in the South.

"Virginia owes white supremacy to the Democratic party," asserted conservative Democrat (and later U.S. senator) Harry F. Byrd in 1928.[11] It was a conviction proudly celebrated by thousands of southern Democratic politicians. In 1940, 98 percent of white southerners supported racial segregation.[12] For *most* whites living in *most* parts of the South during the first half of the twentieth century, being a Democrat and believing wholeheartedly in white supremacy were essential elements of their identities. The beliefs and preferences of most white politicians paralleled those of most white Democratic voters. Political leadership rested completely in the hands of native white southern Democrats. By their socialization as well as their mature inclinations and calculations, these politicians were trained racial militants, periodically scanning the horizon to detect the slightest hint of northern uneasiness with the region's compulsory racial segregation. Because they were nominated in Democratic primaries in which blacks had no opportunity to vote, victorious Democrats necessarily enjoyed the support of white majorities.

Democratic strength in the southern electorate was reinforced by the performance of the party's veteran senators and representatives in Washington.[13] As an isolated and defeated minority after the Civil War, generations of white southerners believed that the best way to wield influence in the nation's capital was to concentrate their political resources in a single party and take maximum advantage of their most talented, skillful, and experienced politicians. To prevent federal interference with southern racial practices, the region's white voters sent only Democrats with impeccable segregationist credentials to Congress. Southerners acquired seniority on significant committees, served as national party leaders, and then used their influence in the congressional Democratic caucuses to keep the party prosouthern on racial issues.

Some southern Democratic politicians were more compulsively demagogic and aggressively racist than others, but a consensus on Jim Crow united the region's politicians. The most vociferous racists—John Rankin, Theodore J. Bilbo, Tom Heflin, Eugene Cox, and "Cotton Ed" Smith come to mind—frequently represented states or congressional districts with many nonvoting blacks, but the defense of segregation extended far beyond the region's black belts. Rayburn's example is again instructive. A respected southern leader who could deal effectively with Democrats across the nation, he represented a rural district in northeastern Texas with relatively few blacks and did not make openly racist speeches on the House floor. Yet "Mr. Sam" was perfectly capable of crafting racist appeals at home if he deemed them necessary. Born in 1882, he held orthodox racist views for most of his life. Rayburn "believed as a race Negroes were inferior to the white race, especially to old-line Anglo-Saxon stock. Complete social equality, which he felt was the aim of integration, would lead to intermarriage—and that was unthinkable." In 1948, after Democratic president Harry S Truman had sent civil rights proposals to the Congress, Speaker Rayburn reminded his Fourth District constituents that he "was opposed to the whole civil-rights program" of the Truman administration. "I voted against everything that looked like an attack on our segregation laws." As part of the southern leadership of the national party, throughout most of his career Rayburn—as did all the other southerners—regularly defended and explained the white southern "point of view" to northern Democrats.[14]

Southern voters generally treated their senators and representatives as long-term investments whose value to their states and districts would multiply over time. "It takes a while for a man to learn and get established and gain his full influence," Rayburn once explained. "He doesn't reach his full usefulness his first term or two, and the worst thing a district can do for itself, if it's got someone here doing his job, is to keep changing its congressman. A man makes a record here about the way he does in business, or the law, or anything else; it's hard work that makes the difference."[15] Reelection posed few difficulties once a southern Democrat had convincingly won office and performed adequately.

Following Reconstruction conservative southern Democrats established the most comprehensive, the most durable, and by all odds the most consequential officeholding juggernaut in American history. "The Solid South in Congress" (see Figure 2.1) provides powerful images of

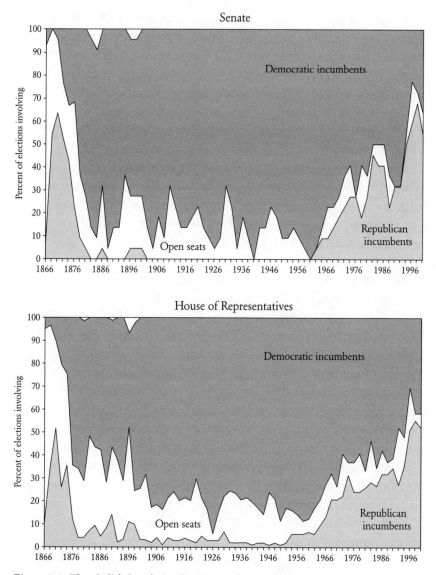

Figure 2.1 The Solid South in Congress: the Democratic juggernaut after the Civil War. *Sources: Congressional Quarterly's Guide to U.S. Elections,* 3d ed. (Washington, D.C., 1994); and *Congressional Quarterly Weekly Report,* various issues.

sustained partisan suffocation, images that are well worth pondering in light of the southern Democrats' determination to preserve the region's segregationist racial order. Figure 2.1 charts Senate and House elections from 1866 through 2000 in terms of the space occupied by Democratic incumbents (the black bands), open-seat elections (the white bands), and Republican incumbents (the gray bands). Not just Democrats but racially conservative incumbent Democrats traditionally dominated the South's delegations to the Senate and House of Representatives.

Once firmly established, the southern Democratic juggernaut was self-perpetuating and operated to permanently discourage serious and even token Republican competition. Beginning in the early 1960s the percentage of Republican incumbent senators in the southern delegation has fluctuated, but over time it has gradually increased. Only as the twentieth century drew to a close were southern Republicans finally converting incumbency to their advantage. A similar Democratic juggernaut structured elections to the House of Representatives, although in the House a molehill of incumbent Republicans always accompanied the mountain of Democratic incumbents. Because most Democratic incumbents thoroughly understood their districts' interests and knew how to secure big favors for their principal contributors and small favors for their ordinary constituents, the Republican party frequently conceded many elections or ran only token campaigns. Through the 1950s the percentage of southern House elections involving Republican incumbents registered only faintly. Although southern Republicans subsequently established a significant minority of safe seats, not until 1996 was there a House election in which Republican incumbents outnumbered Democratic incumbents.

During the first half of the twentieth century, the vast majority of congressional elections featured veteran Democrats who were almost always reelected. Because of the huge Democratic advantage among the electorate, the party's success at the ballot box did not rest simply upon the presence of intimidating incumbents. Open-seat elections in the southern one-party system were usually waged in states and districts where Republican voters were a minuscule fraction of the active electorate. When Republicans did choose to contest vacancies, typically an inexperienced Republican candidate faced an experienced Democratic nominee. So worthless was the minority party nomination that few Republicans ever competed for it. Democratic primaries, not November general elections, almost always determined who would represent the South in the House and Senate. When a vacancy occurred, usually a sizable pool of young and ambitious southern Democrats—politicians such as John Nance Garner, Rayburn, Lyndon Johnson, Carl Vinson, Wright Patman, and Hale Boggs—eagerly competed to become the next senator or representative.

The Democratic practice of reelecting incumbents and nominating strong and experienced candidates in open-seat primaries paid off in national politics. By the early 1870s the South became the largest regional bloc among House and Senate Democrats. Even more important, the southerners became a permanent majority among the most senior House and Senate Democrats. From this group came the elected leaders, committee chairs, and most senior members of the key committees. By virtue of their seniority and networks of allies, southern leaders were well positioned to exert leverage over the policies of the Democratic party from the late 1890s until the early 1960s.

Many veteran southerners acquired seniority on important committees and served as the party's most significant leaders. The whole idea was to enter Congress at a reasonably early age, gradually acquire attractive committee assignments, and then bide one's time until seniority elevated the veteran (from the New Deal onward) to a committee chairmanship. With seniority frequently came the power to truly look after a district or state, power that filtered back home and discouraged serious challenges in Democratic primaries as well as Republican competition in general elections.

Georgia senator Herman Talmadge once explained the realities of power. "Let me tell you," Talmadge asserted, "you don't gain influence in the United States Senate because you work hard or because you're intelligent . . . You gain it for one reason and one reason alone—you stay there long enough to get chairmanships of committees and subcommittees." Then Talmadge connected the political dots: "That's the only way you get your hands on the levers of power."[16] Skilled southern Democrats in Congress could make incumbency work wonders. The veterans could pursue the vital interests of their districts, states, and the entire region. Patience and good health became the keys to long-term influence via the committee system; ability and a willingness to "go along" were also needed to climb the Democratic leadership ladders. For decades the South was represented in Washington by experienced, professional politicians whose careers were devoted to exercising political influence in the central representative institutions of American government.

At the top of the formal hierarchy were the southerners who were chosen by the party caucus to lead the House and Senate Democrats after long experience in other leadership positions. From the election of Georgia Democrat Charles Crisp as Speaker in 1891 to the death of Speaker Rayburn of Texas in 1961, a southerner usually led the Democratic party in the House of Representatives. During these seven decades the South supplied ten of the twelve men who acted as either Speaker or minority leader. Rayburn's long career illustrates the process. Elected to the House in 1912 at the age of thirty, the Texan initially secured an appointment to the Interstate and Foreign Commerce Committee. There he worked diligently to become the protégé of its veteran chairman, William Adamson of Georgia. Later Rayburn's political abilities brought him to the helpful attention of Garner, his more senior Texas colleague, who was an influential figure in the House Democratic leadership. In the fullness of time Rayburn rose through the seniority system to chair the Commerce Committee before making his way into the House Democratic leadership, first as majority leader and later, in 1940, as Speaker of the House. For the next two decades Rayburn remained the Democratic leader.[17]

In the Senate Thomas Martin of Virginia, Oscar Underwood of Alabama, and Joseph Robinson of Arkansas held similar leadership roles. Robinson served as party leader from 1923 until his death in 1937. President Roosevelt blocked the conservative Mississippi senator Pat Harrison from succeeding Robinson, preferring instead the more pliant Kentuckian Alben Barkley, who remained leader until 1949. During much of Barkley's tenure the real leadership lay in the hands of Richard Russell of Georgia. A naturally gifted politician, he became Speaker of the Georgia General Assembly in his twenties and was the youngest governor in the history of the state. Elected to the Senate in 1933, Russell enthusiastically supported Roosevelt's New Deal. In his later years, his principal concerns were civil rights and national defense. "The intellectual leader of the Southern hierarchy," according to Paul H. Douglas, he "mastered the rules and procedures of the Senate and used them to defeat and emasculate any proposal aimed at improving the status of Ne-groes." Russell became the leader of the Dixie caucus after Senator Har-rison died in 1941, but his influence went far beyond the southerners. "Without his approval," Rowland W. Evans and Robert Novak reported, "no Democratic senator became his party's floor leader or whip." Far too rigid a segregationist to serve as the party's elected leader, Russell was always on the lookout for rising politicians sympathetic to the southern cause. In 1949 he became mightily impressed with Lyndon Johnson, a freshman from Texas who had served in the House since 1937.[18]

Johnson had begun his meteoric Senate rise in 1948 after surviving a controversial election by the narrowest of margins—an "official" eighty-seven votes. Johnson defined himself as a Texan rather than a south-erner, and he did not formally join the southern caucus. However, he had always opposed federal civil rights legislation—his first speech in the Senate supported the southern position on the cloture rule—and he im-mediately gravitated toward pleasing Russell as the surest route to lead-ership in the Senate. With Russell's behind-the-scenes help Johnson was elected majority whip in 1951, minority leader in 1953, and majority leader in 1955. Until he resigned to become vice president in 1961, Johnson led the Senate Democrats.[19]

Many of the chairmen and senior members of the most consequen-tial House and Senate committees were also southern Democrats. Their leadership roles were acquired and protected by a seniority rule that strongly benefited members of the majority party with safe seats. South-ern Democrats stacked themselves on committees that might help them service their states and districts as well as generate influence within their institutions. Many acquired reputations as effective, practical, "can-do" legislators. Such southern conservatives as Russell, Byrd, Walter George, Tom Connally, James Eastland, and John Stennis in the Senate, and Cox, Howard Smith, John McMillan, and Graham Barden in the House, could lead their committees without interference from the elected party leadership. Representing mainly the interests, values, and prejudices of the voters who sent them to Congress, the southern com-mittee chairs often pursued agendas that differed from the preferences of majorities of House and Senate Democrats.[20]

Thus southern Democrats could be party leaders in the Senate and

House and safe incumbents in their states and districts. The moderates among them could command enough influence to lead the party, while the more conservative committee chairs could depart from party orthodoxy, keep their leadership positions, and vote on the floor according to their calculations of constituency interests. Not all southerners were as effective or as influential as the chairs, of course, but it would be a remarkably inept incumbent who could not return home to point with pride to benefits that he had brought to the state or district.[21] Midway through the twentieth century, southern whites still set much of the tone and priorities of the House and Senate Democratic parties.

Most important, the southern Democrats' juggernaut enabled them to control racial issues. Whether or not the Democratic party held a majority in the Senate, southern Democrats skilled in parliamentary procedure could always use filibusters or threats of filibusters to discourage if possible—and kill whenever necessary—any serious consideration of civil rights issues. Democratic solidarity was especially important in the Senate because the filibuster was the final weapon of the southern segregationists in blocking national action on civil rights. The Senate's tradition of unlimited debate enabled the southern Democrats to say "no!" with authority. For many generations the solidarity of southern Democrats in Congress constrained American politics in the most fundamental way. Because of their power, significant changes in southern race relations could not be legislated.

Even on the crucial racial issues, however, there had been indications of waning southern influence within the congressional Democratic party. The New Deal brought many northern Democrats into Congress, a development that transformed the relative size of the southern delegations within the Democratic party. After the 1932 elections, as David Potter has pointed out, the South "passed from constituting a majority wing in a minority party to constituting a minority wing in a majority party." Some northern liberal Democrats began to object to the southerners' influence over the party's leadership and agenda. Representing racially and ethnically diverse states and districts with sizable labor-union constituencies, they wanted the party to pass programs of economic and racial liberalism.[22]

Southern Democrats went on the offensive against their northern colleagues. In 1938, for example, while filibustering antilynching legislation demanded by northern liberals, North Carolina senator Josiah W. Bailey warned of "internecine war" if northern Democrats attacked the southern caste system. The South's most influential Democratic senator, James R. Byrnes of South Carolina, told senators that the bill should be retitled as "a bill to arouse ill-feeling between the sections, inspire race hatred in the South, and destroy the Democratic Party." Southern Democrats were even more distressed in 1948 when President Truman included civil rights legislation as part of his Fair Deal agenda. It was the first time in American history that a Democratic president had actually proposed civil rights legislation. Russell characterized Truman's proposals as the "most outrageous affront to the people of our section that we have had to face since Reconstruction days." Quickly mobilizing his fellow southern Democrats, "Russell told a newsman that he had never seen southerners so upset about the racial question. This was because they saw Truman's demand for an end to Jim Crow legislation as 'an opening wedge in the fight to stop all segregation,' which would mean that blacks and whites would 'attend the same schools, swim in the same pools, eat together, and, eventually, intermarry.'"[23]

Truman's racial policies undercut an "unwritten understanding" between the northern and southern wings of the Democratic party. "Until the Truman Administration," historian George W. Mowry has argued, "the southern governing elite received from the national Democratic party something far more important than individual perquisites and sectional grants: an understanding that their support of the party in its decided leftward movement from 1912 to the present would be repaid by a willingness to permit the South to maintain the existing patterns of racial relations and, to a lesser degree, those characterizing the relations between capital and labor throughout the section." As Mowry emphasized, "This seldom-mentioned, unwritten understanding, never formally negotiated and always precarious, especially when a new reforming president took power, was nevertheless the glue by which diverse and often contradictory elements of the party were held together."[24]

Eventually the congressional Democratic parties became so divided over irreconcilable issues that Democratic leaders tried to suppress these conflicts by refusing to call party meetings. When Garner advised Rayburn to use the House Democratic caucus to bind all members to support the position of the majority, the Speaker exploded. "You don't know what the hell you're talking about," Rayburn said. "You can't do that any more. This is a different group of men. You get in that caucus and a wild man from the North will get up and make a wild speech. Then someone from another section will answer him with a wilder speech. First thing you know, you've got the Democratic party so divided that you can't pass anything."[25] Likewise, Johnson saw no point in bringing Senate Democrats together except for a perfunctory formal meeting at the beginning of each Congress.

Confronted with growing northern opposition within their own party, southern Democrats began to exploit the possibilities of a relatively new and untested political alliance with conservative northern and western Republicans. From the shared interests of these two blocs emerged the politics of the "conservative coalition" and the "Inner Club." "During and after the war, Southerners and Republicans found it increasingly easy to work together and perfected the technique of interparty co-operation," Douglas noted. "While neither had a majority alone, when united they did. This conservative coalition dominated Congress during these years. Its members always showed up for roll calls, and its power was occasionally openly flaunted, as when Harry F. Byrd and Robert A. Taft sat together on the floor, checking the list of Senators and sending out for the absent or the few recalcitrants."[26]

In this environment influential Democratic and Republican conservatives informally set the limits on passable legislation. Accounts of the Senate during the late 1940s and most of the 1950s repeatedly describe an institution dominated by an Inner Club of Republicans and southern Democrats. "The heart of the coalition," Evans and Novak reported, "was a *quid pro quo:* the Republicans agreeing to vote with the South against civil rights legislation, the Southern Democrats agreeing to vote with the Republicans against Truman's economic legislation." Douglas emphasized the "tacit protection the Northern Republicans gave the Southern Democrats on racial matters. They did not openly espouse white supremacy or denounce efforts to improve the position of blacks. This would have been politically fatal in many parts of the North. In the Senate they did it by protecting the Southerners' right to filibuster."[27] As the 1950s began, strict segregation was still thoroughly entrenched in the South. The explosive, unresolvable, and largely suppressed issue facing northern Democrats was what to do about pervasive southern racism.

Although preserving the racial status quo was always the paramount concern of southern senators and representatives, this objective by no means exhausted their legislative interests and concerns. To understand why nearly all the southern Democrats remained within the party after they were decisively defeated on civil rights issues in the 1960s, it is crucial to identify other interests—opposition to organized labor and taxation of their constituents as well as support for scores of governmental programs—that linked southern members of Congress with the Democratic party.

Most southern Democrats opposed organized labor. In the rural and small-town South Democrats usually enjoyed the support of the business community and leading farmers. Garner controlled much of the economic activity in Uvalde, Texas. As Speaker of the House and later vice president under Franklin Roosevelt, he epitomized southern opposition to the growing power of organized labor. "Garner's sizeable fortune, as well as that of his Texas friends and of his Southern friends in Congress, had been built on cheap labor," Robert A. Caro has written. Unions were no more welcome in Uvalde than they were in most other southern small towns in the first half of the twentieth century. "To men accustomed to treating laborers like serfs, the very idea of unions was anathema," Caro stressed. "Mr. Garner, he don't like unions," a Uvalde carpenter told Caro. "The plumbers, they had a union once, but they don't now."[28]

Garner's stance accurately reflected the viewpoint of most southern congressmen about the proper relationship between employers and workers. "In spite of their willingness to support an assertive role in the national state in economic affairs with approximately the same degree of enthusiasm as nonsouthern Democrats," Ira Katznelson, Kim Geiger, and Daniel Kryder have argued, southern Democrats "broke ranks on labor-centered questions—whether to facilitate the establishment of a genuinely national labor market and create a favorable climate for trade union organization."[29] The Taft-Hartley Act, strenuously fought by organized labor, passed in 1947 with the overwhelming support of most southern senators and representatives in alliance with northern Republicans. Because many southern Democrats were lifelong allies of the business community and opponents of organized labor, conservatives did not need southern Republicans to represent their views on labor issues.

Taxes also produced considerable agreement among southern Democrats. They wanted taxes kept as low as possible and resisted federal programs whose complex rules and regulations might anger or annoy local elites. Again Garner's attitude was typical. Obsessed with economy in government, his first inclination was to minimize taxation. "In his short life," a biographer wrote, "he had learned how hard men worked to make the money that went into taxes. He hated to see public money frittered away . . . People [in his district] were struggling to get along in stock raising and were building their family lives for future generations. There had to be, as Garner saw it, a good reason for every dollar the government took from these people's toil."[30]

The Great Depression further devastated the already impoverished southern economy. Southern Democrats, embedded in influential leadership and committee positions after President Roosevelt took charge in 1933, proved adept at getting federal dollars flowing into the region with few restrictions on their use. President Roosevelt's New Deal programs paid for Social Security, old-age assistance, and farm programs and put unemployed southerners to work.[31] Millions of dollars helped to construct dams, reservoirs, harbors, highways, and airports. Federal money was political magic, a regional free lunch. It cost the South little because most southerners did not earn enough money to pay federal income taxes. A study of the First Congressional District of Texas during the 1930s, for example, estimated that less than two-thirds of one percent of its citizens paid federal income taxes.[32] New Deal economic policies extracted tax revenues from wealthier individuals and corporations in the more affluent areas of the nation and then redistributed goods and services to citizens living in the poorest parts of the nation. The South received far more in federal expenditures than it sent to Washington in taxes.

Johnson (then a Texas representative) often emphasized these practical economic benefits to his conservative financial backers, Herman Brown and George Brown of the growing Texas construction firm Brown and Root. As George Brown later explained, "Herman would be ranting and raving about New Deal spending, and Lyndon would say,

'What are you worried about? It's not coming out of *your* pocket. Any money that's spent down here on New Deal projects, the East is paying for. We don't pay taxes in Texas . . . They're paying for our projects.'" Other southern politicians emphasized this important point. "Lyndon would take me to these meetings of the Southern Congressmen, and that's the way they'd be talking," George Brown told Caro. "That the South would get these dams and these other projects, and it would come out of the other fellow's pocket. The Presidents before Roosevelt—Coolidge, Hoover—they never gave the South anything. Roosevelt was the first one who gave the South a break. That's why he had more plusses than minuses, because he was getting them all this money."[33]

Liberal spending policies, combined with conservative policies on race, taxation, and union matters, enabled southern Democrats to give most white voters what they wanted while protecting them from what they opposed. The southerners' seniority advantage in the majority party enabled them to deliver services and benefits at little immediate direct cost to their constituents. Moreover, the southern Democrats were a powerful swing force in the Senate and House of Representatives. They could vote with their fellow Democrats in favor of programs that kept mainly northern federal dollars flowing into their districts and states on terms that did not challenge the racial status quo; and they could join with the Republicans to block truly consequential civil rights legislation and craft conservative labor legislation. Because they dominated the most senior levels of the Democratic party leadership, southerners contributed mightily to the tone and priorities of the House and Senate Democratic parties. As a result the Democratic party and Democratic Congresses remained exceedingly useful to a majority of white southerners.

THE REPUBLICAN CONCESSION

As of 1950 the southern Republican party had almost no followers, no leaders, and no candidates for public office. Many native whites, raised to love Democrats and hate Republicans, still used "Republican!" as a defiant cussword. In most of the South any signs of genuine Republican efforts to unseat incumbent Democrats outraged white conservatives and astonished the local media. "It would be tragic, it would be horrible, it would be unbelievable," insisted conservative Georgia Democrat Jack Flynt in 1956, "for Democrats to knowingly or inadvertently help replace [incumbent Democrat] Jim Davis by a Republican congressman for the Fifth District." "For the first time in memory," reported the *Atlanta Journal,* "Democrats have shown some real concern about Republican opposition. The district has seen what politicking must be like in states where two-party fights are the usual thing."[34]

Although Democrats usually ignored or joked about the few harmless local Republicans, sometimes they treated them as enemies to be ostracized and financially punished. For example, "when a small-town Georgia Ford dealer has the temerity to favor a Republican presidential candidate, he loses '17 trade-in customers' to the Chevrolet dealer across the square." Likewise, "A retail merchant attributes a drop of one-third in his trade to the fact that he bolted the Democratic ticket." Anticipated reactions of prominent Democrats to partisan apostasy could keep conservatives from straying. A lawyer who acted as secretary for a southern Democratic party "would like to vote Republican. Most Americans who think and live and act as he does are Republicans. The Democratic party has become, according to him, the party of Negroes, labor, and all the people who can't or won't make a living. They're not his kind. But if he voted Republican once, he says, and even if the Republicans won in that election, he might as well 'turn in his papers' and abandon any ambition for a successful law practice." In another instance, "A Texan of substance fairly hated F.D.R. He expressed good will toward the Republican party but protested, 'If you join, you lose your influence.'"[35]

"The most signal characteristic of the party's southern 'leadership,'" Heard concluded in 1952, was its "lack of interest in winning elections." In the words of James L. Sundquist, the southern Republicans appeared to be a "hopeless, discredited band of stragglers, disreputably led, without tradition of victory or prospect of it." "Southern Republican leaders," Key observed, "are usually pictured as vultures awaiting the day when the party wins the nation and they can distribute patronage in the South. Meantime, they exert themselves only to keep the party weak in the South in order that there will be fewer faithful to reward." With an exception here and there, Republican leaders were uninterested in building a thriving party that regularly fielded candidates and sincerely attempted to win elections.[36]

Most southern Republican leaders were experienced defeatists. "'There's no use fooling ourselves about' winning any seats in South Carolina in the congressional elections, J. Bates Gerald, the Republican state chairman announced in 1946. 'So we're offering no candidates in the general election, in order that every cent of money contributed in the state can be sent into doubtful states to finance campaigns there.'" Gerald was a realist who knew what he was talking about. For generations southern Republicans had adapted to the expectation of defeat by forfeiting elections. Outside the minority party's few traditional rural enclaves in the Peripheral South highlands there were simply not enough Republican voters to generate competitive campaigns. "I am glad to see here under one roof today practically the entire Republican party of the Fifth District," conservative Georgia Democrat Jim Davis chided his Republican opponent during a debate at Atlanta's Henry Grady Hotel in 1956. Southern Republicans could not realistically believe they could unseat many sitting Democrats or win open-seat elections.[37]

In the first half of the twentieth century, Republicans won only 80 of 2,565 congressional elections in the South. Most of these victories occurred in a tiny number of congressional districts in the mountains and valleys of Appalachia, where the strongest white opposition to secession and the Confederacy had appeared. Fifty Republican victories were in two East Tennessee congressional districts, and another 17 took place in 3 neighboring Blue Ridge seats in western North Carolina and southwestern Virginia. An additional 6 victories occurred during the 1920s in a Texas district that included San Antonio and several counties with German populations. With the exception of these six unusual districts, the Democratic electoral juggernaut in the rest of the South was astonishing: southern Republicans won only 7 of 2,434 congressional elections during the first half of the twentieth century! Matters were even worse for southern Republicans with senatorial ambitions. The last Republican senator was Jeter Pritchard, who had been chosen by the North Carolina legislature in 1895. After Pritchard's term expired in 1903, every southern senator had been a Democrat.

Capitulation was plainly evident in the minority party's paltry efforts to compete in southern senatorial and congressional elections in the 1930s and 1940s (see Figure 2.2). Republicans forfeited two-thirds of the House elections, ran candidates who received less than 40 percent of the vote in another quarter of the elections, and fought truly challenging but losing campaigns in 3 percent of the contests. Only in Tennessee, North Carolina, and Virginia did the minority party contest more congressional seats than it forfeited. All twenty victories occurred in Tennessee's Second (Republican since 1867) and First (Republican since 1880) congressional districts. In the remaining eight southern states Republicans typically did not even engage in token efforts. They forfeited more than three-fourths of House elections in Arkansas, Florida, and Texas; and they were especially moribund in the Deep South, failing to compete in almost nine-tenths of all congressional elections. During the 1930s and 1940s Republicans also forfeited more than half the Senate elections. Token contesting for Senate seats was the central tendency of North Carolina, Tennessee, and Virginia. Elsewhere, particularly in the Deep South, Republicans did not bother Democratic senators.[38]

"The greatest stimulus to party growth," Heard argued, "lies in a continuous stream of serious candidates." Republican acquiescence, however understandable, was thoroughly self-defeating. "The easiest way to keep a political party small," he further emphasized, "is to fail to put up candidates."[39] Local Republicans would need to campaign energetically if the party were ever to grow. Exceptionally motivated candidates, unique districts, favorable short-term forces—all these circumstances would be required before southern Republicans could wrest many seats from the dominant Democrats.

Southern Republicans needed outside help. At midcentury challenging the Democrats in southern presidential elections became the first priority for national Republican campaign strategists. Successful and sustained presidential Republicanism might slowly expand the party's grassroots base. "The development of an opposition party in the South will probably depend more on events outside the South than on the exertions of native Republicans," Key asserted. "If the balance of power becomes one that clearly requires a Republican fight for southern votes to win the Presidency, presumably the national party could no longer tolerate its ineffective southern leadership." Heard, too, suggested that "rivalry for the presidency and control of the Congress promises to be

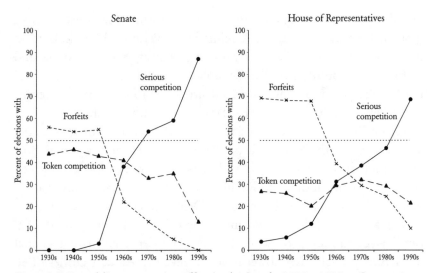

Figure 2.2 Republican campaign effort in the South, 1930s–1990s. *Sources:* Same as Figure 2.1.

the chief prod to Republican growth." Should Republican presidential candidates begin to target southern states that had concentrations of traditional Republicans and/or growing middle-class metropolitan areas, the Solid Democratic South might be disrupted, enabling Republicans to compete more effectively for lesser offices.[40]

By 1952 national Republicans *were* actively in search of southern electoral votes. Their Lincoln Strategy of writing off the South had failed in five consecutive presidential elections. Although the Republicans had no hope of carrying the entire South, they believed that the personal appeal of a popular candidate might enable the party to win several southern states and neutralize the usual Democratic advantage in the region. General Dwight D. Eisenhower was the human triggering mechanism for the first Republican breakthrough in the South. The immensely popular former commander-in-chief of Allied forces in World War II was an ideal Republican candidate to attract southern support. A smiling moderate conservative who did not repudiate popular New Deal programs, a trusted figure who exemplified common sense and leaned toward states' rights, Eisenhower united the small number of southern Republicans and appealed to many conservative independents and Democrats.[41]

His presidential campaign divided the South along the fault lines of subregion, racial composition, and urbanism. Eisenhower carried Florida, Tennessee, Texas, and Virginia in the Peripheral South, but lost to Illinois Democrat Adlai Stevenson in Arkansas, North Carolina, and all five Deep South states. The Republican candidate won a majority of the Peripheral South congressional districts but lost almost nine-tenths of the Deep South districts. In the Peripheral South Eisenhower ran best in urban districts with few blacks, exactly where white voters were the least obsessed with Democratic party orthodoxy. He also captured most of the rural districts with very low black populations, almost all of which contained many mountain Republicans. His moderate conservatism had far less appeal in the Deep South. Democratic party leaders had put Alabama Senator John Sparkman on the ticket as the vice presidential candidate, and Stevenson won 35 of the 39 Deep South congressional districts. Although Eisenhower never achieved landslide victories of 60 percent or better in any southern state, he did so in 13 House districts. The Republican nominee had smaller majorities in 26 other districts and lost to Stevenson in 67 districts.

Eisenhower's limited success in the South did not produce many new Republican victories in House elections and was not associated with any Senate gains. Winning seats in the House of Representatives and Senate was *not* a major objective for southern Republican leaders during the 1950s. Their top priority was electing a presidential candidate by attracting conservative Democrats and independents. A memo circulating among southern Republican leaders in 1952 clearly revealed the minority party's strategy in the South. "Wean the Southerner to EISENHOWER, hero of America and the world—give them, in full measure, a hero to worship—they'll love it," so advised a confidential memorandum to Virginia supporters of presidential candidate Eisenhower in 1952. "Do not try to sell the Republican party to Southern voters—sell Eisenhower as the great American he is—whose principles of governing have been accepted by the Republican Party in making him their candidate." By employing this strategy, southern Republicans could recruit southern Democrats "to work for Eisenhower without sacrificing their Democratic standing in state politics."[42]

However helpful this approach may have been for Eisenhower, it simultaneously blunted progress in electing more Republicans to Congress. Republican candidates clung to the popular Eisenhower ("Send

Dick to help Ike," was the slogan of Virginia Republican Richard Poff, who upset an incumbent Democrat), but the presidential candidate did not ask southern voters to elect Republicans to Congress.[43] Stimulated by Eisenhower's 1952 presidential campaign, a small number of southern Republicans began to campaign aggressively for congressional seats, though it would be another eight years before a southern GOP candidate campaigned seriously against an incumbent Democratic senator.

Eisenhower's weak appeal across the South is visible in Figure 2.3. Consider first the relationship between Eisenhower's 1952 vote and the patterns of southern Republican contesting for Congress, which appears in Figure 2.3 as "House Enclaves." Southern Republicans won 6 of the region's 106 House seats. Republican congressional candidates won 31 percent (4 victories) of the 13 Eisenhower landslide districts, those where Ike won 60 percent or more of the total vote. They won only 8 percent (2 victories) of the 26 districts with smaller Eisenhower majorities. Although all the Republican congressional victories occurred in districts that Eisenhower carried, the central partisan tendency in these districts was the election (or reelection) of a Democrat. Only in the Eisenhower landslide districts did many Republicans obtain at least 40 percent of the total vote, our threshold for a serious competition. Potential Republican candidates were typically on the sidelines in the districts that Eisenhower carried with small majorities. In only 5 of these contests did Republicans poll two-fifths or more of the vote.

Republican failure to compete was even starker in the remaining 67 southern districts where Stevenson defeated Eisenhower. These districts, located throughout the Deep South, Arkansas, Middle and West Tennessee, eastern and central Texas, eastern North Carolina, the panhandle of Florida, and Southside Virginia, constituted the most hostile environments for Republican challengers. If Eisenhower could not carry these districts against an Illinois Democrat, what chance had Republican congressional candidates against southern Democrats? No Republican won a House election in any of these districts. "District is Democratic stronghold," concluded one of the losing Republicans; "Eisenhower defeated here nearly 2 to 1." Republican elites forfeited four-fifths of the potential contests in these settings.[44]

Eisenhower's 1952 vote never reached 60 percent in any state (see the "Senate Concession" in Figure 2.3). Southern Republican politicians

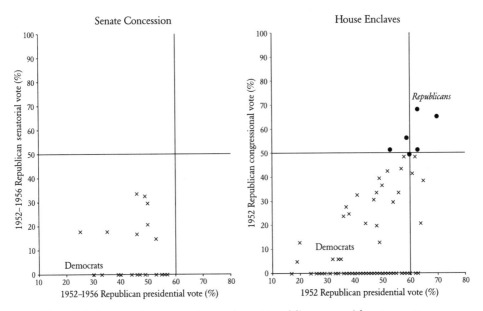

Figure 2.3 Starting from scratch: southern Republicans at midcentury. *Sources:* Same as Figure 2.1.

continued to concede Senate seats, either through outright forfeits or through nominal campaigns. During the 1952–1960 cycle only a single southern Republican, John Tower of Texas, secured as much as 40 percent of the vote. Republican weakness is symbolized by the empty upper right cell, the space representing landslide Republican presidential victories linked to the election of Republican senators.

ENCLAVE REPUBLICANISM IN THE 1950s

In House elections the first thrust of southern Republicanism expanded the party's traditional rural mountain base and made modest inroads in the region's metropolitan areas. Five of the party's six victories in 1952 occurred in contiguous Blue Ridge districts. Tennessee representatives B. Carroll Reece and Howard Baker, the party's only incumbents, easily won reelection. In the neighboring Virginia Ninth District, twenty-six-year-old Republican William Wampler "traveled 35,000 miles and made 250 speeches" to win an open seat. Although Eisenhower carried the district with only a small majority (53 percent), Wampler benefited from a brutal Democratic primary fight that weakened his opponent. Aggressive Republican challengers unseated veteran Democrats in two districts that combined traditional Republican rural supporters with urban middle-class conservatives. In Virginia's Sixth District (Roanoke and Lynchburg) the victor was Poff, a twenty-nine-year-old conservative activist who "shook 10,000 hands and gave 130 speeches." Charles R. Jonas, the son of a Republican who had been elected to Congress in 1928, also capitalized upon Eisenhower's appeal to win the North Carolina Tenth District, a constituency that blended rural Republicans with Charlotte's rising middle class. And southern Republicans broke out of the Blue Ridge in 1952 when real estate developer Joel Broyhill captured a newly created suburban district in northern Virginia. "GOP organizing typically was easier there than elsewhere," explains Frank Atkinson, "because of the influx of Republicans from outside the state and the tendency of many northern Virginia Democrats to align themselves with the more liberal northern Democratic Party."[45]

Two years later the Republicans had a net gain of one seat. Wampler was unseated by a united Democratic party in Virginia's Ninth District, but the GOP picked up two more urban districts. Dallas's Bruce Alger won an open seat with 53 percent of the vote in a district that Eisenhower had swept two years earlier. "In Texas," according to *Time*, "the time-tested Democratic campaign principle is to ignore Republican candidates." However, "Alger refused to be ignored. He campaigned so busily that he even wandered into his opponent's own office in search of votes." William Cramer's sustained organizational efforts paid off in the Florida First, an Eisenhower landslide district "peopled by thousands of retired Northerners." The young lawyer "came close in 1952 in the Tampa–St. Petersburg district, lost only on the count of absentee ballots—and never stopped running." Cramer's success illustrated how an energetic local Republican leadership could capitalize upon the migration of new voters into the retirement areas of the region.[46]

After the 1954 elections the Republicans made no more southern gains during the rest of the decade. Southern conservatives became disenchanted with President Eisenhower in 1954 after the Supreme Court, led by Eisenhower appointee Earl Warren, declared school segregation laws unconstitutional. Three years later the president sent U.S. Army troops to Little Rock, Arkansas, to enforce a federal court order requiring desegregation of a local high school. Angry southern Democrats charged that the Republicans were once again forcing unwanted racial changes in the South. As this racial controversy blew across the region, Republican politicians lay low in the 1958 congressional elections. The seven "embattled" GOP incumbents "held firm," but only fifteen Republican candidates appeared on the ballot in the remaining ninety-nine districts.[47]

Events in the Fifth District of Florida illustrated how military intervention in Arkansas affected the political climate. Eisenhower had twice carried this district with more than 60 percent of the vote, and in 1956 a Republican challenger had nearly ousted incumbent Democrat Sydney Herlong. In 1958, however, the conservative Democrat defeated his Republican opponent, William C. Coleman, by two to one. Herlong explained that his victory was due "largely to the fact that I ran solely on the basis of States' rights." Coleman was much more specific. "'I lost because of Little Rock,'" he told *U.S. News and World Report.* "For three days radio and TV stations every 15 minutes blared out—to a background of 'Dixie'—the appeal: 'Protest use of American troops against American citizens; protect and assure States' rights; vote the State Democratic ticket; keep the Solid South solid.'" The political message was clear: presidential intervention to enforce school desegregation placed tremendous burdens on the president's party in the South among white voters.[48]

For a minority political party, growth requires reelecting any incumbents, winning most open-seat opportunities, and defeating incumbents of the majority party. In 1952 the southern Republicans had no incumbent senators and only two incumbent representatives. In the next two elections, the Republicans combined three defeats of incumbent Democrats, three open-seat victories, and only one loss among their incumbents to reach seven representatives. No Republican was elected to the Senate from a southern state during the 1950s.

The magnitude of the southern Republicans' persistent "Democratic problem" can be illustrated by sorting congressional elections into those involving Democratic incumbents, those with open seats, and those containing Republican incumbents. Defeating an incumbent Democrat would typically be the most daunting task of all. Few Republicans relished the fool's errand of taking on veteran Democrats. Open-seat elections might tempt occasional Republican challenges. However, because of the stupendous Democratic advantage among likely voters *and* experienced candidates, Republican prospects remained grim even when a House seat became vacant. Republican challengers would obviously be underdogs in the vast majority of these constituencies. Any elections, involving Republican incumbents, on the other hand, would offer the greatest likelihood of Republican victories.

Figure 2.4 separates the southern House delegations elected from 1952 through 1960 into Democratic incumbents, open-seat winners, and Republican incumbents, and plots outcomes according to shares of the popular votes and Democratic party unity scores.[49] The vertical line at 60 percent separates winners with safe seats from those without them. Horizontal lines divide *national or liberal* Democrats (those with Democratic party unity scores of 80 to 100) from *moderate* Democrats (those with Democratic party unity scores of 60–79) and from *conservative or nominal* Democrats (those with Democratic party unity scores of 0 to 59) and Republicans.

In practice as well as in theory, of course, it was extraordinarily difficult for a southern Republican to defeat a sitting southern Democrat. Eighty-five percent of the South's 530 congressional elections in the 1950s featured an incumbent Democrat who wanted to return to Washington. These veterans compiled a reelection rate of 99 percent, prevailing in all but 3 of 452 elections. Democratic incumbents ordinarily returned to Congress with huge landslide victories. Almost 95 percent of the incumbent Democrats were either unopposed or captured more than three-fifths of the vote. During the 1950s, before the conservative white South's decisive defeats on civil rights, southern Democrats varied considerably in their degree of support for the positions of majorities of House Democrats. Nominal support for the party was their most frequent response, but many southern Democrats behaved as moderates, and more than a few acted as national Democrats.[50]

One of the most powerful indicators of Democratic dominance during the 1950s is the Republican failure to field candidates in a majority of the open-seat elections. Nine percent of the southern House elections were open, and Democrats won 94 percent of these contests. Judging by their party unity scores, the central tendency of the newly elected Democrats was to act as moderates. An open seat in Nashville,

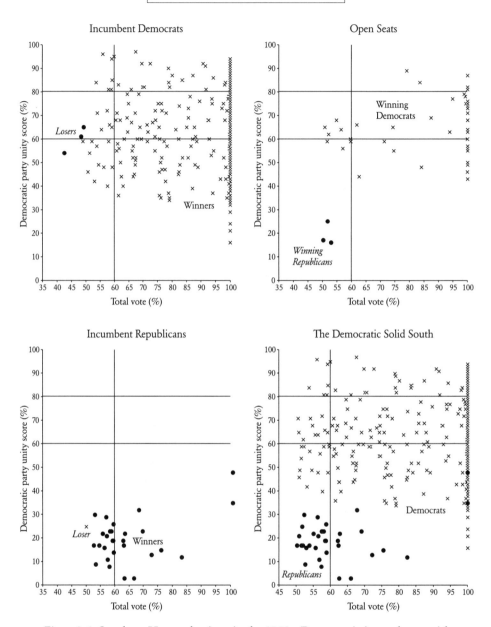

Figure 2.4 Southern House elections in the 1950s: Democratic incumbents with safe seats preserve the Solid South. *Sources:* Same as Figure 2.1.

Tennessee, in 1956 illustrates the enduring Republican disadvantage in open-seat elections. The winning Democrat stressed two fundamental advantages: the seat was "normally Democratic," and his Republican opponent was "virtually unknown." The losing Republican challenger emphasized the absence of Republican party organization in the district. "Had 200 names on file at start of campaign from district with 150,000 registered voters," he told *U.S. News and World Report.* "Party organized only 60 days prior to election."[51]

Although the few Republican incumbents won 97 percent of their reelection efforts, they were on the ballot in only 5 percent of the elections. All Republicans who established secure reelection constituencies represented districts where Eisenhower had polled landslide majorities in 1952 and/or 1956. Energetic campaigning was essential to the incumbents' success. After winning reelection in 1956, for example, Alger emphasized several reasons for his success: "Voters believed in Eisenhower" and "complete acceptance of this premise: 'The Lord helps those who help themselves.' We all worked like dogs." Conservative philosophy was important. "My re-election re-emphasizes Dallas's basic conservatism and our belief in a limited role for government in our lives," Alger told *U.S. News and World Report* after the 1960 election. "This was the whole campaign here." From suburban northern Virginia, Broyhill attributed his 1960 reelection to "A consistent eight-year Republican voting record in national and international legislation [that] gained wholehearted support from a remarkably efficient Republican organization."[52] Only Wampler, competing in a rural district that Eisenhower had carried with a small majority, failed to win reelection. The seven surviving Republican incumbents expanded the party's small niche in the southern House delegation.

"The Democratic Solid South," the final panel in Figure 2.4, reconstructs the party battle in the 1950s for southern House seats. It displays the winning Democrats and winning Republicans according to their vote shares and political ideology. Before federal intervention in southern race relations, the Democratic Solid South remained largely intact. Safe-seat Democratic incumbents continued to overwhelm (mainly) non-safe-seat Republican incumbents. The northern challenge to southern race relations emerged periodically, but not with the force that would soon characterize House debates over civil rights. The southern

Democrats' racial conservatism was not in doubt. Seventy-seven percent of the delegation, including every Deep South Democrat, signed a "Southern Manifesto" in 1956 denouncing the *Brown* decision on school desegregation. Texas Democrats accounted for two-thirds of the nonsigners.[53]

By the 1950s House Speaker Rayburn had sufficiently moderated his racial views to urge some of his younger southern colleagues to support the Civil Rights Act of 1957, legislation that created the U.S. Commission on Civil Rights. In private—strictly in private—the aging Texas politician agreed with the Supreme Court's 1954 decision in *Brown v. Board of Education.* "If you had been on that Court," Rayburn told a legislative aide, "you'd have voted exactly as they voted—if you were an honest man."[54] Indeed, with Rayburn in charge of the Democratic agenda, southern Democrats did not necessarily have to position themselves as conservatives on the much broader set of issues that separated majorities of Democrats from majorities of Republicans. Although only 15 percent of the Democrats voted with their national party 80 percent or more of the time, during the 1950s there were slightly more moderate Democrats (45 percent) than nominal or conservative Democrats (40 percent). The small group of southern Republicans gave little support to Democratic party positions and stood out as much more conservative than most of the southern Democrats.

Both the location and the racial composition of the Republicans' southern districts bear emphasis. Each Republican congressional victory occurred in a Peripheral South district that had a black population of less than 15 percent. Beyond the traditional Republicanism of the Blue Ridge, the central thrust of the successful Republican candidates was an appeal to the economic and social conservatism of the expanding white middle class. By and large, the House Republicans were not conspicuous racial conservatives. The Eisenhower administration, after all, was identified with enforcing the school desegregation decision. There matters stood as the civil rights movement gradually awakened the northern electorates and politicians to the injustice of southern segregation.

The abject failure of southern Republicans to seriously contest—much less win—many elections during the 1950s resembled the party's past more than its future. Despite the GOP's effort to make the South a presidential battleground, the region generally remained a vast Republican wasteland in elections for Congress. Republicans forfeited a majority of House and Senate elections. When they did field candidates, token efforts were more common than serious campaigns (see Figure 2.2). From 1952 through 1960 Republicans won only 34 of 530 southern House elections. Three-fourths of their victories occurred in the three Peripheral South states—Tennessee, Virginia, and North Carolina—where there had always been mountain Republicans; and the party advanced slightly in Texas and Florida, states that would eventually contribute far more to Republican successes. Nonetheless, southern Republicans never solved their candidate problem in senatorial and congressional elections, never overcame the Democratic juggernaut among voters and candidates. Only in a few enclaves did the Republicans operate as a real political party capable of seriously contesting and actually winning elections. After the 1960 elections the Republicans controlled none of the region's senators and merely 7 percent of the southern House delegation. They were still starting from scratch.

3

THE PROMISING
PERIPHERAL SOUTH

When John F. Kennedy became president in January 1961, the Senate juggernaut of southern Democrats was intact. The southern delegation contained neither any Republican senators nor any veteran Democrats who appeared vulnerable to Republican challenges. One seat was vacant because Lyndon Johnson of Texas had become the new vice president—his replacement would soon be chosen in a special election—but the remaining twenty-one senators were all Democrats. Three decades later, after the 1990 elections, the Republicans had made a modest advance: they held seven of the twenty-two southern Senate seats. Only a handful of southern Republican politicians—John Tower and Phil Gramm of Texas, Strom Thurmond of South Carolina, Howard Baker of Tennessee, Jesse Helms of North Carolina, John Warner of Virginia, and Thad Cochran of Mississippi—had been able to construct careers in the Senate. Other Republicans, however, such as Edward Gurney of Florida, Bill Brock of Tennessee, William Scott of Virginia, and Mack Mattingly of Georgia, had been one-termers, senators who failed to convert incumbency into secure seats. Evaluated against the standard of a partisan realignment in officeholding, Republicans had broken the Democratic monopoly but remained a small minority of the region's senators.

The initial Republican advance commenced during the Kennedy and Johnson administrations. Democratic presidents were now finally compelled to deal with southern racism. In the mid-1960s southern Democrats lost their informal veto over racial legislation when majorities of northern Democrats and northern Republicans combined to pass the Civil Rights Act and the Voting Rights Act. Despite these historic defeats southern Democratic officeholders did not abandon their traditional party. Too many other vital state, local, and regional interests were at stake for the southern Democrats to walk away from the political party that still organized the Senate and enabled southerners to hold important leadership positions. In the 1960s and 1970s most southern Democrats distanced themselves from their national party and thereby suffocated many Republican challenges. Over time, however, as the Voting Rights Act worked its "quiet revolution," black voters became a vital component of the Democrats' electoral coalitions.[1] Younger conservative Democrats began to vote as moderate Democrats and to support voting-rights legislation, shifts that further frustrated Republican efforts to win and hold Senate seats in the 1980s.

This chapter and the next analyze the limited rise of southern Republicans in the Senate from 1961 to 1990. Long after federal intervention, the central tendency of the southern party battle in the Senate remained Democratic domination, a pattern broken in the early 1980s by a Republican surge but soon countered by a Democratic revival. Lacking competitive grassroots electoral bases, Republicans operated at a fundamental disadvantage in statewide campaigns. They ordinarily failed to defeat incumbent Democratic senators, lost more open-seat elections than they won, and protected barely half of their few incumbents.

In order to win Senate elections, southern Republicans needed to create short-term advantages to offset their long-term liabilities among the electorate. "Republicans in the South could not win elections by talking about issues," strategist Lee Atwater later told John Brady. "You had to make the case that the other candidate was a bad guy."[2] Republican Senate candidates needed egregious Democratic blunders in order to compete. They needed Democratic opponents who behaved in self-destructive ways, failed to take their Republican opponents seriously, adopted issue positions that did not unify all the ideological wings of the southern Democratic parties, and/or achieved their Democratic nominations in ways that left their Democratic rivals unwilling to rally behind the winner in the general election. And even these Democratic weaknesses were usually insufficient, by themselves, to produce Republican victories. In virtually every instance of successful Republican contesting, GOP Senate candidates needed to put up energetic, visible fights in which they combined some positive messages about themselves (and perhaps their party) with slashing negative attacks against their Democratic opponents. In this sense, general elections in the South became extensions of the often bitterly personal attacks that had long been commonplace in southern Democratic primary fights.

Once in office, Republicans had to face the challenge of winning reelection when the factors that had contributed to their original victory might no longer be at work. "As a challenger, the candidate can run a positive campaign based on name recognition and qualifications and a negative campaign that calls for a referendum on the incumbent," Richard F. Fenno Jr. has argued. "But the requirements of an incumbent campaign are different and more difficult. To be sure, name recognition and general qualifications must be enhanced, but the beginning of a reputation for some kind of positive on-the-job performance must be added." The freshman incumbent seeking reelection needs a "representational theme" or "an incumbent-related message."[3] Many of the freshmen Republican senators from the South during the three decades after federal intervention found themselves vulnerable to campaigns waged by experienced Democratic politicians.

THE TURNING POINT:
DEFEATING THE SOUTHERN FILIBUSTER ON CIVIL RIGHTS

From Reconstruction onward the ultimate weapon of southern segregationists had been their ability to sustain a Senate filibuster against any legislation that attempted to reform southern racial practices and institutions. Before the Senate adopted a cloture rule in 1917, southern Democrats could use the tradition of unlimited debate to force the withdrawal of any legislation that challenged the region's institutions of white supremacy. Between 1917 and 1964 cloture had never been invoked on behalf of civil rights legislation. All experienced senators understood the southern advantage. Under Senate rules two-thirds of all senators were needed to defeat a filibuster. A completely Solid Democratic South would produce 22 votes against cloture. Under conditions of maximum southern Democratic unity, the southern Democrats needed to secure only 12 northern votes—a mere 15 percent of the 78 senators from the 39 northern states—in order to form a blocking coalition of one-third plus one. Assuming no southern support for cloture, a minimum of 67 northern senators (86 percent) would have to join forces in order to defeat Georgia Senator Richard Russell, the acknowledged leader of the southerners. Uniting the southern delegation and lining up 12 northern allies was ordinarily child's play for Russell.[4]

By the early 1960s, however, southern Democrats in Congress were finding it increasingly difficult to kill national intervention in the region's racial practices. The Supreme Court's school desegregation decisions, though widely ignored in the South, had established a clear constitutional rationale for attacking other segregated southern institutions. Activists in the southern civil rights movement, often at great personal sacrifice, were challenging segregation in public accommodations and voting rights. Through sit-in demonstrations at lunch counters and in restaurants, through voter registration drives in localities that historically obstructed black political participation, and through other risky forms of protest, the civil rights movement effectively dramatized the evils of southern racial discrimination in ways that outraged and activated northern public opinion. With network television communicating shocking images of southern injustice, Jim Crow became impossible to ignore and much harder to defend.[5]

President Kennedy's assassination put Vice President Johnson in the White House. "We have talked long enough in this country about equal rights," he told the nation in his first presidential address. "We have talked for 100 years or more. It is time to write the next chapter—and to write it in the books of law." President Johnson also told Senator Russell exactly what he was going to do. "Dick," he said, "I love you. I owe you. But I'm going to run over you if you challenge me or get in my way. I aim to pass the civil rights bill, only this time, Dick, there will be no caviling, no compromise, no falling back. This bill is going to pass."[6]

After a three-month filibuster, a bipartisan coalition of northern Democrats and northern Republicans led by Minnesota Democrat Hubert Humphrey and Illinois Republican Everett Dirksen broke the southern filibuster and passed the legislation. Ninety percent of the northern senators (93 percent of Democrats and 84 percent of Republicans) joined with one southern Democrat–Ralph Yarborough of Texas–to end the debate. "By the time the Senate imposed cloture," Robert Mann writes, "it was too late for compromise. Russell's bargaining power had vanished. He watched helplessly as the Senate defeated hundreds of southern amendments in lopsided roll calls. 'Dick Russell just couldn't believe that so many of his friends would desert him,' said an aide to one southern senator."[7] On final passage the southern Democrats were whipped even more soundly. With 95 percent of the southerners opposing 92 percent of the northerners, the result was a landslide northern bipartisan majority for civil rights. Arizona senator Barry Goldwater, soon to become the Republican presidential nominee, was the most conspicuous of only five northern Republicans to reject the Civil Rights Act of 1964.

As important as it was in changing race relations in the South, the Civil Rights Act did not destroy the barriers to black participation in many parts of the region. Soon President Johnson "was telling Nick Katzenbach about the bill he had in mind for passage in 1965 . . . 'I want you to write me the goddamndest, toughest voting rights act that you can devise.'" Humphrey recalled that Johnson "used to tell me, 'Yes, Hubert, I want all those other things–buses, restaurants, all of that–but the right to vote with no ifs, ands, or buts, that's the key.'" On March 7, 1965, Alabama state troopers and local law-enforcement forces clubbed and tear gassed around six hundred civil rights demonstrators who were trying to march from Selma to Montgomery, the state capital. The brutality of the assault against citizens who were seeking to register to vote–a totally uncontroversial right for most Americans–ignited national public opinion and stimulated the introduction of the voting-rights legislation that President Johnson was already planning to send to Congress.[8]

On March 15, 1965, Johnson again addressed the nation in a speech to a joint session of Congress. "There can be and should be no argument," the president declared. "Every American citizen must have an equal right to vote." The time for a national law to implement the Fifteenth Amendment, to make the right to vote more than words on a piece of paper, was at hand: "The time of justice has now come. And I tell you that I believe sincerely that no force can hold it back. It is right–

in the eyes of men and God—that it should come. And when it does, I think that day will brighten the lives of every American."[9]

Passing the Civil Rights Act had demonstrated that a united and bipartisan northern coalition could overcome southern obstruction, and the Selma tragedy ensured that Johnson's voting-rights bill would receive prompt attention. In 1964 Yarborough had been the lone southern Democrat favoring the Civil Rights Act. Now he was joined by both Tennessee Democrats, Albert Gore and Ross Bass. The northern bipartisan coalition prevailed, as 92 percent of northern Democrats joined with 77 percent of northern Republicans to stop the southerners' filibuster. The Senate then overwhelmingly passed the Voting Rights Act. Every northern senator who cast a recorded vote supported passage.

In 1964 and 1965 the southern Democrats' traditional strategy of legislative obstruction on civil rights was finally and convincingly repudiated. Northern size and unity—the cohesion of the large majority of senators and representatives who lived in the North—overwhelmed the southern segregationists, whose main resource as a sectional minority was their unity and whose chief liability was their small size. These laws marked a historic turning point in American politics. The Civil Rights Act and the Voting Rights Act amounted to successful and irreversible federal intervention in southern race relations. Desegregating public accommodations and protecting black voting rights meant that white supremacy no longer defined the southern political order and that black citizens would be an integral part of the political community. Taken together, these national laws pushed the South in the direction of fundamental racial change.[10]

Federal intervention in southern race relations was also a watershed development in southern party politics. The new civil rights laws had been enacted under the determined leadership of a southern Democratic president, Lyndon Johnson, and with the almost complete support of northern Democrats and northern Republicans. Many racially conservative white southerners felt betrayed by the national Democratic party and began to reassess their partisan options. Some whites who had been trained from childhood to hate Republicans and revere Democrats now saw in the Goldwater wing of the Republican party an alternative to the Democratic party. Conservative whites who despised the party of Lincoln might appreciate the party of Goldwater.

PERSISTENT DEMOCRATIC DOMINANCE

The Democrats' southern juggernaut did not immediately collapse. For another three decades Democrats continued to dominate southern senatorial politics. Their hold on the Senate delegation was seriously disrupted only by a short-lived Republican surge in the early 1980s. Having concentrated their political capital in the Democratic party, the southerners could not afford to abandon their investment in the organization that still controlled Congress.

Senator Russell's perspective explains why almost all southern Democratic officeholders remained nominal party members long after they had lost the civil rights fight. Answering letters from constituents praising Senator Thurmond's switch to the Republicans, the Georgia senator reminded his supporters that "he had always held office under the Democratic banner and had an obligation to the party."[11] Like most racially conservative white southerners, Russell had never remotely thought of himself as a potential Republican. During the 1960s two-thirds of southern whites were Democrats or independents who leaned toward the Democratic party, while only one-fourth were Republicans or independents who favored the Republican party. As long as Democratic primaries produced Senate candidates who could unite the party, southern Democrats could easily win statewide elections simply by mobilizing Democratic voters. They did not need to appeal to independents or Republicans. Almost everywhere in the South in the 1960s, seeking office as a Republican was campaigning the hard way.

Compelling practical advantages encouraged southern Senators to remain Democrats. According to Gilbert Fite, "Russell explained that he could best serve Georgia as a Democrat with his long seniority. He had worked too long and hard, he said, 'for valuable public projects and military installations that are now almost vital to the economy of our state to sign them away with one stroke of the pen' by changing parties. He argued that Georgia needed his seniority to protect the state's economic interests."[12] Southerners still possessed their most important asset for wielding power–their accumulated seniority in the majority party on many key committees of the Senate and House. As shrewd practical politicians, they were not about to compound their weakness by voluntarily surrendering their one last advantage. Experienced Democrats chaired many Senate committees and appropriations subcommittees and were thus able to shape countless public policies in countless ways favorable to their constituents. They could do so because leadership positions were awarded on the basis of seniority on the committee without regard to a member's record of support for the policies favored by a majority of Democrats. These rules enabled the southerners to vote against their northern colleagues whenever they wished and still chair prestigious and powerful committees.

The Georgia senator further emphasized that his duty to the Democratic party "did not mean . . . that he had to follow every party line. Indeed, Russell had always boasted of his independence." For southern Democrats, "independence" ordinarily meant the freedom to oppose northern Democrats. In the late 1950s, as northern Democrats began to take more liberal positions on racial issues, many southerners reduced their support for the policies of the national party. Using a political code that signaled distance from their more liberal colleagues, they presented themselves to voters as "conservative Democrats" or "southern Democrats."[13]

After federal intervention even more southern Democrats asserted their independence by revolting against the national party. During the 1960s and 1970s the South was represented in the Senate mainly by conservative Democrats who controlled myriad leverage points in committees and subcommittees that directed millions of dollars into the region. Figure 3.1 charts the relative prominence of nationals, moderates, and nominals among southern Democratic senators from 1953–54 onward. It shows a huge surge in the percentage of southern Democratic senators who rebelled against the positions of their party colleagues in the mid-1960s. The revolt of the conservative Democrats lasted until the early 1980s.

By repudiating unpopular positions of the national Democrats yet retaining nominal membership in the majority party, sophisticated southern Democratic senators could persuasively market themselves as "practical conservatives." Since few philosophical differences separated southern Democrats from southern Republicans on racial issues, and since the Democratic party still controlled impressive congressional majorities, most white voters preferred to elect practical and powerful conservative Democrats rather than impractical and powerless Republicans.

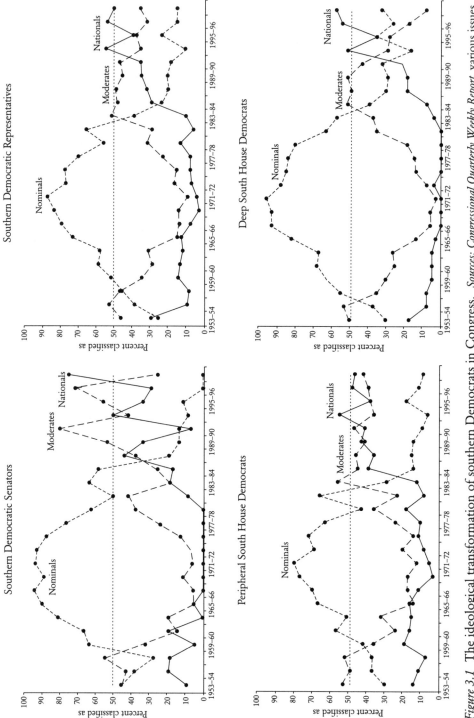

Figure 3.1 The ideological transformation of southern Democrats in Congress. *Sources: Congressional Quarterly Weekly Report*, various issues.

The revolt within the southern Democratic party absorbed much of the increased white demand for conservatism. Conservative southern Democrats thus defused Republican hopes for an immediate partisan realignment based on dissatisfaction with the civil rights policies of the national Democratic party.

The conservative Democratic advantage was especially strong in the aftermath of federal intervention. There was really not much point in encouraging unknown Republicans to take on experienced, well-placed conservatives like Russell (the chair of the Armed Services Committee and Appropriations' defense subcommittee), Louisiana's Allen Ellender (chair of Agriculture and the public-works subcommittee of Appropriations), Arkansas's John McClellan (chair of both Government Operations and the Appropriations subcommittee on Justice and other departments), or Florida's Spessard Holland (chair of the Appropriations subcommittee on agriculture). When they did engage in such windmill-tilting, as Republican congressman Prentiss Walker discovered in 1966 when he rashly challenged veteran Mississippi segregationist Jim Eastland, the result was an embarrassing defeat. With almost no Republican incumbents and with generally poor prospects of defeating Democratic incumbents, southern Republicans were forced to bide their time until senior Democrats died, retired, or were defeated in Democratic primaries.

Even when seats became open, the most common replacement was another conservative Democrat, such as Fritz Hollings in South Carolina, J. Bennett Johnston in Louisiana, and Sam Nunn in Georgia. Nunn was typical of the newly elected conservative Democrats who entered the Senate during the 1960s and early 1970s. He complained that his conservative Republican opponent "was trying to make me out as some sort of liberal, but nothing could be further from the truth. I am a Houston County conservative. I am a common-sense conservative from one of the most conservative, common-sense counties in our great state." As the election approached, Nunn played his racial trump card—his seal of approval from Alabama Democratic governor George C. Wallace, the most influential white politician in the Deep South. "I am very honored to have Gov. Wallace's endorsement," the Georgia Democrat emphasized. "George Wallace is one of us. I don't consider him in the class of Yankee invaders."[14] The emergence of Democratic politicians like Nunn to replace the Richard Russells made it difficult for conservative southern Republicans to find much political traction.

Thus newly elected Democrats as well as veteran conservative Democrats checked Republican party growth by continuing to offer southern white voters the option of being represented by conservative members of the Senate's majority party. The few Republicans who won Senate seats in the South during the 1960s and 1970s usually prevailed only when they faced Democratic nominees who had failed to unite all wings of their party and/or candidates who could be convincingly attacked as liberals or moderates.

Although conservatism generally prevailed during the 1970s, some of the southern Democratic senators began to alter their views about federal voting-rights legislation. The southern Democrats' changing position on voting rights signified a gradual acceptance of the region's new biracial order. In 1970 fourteen of the eighteen southern Democratic senators voted against extending the Voting Rights Act for another five years. By 1975, however, nine southern Democrats supported another five-year extension of the Voting Rights Act, while only five opposed it. For the first time in American history a majority of southern Democratic senators supported the principle of federal supervision of minority voting rights, even if many of them otherwise continued to behave as nominal Democrats. Opposition to the Voting Rights Act was limited to four conservatives (McClellan, John Sparkman of Alabama, John Stennis of Mississippi, and Herman Talmadge of Georgia) who had voted against the original legislation, plus the newly elected Alabama conservative, Jim Allen. Supporting the Voting Rights Act were one veteran senator—Russell Long of Louisiana—and eight Democrats who had been elected to the Senate after the Voting Rights Act had gone into effect: Nunn, Hollings, Johnston, Lloyd Bentsen of Texas, Lawton Chiles and Richard Stone of Florida, Dale Bumpers of Arkansas, and Robert Morgan of North Carolina. Most of these senators generally voted as nominal Democrats, although a few, such as Bumpers and later David Pryor of Arkansas, were beginning to position themselves as moderate Democrats. Even most of the new conservative Democrats were prepared to defend legislation that protected a large group of voters who were now part of their own renomination and reelection constituencies.

Minor tendencies in the 1970s became central tendencies of the southern Democratic senators in the next decades. And as the Democratic senators born and reared in the old southern politics of racial segregation and white supremacy finally passed from the scene, they were usually replaced either by Republicans who primarily targeted conservative white southerners or—most conspicuously in the Peripheral South—by a new generation of Democrats who grasped the necessity and advantage of forming overt biracial coalitions. In 1982 all eleven southern Democrats—the remaining two veterans, Long and Stennis, plus the nine newcomers elected after the original 1965 legislation—voted to extend the Voting Rights Act for twenty-five years. In every southern state, with blacks accounting for sizable fractions of the electorate in Democratic primaries and general elections, Democratic senators from the South now supported national legislation to protect the voting rights of black southerners.

The white Democrats' need for black support was increasingly important because more white voters—especially conservatives but also some moderates—were thinking of themselves as Republicans or leaning toward the GOP. In 1984, for the first time in the twentieth century, fewer than half of southern whites—43 percent—called themselves Democrats or were independents who leaned toward the Democrats. In statewide elections most Democratic politicians could no longer be renominated or reelected by relying exclusively on white Democrats. As conservative white voters left the Democratic party, statewide political power within the Democratic party began to shift to politicians who could appeal to blacks and moderate to liberal whites. Increasingly, southern Democratic senators represented their states as moderates rather than as conservatives (see Figure 3.1). Indeed, some Democratic senators—Bumpers and Pryor, Jim Sasser of Tennessee, Bob Graham of Florida, Wyche Fowler of Georgia, and Terry Sanford of North Carolina—appeared to be so secure in their biracial support that they sometimes voted as liberal or national Democrats during the late 1980s.

THE REPUBLICAN PREDICAMENT

Republican candidates for the Senate confronted utterly different electoral situations. As members of a small minority party in a region long dominated by a Democratic juggernaut of voters and politicians, they were forced to overcome tremendous practical barriers. The path to power for a minority political party involves reelecting its incumbents, winning open-seat elections, and occasionally defeating incumbents of the opposition party. In the South, these uphill GOP efforts had to be sustained over many years. Incumbency, of course, was precisely what southern Republicans lacked and southern Democrats possessed. Democratic incumbency in the 1960s and 1970s was especially powerful because of its tight linkage—in most cases—with southern conservatism.

The only way to break the Democratic monopoly was to mount aggressive and well-financed campaigns when retirement or death created open seats. Many southern Republicans held a minority-party worldview that rejected continuous contesting for (apparently) unwinnable seats. Clarke Reed, who led the Mississippi Republican party for many years, expressed a widespread attitude toward party development. "You pick up most of your gains through attrition," he said, "and pick the others off whenever you can."[15] It was essentially a passive approach in which success depended upon external events (the retirement, death, defeat, or unpopularity of particular Democratic candidates) to create vacancies or opportunities for which Republican candidates might seriously compete. If promising candidates could be persuaded to run, and if those campaigners could be properly financed, the Republicans might be able to compete against nonincumbent Democrats. Even here any Republican candidate would be at a severe disadvantage because of the Democrats' persisting strength in the electorate.

During the 1960s the southern Republicans stopped forfeiting and began to challenge Democrats in a majority of elections for the U.S. Senate (see Figure 2.2). Nonetheless, token contests—those in which the Republican won less than 40 percent of the vote—were still more common than truly serious challenges. Signs of greater competitive effort appeared in the 1970s; for the first time in history, a majority (54 percent) of Senate contests in the South involved seriously competitive Republican candidates. Despite their more vigorous contesting efforts, Republicans experienced only modest success. They won merely a quarter of the Senate elections held in the South from 1961 to 1979, and only five of the eight southern Republican senators served for more than a single term. Serious Republican competition increased slightly during the 1980s, to nearly three-fifths of the elections, and the Republicans' success rate increased to 39 percent. However, most of the newly elected Republican senators were so inexperienced as officeholders that they failed to consolidate, much less expand, their original electoral coalitions.

During the 1970s fewer than 30 percent of southern whites were Republicans or leaned toward the GOP. Southern Republicans who sought the Senate could mount merely token and largely symbolic campaigns if their appeal reached only fellow Republicans. Serious challenges required Republican candidates capable of uniting their partisans, appealing to independents, and attracting the votes of Democrats dissatisfied with their party's nominee. To be competitive in a given election, the GOP needed to find sufficiently large numbers of "persuadable" Democrats or independents who could be combined with diehard Republicans to form temporary, ad hoc, winning coalitions. Many of the early Republican victories were electoral flukes, outcomes based upon unlikely factors that temporarily allowed candidates of the minority party to prevail. Voters were generally more interested in rejecting particular Democrats than in electing Republicans. During the 1960s and 1970s Republican senatorial candidates rarely won open seats; in the 1980s they won more open seats than they lost but had great trouble reelecting these incumbents.

Incumbency was potentially a valuable resource for newly elected Republican senators, provided they could learn how to become visibly responsive to their states' interests and voting constituencies. Yet because Republican success hinged upon candidates who could appeal to non-Republicans, taking advantage of incumbency was no sure thing. Once elected, Republican senators faced the challenge of building careers in political systems in which the Democrats had many more grassroots partisans and a much larger pool of experienced politicians to challenge the freshmen Republicans. Just as many southern Republicans initially elected as governors of southern states in the 1960s and 1970s had great difficulty winning reelection (or being succeeded by a fellow Republican if they were not permitted to seek a second term), so, too, reelection was a very difficult hurdle for freshmen Republican senators from the South.

The southern Republicans who won Senate seats during the 1960s, 1970s, and late 1980s were further handicapped as members of the Senate's minority party. Typically, they were doubly disadvantaged by their minority status in the Senate and at home. Ironically, when the Republicans did become the Senate majority party from 1981 to 1987, none of the five newly elected southern Republicans lasted beyond a single term.

Genuine partisan realignments in officeholding require performances that are confirmed by subsequent reelections. Southern Republican senators had many "success-to-failure" stories.[16] Almost half of the southern Republicans elected to the Senate from 1961 through 1990 failed to secure their political bases. Several incumbent freshmen either decided not to run again or were defeated for reelection. Because of the unusually high rate of incumbency failure among their freshman senators, southern Republicans could not fully consolidate their gains.

Table 3.1 separates the successful southern Republican senators (those who were reelected at least once) from the Republicans who served for one term or less. For the period 1961–1988, it lists each senator by original election year, electoral situation (open seat, Democratic incumbent, party switch), and statewide vote term by term. With the exception of Strom Thurmond, who became a Republican by switching parties, all the successful Republicans entered the Senate by capturing an open-seat election. Only four of the eight one-termers had prevailed in an open-seat election; the other four had defeated sitting Democrats, and their upset victories were due more to the weaknesses of their incumbent Democratic opponents than to their own strengths.

Winning Republicans faced the challenge of turning incumbency to their advantage in systems in which their party was an electoral minority. Richard F. Fenno has argued that newly elected senators (and representatives) normally enter an expansionist phase in which they try to solidify their original support and add new supporters until they are able to build a comfortable renomination and reelection constituency.[17] At that point the senators pursue a protectionist strategy in which they are more interested in satisfying the needs of their usual supporters than in adding more voters to their coalitions. A few southern Republicans did manage to build safe reelection coalitions, while others essentially consolidated their initially small majorities and continued to face serious

Table 3.1 Lost opportunities for Senate careers: vote won by southern Republicans initially elected from 1961 through 1988 (%)

Elected in	Senator	Type	First term	Second term	Third term	Fourth term	Fifth term	Sixth term
Republican senators reelected								
Tex. 1961	Tower	Open	51	56	53	50		
S.C. 1966	Thurmond	RI	62	63	56	67	64	53
Tenn. 1966	Baker	Open	56	62	56	*		
N.C. 1972	Helms	Open	54	55	52	53	53	
Miss. 1978	Cochran	Open	45	61	100	71		
Va. 1978	Warner	Open	50	70	81	52		
Tex. 1984	Gramm	Open	59	60	55			
Miss. 1988	Lott	Open	54	69	63			
Fla. 1988	Mack	Open	50	71	*			
Republican senators not reelected								
Fla. 1968	Gurney	Open	56	*				
Tenn. 1970	Brock	DI	51	47				
Va. 1972	Scott	DI	52	*				
Fla. 1980	Hawkins	Open	52	45				
N.C. 1980	East	DI	50	**				
Ala. 1980	Denton	Open	50	49				
Ga. 1980	Mattingly	DI	51	49				
Va. 1982	Trible	Open	51	*				

Note: * = retired; ** = died during first term; RI = Republican incumbent; DI = Democratic incumbent.

Sources: Calculated from *Congressional Quarterly's Guide to U.S. Elections,* 3d ed. (Washington, D.C., 1994); and *Congressional Quarterly Weekly Report,* various issues.

opposition. For nearly half of the newly elected southern Republicans, however, the most pressing problem was to consolidate or to reconstruct small electoral coalitions rather than to expand their support to comfortable reelection coalitions.

THE PARTY BATTLE IN THE PERIPHERAL SOUTH

Although potential Republican senatorial candidates faced hurdles everywhere in the South, voters in the Peripheral South appeared considerably more receptive to two-party competition than did their counterparts in the Deep South. With smaller black populations, larger urbanized new middle classes, and greater emphasis on economic development, the social structures of most Peripheral South states (Arkansas lagged far behind) were approaching national norms. Texas and Florida had no sizable traditional Republican bases but were rapidly urbanizing. Tennessee, Virginia, and North Carolina possessed traditional Republican strongholds in their highlands and were also developing major metropolitan areas. The greater economic and social diversity of the Peripheral South enhanced the possibility of partisan competition, since it was unlikely that a single political party could adequately express the new complexity of the rapidly changing social order. A Republican candidate appeared on the ballot in the vast majority of Senate elections in the Peripheral South from 1961 through 2000.

The obstacles facing Republican challengers, as well as the historic significance of the Republicans' southern breakthrough in Senate elections, can best be appreciated by examining the careers of southern senators. In the rest of this chapter we shall concentrate on the six Peripheral South states. For each state we have charted partisan control of the two Senate seats according to each senator's Democratic party unity scores. By starting in the early 1960s we can appreciate the power of Democratic incumbency as a deterrent to Republican success and track the impact of federal intervention and expanded black participation on the voting behavior of individual senators. Figure 3.2 displays the party battle in Texas, Tennessee, and Florida, three Peripheral South states that displayed exceptional opportunities for strong two-party competition in statewide elections.

Texas

We shall begin with Texas, the first southern state to elect a Republican senator in the twentieth century. Possessing the lowest black population in the South, Texas has historically been the region's least "southern" state. Incumbency has clearly mattered a great deal in Texas Senate elections. During the four decades covered in the chart, only two Democrats and three Republicans were elected to the Senate. The Republicans' first opportunity arose as a consequence of Lyndon Johnson's election as vice president. John Tower, a young conservative Republican who had run a shoestring campaign against Johnson in 1960, won a special election the following year against a divided Democratic field.

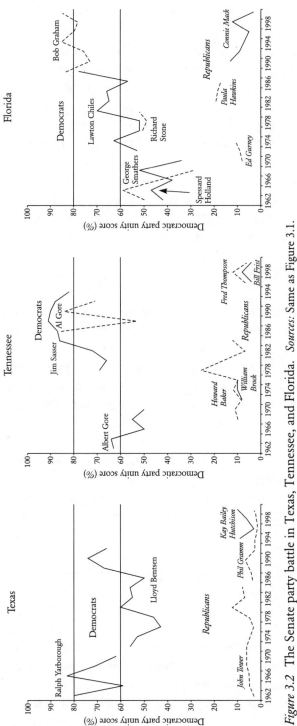

Figure 3.2 The Senate party battle in Texas, Tennessee, and Florida. *Sources*: Same as Figure 3.1.

Characterized by *Time* as "an obscure assistant professor of political science who dabbled in Republican politics but had never won elective office," Tower was a hardline conservative eager to take on the Democrats.[18]

"You practically had to hold a gun on somebody to get him to run as a Republican," Tower later recounted. "They didn't need a gun with me. I guess I was too young and idealistic to know better." Raised in East Texas, Tower had repudiated his Democratic heritage and switched to the Republicans. Attaching himself to Richard Nixon's presidential campaign, the thirty-four-year-old Midwestern State University professor urged Texans to "Double your pleasure, double your fun—scratch Lyndon twice." He attracted over 900,000 votes, 41 percent of the total, an astonishing effort against the Texas Democratic party's strongest officeholder.[19]

The following year Tower won the special election to fill Johnson's seat. As the lone Republican competing against several prominent Democrats, Tower led the first round of balloting with 31 percent. The runoff election matched the young conservative Republican against a much older conservative Democrat, Dallas businessman William Blakely, whom many liberal Democrats refused to support. Drawing on "Anglo voters" in the state's "major urban areas" as his principal sources of support, Tower narrowly upset Blakely with 50.6 percent of the vote. Ideological disagreements among Democrats, combined with Tower's aggressive campaigning, produced the twentieth century's first Republican senator from a former Confederate state. "I am against federal aid to education, medical care for the aged, higher taxes, foreign aid both economic and military, and wasteful domestic spending," the new senator announced. Tower took conservative positions across the board and joined southern Democrats in opposing the Civil Rights Act and the Voting Rights Act.[20]

Tower's fluke victory became a four-term career. Because he represented a state in which Democrats far outnumbered Republicans, Tower—and his political enemies—believed he would be a one-term wonder. Luckily for him, Texas Democrats in 1966 again nominated a conservative, Waggoner Carr, whom liberals refused to support. Tower drew 56 percent with "an inherently shaky liberal-conservative Republican coalition." Once Texas Democrats began to nominate centrist Democrats, however, Tower's share of the vote declined. Despite Nixon's rout of George McGovern in 1972, Tower dropped to 53 percent against moderate Democrat Barefoot Sanders. Six-year congressman Bob Krueger nearly defeated him. Krueger's voting record—"conservative on most issues, liberal on a few"—enabled him to attract "large numbers of liberals and conservatives who [had] abandoned one or the other of Tower's Democratic opponents in past elections."[21] Although Tower prevailed with 49.8 percent of the vote, he never again ran for the Senate.

Tower's conservatism was matched, if not exceeded in scope and fervor, by his successor, Phil Gramm of College Station, a former Democratic congressman who had switched to the Republicans during Reagan's first term. Raised in a military family in Georgia, he was a professor at Texas A & M University. The Aggie economist entered the House in 1978 as a conservative Democrat and became a leader of the "Boll Weevils," the southern Democrats with conservative economic views. Gramm enthusiastically supported President Reagan's economic policies. Accused by his Democratic colleagues of spying for the Republicans, he was stripped of his membership on the Budget Committee in 1983. Gramm then quit the Democratic party, resigned from Congress, and was reelected as a Republican.

The Texas Republican "believes in free markets and very little government, and advocates his positions with a fervor and a disregard for his own political interest that would ordinarily repel practical politicians," observed *The Almanac of American Politics 1984*. When Tower's seat became open, Gramm won the GOP nomination and faced liberal Democrat Lloyd Doggett in the general election. Gramm and Doggett tore into each other early and often. "It has been an unusually negative campaign, even for Texas, where cactus and barbed wire are as common in politics as on the plain," the *New York Times* reported. "Representative Gramm, the Republican, has accused State Senator Doggett, the Democrat, of undermining family values, 'pandering' to homosexuals, unethical advertising and allowing alcohol in the schools." Doggett responded by accusing Gramm "of lying about his campaign contributions, ignoring the elderly and laughing at the handicapped, waging the 'biggest lie-and-buy campaign in the history of Texas,' undermining Social Security and Medicaid and harboring a secret plan to raise taxes and eliminate exemptions for home mortgage interest." It was quite a show.[22]

In a straight liberal-versus-conservative fight Gramm destroyed Doggett by over 900,000 votes. The conservative Republican won 71 percent of white men and 69 percent of white women. He carried huge majorities from whites of every educational level, as well as every income level above $12,500. Gramm won 87 percent of the white conservatives and 60 percent of the white moderates, leaving his Democratic opponent with two-thirds of liberal whites, plus majorities of Hispanics and blacks.[23] No Republican senatorial candidate had ever enjoyed such a lopsided victory in Texas.

Once in office the former Democrat turned Republican knew how to use the powers of incumbency to make his seat safe. Aggressive credit-claiming, conspicuous position-taking, and relentless fundraising became Gramm hallmarks. In 1990, keeping his support among conservative and moderate whites and nearly splitting the Hispanic vote, he coasted to a second term against an underfinanced opponent. Six years later, after his presidential bid ended in an embarrassing defeat, his victory margin fell to 55 percent against a Hispanic Democrat.

Texas Democrats, who had never been seriously challenged before Tower's 1960 campaign, controlled the state's other Senate seat until 1993. Ralph Yarborough was the most successful moderate to liberal Democrat in modern Texas history. After almost capturing the Texas governorship in 1956, he won a special election to the Senate the following year and was reelected in 1958. Avoiding the ideological label "liberal" as political suicide but plainly inclined in that direction, Yarborough was renominated and reelected in 1964 against the wishes of conservative Democrats. No friend of Yarborough, President Lyndon Johnson nonetheless did not want to be accused by northern Democratic liberals of attempting to defeat a Texas liberal in the very year in which he was running against Goldwater. Yarborough held off the challenge of Republican George Bush by tying him to Goldwater.

Conservative Democrats had always been unhappy with Yarborough's moderate to liberal politics, and in 1970 they rallied behind former congressman Lloyd Bentsen. A conservative Democrat with broad appeal in the business community, Bentsen whipped Yarborough in the Democratic primary and then defeated Bush, now a Republican congressman, in the general election. The transition from Yarborough to Bentsen involved an ideological change in a more conservative direction. From the early 1970s through the mid-1980s Bentsen's Democratic party unity scores generally remained in the conservative range; only toward the end of his long Senate career did he vote as a moderate Democrat. Despite his increasing reliance on multiracial coalitions of blacks, Hispanics, and whites, Bentsen never voted as a national Democrat. He held three Republican opponents (1976, 1982, and 1988) to an average of 41 percent. In 1988 he won huge majorities from blacks and Hispanics while only splitting the white vote. The first realistic Republican opportunity to win this seat came when Bentsen entered the Clinton administration as Treasury secretary. Republican Kay Bailey Hutchison won the 1993 special election to become Texas' first female senator. She later won landslide reelections in 1994 and 2000. Conservative Republicans consequently dominated Texas senatorships at the beginning of the twenty-first century.

Tennessee

During the 1950s and into the early 1960s Estes Kefauver and Albert Gore, two of the South's least conservative Democrats, represented Tennessee in the Senate. Kefauver's death in 1963 was followed by a closely contested special Senate election in 1964. The Republican candidate was Howard H. Baker, a lifelong East Tennessee Republican who had "ties to both the mountain Republicans and professional classes of his homeland." Despite the burden of Barry Goldwater at the top of the ticket, Baker drew 47 percent of the vote against Democratic congressman Ross Bass.[24]

Two years later, after Bass lost in the Democratic primary, Baker defeated former Democratic governor Frank Clement to become the second Republican senator elected from a Peripheral South state in the modern era. Baker stressed "fiscal conservatism" to win votes among the "professional classes" and advocated a "constitutional amendment to reinstate voluntary prayer in public schools" to win support among "less well-off socially conservative Tennesseans." Unlike most of the other southern Republicans, he also appealed directly to blacks. Baker won in 1966 by nearly 100,000 votes, attracting a majority of whites and "15 to 20 percent" of blacks. When traditional Republicans in the mountains joined with middle-class whites in the suburbs and the more affluent neighborhoods of Memphis, Republican politicians could seriously contest elections in Tennessee. With the exception of Nashville, a traditional Democratic stronghold, Baker "ran especially strong in the state's urban areas," just as Tower had done in Texas.[25]

Of the first group of southern Republican senators, Baker built the strongest political base. In 1972 he expanded his original support to 62 percent against Ray Blanton, a conservative Democrat. Moderately conservative in ideology and possessing natural leadership skills, he was the first southerner to lead the Senate Republicans and served as majority leader for four years after the Republicans became the majority party in the 1980 elections. Baker lost support among Tennessee conservatives when he helped President Jimmy Carter pass the Panama Canal treaty and fell to 55 percent in 1978 against Democrat Jane Eskind. Baker's retirement in 1984 enabled Representative Al Gore, the son of the former senator, to reclaim the seat for the Democrats. Gore won a landslide reelection in 1990. When Gore vacated his safe seat to become vice president, Baker protégé Fred Thompson brought the seat back under Republican control in the party's 1994 surge. Thompson easily won a full term in 1996.

During the 1960s Albert Gore, a moderate to liberal Democrat, held Tennessee's other Senate seat. Gore had narrowly survived a strong challenge in 1964 from a Goldwater Republican but was unseated in 1970 by another Goldwater disciple, Representative William Brock of Chattanooga. Gore had supported the Voting Rights Act of 1965 and opposed the Vietnam War, positions that put him on the defensive in the Democratic primary. The veteran Democrat barely won renomination and approached the general election as a vulnerable incumbent fighting an uphill battle.

Journalist David Halberstam contrasted Brock's personal style of politicking with the relentless bashing of his advertising. "Though in debates and in personal confrontation and in his own speeches he [Brock] stays away from the issues he has raised," Halberstam reported that the Republican challenger's "newspaper ads and television ads are hitting away daily at the most emotional issues they can touch. His media firm came down here a year and a half ago and found that the five most emotional issues were race, gun control, the war, busing, and prayer, and they are making this the campaign. Keep Gore answering false charges."[26]

"Bill Brock Believes in the Things We Believe In," declared the Republican's billboard advertising. Brock's appeals were directed at the white middle and working classes. Apart from East Tennessee, the Republican party's historical base, the prime new Republican territory lay in the state's growing middle-class suburbs of Memphis and Nashville, as well as the new affluent neighborhoods of smaller cities and towns. "These are your new Republicans," a Nashville lawyer told Halberstam. "Their daddies were all Democrats. But the TVA brought in some jobs and we have some prosperity here. White collar people—gone Republican. We call them $10,000-a-year millionaires. It's socially very respectable for young people here to call themselves Republicans—a sign of breaking from the past, of a new cultural independence." In fact, he emphasized, "To be upwardly mobile down here now, you call yourself a Republican." Brock also benefited from the hostility toward the Democratic party of some working-class whites who had viewed Alabama's George Wallace as their political spokesman during the 1960s. Effectively using television commercials to put the veteran Democrat on the defensive, Brock won a narrow victory.[27]

In 1976 Tennessee Democrats, still angry over Brock's negative campaign, took their revenge. Brock could not hold his original voters, many of whom were more anti-Gore than pro-Brock. Helped by the strong presidential campaign of Georgia's Jimmy Carter, the "virtually unknown [Democratic] state chairman Jim Sasser, who had ties to all Democratic constituencies and enemies in none," attracted a broad biracial coalition and prevailed with 52 percent of the vote.[28] As an incumbent, Sasser was reelected by landslides against weak Republican opponents in 1982 and 1988. The Tennessee Democrat's voting record climbed from the moderate into the liberal range as he made his way up the Democratic leadership ladder. By 1994 Sasser expected to succeed George Mitchell of Maine as the Senate Democratic majority leader. His convincing upset defeat by Republican Bill Frist was undoubtedly the single most shocking event for southern Democratic senators in 1994. If the future leader of Senate Democrats could be humiliated by an unknown Nashville surgeon on the grounds that Sasser (like Gore in 1970) was much too liberal for Tennessee, other veteran Democratic senators might wonder about their own vulnerability. Frist easily won reelection in 2000.

Senate politics in Tennessee has frequently exhibited a pattern of partisan feast or famine not found in other southern states. After Tennessee became the first southern state with two Republican senators (Baker and Brock from 1970 to 1976), Democrats Sasser and Gore served concurrently from 1984 through 1992. The 1994 elections reinstituted Republican control. Beginning with Kefauver and Gore, Tennessee's Democratic senators have been much less conservative than most of the South's Democratic senators. As a result the transition to explicit biracial politics involved less-decisive breaks with the past than occurred in most southern states. By the 1980s both Sasser and Gore generally voted as national Democrats. Ups and downs in Gore's Democratic party unity scores reflect missed votes due to presidential (1988) and vice presidential (1992) ambitions, not ideological moderation. The 1994 elections replaced national Democrats with conservative Republicans.

Florida

Florida illustrates both the power of Democratic incumbency and increased Republican competitiveness. In the early 1960s veteran segregationists Spessard Holland and George Smathers symbolized successful Democratic conservatism. Holland had moved to the Senate in 1946 after serving as Florida's governor, and Smathers had defeated the New Deal Democrat Claude Pepper in the 1950 Democratic primary by attacking him as a liberal. When Smathers retired in 1968, this open-seat election resulted in the Republicans' first Florida victory. Orlando congressman Edward Gurney, a conservative Republican, defeated former Democratic governor LeRoy Collins, a racial moderate. Running against "liberal LeRoy," Gurney framed the alternatives in stark ideological terms. "Here is the issue in the campaign Mr. Collins and I differ on: liberalism and conservatism," he said. "For some reason, my opponent is worried about the label of 'liberal.' I don't see anything wrong with people being called what their labels are. I'm a conservative and proud of it." Generally, the GOP candidate "sought to appeal to the conservative and racist sensibilities of the voters by portraying Collins as an extreme liberal and champion of equal rights for blacks."[29]

In the next three elections possession of this seat shifted back and forth between the parties. Neither Gurney (discredited by financial scandals), conservative Democrat Richard Stone (denied renomination), nor Republican Paula Hawkins (viewed as ineffectual) was able to convert an open-seat victory into a safe seat. The situation changed when Democrat Bob Graham, the state's popular governor, challenged Hawkins' re-election in 1986. Easily defeating the incumbent Republican (55 to 45 percent), Graham used his political skills to make his seat extremely safe, just as Democrats had done in the past. In 1992 and 1998 Republicans more or less conceded the seat; neither of Graham's GOP opponents could mount a serious challenge. Graham's party unity scores have generally hovered close to the 80 percent benchmark for a national Democrat.

Holland's retirement in 1970 produced a seamless transition from an Old South Democrat to a New South Democrat. Lawton Chiles, Florida's first Florida Democratic senator to construct a victorious biracial coalition, retained his seat without difficulty for eighteen years. He won a close contest in 1970, drawing 54 percent against Congressman William Cramer, who suffered the effects of a divided Republican party. In the next two elections Chiles deterred serious challengers and won both contests with landslide majorities. Chiles's decision to retire in 1988 created an important test of Republican growth in Florida.

The result was an exceptionally vigorous ideological battle between two House members, conservative Republican Connie Mack and centrist Democrat Buddy MacKay. The election took place in a state in which Democrats outnumbered Republicans, 54 to 39 percent, among registered voters, but at a time when George Bush routed Michael Dukakis in the presidential contest. Interest in the Senate election, according to Rowland Evans and Robert Novak, focused upon "whether a southern moderate Democrat far from the left-wing liberalism under national attack by Bush and [Dan] Quayle can beat a GOP right-winger. If MacKay loses, the message will sound from Key West to the Potomac River: Republicans are extending their striking electoral college success to the U.S. Senate." Mack repeatedly charged, "Hey Buddy, you're liberal." The Republican candidate's "marching song, repeated over and over in television advertisements, has been 'Less taxes, less spending, less government, more freedom.'"[30]

Greatly helped by Bush's massive presidential victory in Florida, Mack narrowly won with 50.4 percent, a margin of less than 34,000 votes. Having waged a strongly ideological campaign, the new southern Republican senator pledged to be more than simply an ideologue: "I think as the people of Florida get the opportunity to view me as an individual working for the best interests of Florida, they are going to see that, yes, I do have a strong belief, but that I am also trying to find solutions." Mack promised "to fight for Florida's fair share and will do all I can to protect our interests." Six years later, running as an incumbent Republican, Mack drew no serious opposition.[31]

In the 1990s Democrats and Republicans each had a secure incumbent in the Senate. Republican gains in Florida continued to be limited by Democratic incumbency. However, Mack's retirement in 2000 resulted in a Democratic pickup when former representative Bill Nelson defeated Orlando Republican representative Bill McCollum, 52 to 47 percent. Florida illustrates the ideological as well as partisan transformation of Senate seats. Among Democratic senators the changing party unity scores trace the shift from conservative Democratic dominance (Holland, Smathers, and Stone) to conservative to moderate voting records (Chiles), to the frequently liberal voting patterns of Bob Graham. Florida's Republican senators (Gurney, Hawkins, and Mack) have been uniformly conservative. At the beginning of the twenty-first century two experienced Democrats represented Florida in the Senate.

Virginia

In Virginia a similar shift from total conservative Democratic domination to highly competitive battles (not limited to open seats) took place. At the time of federal intervention the Byrd Organization, the highly effective Democratic political machine established by Governor and later Senator Harry F. Byrd Sr. in the 1920s, was in its final decade. After the *Brown* decision Senator Byrd abandoned his taciturn style to urge "Massive Resistance" to school desegregation. He and his equally conservative colleague Willis Robertson (father of evangelist Pat Robertson) were last-ditch opponents of racial change. Because of the state's exceptionally low rates of political participation, Virginia was directly affected by the Voting Rights Act. Increased black participation thus impacted Democratic primaries as well as general elections. When Byrd died in office in 1965 he was replaced by his son, Harry F. Byrd Jr., who continued the family tradition of racial and economic conservatism (see

Figure 3.3 for the party battles in Virginia, North Carolina, and Arkansas). In each of his reelection bids he ran as an independent, lest he be defeated in the Democratic primary, although he continued to participate in the Senate Democratic caucus.[32]

When Byrd retired in 1982 he was replaced by thirty-five-year-old Republican congressman Paul Trible, who benefited mightily from Democratic party infighting and the popularity of President Reagan, who campaigned for the Republican candidate. "'You have a 50-year tradition in Virginia that crosses party lines,' the president said, citing the five decades that Byrd or his father has sat in the Senate," reported the *Washington Post.* "'The best way to continue that tradition on beyond 50 years is to send Paul Trible to the Senate.'" Trible won a very narrow victory over Democratic lieutenant governor Dick Davis, who "spent much of his campaign attempting to shed a liberal image."[33] However, as a freshman senator contemplating reelection Trible faced the same problem that had confronted Hawkins in Florida—opposition from a highly respected Democratic governor. Citing a desire to spend more time with his family, Trible gave up without a fight. His potential opponent, former governor Charles Robb, had united the Democratic party and brought it back into respectability with centrist policies, and he eventually won the Senate seat in 1988 with a landslide vote against a weak and underfunded opponent. Unlike Graham, Robb failed to make his seat secure during his freshman term. In one of 1994's most controversial elections, the Virginia Democrat narrowly defeated ultraconservative Republican Oliver North with only a plurality of the vote, 46 to 43 percent. Six years later, former Republican governor George Allen ended Robb's Senate career with a 52 to 48 percent victory.

The Voting Rights Act ended the careers of prominent Byrd Democrats. Both Senator Robertson and Congressman Howard W. Smith (chairman of the House Rules Committee, who had long used that position to obstruct civil rights legislation) were defeated in the 1966 Democratic primaries. Moderate Democrat William Spong unseated Robertson and then easily won the general election. Spong was Virginia's first Democratic senator to devise a biracial coalition, and his voting record approached around the threshold for moderate Democrats. Indeed, many Virginia Republicans viewed the 1972 election as "a long-shot bid" and an "uphill fight."[34]

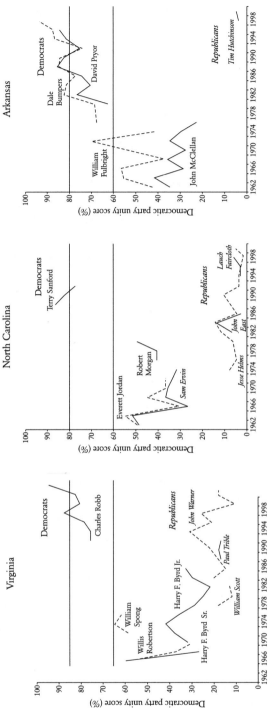

Figure 3.3 The Senate party battle in Virginia, North Carolina, and Arkansas. *Sources:* Same as Figure 3.1.

The only Republican willing to challenge Spong was Congressman William Scott, an "irascible" conservative who had lost his seat in redistricting. With six weeks to go in the campaign, Scott had little money and trailed far behind the sitting Democrat. However, Republican polling revealed that "Spong, the well-known incumbent, was favored by less than 50 percent of the voters sampled. A well-crafted media blitz portraying Scott as a viable conservative alternative could send the dissatisfied undecided voters scurrying to the GOP candidate." A substantial loan to the campaign enabled a "Virginians for Scott" committee to "saturate the airwaves with a simple message—that Scott was conservative and Spong was not." According to Frank Atkinson, "Spong was hammered in the Southwest and in Southside Virginia for his support of gun control measures, in Richmond for his position on voting rights legislation and his failure to oppose mandatory busing forcefully, and in the Hampton Roads area for his lack of support for defense spending and the Vietnam War effort." Spong's supposedly private comment that he "planned to vote for McGovern" in the presidential election became public knowledge before election day and served as the "catalyst" for Scott's late surge. The Republican challenger prevailed by 64,000 votes.[35] Scott's upset victory illustrates the importance of negative media campaigns that temporarily assisted Republican challengers and put Democratic opponents on the defensive. Once in office, however, Scott was unable to represent Virginians effectively in Washington. His tenure in the Senate pleased neither his foes nor his original backers, and he declined to seek a second term.

To fill the open seat in 1978 the Republican convention nominated Richard Obenshain, a longtime party leader. When he died in a plane crash, former Navy secretary John Warner became the party's candidate. Though an inexperienced campaigner, Warner outspent former Democratic attorney general Andrew Miller and effectively used television advertising. Both candidates stressed their conservatism. "Much of the contenders' time," Atkinson points out, "was spent debating which of them was closer in philosophy to—and therefore was the secret choice of—Senator Harry Byrd, Jr." The Democratic candidate failed to mobilize a majority biracial coalition. "Black Democrats, organized labor, and other liberal-leaning partisans would not vote Republican, Miller and his strategists confidently assumed, and so they resolutely targeted the state's conservative voters," Atkinson reported. Warner's victory—an official margin of 4,271 votes—was extraordinarily narrow. "The GOP's sophisticated voter identification and turnout operation," Atkinson argues, "succeeded in getting a large percentage of the Republican's supporters out to the polls on election day, while the Democrats were unable to wage a comparable effort on Miller's behalf."[36]

Starting from this narrow base of support, however, Warner's performance in office was so vigorous and shrewd that he became the first Republican senator from Virginia to secure his seat and enjoy a lengthy career. Using the Armed Services Committee as his political base, and giving special attention to enhancing the Navy in Virginia, Warner deterred strong opponents in 1984 and 1990. His close call came in 1996, when he lost support from the religious right as a result of refusing to back North's bid against Robb.

By the 1990s Virginia's senate delegation mirrored Florida's in its partisan and ideological clarity. Warner was much less of a conservative ideologue than many of his southern Republican counterparts, but his voting record became more conservative after the 1994 elections. Robb, who had led Virginia Democrats back into the governorship by creating a strong biracial coalition, positioned himself in the moderate to somewhat liberal range through 1998 before sharply increasing his party unity voting record in 1999. Allen's victory over Robb in 2000 gave the Republicans full control of Virginia's Senate delegation.

North Carolina

North Carolina has the most traditional demography of any Peripheral South state. Because of its relatively large black population and comparatively small urban population, North Carolina's Senate politics has exhibited a rawer and more persistently racist component than other Peripheral South states.[37] Conservative Democrats Sam Ervin and Everett Jordan, strong opponents of civil rights legislation, predominated before and after federal intervention. The first serious opportunity for the Republicans to win a Senate seat came in 1972, when the Democratic party split over its candidate. Though "tired" and "sick," the elderly Jordan sought to return to the Senate.[38] He was defeated in the Democratic primary by Congressman Nick Galifanakis, a younger, aggressive, and more moderate politician. The disunity and hard feelings resulting from that upset, combined with Richard Nixon's coattails in his landslide defeat of George McGovern, contributed to the victory of an ultraconservative Republican, Jesse Helms, in the November election.

A Republican version of Alabama Democrat George Wallace, Helms expressed without visible embarrassment many of the racial, social, and economic viewpoints characteristic of Old South Democrats. Once settled into the Senate Helms displaced Strom Thurmond of South Carolina in the national news media as the most conspicuously unreconstructed Republican senator from the South. As an exceedingly conservative editorial commentator on a Raleigh television station and a statewide radio network, he had become a "figure of household familiarity among viewers across the state." Helms had denounced as "humbug" the civil rights chant of "freedom now" during the 1960s, and he always provided his audience with plenty to dislike, ridicule, and hate about liberal politicians and policies. Challenged by his twenty-one-year-old daughter–"Will you tell me why you're staying a Democrat? You never vote for a Democratic nominee"–Helms switched his party registration to Republican in 1971. The foundation of Helms's appeal to white Tar Heel voters was a primitive but broadly based and uncompromising conservatism on racial, economic, cultural, and religious issues that separated sheep from goats in no uncertain terms. "Accompanying reporters heard it over and over: 'I'm a strong Democrat, but I'm sure going to vote for you because you used to tell it like it was,'" Ernest Furgurson reported. Helms's slogan in the general election, "He's one of us," implied that Galifanakis was not a "real" North Carolinian. Effectively linking his opponent to the liberal McGovern, who ran 616,000 votes behind Nixon, Helms attracted over three-fifths of white voters and won by almost 118,000 votes. In his first statewide election, Helms carried the traditional Republican vote in the mountains and western Piedmont cities, swept the rural and small-town textile counties in the southwestern part of the state, and began to penetrate Democratic strongholds in the east.[39]

Once in office, Helms became the best-known conservative Republican in the Senate. Helms did more than any other officeholder to shape national images and impressions of the southern Republican party in the 1970s and 1980s. "Beauty is in the eye of the beholder" was Helms's standard response to the question of whether he was a "right-wing extremist." His Senate career involved taking clear positions on an enormous number of conservative causes, using his mastery of the Senate rules to kill or modify liberal legislation, and delivering effective constituency services. *New York Times* reporter Peter Applebome pointed out in 1990 that "Helms remains the most ideologically consistent man in American politics, whose deep-rooted conservatism is as fierce, unvarying and unshakable as it was when he entered the political arena 18 years ago. Helms grew up a Southern Baptist in the segregated South, in an environment where right and wrong were as clear and unassailable as Scripture." As a senator, Helms "has been one of the most consistent voices for cutting domestic programs, for spending on defense, for the moral agenda of the Christian right and for his own militantly anti-Communist foreign policy with its support for the apartheid system in South Africa and the dictatorships of Latin America. He unapologetically favors property rights over countervailing forces like the environment, Christian values over secular ones."[40]

Throughout his career Helms represented the state from the perspective of the values, beliefs, and interests of the most conservative white voters. He had no interest in compromising with his political opponents to expand his original base of support. Newspaper publisher Hoover Adams explained Helms's appeal to his followers. "Jesse Helms doesn't act like a politician, and that's what people like about him. Others start giving in, start compromising, start dealing back and forth. Helms doesn't do that. He stands up for fundamental things he thinks are right. He'd rather come home and play with his grandchildren than compromise."[41] Helms's pattern of representation created and reinforced intense opposition among a sizable minority of North Carolina voters. Yet the senator has won every reelection battle by making his opponent even more disliked than himself.

In the *Washington Post,* Thomas B. Edsall observed that "Helms has demonstrated a consistent willingness to use race as a campaign theme." Throughout his career in the Senate Helms has frequently voted as though the Civil Rights Act and Voting Rights Act did not exist. Unlike South Carolina Republican Strom Thurmond, who voted for the 1982 Voting Rights Act, Helms has never supported any civil rights legislation. He began every election campaign with virtually no support among North Carolina blacks, who accounted for more than one-fifth of the state's population, and therefore needed to poll three-fifths or more among the state's white voters. The Helms approach was simplicity itself. His campaign appeared to calculate the share of the white vote they needed for victory and then worked white Carolinians with divisive and emotionally charged television and radio ads, direct mail, and phone banks until their tracking polls showed they were comfortably exceeding their target. While Helms was "America's most conspicuous spokesman for traditional values, his campaign organization represents the epitome of ruthlessly efficient state-of-the-art politics," according to Applebome. "Helms has fused Bible Belt values with modern technology, like a 19th-century message delivered by a Stealth bomber."[42]

In 1978 Helms had no trouble beating an underfinanced Democrat, but every subsequent reelection campaign was competitive. Helms was involved in especially strident campaigns against Democratic governor Jim Hunt in 1984 and former Charlotte mayor Harvey Gantt in 1990 and 1996. He had so thoroughly alienated blacks and moderate to liberal whites that–unlike Baker, Warner, or Thurmond–the North Carolina Republican could never achieve impressive majorities against serious competitors.[43]

The Helms-Hunt contest illustrates the main features of the incumbent Republican's style. Emphasizing religious, cultural, economic, and racial conservatism, Helms's reelection efforts began in earnest in the fall of 1983 when he conducted a one-month filibuster against a federal holiday honoring civil rights leader Dr. Martin Luther King Jr. "Down 20 percentage points at the start of that campaign," Edsall wrote, "Helms broke the lead of former governor James B. Hunt Jr. (D) with ads describing Helms's battles on the Senate floor against making Martin Luther King Jr.'s birthday a holiday, and then asking: 'Where do you stand, Jim?'" A year later Helms won 74 percent of the votes cast by the nearly four-fifths of white North Carolina voters who opposed this legislation. In 1984 Helms's strongest asset was his ability to frame his reelection as a referendum on the presidency of Republican Ronald Reagan. "If you subscribe to Walter Mondale's liberalism and if you oppose what President Reagan is doing, you should indeed vote for Mr. Hunt," he said. "But if you support what President Reagan is doing and what I do, I hope you will vote for me." On election day Reagan trounced Mondale, 75 to 25 percent, among Tar Heel whites. According to the exit poll, 85 percent of Reagan's white voters also supported Helms, while only 5 percent of Mondale's supporters backed the conservative Republican senator.[44]

Helms's white support in 1984 (65 percent) was formidable. He polled 66 percent of white men and 62 percent of white women. He carried 60 percent or more among every age group. He won 72 percent of whites who said they had been "born again," but he also received 59 percent from whites who did not report such a religious experience. Helms won landslides from white professionals and managers, blue-collar workers, farmers, homemakers, and retirees. Helms carried 95 percent of conservative Republicans, 79 percent of conservative independents, and 71 percent of conservative Democrats—the "Jessecrats." He won 76 percent of moderate to liberal Republicans and split the moderate to liberal independents (49 percent). Helms lost overwhelmingly only among North Carolina blacks and moderate to liberal white Democrats.

In 1990 Helms was seriously challenged by Harvey Gantt, an African-American Democratic politician who told North Carolina voters, "I'm proud to be a liberal." As always, Helms stood on his conservative record. "No political race in memory has so highlighted the complexity and contradictions of the South," Applebome observed. "The contest is being played out in a demographically diverse state that includes not only some of the most yuppified bastions of the New South, such as the high-tech Research Triangle area defined by Raleigh, Durham and Chapel Hill, but also the wary mill towns around Charlotte and the rural and desperately poor outposts of eastern North Carolina." Edsall concluded that "The contest is a titanic struggle between a black liberal who has revived the spirits of a beleaguered North Carolina Democratic Party and a founding father of the 'new right' conservative revolution that was born in the wake of the presidential campaigns of George C. Wallace and his appeal to white, working-class discontent with the civil rights, abortion-rights and gay rights movements." Helms reassured his supporters in January 1990: "On the issues, I am precisely where I was 20 to 30 years ago." For Gantt supporters, Helms's record was precisely the reason they wanted to defeat him. Mel Watt, Gantt's campaign manager, characterized Helms's efforts as "a no, no, no, no, no campaign. It's a negative-Gantt, negative-Gantt, negative-Gantt campaign . . .

You've got the backdrop of all that venom six years ago [in the Helms-Hunt election] that people simply don't want to be reminded of, and you've got 18 years—actually it's probably 25 years—of history with Helms just being an outspoken advocate for division rather than togetherness."[45]

A native of South Carolina, Gantt had broken the color line at Clemson University in 1963, earned an M.A. in architecture from the Massachusetts Institute of Technology, and had twice been elected mayor of Charlotte, North Carolina. After winning the Democratic primary, Gantt was optimistic about his chances in the general election. "The times have really changed, yes they have," Gantt announced. "North Carolina needs a new kind of senator, someone with the very best hopes and aspirations of all the people of North Carolina . . . Folks, I want to tell you, God is good, yes He is. The wonderful people of this state showed their confidence in me. There's a new day in North Carolina." Thad Beyle, a longtime observer of North Carolina politics, injected a more realistic tone into the challenge facing the Democratic nominee: "The key will be for Mr. Gantt to . . . [control] the agenda and . . . not allow Helms to define it."[46]

The Helms campaign expressed "both the down-home, just-folks charm of the candidate and the dangerous, ungodly qualities of his opponent." In 1990 the senator broke bread, from time to time, with his loyal followers in the state's small towns. Campaigning in the eastern part of the state, Helms reminisced about "stopping here in Johnston County during his first campaign in 1972, the year 'I lost my mind and said I'd run for Senator.'" Speaking "in the soft, self-effacing drawl of a small-town preacher," Helms told the audience: "I came down here looking for friends and, by George, I found them. And you're still my friends, and I love you. I'm not very good at saying pretty things. But you mean so much to me, and it means so much to come here tonight." Edsall described similar campaign events: "Helms is greeted by a sea of grizzled white faces, men and women who live along the blacktopped, two-lane highways east of Raleigh, or work in the textile mills around Kannapolis and Concord. Many of them are elderly. For these voters, often former Democrats known as 'Jessecrats,' the $5 chicken barbecue would be worth triple the price as long as it included a chance to hear Helms reiterate his absolute commitment 'that I would never cast a political vote.' Or to hear him joke: 'Harvey, please get it over with,' after a group of black kitchen workers briefly drowned out his speech as they dragged their equipment to a truck."[47]

Unlike virtually all Democratic politicians running statewide campaigns in the South, "Gantt ran as a liberal, embracing the label more openly as the race wound down," Applebome observed. "His stands included increased spending for social programs, opposition to the death penalty and support of abortion rights." Helms's television campaign pounded relentlessly against Gantt's support of liberal social groups and causes. As Edsall reported:

> In one Helms commercial, pictures of a woman lying on the ground, apparently beaten and raped, flash on the screen. "The death penalty for rapists who brutally beat their victims?" the announcer asks, and then answers: "Gantt says 'no.' Helms says 'yes.'" In another, the narrator asks: "Should teenage girls be allowed to have abortions without their mothers being informed?" Gantt's picture appears as the narrator replies to his own question: "Harvey Gantt says 'yes, it's a teenage girl's right.'" Then Helms's picture appears: "Jesse Helms says 'no, we can't undermine families.'"

Helms also denounced "federal subsidies for the 'crude, pornographic, so-called art' of photographer Robert Mapplethorpe and assailed Gantt's support from 'the homosexual lobby.'"[48]

Until the closing days of the election, however, racial conflict was not the central focus of the campaign. Then the situation changed dramatically. Trailing his Democratic challenger, Helms used a television advertisement that "bluntly and directly injected the subject of race into the bitter Senate contest . . . in a television commercial attacking Gantt on the issue of racial job quotas." According to Edsall, "The Helms job quotas commercial shows a white man's hands crumpling what clearly is a job rejection letter. 'You needed that job and you were the best qualified,' the announcer says. 'But they had to give it to a minority because of a racial quota. Is that really fair? Harvey Gantt says it is,' the message continues. 'Gantt supports Ted Kennedy's racial quota law that makes the color of your skin more important than your qualifications.'"[49]

Helms's explicit use of this emotionally charged racial issue transformed the campaign's momentum. "Analysts say that Mr. Helms's ads and campaign speeches both played on racial fears and turned around Mr. Gantt's message of a worrisome, weakening economy by saying the problems were the results of blacks taking jobs from whites," Applebome reported. "I think whites believe blacks are in favor of equal results and quotas if that helps them get results," explained political scientist Ted Arrington. "That may be unfair, but it's there. It was an issue that allowed Helms to bring race into an election in a way that wasn't offensive to many [white] voters."[50]

It worked. Helms defeated Gantt, 53 to 47 percent, with a margin of nearly 106,000 votes. Defeat was a wrenching experience for Gantt and his followers. "On Tuesday night, a mass of faces, black and white, young and old, seemed to fill with tears at once as television sets in the North Raleigh Hilton ballroom flashed the news that Helms had won," observed Michael K. Frisby. "These were abortion-rights activists, environmentalists and traditional Democrats who saw their hopes and dreams crushed by the negative, race-baiting ads. The candidate also was stunned as he witnessed the tide turn against him from his hotel suite in the Hilton." Susan Jetton, Gantt's press secretary, "criticized Helms for playing to racial fears." As Jetton elaborated, "There is in all of us in this country and probably everybody in the world, some racism, and with some people it's way down deep and with others it's closer to the surface, and Jesse Helms has always been a master at playing on that. I think he did it again . . . That was a horrible, horrible, horrible thing for him to do." Meanwhile, Helms savored his victory. "I'm sorry I'm so late," he explained to his waiting supporters, "but I've been at home watching the grim face of [CBS television anchor] Dan Rather." He could not resist the opportunity to gloat. "If the liberal politicians think I've been a thorn in their side in the past," Helms promised, "they haven't seen anything yet."[51]

According to the exit polls, Helms won 63 percent from whites and only 7 percent from blacks. An apparent gender gap—Helms had the support of 57 percent of North Carolina male voters but only 47 percent of the state's female voters—was in fact a racial gap. The Republican senator won 67 percent of white men *and* 58 percent of white women, while merely 10 percent of black men and 4 percent of black women voted for him. Edsall noted that the North Carolina Republican had "turned the New Deal base of the Democratic Party among white voters on its head, winning larger margins among the textile workers and auto mechanics than in the country club bastions of the privileged."[52] In 1990 Helms's strength was inversely related to the income and education of white voters. He led Gantt by 30 percentage points among whites with incomes of less than $50,000, by 21 percentage points among whites with incomes in the $50,000 to 99,000 range, and by only 9 percentage points among white voters whose incomes were $100,000 or more. The Tar Heel Republican did best among white voters with the least formal education. He won 78 percent among high school dropouts, 77 percent among high school graduates, 66 percent among college dropouts, and 56 percent from those who had finished college. Only among North Carolina white voters with postgraduate education did Helms run behind Gantt. Native North Carolina whites gave Helms the edge he needed. He won two-thirds of white voters who had been born in North Carolina, 58 percent of those who had lived in the state for ten or more years, but only 44 percent of more recent white migrants to the state.

As in the past Helms ran strongest among North Carolina white voters who classified themselves as conservatives. He took 94 percent of conservative Republicans, 93 percent of conservative independents, and 79 percent of conservative Democrats. His support dropped to 68 percent of moderate to liberal Republicans. Helms ran well behind Gantt among moderate to liberal white independents and Democrats. "To many observers," Applebome concluded, "Helms's victory was almost a carbon copy of earlier races in which he polarized the electorate and turned the election into an emotional value-laden choice between his view of North Carolina values and alien values."[53] Helms easily won a rematch against Gantt in 1996.

In North Carolina's other Senate seat, incumbent Sam Ervin held his Republican opponents to less than 40 percent of the vote in 1962 and 1968. However, after the veteran conservative Democrat retired in 1974, party control of this seat has shifted every six years. Robert Morgan, who generally continued the conservative Democratic tradition of Ervin and Jordan except that he supported the Voting Rights Act, was elected with 63 percent of the vote. Democratic incumbency no longer deterred

Republican challenges. Morgan was narrowly defeated in 1980 by John East, an East Carolina University political science professor who was an ideological soulmate of Helms. The incumbent Democrat greatly underestimated the tactics, strategy, and financial resources of Senator Helms's Congressional Club, and East won on the basis of a negative advertising television campaign.[54]

Six years later the seat returned to the Democrats. When East committed suicide in 1986, Republican governor James Martin appointed Republican congressman James T. Broyhill as his replacement. After winning a bitter fight in the Republican primary against a candidate backed by Senator Helms, the wounded Broyhill was defeated by former Democratic governor and Duke University president Terry Sanford, 52 to 48 percent. During his single term Sanford voted fairly consistently as a national Democrat. Poor health limited Sanford's ability to campaign in 1992, and he was narrowly defeated by Lauch Faircloth, a former Democratic ally who had converted to the Republican party and had become closely aligned with Helms. Lacking Helms's touch with white North Carolinians, Faircloth became the only incumbent southern Republican senator in the 1990s to be defeated. Democrat John Edwards, a wealthy trial lawyer, defeated more experienced North Carolina Democrats to win the Senate nomination and then marginalized Faircloth as a right-wing extremist to win a close victory (51 to 47 percent) in 1998.

From the mid-1980s onward the party battle for North Carolina's Senate seats generally matched fairly liberal Democrats (Sanford and Edwards) against exceptionally conservative Republicans (Helms and Faircloth). Although Helms won a series of closely contested campaigns, his racially tinged conservatism has not translated into durable success for anyone besides himself and has made it difficult for North Carolina Republicans to recruit less strident and more mainstream conservatives.

Arkansas

For generations Arkansas has been one of the nation's most Democratic states. Until 1996, when Tim Hutchinson became Arkansas's first Republican senator, the most important changes in Senate politics occurred within the Democratic party. From the 1940s though the mid-

1970s, Democrats John McClellan and J. William Fulbright represented Arkansas in the Senate. The plainspoken McClellan was a typical southern conservative, while the patrician Fulbright was somewhat atypical. McClellan rarely faced serious opposition from either Democrats or Republicans. After McClellan died in office he was replaced by Governor David Pryor. A prototypical New South Democrat, Pryor was willing and able to construct biracial coalitions, and his Democratic party unity scores contrast sharply with those of his predecessor. When Pryor decided to retire after the 1994 elections, he gave the revitalized Republican party an opportunity. In 1996 Republican congressman Hutchinson won the open-seat election by a margin of 53 to 47 percent.[55]

Arkansas's other Senate seat underwent a similar ideological shift. In part because of his reputation for aloofness, Fulbright usually drew opposition from Democrats and/or Republicans. In 1974, to his anger and astonishment, he was not only challenged but trounced (65 to 35 percent) by Governor Dale Bumpers in the Democratic primary. Once in the Senate Bumpers encountered no serious opposition during four terms. Without using the term "liberal," both Bumpers and Pryor began their Senate careers as moderates and (after winning their second terms) drifted into the liberal range for most of the rest of their careers. When Bumpers retired after four terms, he was succeeded by Blanche Lincoln, a former Democratic congresswoman with an effective style of campaigning.

PERIPHERAL SOUTH PATTERNS

From 1961 to 1990, Republicans in the Peripheral South not only competed seriously for Senate seats but won 37 percent of the elections, a respectable performance compared to their unrelieved string of defeats during the first six decades of the twentieth century. Republicans won 85 percent of the elections involving their own incumbents, over two-fifths of the open-seat elections, and a tenth of the contests with incumbent Democrats. However, campaigns featuring Republican incumbents (21 percent) were less common than open-seat situations (33 percent) and much less common than battles against Democratic incumbents (46 percent). At this time Republicans had considerable difficulty capitalizing upon their initial victories. Only half of the twelve Peripheral

South Republican senators—Tower, Baker, Helms, Warner, Gramm, and Mack—survived to win a second term in office, a very high rate of incumbency failure. Without a natural majority in the electorate, considerable political skills in position taking, advertising, credit claiming, fundraising, and constituency service—everything involved in mastering the complex job of manifestly representing a state's vital interests—were necessary for political survival. Democratic politicians in the Peripheral South, far from considering Republican incumbents unbeatable, often regarded Republican victories as flukes that could be easily overturned.

4

THE IMPENETRABLE
DEEP SOUTH

None of the Deep South states—Alabama, Georgia, Louisiana, Mississippi, and South Carolina—had impressive traditions of grassroots Republicanism. Nor did these states contain white middle classes large enough to make Republicans competitive in statewide elections. Most Deep South states were still more preoccupied with racial conflicts than with economic development. As they had done for generations, racially conservative white Democrats continued to set the tone of Deep South politics. Republican senatorial candidates who ran as Goldwater conservatives did not produce realistic campaigns against Deep South Democratic candidates, many of whom were veteran segregationists. Before Ronald Reagan's election in 1980, Republican prospects for winning Senate seats were particularly unpromising in the Deep South.

Although Republicans from the Peripheral South gradually became a sizable minority presence in the Senate, they had much greater difficulty doing so in the Deep South. All in all, Republicans won only a fifth of the 1961–1990 Deep South Senate elections. Compared with their Peripheral South counterparts they had lower victory rates when they ran their own few incumbents (78 versus 85 percent), had open-seat opportunities (30 versus 43 percent), or faced Democratic incumbents (3 versus 10 percent). And since elections involving veteran Democrats occurred far more frequently in the Deep South than the Peripheral South (64 versus 46 percent) while open-seat elections were considerably less common (19 versus 33 percent), Deep South Republicans had few realistic opportunities to win Senate elections.

THE PARTY BATTLE IN THE DEEP SOUTH

South Carolina

No state better illustrates the advantage of incumbency for both Democrats and Republicans than South Carolina (see Figure 4.1). On the eve of federal intervention Senators Olin Johnston and Strom Thurmond were the state's experienced Democratic segregationists. Thurmond was the only southern Democrat to surrender the benefits of membership in the Senate's majority party in order to demonstrate his disgust at federal intervention on civil rights. The conservative Democrat switched parties in 1964 and became an even more conservative Republican. In the process, however, Thurmond took care not to distance himself from his conservative Democratic allies. Easily reelected in 1966 and 1972, Thurmond repelled (56 to 44 percent) a more vigorous challenge in 1978. As a practical conservative, he habitually reaped credit from legislation he had voted against. "Thurmond's effrontery at pork barrel politics is almost breathtaking," Jack Bass and Marilyn W. Thompson reported. "After voting against almost all federal legislation aimed at improving health care, education, housing, and other domestic spending programs not involving the military, Thurmond sought every federal dollar he could get for South Carolina, with a press release seeking credit for every grant made to the state."[1]

Eventually Thurmond accepted desegregation and black participation and revised his image more in the direction of economic conservatism. After a protégé was defeated for governor in 1970 by a biracial coalition organized by Democrat John West, Thurmond hired a black staff aide. Nadine Cohodas has clearly explained the evolution of Thurmond's style: "If he voted against civil rights bills in Washington, he paid attention to black concerns at home. Always a hands-on politician who thrived on the human touch, he now turned that considerable skill toward the black community. It wasn't just that he did favors for constituents; it was the way he got things done, turning routine political business into personal gestures that individuals long remembered." In the

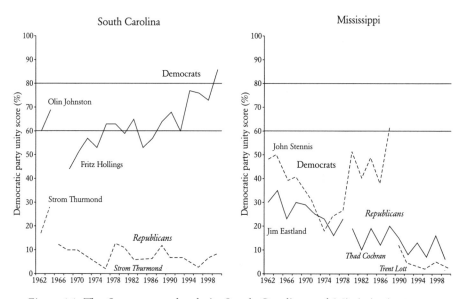

Figure 4.1 The Senate party battle in South Carolina and Mississippi. *Sources: Congressional Quarterly Weekly Report,* various issues.

1980s Thurmond supported the Voting Rights Act and the King federal holiday. All of this paid off in reducing the intensity of his black opposition. "When it came time for reelection," Cohodas concluded, "Thurmond might not get much black support, but he was not going to excite much black opposition, either."[2]

Despite his advanced age Thurmond coasted to victory in 1984 and 1990. "We *killed* him!" was Thurmond's private characterization of one hapless opponent.[3] The senator's "political mastery" of electoral politics, Bass and Thompson have contended, has been based on "(1) political boldness, which reflects both courage and an unsurpassed instinct for timing; (2) a refusal to keep an enemy, which dissipates opposition; (3) a willingness to take a firm stand on issues, which generates respect; and (4) a record of legendary constituent service, which creates goodwill."[4] Thurmond was almost eighty-eight when he was reelected with 64 percent in 1990, winning 80 percent of whites and 20 percent of blacks. In 1996, when Thurmond ran for the last time, he rebuffed a serious Democratic challenge but fell to only 53 percent of the vote.

While Thurmond's defection and subsequent reelections gave South

Carolina Republicans continuous representation in the Senate, the death of Olin Johnston eventually culminated in the 1966 election of an experienced Democrat, former governor Ernest "Fritz" Hollings, who knew how to solidify a Senate seat. Like Thurmond, Hollings had originally been a strong segregationist. In 1959, for example, he used congressional hearings to denounce pending civil rights legislation as "unnecessary laws being enacted against a minority South in the name of civil rights to gain political capital with other minority groups over the nation." According to Hollings, "thinking leaders of both races in the South realize that integration is unwise, impractical and will never be accomplished."[5] Both the Civil Rights Act and the Voting Rights Act were passed before Hollings entered the Senate, and he therefore had more room to maneuver in overcoming his segregationist past. Confronted with the need to gain credibility with black Carolinians, Hollings used the issue of hunger to champion food stamps and other federal programs. By 1972 he was much stronger than he had been in the open-seat election of 1966, and his ability to satisfy both black and white Democrats enabled him to create a safe seat before the 1990s. In 1992 and again in 1998 Hollings survived vigorous challenges from second-tier Republicans, former Charleston congressman Tommy Hartnett in 1992 and Greenville congressman Bob Inglis in 1998.

Figure 4.1 shows the ideological shift in South Carolina Senate elections through the careers of Thurmond and Hollings. Thurmond's Republican conservatism appears as a constant, whereas Hollings' Democratic party unity scores trace a slow shift from conservatism through moderation. In 1999, for the first time in his long Senate career, Hollings voted as a national Democrat. Because these veteran incumbents were nearing the end of their careers, both South Carolina Senate seats will be highly contested in the first decade of the twenty-first century.

Mississippi

No state has produced less ideological change in its Senate delegation than Mississippi. As in South Carolina, incumbency has benefited both political parties. James Eastland and John Stennis, Mississippi's veteran Democratic senators at the time of federal intervention, differed in style (Eastland was more abrasive, Stennis more courtly), but both militantly opposed racial change. Beginning the 1960s as conservative Democrats, they became even more conservative after federal intervention. When Eastland retired in 1978, Republicans seized the opportunity. An independent campaign by a black politician divided Democrats and enabled Republican congressman Thad Cochran to win the open-seat election with a 45 percent plurality. Cochran had been elected to the House of Representatives in 1972, and he marketed himself "almost as an incumbent." As the accidental frontrunner, Cochran explained that his success was "not a resurgence of Republicanism in the South, or anything like that . . . It's a fluke, a most unusual set of circumstances that happen to benefit me. If I had to write a script, I couldn't have done a better job."[6]

Cochran was the sole Republican success story in a Deep South open-seat election during the 1960s and 1970s. His immediate challenge was to convert an accidental victory into a secure seat. Thurmond offered practical advice, telling the Republican freshman "how he could vote against federal government programs drafted to help minorities but not lose black support at home. 'Your black friends will be with you,' he told Cochran, 'if you be sure to help them with their projects.'" In office Cochran represented Mississippi as a "New South Republican" who was much closer in style and temperament to Howard Baker and John Warner than to Jesse Helms. The Mississippi Republican voted to extend the Voting Rights Act and to establish the King holiday. Cochran developed a reputation for effective constituency work, and he "supported funds for the school lunch program, research grants for predominantly black colleges, and home loans for low-income farmers—all popular programs in the nation's poorest state."[7]

Cochran's activities amounted to a textbook example of how to expand a reelection constituency. Running for reelection in 1984 as an integral part of the Republican-controlled Senate, Cochran emphasized his membership in the majority party, just as Democratic incumbents had once done. "There comes a point in all his stump speeches that Sen. Thad Cochran (R–Miss.) pauses to tick off 'the list'—a meticulous accounting of his subcommittee chairmanships and assignments," the *Washington Post* reported.[8] He was reelected with 62 percent of the vote. Although he won only 12 percent of the black vote, he received 82 percent of the white vote and demolished a well-known Democrat, former governor William Winter. Cochran won 94 percent among white Republicans, 86 percent of white independents, and 59 percent of white Democrats. He carried 90 percent of white conservatives, 75 percent of white moderates, and 66 percent of white liberals. After this decisive victory, no major Democrat has chosen to contest Cochran. In 1990 he drew no Democratic opponent, and in 1996 he won going away.

Less of a segregationist ideologue than Eastland, Stennis adapted to the reality of black participation and prolonged his career until his retirement in 1988. During the 1980s his Democratic party unity scores moved upward but they nudged past the 60 percent line only in his final Congress. Stennis' retirement gave the Mississippi Republican party another opportunity. In 1988 Republican congressman Trent Lott gave up a safe seat on the Gulf Coast and excellent prospects of a future leadership role among House Republicans (he was higher on the leadership ladder than Newt Gingrich) in order to run for the Senate. With minimal black support, Lott attracted well over three-fifths of Mississippi's white vote and defeated Democratic Congressman Wayne Dowdy by a margin of 54 to 46 percent. Lott had sufficient skill, experience, and ambition to secure his seat and emerge as a party leader. Easily reelected in 1994, Lott challenged and defeated Alan Simpson for the position of Republican whip. When Republican majority leader Bob Dole resigned to run for president in 1996, Lott defeated the more senior Cochran to become the Senate's new majority leader. However controversial Lott may have been as Senate majority leader, he was utterly secure at home. No major Democrat challenged him in 2000, and Lott won with 67 percent of the vote.

Mississippi's Senate politics, therefore, has basically involved a straightforward shift from conservative Democrats elected by whites to conservative Republicans still elected by whites. The overtly racial features of the old Mississippi politics have generally been absorbed into a broader economic and social conservatism. Racial divisions are now expressed through the party system: a Democratic party usually composed of most blacks and a distinct minority of whites faces a Republican party dependent upon extraordinarily large white majorities. This situation produces competitive battles in open-seat elections but otherwise gives the advantage to incumbents.

Georgia

Richard Russell and Herman Talmadge, Georgia's conservative Democratic senators, had defended southern racial traditions and denounced civil rights legislation throughout their careers. No Republican, no matter how conservative, could hope to defeat them in the years following federal intervention (see Figure 4.2). After Russell's death in 1971, Governor Jimmy Carter appointed Atlanta lawyer David Gambrell to finish his term. The following year, however, when Gambrell sought nomination for a six-year term, he was upset in the Democratic primaries by Sam Nunn, a thirty-four-year-old state legislator. Nunn then became Georgia's first Democratic Senate candidate to face a serious Republican opponent—Atlanta congressman Fletcher Thompson.[9]

The 1972 Nunn-Thompson battle illustrates how conservative Democrats could often suffocate conservative Republicans in the Deep South. Both men campaigned energetically for the votes of racially conservative white Georgians. Thompson made "it a horse race by clinging to the coattails of President Nixon and Vice President Spiro Agnew, while at the same time waving the bloody shirt of the Democrats' national ticket, liberals George McGovern and Sargent Shriver." Nunn repudiated McGovern but also "point[ed] out with disdain that despite the so-called 'southern strategy' of the Nixon administration, 'there has been more [racial] integration under Nixon than under the last two Democratic presidents.'"[10]

Prominent Georgia Democrats, worried that a Republican senator would damage Georgia interests, rushed to Nunn's assistance. After Nunn won the Democratic primary, "The organizations of Sen. Herman Talmadge, Sen. David Gambrell (whom Nunn upset in the party runoff), Gov. Jimmy Carter, former Govs. Carl Sanders, Ernest Vandiver, and Marvin Griffin, and, to a lesser extent, that of Lt. Gov. Lester Maddox . . . produced an abundance of volunteer workers, veteran political strategists, voter registration lists, telephone numbers, financial contributors, and, ultimately, voters, for the Nunn camp to toy with." Thompson's campaign, by comparison, was almost literally a one-man effort. Beginning with "virtually no organization outside his home district," he was forced to "put together an organization from ground

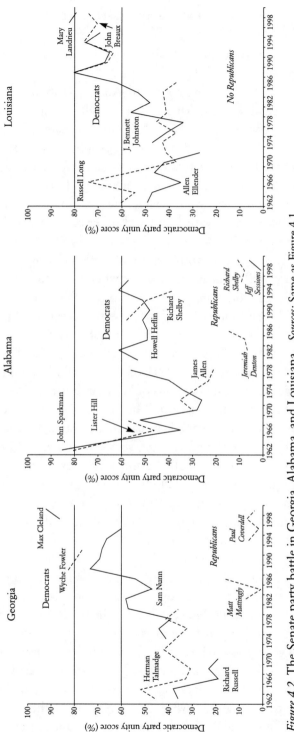

Figure 4.2 The Senate party battle in Georgia, Alabama, and Louisiana. *Sources:* Same as Figure 4.1.

zero." As Thompson conceded, "It's tiring when you have to take on the entire power structure."[11]

As a leader of antibusing forces in Atlanta, Thompson was completely unacceptable to black voters. He sought to undermine Nunn's appeal among conservative whites. "Thompson charged," reported the *Atlanta Journal*, "that Nunn deceived the people of Georgia by openly courting the white conservative vote prior to the primary runoff while meeting secretly with black leaders, including [Julian] Bond, to lure their support. Nunn denied the charge. He said no deceit was involved because in the meetings with Bond and other black leaders he did not solicit their support."[12]

Though closely allied with segregationists Talmadge and George Wallace, Nunn still managed to win overwhelming support from Georgia blacks. "Negro voters are being urged to vote the straight Democratic ticket, [Sen. LeRoy] Johnson said, because the Democratic party offers them 'the best hope for the realization of first class citizenship and opportunity.'" Johnson "predicted that Sam Nunn, who has shunned McGovern, will be the 'incidental beneficiary' of a heavy black vote." Despite avoiding open solicitations of black support, the *Atlanta Journal* reported, "Nunn is counting on it." In the end Nunn's covert biracial coalition overcame the Republican candidate's strength among urban whites. While Nixon carried Georgia with an estimated 90 percent of the white vote, Thompson polled a much smaller white majority and virtually nothing from blacks.[13] Nunn became Georgia's first Democrat to win a Senate election despite losing the white vote.

In Washington the new senator quickly established himself as a serious and effective workhorse. Nunn won Russell's old seat on the Armed Services Committee and became a leader on military matters. "His basic instincts are conservative, particularly on cultural issues; and on many matters his voting record looks like that of an old Dixiecrat," concluded *The Almanac of American Politics 1984*. "But he is not a knee-jerk vote for anything, and he is open to persuasion on most domestic matters."[14] Nunn strongly opposed busing, but he voted to extend the Voting Rights Act in 1975 and 1982. By offering something valuable to majorities of both whites and blacks in Georgia, Nunn united the Georgia Democratic party at a time when 55 percent of southern whites were still favorably disposed toward the Democrats and nearly all blacks supported Democratic candidates. Having expanded his reelection constituency, Nunn never again faced serious Republican opposition.

For more than a decade Nunn positioned himself as a conservative Democrat, with Democratic party unity scores resembling those of Lloyd Bentsen in Texas and J. Bennett Johnston in Louisiana (see below). Only in the mid-1980s, as Nunn's seat became totally secure and as he came to be mentioned as a possible Democratic presidential candidate, did he move into the moderate range. Nunn's unforced retirement in 1996, when no Republican in Georgia could possibly have beaten him, shocked many southern Democrats because it deprived the region of an especially influential voice in national politics. His departure, however, helped clarify the relationship between ideology and party in Georgia's Senate elections. Democrat Max Cleland, the winner of the close open-seat election in 1996, constructed a majority biracial coalition in which heavy black turnout (especially in Atlanta) provided his margin of victory. Cleland's national Democratic party unity scores stand in sharp contrast to those of Nunn, Russell, and Talmadge.

Senator Talmadge, a symbol par excellence of countrified old southern politics, continued to vote as a conservative Democrat long after federal intervention. In 1980 Talmadge faced a difficult reelection challenge. The Senate had denounced him in 1979 "for 'reprehensible conduct' in his handling of campaign and office expense account funds"; his lifestyle as well as his business dealings had come under withering criticism from the Atlanta newspapers; and he had been renominated for a fifth term only after surviving a bitter Democratic runoff against Zell Miller. The veteran senator had never faced a serious Republican challenge and clearly underestimated his opponent, Mack Mattingly, whom he later recalled as "a pleasant looking fellow with a big dimple in his chin . . . [whose] previous political experience consisted of a losing race for Congress and a stint as state chairman of the Republican party."[15]

The bitter Democratic primary fights, Art Harris observed, "allowed Mattingly to conserve his meager cash, stake out the high road and stick to raising his visibility, advancing his image as a budget balancing, tax cutting pragmatist, and to flail Talmadge above the belt with highly memorable TV spots. The ads freeze-framed Talmadge, his mouth in gear, declaring 1980 his most productive year in the Senate, while a narrator hyped his high absentee record." Low on funds, Talmadge "stooped to scare tactics, likening Mattingly, who moved to Georgia after college and service in the Air Force 25 years ago, and his staff to 'carpetbaggers' leading Sherman's army through Georgia. It didn't work. He implored his people to get out and vote. It sounded like a wolf cry. Few could imagine a Talmadge whipped by a Republican."[16]

In the general election Talmadge was caught between the understandable dissatisfaction of many blacks with his segregationist history and the unhappiness of many Atlanta area whites with his country-boy persona. While the early rural returns gave Talmadge a large lead, "some time before the sun rose over Georgia Nov. 5 a gigantic suburban vote from around Atlanta and other major cities came rolling in. Joining the suburbanites were other elements of a classic New South urban coalition: Yankee émigrés, Republicans, Talmadgehaters, some blacks and some young people—all of them unswayed by the Talmadge mystique of seniority and service. And Talmadge came up short by 26,000 votes out of a record of more than 1.6 million cast."[17] Mattingly became the first Republican from the Deep South to defeat an incumbent Democratic senator.

Because the 1980 election was mainly a referendum on Talmadge, Mattingly's unusual electoral coalition—about one-third of Atlanta blacks plus suburban whites—did not constitute a realistic basis for his reelection. The new Republican incumbent's task was to enhance his appeal among rural whites to complement his strength among urban whites. Mattingly, however, was an amateur politician. As Marvin Overby has convincingly shown, Mattingly failed to use the potential resources of incumbency even to consolidate, much less to expand, his original electoral base. "I had never done constituent service work before," the former senator later acknowledged. "I was not a professional politician who came into office knowing how to do such things." He took visible "positions" on issues that were peripheral to the interests of his constituents. "Although [Mattingly] chaired the politically powerful Senate Appropriations Subcommittee on Military Construction," Overby argues, "he was better known for his unflagging defense of a presidential line item veto than for either his expertise on defense or his ability to deliver appropriations projects to his home state." Nor did he seriously cultivate local constituencies. Although the freshman senator "returned fairly often to Georgia, he spent most of his time there either in Atlanta or at his home on St. Simons Island, not out touring the state. Such behavior undermined his ability to portray himself as a hard-working, accessible, 'non–country club' Republican."[18]

In 1986 Mattingly's opponent was an experienced Democratic politician, Atlanta congressman Wyche Fowler. He had represented a majority black Atlanta congressional district as a moderate Democrat. According to R. W. Apple Jr., "Mr. Fowler's overall strategy is simple: to persuade Democrats who now seem ready to vote for Mr. Mattingly that they should 'come home' because he is a safe, mainstream member of their party and not an exotic Atlantan." Fowler campaigned throughout rural Georgia accompanied by prominent state and local Democratic leaders. "Fowler has been reelected five times, and his people have campaigning down to a fine art," Loch Johnson observed. "Out on the hustings, he doesn't really come across as a liberal. He'll talk about his grandfather, who was a farmer, or his mother, who was born just outside of Albany—and he knows every church song down to the fourth verse." Fowler portrayed Mattingly as a country club Republican who ignored the interests of average Georgians while giving tax breaks to large corporations. "Mack Mattingly. Voting Against Georgia. Voting Against Us," was the powerful message of one negative ad. "While Mattingly was trying to make the race a conservative-liberal contest," the *Washington Post* reported, "Fowler's ads were turning it into a battle between a Georgia Democrat and a national Republican."[19]

And yet despite his ineptitude, despite a flawed reelection strategy that kept him working in Washington instead of campaigning in Georgia, and despite the determined opposition of an experienced Democrat, Mattingly very nearly won reelection. Assembling the majority biracial coalition that had eluded Talmadge, Fowler defeated Mattingly by 22,460 votes. Even though only 30 percent of Georgia's white voters were Republicans, Mattingly won 59 percent of the white vote. He carried 92 percent of white Republicans, 72 percent of white independents, and 25 percent of white Democrats. By 1986, only 37 percent of Georgia white voters identified themselves as Democrats. The precariousness of Fowler's victory was indicated by his small share (41 percent) of the white vote. Fowler, too, would have to broaden his appeal beyond his biracial Democratic base in order to build a safe reelection constituency.

In 1992 Republican Paul Coverdell challenged Fowler. Fowler defeated Coverdell but failed to win an outright majority. Under Georgia law (since changed to permit plurality victories) a runoff was required. With the incumbent Democrat on the defensive, Coverdell defeated Fowler 51 to 49 percent. Coverdell was reelected in 1998 but only with a majority of 52 percent. The Republican senator's unexpected death in the summer of 2000 led to the appointment and later election of former Democratic governor Zell Miller to the Senate. Miller easily dispatched former one-term Republican senator Mack Mattingly, 57 to 39 percent. Georgia began the new century with two Democratic senators.

Alabama

During the 1950s and early 1960s Lister Hill and John Sparkman had been among the least conservative Democratic senators from the Deep South. As New Deal Democrats, they were inclined to support the national Democratic party on matters not involving race relations. Their maneuverability diminished with the emergence of civil rights as a national issue and the ascendancy back home of the segregationist crusader Governor George Wallace. Hemmed in by Wallace's immense popularity with whites, Alabama's veteran senators were compelled to put substantial distance between themselves and the national Democrats, who were advocating federal intervention.[20]

In 1962 Hill was caught by surprise and almost lost his Senate seat to James D. Martin, a Goldwater Republican who emphasized racial and economic conservatism. Hill had always voted against civil rights legislation and strongly supported New Deal Democratic programs. As a Democrat, however, in the eyes of many Alabama whites Hill had now become associated with the unpopular Kennedy administration. The Republican Senate candidate, a novice politician, had been nominated by the Republican state convention after "an insurgent group largely representative of the newer and younger urban business-professional wing of the party" took control. As Numan V. Bartley and Hugh D. Graham pointed out, "In his acceptance speech Martin set the tone of attack, calling for 'a return to the spirit of '61–1861, when our fathers formed a new nation' to support their principles. 'God willing,' Martin concluded, 'we will not again be forced to take up rifle and bayonet to preserve these principles . . . Make no mistake, my friends, this will be a fight. The bugle call is loud and clear! The South has risen!'" A majority of Alabama's white voters supported Martin, while Hill's support was greatest among the state's few black voters and rural whites in northern Alabama. Martin's stridently ideological campaign attracted white conservatives and served as a "harbinger of the Goldwater phenomenon shortly to follow" in the Deep South. The veteran Democrat "countered as best he could with appeals to fading memories of the 'Republican depression' and Herbert Hoover and by emphasizing the New Deal's contribution toward alleviating the misery of depression and underdevelopment in Alabama, his own consistent support of TVA, and the advantages of his seniority." Hill barely survived, running ahead of his Republican opponent by only 6,803 votes, a "razor-thin margin of eight-tenths of one percent."[21]

Hill never really recovered from his near-defeat. When he chose to retire in 1968, his replacement was a far more conservative Democrat. Jim Allen was a Wallacite completely uninterested in creating biracial coalitions. After Allen died in office, a bitter intraparty struggle developed over his seat. In 1980 the interim Democrat was defeated in the Democratic primary. Hard feelings between rival Democratic camps helped send Republican Jeremiah Denton, a retired admiral and conservative ideologue, to the Senate with a narrow victory. Denton was closely identified with the religious right, and his performance in office epitomized the zealous pursuit of a rigidly conservative agenda at the expense of practical goals. He had never held elective office, much less served in a legislative body. Of the four southern Republicans elected in 1980, Overby observed, "Denton developed perhaps the worst reputation regarding constituent outreach and service." A former adviser said that Denton "would not travel around the state much, would not go to community events, and this hurt his image as a responsive senator." In a state with sixty-seven counties, "there were 'some thirty to forty counties Denton never set foot in during six years.'" Amazingly, the senator even tried to justify his unorthodox and exceedingly impolitic priorities.

"I can't be down here patting babies on the butt," he told Alabamians in a television interview, "and get [much] done in Washington."[22]

In 1986 conservative Democratic congressman Richard Shelby narrowly defeated Denton. Shelby moderated his previously solid conservatism to win support from blacks and organized labor. He ridiculed Denton by running "the incumbent's 'baby butts' clip in his own ads and distributing handbills that read 'Lost—Sen. Jeremiah Denton . . . Rarely seen in Alabama over the past six years though sporadic sightings have been reported during the campaign season.'"[23] Shelby's biracial coalition—39 percent of whites combined with 93 percent of blacks—produced a 7,000-vote victory. Democrats provided most of Shelby's white support, while the Republican relied heavily on white independents. Once in office, Shelby voted as a conservative Democrat and was easily reelected. In 1994, after the Republicans regained control of the Senate, Shelby immediately switched parties. He breezed to victory in 1998 against token Democratic opposition.

Unlike Hill, Sparkman managed to preserve his career. His party unity scores declined dramatically through the early 1970s, but in his final term he began to vote more frequently with his party. After Hill's near-defeat, however, Sparkman never voted in the moderate range. His successor, Howell Heflin, assembled a majority biracial coalition but generally continued to vote as a conservative or nominal Democrat. Although Republicans could not compete with Heflin's incumbency, in 1996 Republican Jeff Sessions won the open seat created when Heflin retired.

Aside from the early 1960s, conservatism has been the dominant orientation of Democratic and Republican senators in Alabama. Neither Heflin nor Shelby ever shifted decisively into the moderate range as Nunn and Hollings eventually did. Alabama ended the 1990s with two very conservative Republican senators. In 1998 Shelby demonstrated his political skill in winning a landslide reelection after switching parties, but the jury is still out on Sessions' ability to make his seat secure. Alabama Democrats, it should be emphasized, should not be counted out in statewide elections. Biracial politics means that Democratic candidates can win statewide if they can unify blacks and win between 35 and 40 percent of the white vote.

Louisiana

Louisiana's Senate politics is unique. In no other southern state did the Republican party fail to win a single Senate election from 1952 through 2000. Why were the Republicans completely unsuccessful? First of all, Allen Ellender and Russell Long responded to federal intervention by distancing themselves from the national party. Long's moderate Democratic party unity scores (a necessity while he was the Democratic whip) threatened to be a problem. After Edward Kennedy of Massachusetts defeated him for whip, Long's party unity scores dropped well into the conservative range and remained there for the rest of his career. Long's retirement produced a close election between Democratic congressman John Breaux and Republican congressman Henson Moore. Each attempted to implement standard partisan solutions to coalition building. Breaux, a natural "moderate" who knew how to blend conservative and liberal positions to produce a majority coalition of most blacks and a large minority of whites, defeated Moore by the margin of 53 to 47 percent. Moore's coalition of white economic conservatives and white social conservatives resulted in a white majority of 60 percent, insufficiently large to produce victory. Louisiana's Republicans have more or less conceded the seat to Breaux in subsequent elections.[24]

Ellender's death resulted in the election of another conservative Democrat, J. Bennett Johnston, to the Senate. Like Nunn in Georgia, Johnston did not move into the moderate range until the mid-1980s. His severest challenge came in 1990 against David Duke, the notorious right-wing extremist who embarrassed the national GOP and split the Louisiana Republican party by running as a Republican. On the basis of an "analysis of all-white and all-black precincts," Douglas D. Rose concluded that "Duke received under 1 percent of the black vote cast and nearly 57 percent of the white vote cast in the election."[25] In 1996 Democrat Mary Landrieu barely edged out Republican Woody Jenkins, a religious-right conservative, for the seat opened by Johnston's retirement.

Facing an array of skilled and experienced Democratic politicians, Republicans in the Deep South won only three of ten open-seat Senate elections from 1961 through 1990. Two of these open-seat winners—

Cochran and Lott—have enjoyed lengthy Senate careers, while Denton was narrowly defeated in his reelection effort. Only one Deep South Democratic senator, the embattled Talmadge, was unseated by a Republican challenger. Through the 1980s, therefore, the Deep South remained a Democratic stronghold. The Republicans who built careers as senators had strong reputations for constituency service; they behaved as pragmatic conservatives.

THE STRUCTURE OF REPUBLICAN OPPORTUNITIES IN SENATE ELECTIONS

For any political party the ideal situation—as illustrated historically by the Democratic Solid South—is one in which simply reelecting the party's incumbents perpetuates an overwhelming majority. A more competitive party battle exists when neither Republicans nor Democrats can control a delegation just by reelecting incumbents. The worst possible position for a party—illustrated by that of the southern Republicans—is one in which there are no (or very few) incumbents to reelect. Table 4.1 summarizes the Republican opportunity structure in southern Senate elections from the 1950s through the 1980s. It reports the electoral context Republicans confronted, their victory rates, and their yields, three vital components of Republican performance.

The electoral context—the relative proportion of elections involving incumbent Republicans, open seats, or incumbent Democrats—establishes the boundaries of Republican opportunities. Republican victory rates varied enormously with each situation. Republicans enjoyed their greatest success, of course, among their own incumbents. Southern Republican senators might ordinarily be in the minority, but they could nonetheless use their visibility to raise money, deliver services, and become better known to their constituents. Open-seat contests would offer the best opportunities to enlarge the Republican delegation, but in many instances Republican candidates would be facing electorates dominated by Democrats. And very few southern Republicans could hope to defeat veteran Democratic senators. As long as most conservative whites thought of themselves as Democrats, exceptional circumstances would be required to produce any Republican victories.

Table 4.1 The changing Republican opportunity structure in southern Senate elections, 1950s–1980s (%)

Elections with	Electoral context			Republican victory rates			Republican yields		
	1950s	1960s–1970s	1980s	1950s	1960s–1970s	1980s	1950s	1960s–1970s	1980s
Incumbent Reps.	0	14	27	0	90	75	0	13	20
Open seats	19	30	23	0	29	60	0	8	14
Incumbent Dems.	81	56	50	0	5	9	0	3	5
All elections	100	100	100	0	24	39	0	24	39

Note: Electoral context = percentage of Senate elections involving incumbent Republicans, open seats, or incumbent Democrats; Republican victory rates = percentage of each type of election won by Republicans; Republican yields = electoral context times Republican victory rates.
Source: Calculated from *Congressional Quarterly's Guide to U.S. Elections*, 3d ed. (Washington, D.C., 1994).

Republican yields summarize the net impact of electoral context and victory rates. Multiplying the percentage of elections with incumbent Republicans (or open seats or incumbent Democrats) by the percentage of such elections resulting in Republican victories produces the Republican yield. For example, 14 percent of the South's Senate elections in the 1960s and 1970s contained Republican incumbents, and Republicans won 90 percent of these contests. The Republicans' yield from their incumbent senators ($14 \times .90$) thus amounted to 13 percent of all southern Senate elections during this period. Southern Democrats, by comparison, won 95 percent of the 56 percent of elections featuring their incumbents. They controlled a majority of the 1961–1979 senate elections—53 percent—merely by reelecting their veterans.

In the 1950s the Republicans faced an exceedingly bleak opportunity structure. Incumbent Democrats dominated southern Senate elections. They appeared in four-fifths of the campaigns and never lost. And because Democrats also won all the open-seat contests, the southern Republicans' yield for the entire decade was zero.

During the 1960s and 1970s, however, Republicans won a quarter of the region's Senate elections. Their partial breakthrough in the Peripheral South (33 percent) was offset by token victories in the Deep South (13 percent). Republican gains resulted from a less daunting electoral context and improved victory rates. The Democratic incumbency advantage, 81–0 in the 1950s, dropped to 56–14 in the next two decades. Retirements and occasional defeats of incumbents in Democratic primaries created more open-seat elections (rising from 19 to 30 percent). Southern Republicans reelected all but one of their incumbents who stood for reelection (Brock was the exception), and they won a small minority (29 percent) of their open-seat opportunities. Unsurprisingly, apart from Gore and Spong they failed to defeat veteran Democrats. Republicans emerged as a significant minority in the Peripheral South delegation but failed to advance beyond a token presence among Deep South senators.

During the 1980s the Republicans captured almost two-fifths of the Senate campaigns and did only slightly better in the Peripheral South (42 percent) than in the Deep South (35 percent). This modest improvement resulted from two factors. Elections featuring their own incumbents accounted for twice as many elections in the 1980s as in the previous two decades (27 to 14 percent), so that the Republicans could increase their yield from their own incumbents (rising from 13 to 20 percent of all elections) despite having a poorer incumbent victory rate (falling from 90 to 75 percent). At the same time, the Republicans won three-fifths of the open-seat elections and thereby doubled their yield from open-seat opportunities, from 8 percent in the 1960s and 1970s to 17 percent in the 1980s. Democratic incumbency continued to constrain Republican advances, but the Democratic advantage (50 to 27) was now two to one instead of four to one as it had been in the 1960s and 1970s. As the 1990s began, Republicans were gradually closing the incumbency gap that had traditionally perpetuated their minority-party status.

The fundamental weakness of many southern Republican senators was their inability to use incumbency to secure and expand their reelection constituencies. Democrats controlled the Senate during much of this period, and Republican senators could not gain reelection solely by mobilizing their own partisans. As members of a minority party, Republican politicians needed to be unusually skilled in order to unify their party, reach out to independents and sympathetic Democrats, and deliver services and benefits. Several Republican senators lacked officeholding experience, and some behaved as ideological zealots rather than as practical conservatives.

As a result, nearly half of the seventeen southern Republican senators originally elected from 1961 through 1988 (47 percent) were one-termers. Four freshmen senators found their officeholding experience so unsatisfying that they declined to seek a second term, career decisions baffling to southern Democrats. Four other first-term senators were such poor politicians that they were unseated by Democrats. Just as many pioneering southern Republican governors were followed by Democrats, so, too, this experience was common among the first generation of southern Republican senators.

Republicans who entered the Senate during the 1960s and 1970s were actually more likely to win reelection and establish substantial careers (six who did versus three who did not) than those who entered during the 1980s (three to five). In the earlier period blacks were not yet fully mobilized, and fewer white Democrats were interested in or skilled at constructing biracial coalitions. Republican incumbents in the 1980s were more likely to face larger black electorates as well as moderate or centrist Democratic candidates eager to organize majority biracial coalitions.

During the 1980s southern Democrats responded to the threat of increased Republican competition by perfecting their biracial coalitions. Although Deep South Democratic senators such as Hollings, Stennis, Heflin, Nunn (in 1984), and Johnston (again in 1984) continued to position themselves as experienced conservatives while most Peripheral South Democratic senators voted as moderates and/or nationals (Lawton Chiles, Bob Graham, Jim Sasser, Al Gore, Dale Bumpers, David Pryor, and Charles Robb, for example), the common denominator of their victories was their ability to organize and sustain biracial coalitions that added up to statewide majorities. Republicans across the South went to the Senate only by uniting whites across income lines sufficiently to produce white majorities that also summed to statewide majorities.

Drawing on exit polls in (most) southern Senate elections from 1982 through 1990, Figure 4.3 shows the shares of the white vote and the black vote won by victorious Republicans and Democrats in elections involving Democratic incumbents, open seats, and Republican incumbents. Lines drawn at 50 percent divide Democrats with majority black *and* majority white support (the upper right cells) from Democrats with majority black *but* minority white support (the upper left cells) and from Republicans with majority white *and* minority black support (the lower right cells).

Between 1982 and 1990 no Republican defeated an incumbent Democratic senator. All the winning Democrats had solid black support, but their white votes differed considerably. Given the resources of their incumbency, what is most intriguing is the inability of many veteran Democrats to win landslide (60 percent or higher) white votes against relatively weak opponents. Despite their seniority Bentsen and Heflin barely split the white vote. Aside from Gore, who won two-thirds of the white vote against token opposition in 1990, none of the Democratic incumbents in the figure achieved landslide white support. Their reelections were not endangered, yet it was a significant sign of increased com-

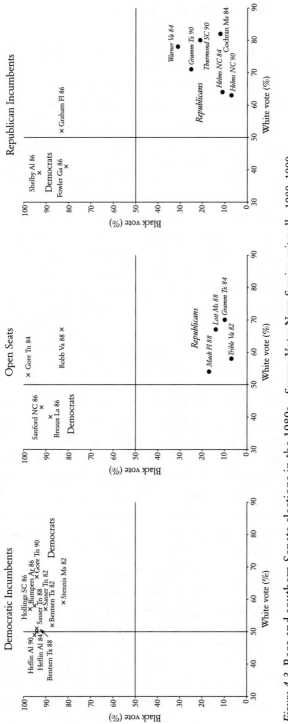

Figure 4.3 Race and southern Senate elections in the 1980s. *Sources:* Voter News Service exit polls, 1980–1990.

petitiveness that many obscure, poorly financed Republicans could attract over 40 percent of the white vote.

In eight open-seat elections, the successful Republicans all secured white majorities large enough to combine with small minorities of the black vote. Gramm and Lott performed especially well among whites in their initial campaigns. Among winning Democrats Gore and (especially) Robb assembled black and white majorities for their landslide open-seat victories, whereas Breaux and Sanford combined overwhelming black support with a minority of the white vote.

Finally, during the 1980s Republicans squandered many opportunities to make incumbency serve their interests. Cochran, Thurmond, Warner, Gramm, and Helms all achieved landslide white votes, but Democratic challengers unseated three Republican incumbents (Hawkins, Mattingly, and Denton). Graham entered the Senate with black and white majorities, while Shelby and Fowler obtained majority support only from blacks. Over the entire decade the Democrats retained their regional majority by assembling majority biracial coalitions. Once black support was secured, the fundamental Democratic advantage was that a sizable minority of the white vote assured their election.

Although the Republicans no longer automatically conceded the South, from the early 1960s to the early 1990s they were never able to control a majority of the South's senators. After the 1982 elections the delegation was evenly divided, but the Democrats reemerged with a majority two years later. Incumbency, ideology, and racial divisions combined to keep the Republicans a minority force in Senate politics. Because Democratic incumbents were plentiful (particularly in the Deep South), Republicans were compelled to concede or nominally contest many Senate elections. Unable to compete against most conservative southern Democrats by running as conservative Republicans, Republicans were often forced to bide their time until seats became open. Because there were far more Democrats than Republicans among likely voters, Republican breakthroughs were generally a result of temporary disarray within the Democratic party rather than the inherent grassroots strength of the Republicans. And as Old South Democrats who relied mainly on white support gradually gave way to New South Democrats who positioned themselves as conservative progressives or progressive conservatives, conservative Republicans were frequently defeated because they were unable to win sufficiently large white majorities.

When Republicans explicitly or implicitly wrote off the black vote, they mortgaged their campaigns to winning majority shares of the white vote that were frequently unrealistic. More whites would have to abandon the Democratic party and become Republicans or independents before Republican candidates could execute their monoracial strategy. That process of ideological resorting might be stimulated by the performance of Republican presidents and particular southern senators. For if conservative Republicans no longer needed to compete against conservative Democrats, the customary advantage of running as a conservative might come into play in many open-seat elections and occasionally in districts where Democratic incumbents might plausibly be attacked as too liberal.

5

THE DEMOCRATIC SMOTHER

After the Civil War southern conservatism—racial, economic, religious, social, cultural—was channeled exclusively through the Democratic party. From 1898 through 1960 the Republican party never elected even a tenth of southern representatives, and few southern Democrats in Congress ever fretted much about Republican opposition. When federal intervention decisively reshaped southern race relations in the mid-1960s, the South's House delegation was still almost completely Democratic. Because southern Democrats had long defended racial segregation, because the Democratic party controlled the avenues to high political office, and because southern Democrats, voters as well as politicians, benefited directly from their party's national congressional majorities, most conservative white voters and most conservative white politicians lacked compelling incentives to switch to the Republican party. Following federal intervention three decades would pass before the southern Republicans finally achieved their first modern majority in the House of Representatives.

Why did it take such a long time for the southern Republicans to become a majority? Reduced to fundamentals, when Republican activists transformed the party of Abraham Lincoln into the party of Barry Goldwater, they foolishly wrote off black southerners at the very time when black participation was dramatically increasing. In repudiating Lincoln and embracing Goldwater, southern Republicans implicitly narrowed their possible targets to those congressional districts in which

Republican candidates could consistently attract sizable majorities of white voters. Yet beyond the Blue Ridge such districts were historically few and far between. By emphatically aligning themselves with white conservatives at a time when few white southerners felt comfortable thinking of themselves as Republicans, the Goldwater Republicans secured modest immediate gains but ensured that their party would long remain a small minority within the southern congressional delegation.

Republican politicians, especially in the Deep South, confronted enormous practical difficulties in winning southern House races. Throughout the 1960s and 1970s Republicans failed to realign southern congressional politics because only about one-fifth of whites were Republicans, far too small to constitute an effective base of reliable support, and because their chief opponents were experienced and pragmatic politicians, most of whom were incumbents and most of whom marketed themselves as conservatives. In the 1980s, despite Ronald Reagan's successful presidency and a growing Republican electorate, Republican campaigners were frequently constrained by a fundamentally different obstacle: the replacement of segregationist and generally conservative Democrats by a new generation of nonsegregationist and typically more moderate Democratic politicians who were skilled at constructing biracial coalitions. This chapter focuses on the 1960s and 1970s, the era of conservative Democratic dominance.

Most southern Republicans viewed Goldwater as their hero and champion. Goldwater conservatism, with its resentment of civil rights legislation, opposition to big government, and hawkish stance vis-à-vis the Soviet Union, became the ideological hallmark of Republican candidates for Congress. An excellent way to grasp the Republican party's new appeal to millions of white southerners, and particularly to whites in the Deep South, is to ponder the obvious racial symbolism of a Goldwater rally held at a football stadium in Montgomery, Alabama. It had been decided, as Richard Rovere explained in his gripping report of the event, "to show the country the 'lily-white' character of Republicanism in Dixie by planting . . . a great field of white lilies—living lilies, in perfect bloom, gorgeously arrayed . . . sown on the turf were seven hundred Alabama girls in long white gowns, all of a whiteness as impossible as the greenness of the field." This amazing spectacle set the stage for Goldwater's stately entrance:

> Then, right on schedule, an especially powerful light played on a stadium gate at about the fifty-yard line, and the candidate of the Republican party rode in as slowly as a car can be made to go, first down past fifty or so yards of choice Southern womanhood, and then, after a sharp left at the goal line, past more girls to the gorgeously draped stand. It was all as solemn and as stylized as a review of troops by some such master of the art as General de Gaulle. The girls did not behave like troops—they swayed a bit as Goldwater passed, and sounds came from them—not squeals or shrieks, but pleasing and ladylike murmurs. And in a sense, of course, they *were* Goldwater's troops, as well as representatives of what the rest of his Southern troops—the thousands in the packed stands, the tens of thousands in Memphis and New Orleans and Atlanta and Shreveport and Greenville—passionately believed they were defending.[1]

By words, deeds, and gestures, as well as by the company he kept on the speaking platforms, the Republican presidential candidate inspired many whites—Goldwater won about half the white vote in the Peripheral South and around seven-tenths of it in the Deep South[2]—but permanently alienated nearly all blacks from the new Republican party. Although Goldwater made economic conservatism his central theme and seldom directly mentioned racial issues, race was undoubtedly the driving force in his Deep South campaigns and one of several driving forces in his Peripheral South campaigns. In the distant past—during Reconstruction—black men had constituted the mass base of the southern Republican party. But now that the Republican party had reinvented itself as an "organization that was secure against integration because it had made itself secure against Negro aspirations," Rovere correctly concluded that "no Negro would ever want in."[3]

Saturated in the imagery of white supremacy, the Republican party became completely dependent on white votes for electoral success. The fundamental practical difficulty with this strategy was that it ran against the grain of southern political experience. White voters in the South were ordinarily born and bred Democrats—conservative to moderate

Democrats for the most part—long accustomed to supporting Democratic politicians for every conceivable political office. Most native white conservatives retained intense emotional as well as practical attachments to the party of their ancestors. Their daddies, their grand-daddies, and assuredly their great-granddaddies had all been *southern* Democrats, and they firmly believed their national party had deserted them rather than the other way around. And yet Republicans needed to attract white majorities—the precise percentage of white voters required would vary according to the size of the black vote in each district—despite the fact that in most districts there would be far more white Democrats than white Republicans in the active electorate.

Only in a few mountain districts would native white Republicans outnumber white Democrats, and only in some rapidly urbanizing areas would middle-class whites find Republican congressional candidates attractive. With such a small base of reliable white Republican voters, the party's candidates generally required extraordinarily powerful short-term forces to disrupt the traditional Democratic majorities and place Democratic incumbents on the defensive. At the time of federal intervention few southern Democrats saw compelling practical reasons to switch parties. Most conservative Democratic voters certainly did not blame their Democratic representatives, whose careers had ordinarily been devoted to maintaining racial segregation, for the passage of civil rights and voting-rights legislation.

Hence southern Democrats, like southern Republicans, reacted decisively to federal intervention. Southern protest was initially expressed as a rebellion *within* the congressional Democratic party. When the Kennedy and Johnson administrations expanded the federal presence in civil rights and finally moved to abolish racial segregation, most southern Democrats in Congress—and especially most Democrats from the Deep South—angrily revolted against the liberal wing of the national Democratic party.[4] (See Figure 3.1 for the huge surge of nominal Democrats in the southern House delegation.) Their survival instincts led them to distance themselves from the national Democratic party by re-emphasizing their conservatism. Many veteran southern Democrats, including some who had generally supported the national Democratic party from the New Deal onward on issues not directly involving race relations, renewed their ties with their most conservative constituents, the identical group of white voters whom Republican candidates were targeting. By their votes and speeches in Washington and by their activities back in their districts, most Democrats emphasized their opposition to the racial changes associated with Lyndon Johnson's Great Society.

In 1965 68 percent of the southern Democrats in the House of Representatives had opposed the Voting Rights Act, with Deep South Democrats (86 percent) providing considerably more resistance than Peripheral South Democrats (59 percent). Five years later the Voting Rights Act came up for reauthorization. There was no net change among Deep South Democrats (86 percent still voted against it), but in the Peripheral South a slightly smaller majority of Democrats (53 percent) continued to reject a law that had tremendously stimulated black registration and voting. All in all, almost two-thirds of the southern Democrats continued to protest federal intervention.

The resurgence of conservative Democratic incumbents and conservative Democratic nominees in open seats suffocated the potential realignment of conservative white voters into the Republican party. By continuing to give their traditional conservative constituents attractive and familiar political options, experienced Democratic representatives held many white conservatives in the Democratic party. Conservative Democratic congressmen, after all, retained the immense practical advantages of membership in the House's majority party, the party that had governed almost without interruption since the New Deal. Democrats—including many experienced southerners—chaired all the committees and allocated resources. Incumbent conservative Democrats were well positioned to deliver goods and services to their districts. The Democratic party had remained very popular among millions of voters for Social Security and agricultural subsidies. Among Johnson's Great Society programs, Medicare would be a welcome benefit for all types of southerners. At the same time, by breaking with the national party leadership on policies that infuriated many white conservatives, southern Democratic representatives could demonstrate enough independence from the liberal leadership to remain trusted and effective in their districts. By continuing to support the party's truly popular programs while attacking the more controversial proposals, many southern Democrats sought to represent majority white opinion in their constituencies.

Against these experienced Democrats, there was initially scant political demand for Republican congressional candidates even among white conservatives. Republican politicians frequently presented voters with a strident and far-reaching conservatism, but stem-winding rhetoric was all they could offer. In the South the Democratic party remained the home of practical conservatism. Throughout the 1960s, 1970s, and 1980s the ability of Democratic incumbents to discourage or defeat Republican challengers, as well as the conservative Democrats' continuing domination of open-seat elections, prevented a partisan realignment in southern congressional elections. To place the Republicans' breakthrough in the 1990s in its proper perspective, it is necessary to understand more specifically the monumental barriers confronting Republicans as southern race relations became the paramount issue of the day. Our analysis begins with the continuing obstacle of demographic traditionalism.

DEMOGRAPHY AS A CONTINUING DEMOCRATIC ASSET

Federal intervention in race relations coincided roughly with the Supreme Court's important 1964 decision that all congressional districts must henceforth represent equal numbers of people. In the 1960 Census the South neither gained nor lost House seats. Within the region, however, the Peripheral South picked up two seats while the Deep South surrendered two. Aside from minor adjustments, by 1966 the southern states had finished redrawing their congressional districts to comply with *Wesberry v. Sanders*.[5]

With Democratic state legislatures and Democratic governors thoroughly alert to their partisan duties, the net result of reapportionment and redistricting was a slight modification of demographic traditionalism. The top half of Figure 5.1 compares the demography of the South's congressional districts in 1952 and 1966. We use 15 percent black and 50 percent urban as cutting points to group the districts into four distinct political arenas: *white New South districts* (less than 15 percent black and majority urban), *white Old South districts* (less than 15 percent black and majority rural), *biracial New South districts* (15 percent black or higher and majority urban) and *biracial Old South districts* (15 percent

black or higher and majority rural). Because of their huge white populations and expanding middle-class electorates, white New South districts
were the settings most likely to generate two-party competition. However, these relatively dynamic districts increased only fractionally, from
16 to 19. Many white Old South districts contained mountain Republicans. This secondary Republican target, far from expanding, actually declined, from 18 to 12 districts. Together the white New South districts
and white Old South districts, the two settings relatively congenial to
Republican campaigning, accounted for only 29 percent of the region's
106 congressional districts during the 1960s.

In biracial New South districts any Republican advantage based on
rising middle-class populations could be offset by larger black electorates. Doubling from 21 to 42, biracial New South districts became the
single largest setting for southern congressional elections during the
1960s. Republican prospects were bleakest in the biracial Old South districts. With higher black populations and smaller middle classes, this
arena was the most traditional setting for congressional elections. Although the biracial Old South districts fell from 51 to 33, they still far
outnumbered the white New South districts.

The bottom half of Figure 5.1 highlights the radically different starting points for congressional elections in the southern subregions. All 19
white New South districts were located in the Peripheral South, and a
single state, Texas, contained two-thirds of them. Biracial Old South districts, though now equally divided between the Peripheral South and
the Deep South (16 versus 17), continued to constitute a much larger
proportion of Deep South than Peripheral South districts (46 versus 23
percent).

Subregional differences were especially important for racial concentrations, always the single most important factor in structuring southern
politics. Congressional districts with very small black populations (less
than 15 percent) are designated *white districts*. Two-fifths of the Peripheral South districts had such relatively small black populations, whereas
less than a tenth of the Deep South districts did so. In fact, all but three
white districts were located in the Peripheral South. In these constituencies Peripheral South Republicans could be elected with relatively small
white majorities. Depending on turnout patterns, white majorities in the
range of 52 to 57 percent would be sufficient to win a white district.

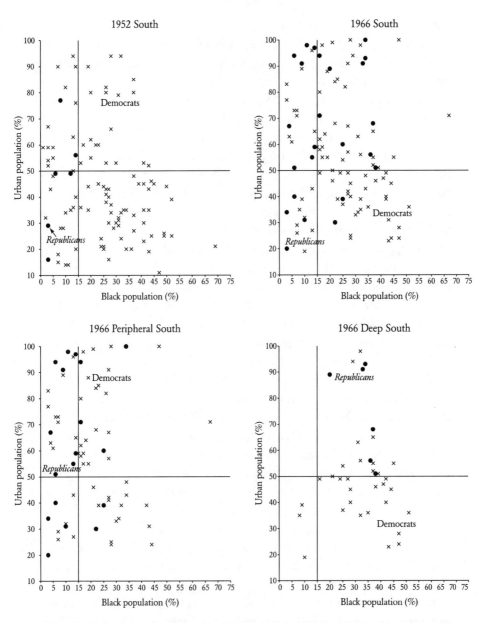

Figure 5.1 Southern demographic traditionalism: House districts in 1952 and 1966. *Sources:* Calculated from *Congressional Quarterly Weekly Report*, various issues.

Inflammatory racial appeals would be unnecessary and probably counterproductive. Peripheral South Republicans running in white districts would assuredly campaign as conservatives, but they were more likely to emphasize economic conservatism than racial conservatism.

Republican candidates in Deep South states, by contrast, almost invariably competed in *biracial districts,* those with black populations exceeding 15 percent. In Alabama, South Carolina, Mississippi, Georgia, and Louisiana, Republican congressional candidates ordinarily needed much larger white majorities than did their Peripheral South counterparts. Deep South Republicans who sought office in districts that were 30 to 35 percent black would need roughly 70 to 75 percent of the white vote. Those staggering white shares could not possibly be achieved without explicit or implicit appeals to racial solidarity.

The black dots in the lower left corner of Figure 5.1 identify the eighteen Republicans who were elected in 1966 from Peripheral South states. Two-thirds of these Republican victories occurred in constituencies with few blacks, and only Dan Kuykendall in Memphis was elected from a district whose black population exceeded 30 percent. Urban districts produced two-thirds of the subregion's Republicans.

Within the white New South districts Republicans did best in *metropolitan* settings, winning four of the seven districts that had urban populations of 80 to 100 percent. In addition to the veteran incumbents Joel Broyhill and William Cramer, Republicans won newly created seats in Dallas with James Collins and in Fort Lauderdale with Herbert Burke. Peripheral South Republicans were less successful, however, in the white New South settings that mixed urban and rural populations. They won only a third of twelve districts with urban populations of 50 to 79 percent. Among the victorious Republicans were incumbents Richard Poff in Roanoke, John Duncan in Knoxville, and William Brock in Chattanooga, all from the Blue Ridge, and Robert Price, newly elected from Amarillo, in the Texas panhandle.

In white Old South settings the GOP prevailed in four mountain Republican districts. Blue Ridge Republicans included incumbents Jimmy Quillen in East Tennessee and James Broyhill in western North Carolina, plus the newly victorious William Wampler in western Virginia. In the Arkansas Ozarks John Paul Hammerschmidt defeated James Trimble, a national Democrat, to give the Republicans the Third

District. No Peripheral South Republican had voted for the Civil Rights Act, but Cramer, Quillen, Duncan, and Brock supported the Voting Rights Act on final passage.

Only six Peripheral South Republicans were elected from districts with black populations exceeding 15 percent. Aside from Kuykendall in Memphis, they were the veterans Charles Raper Jonas (Charlotte) and Edward Gurney (Orlando) as well as the freshmen George Bush (Houston), William Scott (northern Virginia), and James Gardner (Raleigh). North Carolina Democrats had redrawn Jonas' Charlotte district to remove its Blue Ridge component and expand its black population, but Jonas' incumbency and organizational skills enabled him to survive handily. Gurney was unopposed in a mixed urban-rural district that was 16 percent black, and Bush won another 16 percent black district that included metropolitan Houston's wealthiest neighborhoods. Scott benefited from the defeat of veteran conservative and House Rules Committee chairman Howard W. Smith in a divisive Democratic primary. Gardner upset Howard Cooley, the elderly chairman of the Agriculture Committee.

Gardner, Scott, and Gurney were certainly aggressive Goldwater conservatives, but in general the intensity of conservatism among Peripheral South Republicans paled by comparison with the more primitive, racially driven conservatism of the six Deep South Republicans—Jack Edwards (Mobile), William Dickenson (Montgomery), John Buchanan (Birmingham), Albert Watson (Columbia), Ben Blackburn (Atlanta), and Fletcher Thompson (Atlanta)—who were elected in 1966. Two years before, as part of the Deep South's revolt against racial change, Republicans had won an astonishing five districts in Alabama (Dickenson, Buchanan, and Glen Andrews defeated incumbent Democrats; Edwards and James Martin won open seats); one seat in Mississippi, where Prentiss Walker upset a veteran Democrat; and one Georgia district (Howard Callaway won an open seat). After the 1964 election Watson (then a Democrat) resigned, switched parties, and was reelected as a Republican. None of the four Deep South Republicans elected from a *rural* constituency, however, served beyond a single term. Callaway, Martin, and Walker vacated their seats in order to run (unsuccessfully) for governor or the Senate; and Bill Nichols, a deeply conservative Democrat allied with Governor George Wallace, easily defeated Andrews in

1966. Nichols proudly (though misleadingly) characterized himself as a "middle-of-the-road Democrat . . . a Democrat first, last and always."[6] Deep South Republicans found it impossible to hold rural seats.

From their initial surge three biracial New South districts, all of which combined conservative urban whites with even more conservative rural whites, became Republican strongholds. Edwards in Mobile and southwestern Alabama, Dickenson in Montgomery and southeastern Alabama, and Watson and (after 1970) Floyd Spence in Columbia and lowland South Carolina pioneered hard-line Republican conservatism in the Deep South. "Thank God for Barry Goldwater" was the gist of Edwards' message in his 1964 campaign. Edwards believed Goldwater's rejection of the Civil Rights Act represented political "courage."[7] Republicans had less success in purely metropolitan biracial environments. In Birmingham Buchanan later moderated his original conservatism to the point where he was defeated for renomination in 1980. Neither of the Atlanta districts became a safe Republican seat, although the suburban Fourth District seesawed between the parties as it was redrawn over the years.

The most significant contrast between Deep South and Peripheral South Republicans was the racial composition of their districts. In 1966 all but one of the Republicans' Deep South victories occurred in districts with black populations of 30 percent or more, whereas only one Republican victory in the Peripheral South did so. Even if it is assumed that blacks were still considerably undermobilized (the full impact of the Voting Rights Act would take years to develop), extraordinary white majorities were required for Republican victories in the Deep South.

THE CONSERVATIVE ADVANTAGE IN WHITE PUBLIC OPINION

Federal intervention made racial issues exceedingly salient, especially in the states with the largest black populations and in those sections of both subregions where blacks constituted substantial percentages of the population. White racism was most intense and universal in higher-black areas of higher-black states. Most white politicians from the Deep South—Democrats and Republicans—were immersed in traditional racial politics to a much greater degree than most white politicians—Democrats or Republicans—from the Peripheral South. Furthermore, the spread of big-city and suburban districts was much more advanced in the Peripheral South than in the Deep South. With exceptions here and there, for many years the conservatism of the Deep South states would be grounded in race and economics, with racial considerations omnipresent. Conservatism in the Peripheral South states, though widespread, would be less dominant and focused relatively more on the economic interests of the growing white middle class. Racial considerations would generally manifest themselves in more subtle ways.

The intensified conservatism of many congressional Democrats reflected white public opinion. Federal intervention produced a counterreaction among many white southerners that varied immensely by subregion. In presidential elections racially conservative whites could express their dissatisfaction with the federal presence by supporting Goldwater in 1964 and Wallace in 1968.[8] These grassroots presidential votes reveal the relative breadth and magnitude of white anger and resentment at federal intervention into southern race relations. The 1964 presidential election occurred only months after Congress had passed the monumental Civil Rights Act outlawing racial segregation in public accommodations. Four years later, following continuing protests against discrimination in voter registration, passage and enforcement of the Voting Rights Act, and the emergence of a Black Power movement, former Alabama governor Wallace ran for president as a third-party candidate. Only the least astute could fail to understand that Wallace hoped to nationalize the politics of race.[9]

Goldwater and Wallace diverged significantly on economic issues. Goldwater was a thoroughgoing economic conservative, the friend of upwardly mobile whites who believed they were overtaxed and overregulated by the federal government; Wallace ran as an economic populist, the best friend of "little" white men and women. Racial conservatism, not economic conservatism, was the common denominator of their presidential candidacies. In each election they symbolized, more dramatically than any other option, vigorous disapproval of federally mandated racial change. Because neither Goldwater nor Wallace received any votes from blacks, the county-level results *underestimate* their white support. Wallace won 63 percent of the white vote in the Deep South but only 31 percent in the Peripheral South.[10] Because of the Voting Rights Act, far more blacks voted in 1968 than they did in 1964.

Four intriguing situations emerge when Peripheral South and Deep South counties are grouped according to their votes for Goldwater and Wallace (see Figure 5.2). Counties in which both Goldwater and Wallace achieved majorities (the upper right cells) represent areas of extraordinary white opposition to racial change. In "high-high" counties the climate of white public opinion was extremely conservative on race. Counties in which neither Goldwater nor Wallace won majorities (the lower left cells) identify areas characterized by less pervasive white opposition to racial change. The upper left cells include those counties in which Wallace won a majority but Goldwater did not; they identify normally Democratic counties responsive to Wallace's racial conservatism and "little man" economics; and the lower right cells contain the counties that favored Goldwater but did not give Wallace a majority. These counties embody three different situations: traditionally Republican counties disinclined to support Wallace (as in East Tennessee), counties (the Mississippi Delta, for example) where increased black voting reduced Wallace's share of the total county vote below 50 percent, and still other counties (especially in South Carolina) where Republican senator Strom Thurmond persuaded many whites that Richard Nixon was a wiser choice than Wallace.

The results isolate contrasting grassroots centers of gravity between the Peripheral South and the Deep South. White racial protest was prominent and pervasive in the Deep South. Almost three-fifths of the 418 counties in the Deep South were "high-high" counties, and only a tenth were "low-low." White public opinion in the Deep South was incredibly "solid." Before the 1964 presidential election the Republican party had not carried any Deep South state for eighty-eight years. Yet shortly after Congress passed the Civil Rights Act, hundreds of Deep South counties gave Barry Goldwater landslide majorities. Four years later, with far more black participation, Wallace nonetheless achieved broad majority backing at the county level.

Peripheral South whites were much less willing to support the presidential candidacies of racially intransigent politicians. In the Peripheral South 70 percent of the 728 counties were "low-low," and merely 4 percent were "high-high." The Florida panhandle, functionally an extension of the Deep South to the Gulf of Mexico, was the principal source of joint Goldwater and Wallace majorities. Although white public opin-

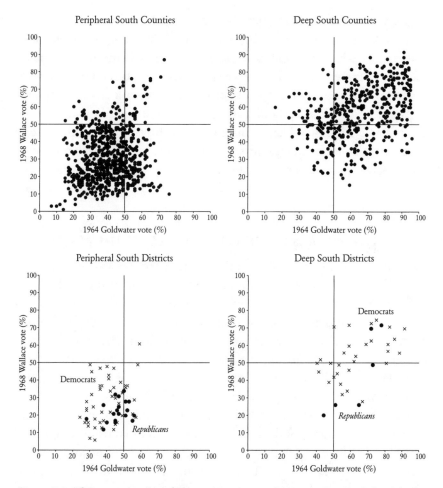

Figure 5.2 The conservative climate: grassroots white reaction to federal intervention. *Sources:* Calculated from *Congressional Quarterly Weekly Report*, various issues; and Richard M. Scammon, ed., *America Votes* (Washington, D.C.: Congressional Quarterly), various years.

ion in the Peripheral South states was less overwhelmingly conservative than in the Deep South, the results of the two votes suggest widespread patterns of white conservatism in that subregion as well. Wallace won at least 25 percent of the vote in three-fifths of the Peripheral South counties.

Racial conservatism would thus be majority white opinion in most Deep South districts and many Peripheral South districts, and it would be the viewpoint of substantial minorities of whites in many other Peripheral South districts (see the bottom of Figure 5.2). As a practical matter, the white reaction to federal intervention meant that most southern representatives, Republicans and Democrats, could not afford to ignore grassroots white conservatism. Aside from a few big-city districts in Texas (Houston and San Antonio) and Florida (Miami and Tampa) where national Democrats could still thrive, most southern representatives could not forget (even if they wished to do so) that conservatism—racial, economic, or both—was firmly embedded in their districts.

INCUMBENCY AND CONSERVATISM AS DEMOCRATIC ASSETS

Incumbency is the most powerful resource in congressional elections. The advantages in name recognition, campaign fundraising, and credit-claiming that are rooted in being a U.S. representative are obvious. Across the South incumbency insulated practically all but the most complacent Democrats from serious Republican challenges. Once elected, southern Democrats devoted their entire congressional careers to making their districts safe from other Democrats or Republicans. Many a potential challenger would finally decide not to take on Congressman X after carefully considering his or her prospects. Veteran southern Democrats could easily build the kinds of landslide majorities that would discourage opposition. As members of the majority party, often serving on key committees that handled legislation vital to their districts, southern Democrats could represent their constituents far better than Republicans could plausibly claim to do. Yet the Democrats' incumbency advantages rested on more than their mastery of practical politics, and on more than their ability to win landslide reelections. After federal intervention, by positioning themselves (or in some cases by repositioning themselves) as conservative Democrats, they could simultaneously take credit for popular Democratic programs like Social Security and Medicare while voting against the Democratic leadership on issues that were controversial in their districts. Ideology and incumbency were mutually reinforcing and thus provided double protection for Democrats against Republican challengers.

Thus the fundamental constraint on Republican advances was the hard reality that Democratic incumbents representing primarily Democratic electorates occupied most southern seats. Defeating Democratic incumbents would ordinarily be all but impossible. Republicans would therefore have to watch and wait for open-seat elections, and even in these they would commonly face formidable Democratic opposition. If open seats could be won, however, skillful politicking might shift the incumbency advantage to Republicans. The basic model for Republican growth was straightforward: nurture and reelect any Republican incumbents, try hard to win any open-seat elections, and occasionally capitalize on fortuitous circumstances to defeat an unexpectedly vulnerable incumbent Democrat.

Alexander Heard had recommended in 1952 that Republicans seriously challenge Democratic incumbents over a long series of elections in order to build strength in the constituencies.[11] It was advice seldom taken. By tracing one exceptional case that ultimately succeeded, we can illustrate what was ordinarily missing in the Republicans' pursuit of southern congressional seats. A rare truly persistent challenge of a sitting conservative Democrat by a Republican took place in Georgia's Sixth Congressional District. Jack Flynt, the epitome of a rural conservative Democrat, had first been elected to Congress in 1954. His seat originally covered the countryside of west-central Georgia. As Richard F. Fenno has persuasively shown, it was ideally suited to Flynt's talent for personal politicking among like-minded conservative Democrats in the district's rural areas and small towns.[12] Flynt was an unapologetic segregationist who never supported any civil rights bills, and his idea of outreach to the black community did not extend much beyond arranging an occasional private word with a respected black mortician. He was, to say the least, incapable of imagining—much less building—a true biracial coalition. Conservative rural and small-town whites were his core constituents.

For a decade Flynt never faced a Republican opponent. In 1966, however, Republican state representative G. Paul Jones Jr., of Macon, the chairman of the Georgia Republican party, decided to challenge the veteran Democrat. The young Republican's base of support was confined to urbanized Bibb County while most of the district's vote was cast in rural and small-town counties dominated by conservative Democrats. In a familiar pattern, the incumbent Democrat's conservatism suffocated the Republican candidate. "He tried at first to paint me as a liberal . . . and, failing that, he tried to out-conservative me," Flynt later explained to Fenno. "No matter how hard he tried, he couldn't out-conservative me. There just wasn't any room. If he got on the conservative side of me, he'd fall off into the air." Jones could not plausibly attack Flynt as a liberal or even a moderate Democrat. "Both candidates are conservatives," reported the *Congressional Quarterly,* and "Jones admits that it has been difficult to tie Flynt to the Johnson Administration. 'People have gotten used to thinking of him as a conservative,'" complained the Republican challenger. Flynt's conservatism, after all, had been cultivated during a lifetime in Democratic politics. "If anything," Flynt stressed, "I've probably voted more conservatively than the people in the district would have wanted."[13] The result was a runaway victory—68 to 32 percent—for the conservative Democratic incumbent. Flynt's decisive win chilled any future Republican aspirations for victory in Georgia's Sixth District, just as most other southern Democrats had easily stomped out sporadic Republican efforts in the aftermath of federal intervention.

In 1972 the Georgia legislature significantly reshaped the district by removing Bibb County and some rural counties and by adding wholly unfamiliar and potentially troublesome territory in Atlanta's southern suburbs. A familiar and comfortable district now became unknown and somewhat mysterious. When predominantly rural districts were diluted through the addition of larger cities or suburbs of metropolitan areas, Democratic incumbents faced the problem of extracting support from strangers who were not part of the member's original rural network. The veteran congressman was lost—sometimes he quite literally did not know where he was—when he tried to campaign in the Atlanta suburbs.[14] His new suburban constituents were not his kind of people.

White suburbanites, however, were exactly the people who were increasingly attracted to the conservative message of the Republican party. In these new suburban neighborhoods a young history professor at West Georgia College, Newt Gingrich, began to find and mobilize Republican voters. Charismatic and energetic, Gingrich organized numerous volunteers, stressed issues, raised money, and galvanized Republican contesting efforts. Running only months after Republican president Richard M. Nixon had resigned in disgrace, and in a year in which the Republican party lost forty-three seats in the House of Representatives, Gingrich nevertheless drew an amazing 49 percent of the vote. In his first race for Congress, Gingrich came within 2,773 votes of unseating the veteran conservative Democrat. No one was more astonished and shocked than Flynt himself. When Fenno telephoned him to seek an explanation for the unexpectedly tight race, Flynt "shouted, 'I damn near got my ass beat off, that's what happened!'"[15]

Two years later Gingrich tried again, lost a little ground, but still managed to poll 48 percent of the vote—achieving levels of highly competitive campaigning in consecutive elections against a conservative Democrat that were unmatched by other Republican candidates in the 1970s. Normally a Democrat with an unanticipated narrow victory would have reworked the district, rebuilt support, and avoided a second close call. Flynt's inability to reestablish a comfortable lead after his narrow escape indicated that he had lost the support of almost half the district. Two years later, citing poor health, Flynt retired from congressional politics. Without actually defeating Flynt, Gingrich had run the veteran Democratic conservative out of Congress. Now the 1978 frontrunner because of his previous campaigns, Gingrich won the Sixth District on his third try with 54 percent of the vote.

Gingrich was not building a political career the normal Republican way. Although the Gingrich model of aggressive and repeated efforts to build a consistent base of support eventually paid off, very few Republican candidates pursued this type of persistent campaigning against conservative incumbent Democrats. Most of them waited patiently for open-seat opportunities.

Elections with Democratic Incumbents

Throughout the 1960s and 1970s, as the Republicans struggled to win southern House seats in districts in which Democrats greatly outnumbered Republicans, their biggest immediate obstacle, election after election, was the formidable reality that veteran incumbent Democrats already occupied most seats. Fully two-thirds of all the southern congressional elections from 1961 through 1981 involved incumbent Democrats. Even during this extraordinarily turbulent period, as the politics of racial change played out across the region, their reelection rate was a robust 97 percent. In ten southern states Democratic incumbents were involved in a majority of the congressional elections, ranging from 78 percent of the Texas elections (the big Texas delegation, for decades trained and supervised by Speaker of the House Sam Rayburn, was a powerful force in House Democratic politics) to merely 51 percent in Tennessee. Democratic incumbents maintained only a tiny advantage over Republican incumbents (46 to 44 percent) in Virginia, where increased political participation temporarily threw the Democrats on the defensive. Democrats could easily control huge majorities of the southern delegation just by reelecting their incumbents. In the 1960s and 1970s the Solid Democratic South could perpetuate itself even without winning open seats or defeating Republican incumbents.

Although the southern Democrats began their defense against the challenge of Goldwater Republicanism with the obvious advantage of holding most southern seats, incumbency was only the beginning of their advantage. The most secure incumbent is the experienced politician who can be reelected, time and again, with landslide majorities. We consider a district safe whenever a representative is elected with 60 percent or more of the vote. Southern Democrats were not only incumbents but *safe-seat incumbents*. Safe-seat incumbent Democrats captured almost three-fifths of the 1,091 southern elections held from 1961 through 1981. They won at least two-thirds of all the House elections in Mississippi, Louisiana, Texas, and Georgia. Simply by reelecting their safe-seat incumbents, Democrats could still control a majority of the regional delegation.

Incumbency and safe-seat incumbency did not exhaust the Democrats' fundamental advantage vis-à-vis Goldwater Republicans. Southern Democrats were not only incumbents, and they were not only safe-seat incumbents; many of them were *conservative safe-seat incumbents*. By themselves, conservative safe-seat incumbent Democrats won 41 percent of all the southern elections, including 53 percent in the Deep South and 34 percent in the Peripheral South. They accounted for half or more of all elections in Mississippi, Georgia, South Carolina, and Louisiana. Before the widespread creation of Democratic biracial coalitions in the 1980s, conservative ideology, safe seats, and incumbency mutually reinforced one another to give the Democrats a triple-threat defense against conservative Republicans.

Many of these conservative, safe-seat, incumbent Democrats chaired important congressional committees or subcommittees of the powerful Appropriations Committee. They included such men as Mississippi's William Colmer (Rules) and Jamie Whitten (Appropriations subcommittee on agriculture), South Carolina's Mendel Rivers (Armed Services), Arkansas's Wilbur Mills (Ways and Means), Texas' William Pogue (Agriculture Committee) and Olin Teague (Veterans' Affairs), and Florida's Robert Sikes (Appropriations subcommittee on military construction).

Figure 5.3 places ideology and safe seats in the context of Democratic incumbents, open seats, and Republican incumbents, the three mutually exclusive settings for House elections. Observing the 1961–1981 House elections from the analytical standpoint of minority-party development, the figure presents the structuring of election results according to the fundamental obstacle of Democratic incumbency, the promise of open seats, and the potential advantage of Republican incumbents. Each black dot (for Republicans) and each X (for Democrats) represents a single election. The patterns provide valuable collective portraits of the southern politicians who struggled to win House seats immediately before and after federal intervention. The clusters reveal the partisan and ideological orientation of the southern delegation to the House of Representatives at a critical juncture in American history.

Southern Democrats operated from a stupendous incumbency advantage. Figure 5.3 demonstrates the smothering effect of conservative, safe-seat Democratic incumbents vis-à-vis conservative Republicans. The vast majority—86 percent—of all southern Democratic incumbents won safe-seat victories. Conservatives with safe seats accounted for 60 percent of all Democratic incumbents, compared to 18 percent for safe-seat moderates and 8 percent for safe-seat liberals. The lower right-hand cell of the scatter plot for Democratic incumbents—the space containing all the conservatives with safe-seat reelections—defines the principal response of congressional Democrats to the threat of competition from Goldwater Republicans. Given that many of the elections involving Democrats with liberal and moderate voting records occurred *in the early*

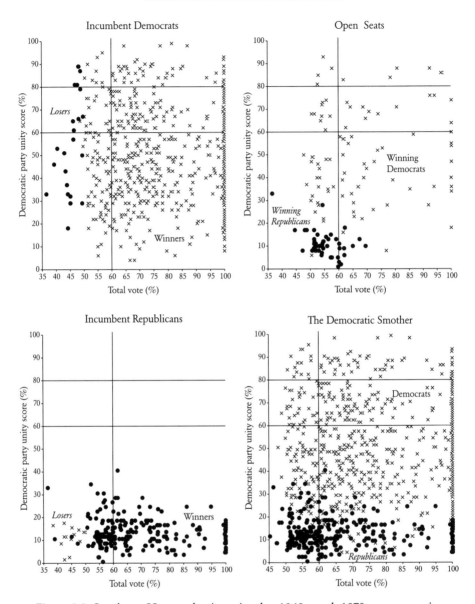

Figure 5.3 Southern House elections in the 1960s and 1970s: conservative Democrats smother the Republican challenge. *Sources:* calculated from *Congressional Quarterly's Guide to U.S. Elections,* 3d ed. (Washington, D.C., 1994); and *Congressional Quarterly Weekly Report,* various issues.

1960s, before the white reaction against federal intervention reached its peak, the profoundly conservative nature of the initial Democratic reaction is clear. Conservatism especially prevailed among Democratic incumbents in the Deep South. Safe-seat conservatives there won 76 percent of the 1961–1981 elections involving Democratic incumbents, versus 52 percent in the Peripheral South.

In the Peripheral South four-fifths of the incumbent Democrats emerged with safe seats. Ideologically, most Peripheral South Democrats were conservative. Far more Peripheral South incumbent Democrats were conservative (63 percent) than moderate (24 percent) or liberal (14 percent) in their party unity scores. Conservatives with safe seats—Democrats like David Satterfield (Virginia), Don Fuqua (Florida), H. L. Fountain (North Carolina), Ed Jones (Tennessee), and O. C. Fisher and Bob Casey (Texas)—accounted for half of all the elections involving Democratic incumbents. As a group, they offered formidable competition to Republicans.

Even during the first two decades following federal intervention, about a quarter of the Democratic incumbents had moderate records (60 to 79) of support for the Democratic party, and 14 percent of them could be classified as national Democrats. Among the Democratic incumbents whose voting records were predominantly moderate were Claude Pepper (Miami), Sam Gibbons (Tampa), Richardson Preyer (Greensboro), Richard Fulton (Nashville), future Speaker Jim Wright (Fort Worth), and Jack Brooks (Beaumont). National or liberal Democrats came primarily from Florida (Dante Fascell and William Lehman from Miami), Texas (Henry Gonzales of San Antonio and Houstonians Albert Thomas, Bob Eckhardt, and Barbara Jordan), and Virginia (Herb Harris and Joe Fisher in the Washington suburbs).

Democrats were even more entrenched in the Deep South. Ninety-two percent of all the Democratic incumbents were elected with more than three-fifths of the vote, and 76 percent of the Democratic incumbents were conservatives with safe seats. Among all Democratic incumbents in the Deep South, 82 percent had party unity scores of less than 60, 15 percent scored in the moderate range, and only 2 percent voted with their party at least 80 percent of the time. After 1964 Republicans defeated no conservative Democrat for twenty years.

Some of the Deep South's most conspicuous conservatives, such as Alabama's George Andrews, Louisiana's Edward Hebert, Otto Passman, and Joe Waggonner, Mississippi's Tom Abernethy, and South Carolina's Rivers, were so entrenched among the conservative voters in their districts that they never faced a Republican opponent. When the Republicans did field candidates, the usual result was a obvious mismatch between a popular, well-known, experienced, and highly respected Democrat and an unknown, inexperienced, and poorly funded Republican challenger. Men like Alabama's Bill Nichols, Georgia's Jack Brinkley, Louisiana's John Breaux, Mississippi's Whitten, and South Carolina's William Jennings Bryan Dorn occasionally drew Republican opposition after federal intervention but never came close to losing their seats.

In theory, Republicans should have been more competitive against Deep South Democrats who continued to champion their national party. Presumably conservative white voters faced with a choice between a moderate to liberal Democrat versus a conservative Republican might have been more inclined to vote Republican. Before federal intervention many Deep South Democrats had behaved as moderate or even national Democrats. After federal intervention conspicuous identification with the national Democratic party carried grave political risks. So strong was white conservatism within the Democratic party in the Deep South that more loyalist Democrats were defeated in Democratic primaries than in general elections. To a greater degree than occurred in the Peripheral South, the dominant stream of Deep South protest against the national Democratic party took place in Democratic primaries rather than in general elections. By eliminating several less conservative Democrats before Republicans had the opportunity to challenge them, the Democrats' ideological housecleaning delayed partisan realignment in the Deep South congressional delegation.

What happened to those Deep South Democrats who stuck their heads up, so to speak, in defiance of the general Deep South revolt against the national Democratic party? Although no Deep South Democrat voted for the 1964 Civil Rights Act, thirteen of them—35 percent of the delegation—voted with the majority of their party on at least 60 percent of the *Congressional Quarterly* party unity roll calls in 1963–64. Two of the moderates, Carl Vinson of Georgia and Robert Hemphill of

South Carolina, did not seek reelection. Two other loyalists, Carl Elliott of Alabama and Gillis Long of Louisiana, were denied renomination in Democratic primaries. Elliott had been one of the most effective legislators on education issues, but his racial moderation had ensnared him by the early 1960s. In 1964 he was eliminated in the Alabama Democrats' unusual "nine-for-eight" statewide slating (Alabama had lost a congressional seat in 1962 but failed to draw the new districts before the 1964 Democratic primaries) when the Wallace-influenced Democratic party failed to endorse him.[16] Gillis Long was beaten in a Louisiana primary by his outspokenly conservative cousin, Speedy O. Long.

Nine moderates survived the 1964 general election—four of them experiencing seriously contested races—and returned for the Great Society Congress of 1965–66. Six of the moderates resolved their potential electoral problems by joining the conservative bloc. Georgia's John W. Davis, Elliott Hagan, J. Russell Tuten, Robert Stephens, and Phil Landrum, along with Louisiana's Edwin Willis, no longer voted as loyalist Democrats. Three loyalist Democrats were reelected in 1964 and continued to back the party in the Eighty-ninth Congress: Hale Boggs of New Orleans, Louisiana, the only Deep South member who voted as a national Democrat, and moderates Jimmy Morrison of Baton Rouge, Louisiana, and Charles Weltner of Atlanta, Georgia. Joining this group were one freshman, James Mackay of suburban Atlanta, and one veteran, Robert Jones of northern Alabama.

The 1966 elections further cleared the ranks of loyalist Democrats in the Deep South. Despite his new conservatism, Tuten was defeated in the Democratic primary by the much more conservative W. S. Stuckey. Morrison was likewise defeated in his primary by Judge John Rarick, an ultraconservative who belonged to the John Birch Society. In Atlanta Weltner abandoned his congressional career a month before the November 1966 election because, he announced, he could not run on the same ticket with segregationist gubernatorial candidate Lester Maddox. In the same election Mackay lost to conservative Republican Ben Blackburn.

Alabama's Jones was the Deep South's only rural moderate. Representing a district heavily influenced by the Tennessee Valley Authority, Jones typically drew no Republican challenger. After opposing both the Civil Rights Act and the Voting Rights Act, he began to moderate his views in the late 1960s. Toward the end of his career, however, Jones's party support again dropped. When he retired in 1976, Jones had behaved as a nominal Democrat in his final three Congresses. Boggs was the Deep South's most consistently loyal Democrat. A protégé of Democratic Speaker John McCormick, he was an influential House Democratic leader with national aspirations. Boggs had voted as a national Democrat early in his career, regularly scoring above 80 percent in party loyalty. By the early 1970s Boggs was the only party loyalist remaining among the Deep South's thirty Democrats.

Conservative Democrats, not conservative Republicans, were thus the main beneficiaries of the national Democrats' unpopularity among Deep South whites. The disappearance of moderates as "easy" targets in conservative Deep South districts—whether as a result of shifts to the right by Democratic incumbents or as a result of loyalist defeats in Democratic primaries—sharply reduced the opportunities for Republican candidates to market their brand of conservatism.

Open-Seat Elections

Finding it extraordinarily difficult—especially after surprising a few complacent veteran Democrats in 1964 and 1966—to defeat sitting Democrats, the Republican party's only route to power lay in holding their own few seats and winning open seats. For a tiny minority party the main limitation on leveraging open seats was that such elections were uncommon. They were especially rare in the South, where the tradition was to elect a man—almost invariably a man—and keep returning him until seniority gave him the experience and power to deliver goods and services to his district and state.

Only 13 percent of the 1961–1981 southern House elections involved open seats. Republicans won a third of these contests, performing slightly better in the Peripheral South (35 percent) than in the Deep South (29 percent). Far more Democrats than Republicans achieved safe-seat margins in open-seat settings (see Figure 5.3). Democrats were entrenched in many districts with open seats. When Republicans prevailed, they usually did so with narrow victories. Over half of the Republican winners, versus a quarter of the Democratic winners, were elected with less than 55 percent of the total vote. All in all, Democrats won 41 percent of the open-seat elections with at least 60 percent of the vote. Republicans achieved similarly impressive victories in less than a tenth of the open seats. All the "safe-seat" Republican victories in the Deep South were actually protest votes concentrated in the 1964–1966 period; "safe-seat" Republican successes in the Peripheral South generally involved winning newly established districts or replacing veteran Republicans in urban areas of Florida and Texas.

Not only were there few open-seat elections, but not all of them represented new Republican opportunities. About three-quarters of the open seats resulted from Democratic vacancies, and among this large number of elections the Republicans won only 25 percent of the contests. Democratic congressional staffer Trent Lott, for example, had the good fortune to pursue an open-seat opportunity in 1972, the year of President Richard Nixon's landslide defeat of George McGovern. His boss, conservative Democrat William Colmer, decided to give up his Rules Committee chairmanship and retire. Switching parties, Lott ran for Mississippi's Gulf Coast district as a conservative Republican. As he explained, "I'm tired of the Muskies and the Kennedys and the Humphreys and the whole lot . . . I will fight against the efforts of the so-called liberals to concentrate more power in the government in Washington."[17] Lott won with 55 percent of the vote.

A tenth of the open-seat elections took place in newly created districts. In these contests the Republicans' victory rate rose to 44 percent. Aside from two reconfigured Deep South districts in Atlanta and New Orleans, the new districts were located in Texas and Florida. The most significant Republican gains from new districts came in Dallas, Houston, Orlando, Fort Lauderdale, and the Florida Suncoast. At the same time reliably Democratic districts were established in Miami, Tampa, Dallas, and Houston. The Texas delegation, 22 strong in the 1950s, grew by one seat per decade to give it 24 seats during the 1970s. Truly explosive population growth occurred only in Florida, where the delegation rose from 8 in the 1950s to 12 in the 1960s and 15 in the 1970s. Democratic legislatures and Democratic governors in Florida and Texas took care to enhance Democratic prospects by carefully limiting the number of seats Republicans might expect to win. Apart from Florida and Texas no southern state gained new districts in the 1960s or 1970s. Virginia (10), Georgia (10), Louisiana (8), and South Carolina (6) remained stable from the 1950s through the 1970s. The remaining states lost representation. Alabama (9 to 7) and Arkansas (6 to 4) were the region's biggest losers, and North Carolina (12 to 11) and Tennessee (9 to 8) lost single seats.

The remaining southern open-seat elections (15 percent) involved Republican vacancies, situations usually occurring when the departing congressman sought a statewide office. One of the real problems confronting Republicans was their vulnerability whenever their incumbency advantage disappeared. Republicans kept only three-fifths of the open seats they had to defend. The subregional contrast is striking. Republicans were quite successful in the Peripheral South, where they won ten of the twelve open seats they had previously controlled. Although these victories merely maintained the Republicans' advantage, they demonstrated Republican penetration of many districts. These victories included both Republican strongholds in East Tennessee, Charlotte, Roanoke, and St. Petersburg and new centers of strength in Houston and Orlando. In the Deep South many of the Republican victories (especially in 1964 and 1966) had been political flukes. Some had surprised veteran Democrats; all had won among electorates in which blacks were incompletely organized. As a result, Republicans held only three of their nine vacancies. Furthermore, of the Deep South Republicans who were elected in such open-seat contests, only Floyd Spence (winning the Second District of South Carolina when Albert Watson vacated it to run unsuccessfully for governor) secured the overwhelming white support he needed to sustain a long congressional career.

For approximately the first decade after federal intervention, younger conservative Democrats replaced veteran conservative Democrats in most open-seat elections. Passage of the Voting Rights Act and the entry of hundreds of thousands of black voters in the Deep South and Virginia, as well as increased black participation elsewhere in the Peripheral South, did not immediately transform the Democratic party in most congressional districts. The strategy of most aspiring Democratic candidates was to draw support from discontented white voters by publicly disavowing the national Democratic party. "I am against the 'Great Society' and the give-away programs just as conservative-thinking Americans are against these programs," Mississippi Democrat Sonny Montgomery told white voters in his successful 1966 campaign for the seat that one-term Republican congressman Prentiss Walker had just vacated.[18] Republican candidates usually faced Democratic politicians who were more comfortable appealing to white conservatives than to newly enfranchised blacks in an explicit biracial coalition. By the 1970s, white politicians might well reach private understandings with black leaders, but there was little openly biracial campaigning except in some big-city districts.

The ability of conservative Democrats to defeat most conservative Republican challengers in open-seat situations is illustrated by the outcome of the earliest example of a serious effort by a Deep South Republican to appeal to white conservatives after the Kennedy administration took office. It occurred in a 1961 special election in the Fourth Congressional District of Louisiana. The seat, long held by conservative Democrat Overton Brooks, consisted of Shreveport and six surrounding rural parishes. When Brooks died in office, Republicans recognized "a 'now or never' opportunity to crack the monolithic Democratic orientation of Louisiana." The Republican candidate was conservative Charlton Lyons, a wealthy oilman. According to the *Congressional Quarterly Weekly Report*, local Republicans were "going all out to elect Lyons, with liberal financing, organization, and manpower."[19]

Whether or not it was true that Shreveport contained "more haters per square mile than anywhere else in the country,"[20] it was assuredly true that this city had "the best-organized, best financed and most enthusiastic Republican organization in Louisiana, a fruit of enthusiasm generated by President Eisenhower's strong races in the area and subsequent successful GOP tries for city offices in Shreveport."[21] Voters in this northwestern Louisiana district had twice given majorities to Eisenhower and would have done the same for Richard Nixon had it not been for a well-organized states'-rights candidate in 1960.

Although these factors were encouraging, Lyons still had to defeat a conservative Democrat to get to Congress. Democrats countered with Joe Waggonner, a politician who was not—by any stretch of the imagination—a "New South" Democrat. Far from it. Waggonner was a militant segregationist from the small Bossier Parish community of Plain Dealing, the sort of unreconstructed conservative Democrat who "pointed with pride to the fact that the Negro vote in Shreveport went solidly against him in the Oct. 28 Democratic primary." His racist credentials were undisputed. Waggonner had "served as president of the Fourth

District Citizens Councils, the counterpart of White Citizens Councils in other states."[22] Positions on the Bossier Parish school board and state board of education had given Waggonner platforms from which to fight school desegregation.

Thus voters could choose "between two strong conservatives, one a Democrat and one a Republican." Both nominees were "running on anti-Kennedy Administration platforms, attacking socialism in government, high federal spending and aid to education," and both expressed "strong support for states' rights and segregation of the races." Lyons argued that "it would be a 'tragedy' to send a Democrat to Congress since this would be interpreted nationally as a Kennedy Administration victory." Waggonner countered with his own appeal to conservative Democrats. According to *Congressional Quarterly,* Waggonner "says Lyons' election and the emergence of a two party system in the area would make it possible for minority groups—Negroes, in particular—to swing the balance of power between the parties. He says this happened nationally in the 1960 elections, electing President Kennedy, and should not be allowed to happen in Louisiana."[23]

Although this open-seat election was close by Louisiana standards, the conservative Democrat won with 54 percent of the vote. Support for the Republican challenger was much stronger in the urban sections of the district than in the rural areas. Lyons led in Shreveport by about 6,500 votes but ran more than 12,000 votes behind Waggonner in the district's rural parishes. Lyons was the apparent beneficiary, purely by default, of a small black vote, but he lost because white majorities still preferred an ultraconservative Democrat to a conservative Republican.[24]

Having survived an unusually close election, Waggonner then developed a Washington style that made him invulnerable at home. He became one of the most outspoken southern conservatives on racial issues in the House of Representatives. No Republican, no matter how obstreperous, could have got to the right of Waggonner on these issues. On the floor Waggonner voted with Republicans more often than with Democrats (his highest Democratic party unity score was 35). He never again faced a Republican challenger. Louisiana Republicans had no quarrel with his voting record, and, even if they had, Waggonner could not have been defeated.

Joe Waggonner's success as a conservative Democrat was typical of many other southern Democrats who won open-seat elections in the 1960s and 1970s. The "Shreveport" example of conservative Republicans challenging conservative Democrats established the main pattern—particularly in the Deep South—of ideological dispute between Republicans and Democrats in open-seat contests for the next two decades. Many Republicans sought to become the functional equivalents of racially conservative Democrats. This strategy required landslide majorities among white voters; any black votes cast for Republicans would be limited to those elections in which the Republican candidate was seen as a lesser evil.

Elections with Republican Incumbents

Republican incumbents were present in a fifth of the 1961–1981 elections (see Figure 5.3). Once in office, most House Republicans could make incumbency work for them. Their principal frustration was that—as far ahead as anyone could see—Republicans were bound to remain the minority party in the House of Representatives. No matter how much seniority any of them might acquire and no matter how able or energetic any of them might be, they could not realistically expect to chair a House committee or become part of a majority leadership team. This hard reality would encourage some Republican incumbents to run for governor or the Senate (where the same reality of minority status would prevail until the 1980 elections). From 1961 through 1981 the victory rate of incumbent Republicans was 93 percent, only four points lower than that of the much larger group of incumbent Democrats.

Because they started from such a small base, the southern Republicans were fundamentally constrained by Democratic incumbency. Republicans faced a formidable opportunity structure. Their chances for victory were obviously greatest when they were in a position to run their own incumbents and poorest when they were compelled to face veteran Democrats. Open-seat elections were less daunting to Republicans than running against sitting Democrats, but such elections were infrequent and sometimes involved defending their own vacant seats.

The distribution of elections among these three possibilities established the Republicans' bleak opportunity structure. Republicans could not possibly grow rapidly when the Democrats had better than a three-to-one advantage (67 to 20 percent) in elections involving incumbents. Republicans managed to win a quarter of the House elections, but that regional victory rate was due primarily to reelecting their own incumbents (93 percent) rather than to defeating veteran Democrats (3 percent).

Meanwhile, the southern Democrats—in a classic example of maintaining an original advantage despite a rapidly changing environment—continued to prosper by consistently reelecting their incumbents. The yield to Democrats from their veterans alone—67 percent of all the elections times a Democratic victory rate of 97 percent—was a robust 65 percent of all southern House seats. Combined with many open-seat victories and occasional defeats of incumbent Republicans, southern Democrats won 75 percent of the congressional elections in the 1960s and 1970s.

Republican victory rates varied according to the districts' racial and urban composition. GOP candidates won 42 percent of the elections in very low-black districts but only 18 percent of those in constituencies where blacks made up larger portions of the population. Candidates of the minority party prevailed in 30 percent of the contests in urban districts but merely 16 percent of the elections in rural seats. The Republicans' highest rate of success—43 percent—occurred in white New South districts, followed closely by a 40 percent rate of victory in white Old South districts. Beyond these two demographic settings, however, the Republicans fared poorly. They won only 24 percent of the elections in biracial New South districts and plummeted to 6 percent in the biracial Old South districts.

Republican candidates for Congress won slightly more often in the Peripheral South than in the Deep South (27 versus 20 percent). The constituency foundations of congressional Republicanism differed considerably between the two subregions. Two-thirds of the Republican victories in the Peripheral South occurred in white districts, whereas three-quarters of them in the Deep South took place in districts in which blacks made up 30 percent or more of the population.

Because of the Peripheral South's large size and the Republicans' higher rate of success, most of the southern Republicans' House victories in the 1960s and 1970s—72 percent—occurred in this subregion.

Thirty-nine percent of the Peripheral South congressional elections took place in districts with very low black populations, and the GOP won an impressive 47 percent of these contests. Only small white majorities were needed for victory in these constituencies. However, Republican congressional candidates did not do well in the subregion's biracial districts. Here larger white majorities were necessary for victories, and Republicans prevailed in only 14 percent of the elections.

Building on the historical foundations of mountain Republicanism, GOP congressional candidates won 51 percent of the elections during the 1960s and 1970s in the subregion's white Old South districts. Several of these rural districts, such as Tennessee's First (East Tennessee with Jimmy Quillen), Virginia's Ninth (western Virginia with William Wampler), North Carolina's Tenth (Blue Ridge with James Broyhill), and Arkansas's Third (Ozarks with John Paul Hammerschmidt), had traditions of rural Republicanism that traced back to the Civil War.

Perhaps surprisingly, Peripheral South Republicans won a smaller share of elections (46 percent) in the subregion's white New South districts. Their shortfall did not stem from weakness in the few genuinely metropolitan districts that had very low black populations. Peripheral South Republicans won 54 percent of all elections that took place in white New South districts whose urban populations ranged from 80 to 100 percent. Republican successes in these contexts are illustrated by such districts as Texas' Seventh (Houston with George Bush and Bill Archer) and Third (Dallas with James Collins), Florida's Sixth (St. Petersburg with William Cramer and Bill Young) and Ninth/Fifth (Orlando with Edward Gurney, Louis Frey, and Bill McCollum), and Virginia's Tenth (northern Virginia with Joel Broyhill). The subregion's Republicans also did well in very low-black constituencies where cities had been joined with rural areas that held significant pockets of traditional mountain Republicans, such as Tennessee's Second (Knoxville and rural East Tennessee with John Duncan) and Virginia's Sixth (Roanoke and western Virginia with Richard Poff and Caldwell Butler). Republicans also established themselves in Florida's Tenth (Suncoast with Skip Bafalis) and (starting in 1978) Texas' Twenty-first (San Antonio and West Texas). Republican weakness in the Peripheral South's white New South districts occurred principally in districts that combined city voters with traditionally Democratic rural voters. In numerous mixed urban-rural districts, many of them located in Texas, conservative Democratic strength in the rural areas made Republican victories difficult. Accordingly Republicans won only 39 percent of the white New South districts whose urban populations ranged from 50 to 79 percent.

The Republican victory rate fell to 17 percent of the elections held in the subregion's biracial New South constituencies. Examples of Republican success include North Carolina's Ninth (Charlotte with Jonas and James Martin), Virginia's Third (Richmond with Thomas Bliley in 1980), Second (Virginia Beach with William Whitehurst), First (Hampton Roads with Paul Trible), and Seventh (Blue Ridge with Kenneth Robinson). Although a Republican challenger could occasionally upset a veteran Democrat in this type of district, as Jack Fields did against Bob Eckhardt in Texas' Eighth (Houston) in 1980, Republicans were potentially vulnerable against Democrats who could effectively mobilize black voters. Dan Kuykendall served four terms before being defeated by Harold Ford, a black Democrat, in 1974. Kuykendall's Memphis district had been redrawn to increase its black population to 48 percent. Republican Robert Daniel won a plurality victory in 1972 to fill Virginia's Fourth (Southside), a seat long controlled by conservative Democrat Watkins Abbitt. Daniel was the most racially conservative Peripheral South Republican, and his intransigence invited opposition from any moderate Democrat who could forge a biracial coalition. Norman Sisisky would use that approach to reclaim the seat for the Democrats in 1982.

The Deep South accounted for 28 percent of the southern Republicans' congressional victories during the 1960s and 1970s. Nearly all Deep South districts (91 percent) had black populations greater than 15 percent, and all Republican victories in the Deep South occurred in biracial districts. In these situations Republicans could win only by virtue of large white majorities, low black participation, or some combination of both factors. In the Deep South Republicans became a competitive force only in biracial New South districts, where they won 34 percent of the elections. Their earliest sustained breakthroughs occurred in Alabama and South Carolina during the 1960s. In these settings the racial dimension of Goldwater conservatism was particularly potent. Republican breakthrough districts originally included Alabama's First (Mobile and southwestern Alabama with Jack Edwards), Second (Montgomery and southeastern Alabama with William Dickenson), and Sixth (Birmingham with John Buchanan) and South Carolina's Second (Columbia and rural central South Carolina with Albert Watson and Floyd Spence).

In the 1970s Republicans advanced in several other biracial New South districts. Mississippi's Fourth (Jackson and southwestern Mississippi with Thad Cochran and Jon Hinson) and Fifth (Biloxi and southeastern Mississippi with Trent Lott), Louisiana's Sixth (Baton Rouge with Henson Moore), First (New Orleans with Robert Livingston), and Third (New Orleans suburbs with David Treen), Georgia's Sixth (Atlanta suburbs and south-central Georgia with Newt Gingrich), South Carolina's Fourth (Greenville with Carroll Campbell) and First (Charleston with Tommy Hartnett) became constituencies friendly to the GOP. Two of these Deep South Republicans—Lott and Gingrich—would build impressive careers as congressional leaders of the national Republican party.

THE DEMOCRATIC SUFFOCATION

The civil rights movement and federal intervention set in motion the reenfranchisement of black southerners and the growth of two-party politics. Neither of these developments reached its full potential for many years. Black participation sharply increased and converted many white politicians from segregationists to nonsegregationists, but in a great many congressional districts blacks were not yet sufficiently mobilized to effectively challenge conservative Democratic incumbents. In the short run it was generally easier for veteran Democrats to smother the conservative Republican threat by emphasizing their own conservatism and acute unhappiness with the national Democratic party rather than reinventing themselves as New South Democrats.

For Republicans hoping to win congressional elections, the Goldwater movement as well as their own inclinations and actions meant that they had no standing at all among black southerners. Whether or not they emphasized racial matters (and aggressive racial campaigning was much more prevalent in the Deep South), Republicans opted to rely totally on white votes at a time when more blacks than ever were registering and voting. Unless and until white electorates emerged who were less tied to the Democratic party and more receptive to Republican appeals, in most congressional districts southern Republicans could not possibly execute their implicit strategy of winning substantial white majorities.

In the 1960s and 1970s, Democratic incumbents suffocated the conservative Republican challenge with conservative ideology and safe seats (see the final panel in Figure 5.3). "The Democratic Smother" provides a powerful image of southern congressional conservatism at the time of federal intervention. Within both political parties an exceptionally widespread and protracted conservative protest formed the common denominator of the southern response to federal intervention and the liberal wing of the national Democratic party. Nonetheless, the triumph of the conservative southern Democrats was also their swan song. When the broad issue of race relations was resolved against the preferences of white segregationists, conservative Democrats reasserted their traditional advantage in congressional elections. Republicans, after all, were comparatively inexperienced practitioners of openly racist politics, while southern Democrats were past masters at whipping up antagonism between the races. The possibility of partisan realignment based on racial cleavages was smothered by the conservative Democrats, many of whom continued to act as though blacks were not really part of their nomination or election constituencies.

Although most Democratic incumbents used conservatism to prolong their congressional careers, as time passed the new politics of Democratic primaries would make it much more difficult for white Democrats to win congressional nominations by running as unqualified conservatives. In district after district, as veteran Democrats retired or died, it would become much easier for white Democrats to capture nominations and win general elections by building biracial coalitions. A telling sign of the unfolding Democratic transformation appeared in the 1975 vote to extend the Voting Rights Act. Deep South Democrats still opposed it, but they did so by the comparatively small margin of 56 to 44 percent. And Peripheral South Democrats, who had been almost evenly divided in 1970, favored extending the Voting Rights Act by 78 to 22 percent. On final passage two-thirds of the southern Democrats supported the Voting Rights Act of 1975.[25] Increased black participation was reshaping Democratic primaries and general elections. The following decade would see the emergence of many moderate Democrats, Democrats who would vote with their party much more frequently than their predecessors yet still keep enough distance from northern liberal Democrats to retain the white shares they needed to combine with black support to be reelected.

Initially the resurgence of conservative or nominal southern Democrats frustrated the Republican congressional realignment. The Goldwater approach to party development left the Republicans a small minority in the Deep South delegation, while the less traditional demography of the Peripheral South gave the Republicans a slightly larger number of attractive targets. At no point during the 1960s and 1970s did the Republicans control as much as two-fifths of the regional or subregional delegations. National events, especially those involving presidential politics, could both make and break congressional careers. After their protest victories in 1964, Republicans lost ground and stalled in the Deep South for the rest of the decade. In the Peripheral South Republicans continued to make incremental gains. Republicans advanced in both subregions in 1972, the year of Nixon's decisive reelection, but the Watergate scandal erased those gains two years later. In 1974 the Republicans lost seven Peripheral South incumbents and two Deep South incumbents. Only toward the end of the period did the Republicans revive. After the 1980 election, when Ronald Reagan's success helped the Republicans defeat six incumbent Democrats, the Republicans remained well in the minority of the southern House delegation.

By the late 1970s some southern Democrats were beginning to reposition themselves as moderate Democrats. Many Republicans had been defeated or deterred from competing in the 1960s and 1970s when they had to face conservative Democrats. What would happen if more Democrats began to devise biracial coalitions and, as part of that process, began to recast themselves not as conservatives pure and simple but as an ideological mixture, conservative on some issues but liberal on others? Such an ideological blurring might well present southern Republicans with a quite different but equally formidable obstacle in House elections.

6

THE DEMOCRATIC
DOMINATION

A central irony permeated southern politics in the 1980s. Democrats easily dominated the congressional delegation even as Republicans won thirty-two of thirty-three state presidential elections. Presidential realignment did not immediately lead to congressional realignment. Seriously competing against Democrats less than half the time, from 1982 through 1991 southern Republicans won only a third of the elections to the House of Representatives. Although their overall performance was marginally better than their victory rate of 25 percent in the previous two decades, Republicans remained far short of controlling the South's congressional delegation. The ideological repositioning of their Democratic opponents helps explain the continuing electoral predicament of the southern Republicans.

Starting in the late 1970s and accelerating throughout the 1980s, many newly elected southern Democrats entered Congress as moderates, and some veteran conservatives redefined themselves as moderates. A few others, usually politicians representing districts with few white conservatives, began to vote as national Democrats. Developments at home and in Washington encouraged and mutually reinforced these important shifts. Ronald Reagan's presidency persuaded many conservative whites to abandon the Democratic party. At the same time many blacks were assimilated into southern party politics as committed Democrats. In numerous congressional districts the growing importance of blacks and moderate to liberal whites in Democratic primaries and general elections gradually gave the Democratic party a less conservative, more centrist image.

As a result Republican congressional candidates often faced a different challenge in the 1980s. Whereas conservative safe-seat incumbent Democrats had frequently smothered conservative Republicans in the 1960s and 1970s, many Republicans now confronted moderate or centrist Democratic opponents as they sought to expand their ranks in the southern House delegation. The revised Democratic advantage flowed from the Republicans' persistent inability to attract significant black support. Moderate safe-seat incumbent Democrats contained the Republican challenge with majority biracial coalitions. These experienced Democratic politicians campaigned in their districts and voted in Washington neither as staunch conservatives nor as resolute liberals. Modifying their ideology, many situated themselves as centrist Democrats, politicians who mixed liberal positions on some issues with conservative positions on others.[1]

When conservative Democrats left Congress in the 1980s, they were increasingly replaced not by other conservative Democrats but by younger white Democrats who readily understood the strategic advantage and practical necessity of organizing durable biracial coalitions. These moderate Democrats, unlike many of their predecessors, were at ease with the ebb and flow of biracial politics.[2] In many traditionally Democratic districts ambitious younger white Democrats recognized that it was no longer possible to win nominations in Democratic primaries, much less sustain their congressional careers, if they marketed themselves as unqualified conservatives.

By giving black constituents some of what they wanted (casting pro–civil rights votes without hesitation) while also giving white constituents part of what they wanted (voting conservative on many economic and social issues), "moderate" white Democratic incumbents could ordinarily defeat conservative Republican challengers. In 1982 91 percent of the southern House Democrats voted to extend the Voting Rights Act for twenty-five years. Only six Democrats—Richard Shelby and Bill Nichols of Alabama, Sonny Montgomery of Mississippi, Jack Brinkley and Larry McDonald of Georgia, and Dan Daniel of Virginia— opposed the Voting Rights Act. Across the South it was now smart

Democratic politics to protect the voting rights of a vital Democratic constituency.

The white Democrats' shift to overt biracial politics had important national consequences. Southern Democratic majorities continued to provide a cushion of surplus Democratic seats that ensured continuous Democratic control of the House of Representatives. On Capitol Hill senior southern Democrats learned that outright rebellion against the national Democratic party would no longer be tolerated. After federal intervention most committee chairmen from the South had revolted against the liberalism of the national party. During the first five Congresses after the Voting Rights Act, 91 percent of the committee chairsmen such as Wilbur Mills of Ways and Means, George Mahon of Appropriations, William Colmer of Rules, Bob Poage of Agriculture, Mendel Rivers and Edward Hebert of Armed Services, Wright Patman of Banking, John McMillan of District of Columbia, Olin Teague (Science and Astronautics), and William Jennings Bryan Dorn (Veterans' Affairs)—had supported their party's position on well less than half of the party unity roll calls. Many southern committee chairmen were unreliable Democrats at best, and some of them voted more often with the Republicans than with their fellow Democrats.

As time passed liberal northern Democrats were even less inclined to put up with the powerful southern conservatives. More was at stake than ideological differences. It was one thing for conservative southerners to chair committees before national legislation reshaped southern race relations; it was something else to permit southern conservatives to continue using their institutional power to undermine or dilute the northerners' liberal policy objectives. Following their gains in the 1974 Watergate elections, northern Democrats moved to discipline conservative committee chairs by instituting secret ballots for leadership elections. This reform sent a powerful message to southern conservatives. No longer would seniority automatically determine Democratic committee chairmanships. The shift to secret ballots undermined the autonomy of the southern conservative Democrats in the committee system.[3]

During the 1980s it became increasingly evident that southern Democrats would have to demonstrate considerable party loyalty in order to win secret ballots for major elected leadership positions and committee chairmanships or to secure appointment to the most prestigious committees. Pressure from party leaders and northern Democrats to support the leadership coincided with—and powerfully reinforced—the new politics of maintaining biracial coalitions in their constituencies. Consequently, most ambitious southern Democratic congressmen shifted away from purely conservative positions.

To understand the changing dynamics of Democratic practical politics, consider the Democratic party unity scores recorded by two senior Democrats, Jamie Whitten of Mississippi and Jim Wright of Texas, and two comparative newcomers, Butler Derrick of South Carolina and Charles Stenholm of Texas (see Figure 6.1). A leading Deep South Democrat from a biracial Old South district, Whitten had entered Congress in 1941 as a proud, unreconstructed segregationist elected by a totally white electorate. Much too "southern" to become a national leader of the Democratic party in the House of Representatives, Whitten could nonetheless use the committee system and its norm of seniority to construct his own powerful domain. Because he chaired the Agriculture Subcommittee of the House Appropriations Committee, Whitten effectively controlled the entire budget of the Department of Agriculture. He could simultaneously take care of white cotton farmers in his rural northern Mississippi district and use his influence over the Department of Agriculture to fight racial change. In 1967, for example, when an experienced bureaucrat in the Department of Agriculture discovered plans to survey hunger in Mississippi, his immediate response was to telephone this disturbing information to the "permanent secretary of agriculture." Only a few seconds of Whitten's time were required to kill any study of Mississippi's massive nutritional deficiencies. "'George, we're not going to have another smear campaign against Mississippi, are we,' declared Whitten to his informant. 'You boys should be thinking about a *national* survey—and do some studies in Watts and Hough and Harlem!' "[4] From 1962 through 1980 his party unity scores never reached 50.

In the House Democratic caucus, however, Whitten's lifelong conservatism threatened his succession to the chairmanship of the Appropriations Committee, the largest and most powerful committee in the House of Representatives. Chairing Appropriations had been Whitten's ultimate institutional goal. His survival of a secret ballot to succeed the retiring George Mahon of Texas apparently came with the understand-

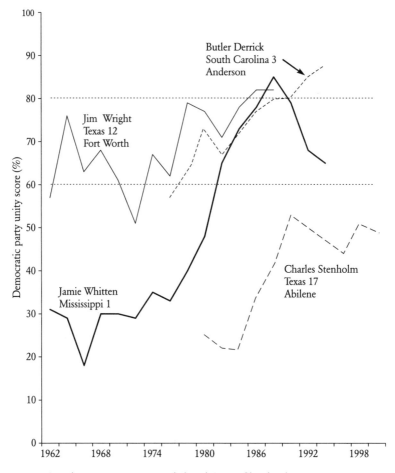

Figure 6.1 Southern Democrats and the claims of leadership. *Sources:* Calculated from *Congressional Quarterly Weekly Report,* various issues.

ing that he would genuinely cooperate with the Democratic leadership and support the Democratic agenda. The claims of the party leadership for increased loyalty coincided with increased black participation in Whitten's district, and his party unity scores soared into the moderate range. In 1987–88 Whitten voted with the Democratic majority on 85 percent of the party unity roll calls. It was a remarkable shift for the Mississippi congressman. "A lawyer who doesn't realize when you've changed the judge and jury is not much for you," Whitten once remarked. "I have adjusted to changing conditions."[5] No doubt Whitten's newfound moderation (including supporting the 1982 Voting Rights Act) disappointed and puzzled many of his longtime conservative white constituents. Yet as an experienced Democratic incumbent who knew personally thousands of the voters in his district and who had undoubtedly done countless favors, Whitten's standing in his district gave him a relatively free hand.

Jim Wright, first elected from Fort Worth in 1954, had more options than Jamie Whitten. He neither represented a district nor lived in a state where many whites would fight to the last ditch to preserve racial segregation. As an ambitious Texan from a white New South district, Wright did not have to conform to the militantly segregationist norms of the Deep South. Although he voted (to his later regret) against the 1964 Civil Rights Act, subsequently he was always pro–civil rights.[6] Moreover, Wright served in a delegation that prided itself on carefully grooming national Democratic leaders. Sam Rayburn and Lyndon Johnson had previously exemplified Texas Democrats with national ambitions. Hence it is not surprising that Wright generally positioned himself as a moderate Democrat over most of his career. He was elected majority leader in 1976 and advanced to the Speakership in 1986 following the retirement of Tip O'Neill of Massachusetts. Only during his final two Congresses as majority leader did his party unity scores reach the low 80s.

Unlike his fellow Deep South colleague Whitten, Butler Derrick began his congressional career in a biracial Old South district *after* blacks had entered the electorate. In 1974 Derrick forged a majority biracial coalition in the rural Third District of South Carolina. Derrick's strong party unity scores (which entered the moderate range by his second term) and obvious eagerness to support the Democratic leadership helped secure his early appointment to the prestigious Rules Committee. Although Derrick voted as a national Democrat in his final four terms and his reelection was never in doubt, the rise of presidential Republicanism indirectly threatened his insider aspirations. When he retired prematurely in 1994 he was the second ranking Democrat on Rules.

Charles Stenholm, the final Democrat shown in the chart, is an exception to the general rule of fewer conservative Democrats with institutional power. Stenholm was elected from a white New South district in West Texas long held by another conservative Democrat, Omar Burleson. In the early 1980s he was a leader of the Democratic "Boll Weevils" who supported much of President Reagan's tax and budgetary cuts. Unlike Wright, Stenholm was far too conservative to win a major leadership position. His best bet for achieving power was to rise within the committee system, and by the late 1990s Stenholm was the ranking Democrat on the Agriculture Committee. Agriculture is the sort of second-tier committee that northern liberal Democrats are willing to cede to their party's few conservatives.

All of these Democrats accommodated constituency opinion and institutional demands in ways that allowed them to have lengthy congressional careers. Whitten, Wright, Derrick, and Stenholm all knew how to leverage their incumbency back in their districts. Although none of these skilled Democrats were defeated by Republican challengers, they were nevertheless all operating to some extent on borrowed time. Each served in a district that was trending Republican in presidential politics. Derrick and Stenholm especially had to devote considerable time and energy to raising money to defend their seats. Conservative Republicans—Roger Wicker in Mississippi's First and Lindsay Graham in South Carolina's Third—replaced Whitten and Derrick when they retired. After a brief Democratic interlude, Republican Kay Granger, the mayor of Fort Worth, won Wright's seat. Stenholm's district is a probable Republican pickup if and when he retires or his district is significantly reconfigured.

Because of these new constituency and institutional claims on southern Democrats, conservative Republican challengers in the 1980s frequently faced not conservative Democrats but moderate to liberal Democrats. Under these evolving realities white and black voters in general elections now had a broader range of partisan and ideological choice. Ordinarily the advantage remained with incumbent Democrats. Veteran Democrats could typically hold their districts because the addition of exceptionally loyal black Democrats—voters who might not have been enthusiastic about particular white incumbents but who certainly wanted to maintain a Democratic majority in the House of Representatives—more than compensated for defections among white conservatives. Furthermore, moderate white Democratic representatives, politicians who knew how to mix things up ideologically in order to appeal to different segments of their biracial coalitions, could still attract many white conservatives on practical grounds. A Democrat who could unite the key party constituencies and appeal to moderate independents could thus gain sufficient white support to combine with an overwhelming share of black voters for a party victory. Realistic appraisals of the biracial coalitions devised by experienced southern Democrats would often discourage all but the most determined or wealthiest Republicans from even trying to compete.

Over the longer run, however, many southern Democrats faced increasing strains and mismatches between district imperatives and institutional demands. They were significantly cross-pressured, caught between their need to balance conservative and liberal positions in order to retain majority biracial grassroots support versus the insistence of national party leaders that they demonstrate substantial loyalty to the liberal agenda favored by many northern Democrats. Southern Democrats who represented liberal constituencies had no problem winning reelection and serving as party leaders, and Democrats who faced moderate constituencies could usually finesse the conflicting expectations of the district and the Capitol. Democrats still running in conservative districts, however, faced difficult challenges. On the one hand, they could choose the risky but possibly rewarding approach of establishing the moderate to liberal voting records needed to impress House Democratic leaders. Alternatively, they could adopt the safer yet probably less satisfying strategy of voting more conservatively and thereby surrendering any ambition to become a significant party leader or to chair any congressional committee or subcommittee that liberal Democrats wished to control. Younger southern conservatives, understanding the dilemma clearly, would increasingly run for Congress not as Democrats but as Republicans.

INCUMBENCY AND "MODERATION" AS DEMOCRATIC ASSETS

Elections with Democratic Incumbents

Democratic incumbency continued to stifle Republican growth. Democratic incumbents were on the ballot in three-fifths of the elections, and 97 percent of them were reelected. Without winning any open seats or defeating any Republican incumbents, the Democrats controlled 57 percent of the southern seats merely by reelecting their officeholders. In every state except Virginia, most House elections during this period involved Democratic veterans. Democratic incumbents achieved safe-seat victories in half of all the elections, whereas Republicans had similarly impressive wins in a fifth of the contests. In these comparisons the Republicans were fractionally stronger, and the Democrats slightly weaker, than they had been in the 1960s and 1970s.

By the 1980s tremendous ideological shifts characterized the southern Democrats. The principal ideological change was reflected in the decline of conservative safe-seat Democratic incumbents. Conservative safe-seat Democratic veterans, who had won two-fifths of the 1961–1981 elections, accounted for only 15 percent of the 1982–1991 elections. Many Democratic representatives were no longer in full-fledged revolt against their party (compare Figure 6.2 with Figure 5.1). Among successful southern Democrats the main ideological focus shifted from conservatism to moderation. Forty-five percent of the Democratic incumbents voted as moderates in the 1980s; and national Democrats, who had accounted for only a tenth of the Democratic incumbents in the 1960s and 1970s, were only slightly less common than nominal Democrats (25 versus 30 percent). Moderates constituted the single largest category of Democratic incumbents in both the Peripheral South (44 percent) and the Deep South (48 percent). Peripheral South Democrats abandoned conservatism far more readily than Deep South Democrats. Among Peripheral South Democrats, liberals slightly outnumbered conservatives (31 to 25 percent), while in the Deep South there were still four times as many conservative as liberal Democrats (40 to 11 percent).

Over four-fifths of the Democratic incumbents won safe-seat reelections, and more of these landslide victories now involved moderates (43 percent) rather than conservatives (30 percent). Moderate Democratic incumbents doubled their share of safe-seat victories from the 1960s and 1970s, while conservative Democratic incumbents saw their previous domination (70 percent) severely diminished. Liberal Democrats, who had previously won only a tenth of the safe-seat Democratic incumbent elections, accounted for a quarter of them during the 1980s.

Democratic conservatism declined because it was increasingly incompatible with the theory and practice of biracial politics. The new realities affected both veterans and newcomers. Among the Peripheral South

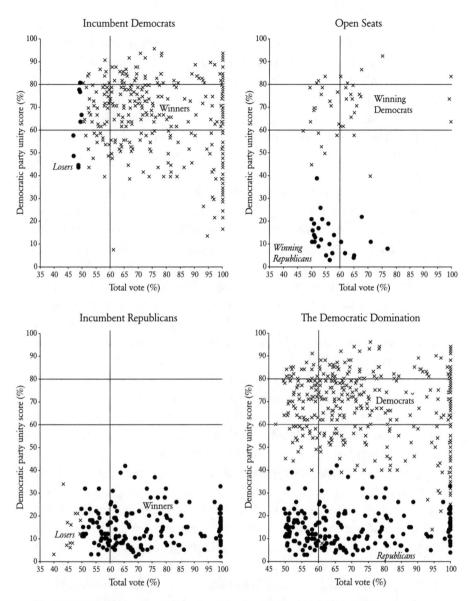

Figure 6.2 Southern House elections in the 1980s: moderate Democrats domi-
nate the Republican challenge. *Sources:* Calculated from *Congressional Quarterly's
Guide to U.S. Elections,* 3d ed. (Washington, D.C., 1994); and *Congressional Quarterly
Weekly Report,* various issues.

veterans whose original ideology was totally or predominantly conservative but who emerged as moderates and/or liberals in the 1980s were Bill Hefner of North Carolina, Bill Alexander of Arkansas, and Charles Bennett of Florida. In the Deep South similar repositionings involved Whitten and Tom Bevill of Alabama. Derrick and John Jenerett pioneered "moderate" politics in South Carolina. All these Democrats understood the necessity of demonstrably supporting their party in order to promote their institutional careers and sustain their biracial coalitions at home.

The Democratic newcomers, representatives who entered the House in the late 1970s or during the 1980s, confronted far different situations from the Democrats whose careers began either before or immediately after federal intervention. Many newcomers established themselves from the outset as moderates (sometimes after a freshman term when their party unity scores were in the 50s). Others shifted from the moderate into the liberal range as their careers progressed, and a few white Democrats regularly voted as nationals. Among the successful moderate newcomers from the Peripheral South were Norman Sisisky and Owen Pickett (Virginia), Mike Andrews (Texas), and John Tanner (Tennessee). In the Deep South states, where blacks were often a larger proportion of a successful Democratic campaign, many of the Democrats who emerged in the late 1970s or in the 1980s—such as Robin Tallon in South Carolina, Buddy Darden in Georgia, and Glen Browder in Alabama—were far less conservative than the men they replaced.

A few newcomers—Martin Frost of Texas and John Spratt of South Carolina are good examples—began as moderates but gradually developed reputations as national Democrats. Although white Democrats rarely used the term "liberal" to describe themselves, still other newcomers positioned themselves as national Democrats from the outset. In addition to black politicians elected from majority or near-majority black districts, such as Mickey Leland (Houston) and John Lewis (Atlanta), the national Democrats included Al Gore in Tennessee, John Bryant in Texas, and David Price in North Carolina.

If most of the southern Democrats who entered Congress from the late 1970s onward did not do so as conservatives, Democratic conservatism persisted to some degree in six states. In the Peripheral South it was confined to Texans such as Stenholm, Phil Gramm (before he became a

Republican), and Ralph Hall and to such Floridians as Earl Hutto and Bill Nelson. Among Deep South newcomers the conservative tradition was strongest in Louisiana (Jerry Huckaby, Buddy Roemer, and Billy Tauzin) and Mississippi (Mike Parker and Gene Taylor), very weak in Georgia (Doug Barnard and Richard Ray) and Alabama (Richard Shelby), and nonexistent among South Carolina Democrats.

Open-Seat Elections

During the 1980s the Republicans again failed to capitalize upon the opportunities presented by open-seat elections (see Figure 6.2). Only 11 percent of the House elections involved open seats, and the Republicans won merely two-fifths of these campaigns. Democrats continued to dominate the open-seat campaigns, and in many instances they were able to achieve landslide majorities.[7] Democrats won three times as many open-seat elections, with 60 percent or more of the vote, as the Republicans (33 to 10 percent).

Although the Republicans won a slightly larger share of open-seat elections in the 1980s than they had done in the 1960s and 1970s (33 percent), much of this modest improvement was due to holding their own vacancies rather than to capturing Democratic vacancies. Between the periods 1961–1981 and 1982–1991 the percentage of open-seat elections involving previously Republican seats more than doubled (from 15 to 34 percent), and Republicans won 70 percent of these campaigns. For example, Tom DeLay and Lamar Smith (Texas), Herb Bateman (Virginia), Porter Goss (Florida), and Cass Ballenger (North Carolina) all replaced Peripheral South Republicans. In the Deep South the open-seat victories of Alabama's Sonny Callahan, Louisiana's Richard Baker, and South Carolina's Arthur Ravenel took place in districts previously held by Republicans. All in all, however, the Republicans kept only sixteen of their twenty-three open seats. It was not a spectacular performance for a minority party.

Moreover, the Republicans won only 17 percent of the open-seat elections in districts previously held by Democrats. These modest Republican gains were limited to Texas, Florida, and Louisiana. Phil Gramm (Texas' Sixth District) switched parties in 1983 and won the special election called after he resigned his seat in order to run as a Republican. Joe Barton followed Gramm in 1984 when Gramm was elected to the Senate. In the same year Larry Combest (Texas' Nineteenth) became the first Republican to win the Lubbock seat. In Florida Cliff Stearns won the Sixth District in 1988 when Democrat Buddy MacKay vacated it to run (unsuccessfully) for the Senate; and Claude Pepper's death in 1989 resulted in a Republican pickup of Florida's Eighteenth (Miami) with Ileana Ros-Lehtinen. Gillis Long's death in 1985 produced a Republican victory for Clyde Holloway (Louisiana's Eighth). And when Democrat Buddy Roemer resigned his Shreveport seat in 1988 (Louisiana's Fourth) after winning the governorship, he was succeeded by his former staffer, Jim McCrery. As Trent Lott had done when he was first elected to the House, McCrery switched to the Republican party to make the race.

The 1980 reapportionment did not create many new districts congenial to southern Republicans. New districts appeared only in Florida, Texas, and Mississippi, and Democrats were slightly more successful than Republicans in controlling these seats. Population gains in Florida and Texas produced eight new seats. The Democrats won all three new House seats in Texas (Houston, Corpus Christi, and Dallas). In 1984, however, Dick Armey defeated Tom Vandergriff to give the Republicans additional representation in the Dallas suburbs. In Florida the parties divided the new districts, with the Republicans winning in Sarasota–Fort Myers, Clearwater, and Palm Beach and the Democrats taking a new Miami district and a new central Florida district. Mississippi's new district was based on compliance with the Voting Rights Act rather than on population growth. Republicans temporarily claimed a new black-majority district in the Mississippi Delta when Webb Franklin won a narrow victory in 1982. In 1986 Mike Espy defeated Franklin to become Mississippi's first black representative in the twentieth century.

Elections with Republican Incumbents

Because they could neither defeat many incumbent Democrats nor win a majority of open-seat elections, southern Republicans survived by systematically reelecting their slightly larger group of Republican incumbents. In the 1980s Republican incumbents did not improve their victory rate over previous decades—it remained at 93 percent—but they had more incumbents to reelect (30 percent of the elections versus 20 percent in the 1960s and 1970s). Marginal gains occurred in the proportion of Republican incumbents who were reelected with landslides. Seven-tenths of the Republican incumbents, compared to over four-fifths of the Democrats, achieved safe-seat victories. In the Peripheral South Republican incumbents were about as likely as Democratic incumbents (76 to 79 percent) to win decisively. The Democratic advantage in safe-seat victories persisted in the Deep South, where 91 percent of veteran Democrats but only 59 percent of Republican incumbents were similarly successful.

In metropolitan white New South districts Republicans used incumbency to hold their established bases in Dallas, Houston, St. Petersburg, the Florida Suncoast, and northern Virginia. During the decade Republicans secured other metropolitan seats, in Clearwater and Dallas. Republican incumbents also had considerable success in the white New South districts that mixed urban and rural populations. Retaining their seats in Knoxville, Memphis, and San Antonio, they then picked up similar districts involving the (far) Dallas suburbs, Lubbock, Lakeland, and central Florida. In white Old South settings Republicans kept their traditional advantage in East Tennessee, the Arkansas Ozarks, western North Carolina, and Virginia's Shenandoah Valley. Late in the decade they won Ocala with Cliff Stearns and Asheville with Charles Taylor.

Republicans had more limited success in the biracial New South districts. Nonetheless, in metropolitan settings incumbency protected Republicans in Houston, Orlando, Fort Lauderdale, Richmond, and New Orleans; and Ros-Lehtinen added a Miami seat in 1989. Republicans held their mixed urban-rural biracial New South districts in Charlotte, Newport News, Mobile, Montgomery, Columbia, Charleston, Atlanta, and Baton Rouge. During the decade they picked up Greensboro, West Palm Beach, and Shreveport. Democrats continued to dominate congressional elections in the biracial Old South districts. Sporadic Republican success—Clyde Holloway's three victories in Louisiana's Eighth District and Webb Franklin's two victories in Mississippi's black-majority Second—were based on extreme racial polarization.

Table 6.1 presents the Republican opportunity structure for House elections in the 1950s, the 1960s and 1970s, and the 1980s. It reports the changing electoral context (the distribution of contests involving incumbent Republicans, open seats, or incumbent Democrats in a given period), Republican victory rates in each type of election, and the conse-

Table 6.1 The changing Republican opportunity structure in southern House elections, 1950s–1980s

Elections with	Electoral context			Republican victory rates			Republican yields		
	1950s	1960s–1970s	1980s	1950s	1960s–1970s	1980s	1950s	1960s–1970s	1980s
Incumbent Reps.	5	20	30	97	93	93	5	18	28
Open seats	9	13	11	6	33	39	1	4	4
Incumbent Dems.	85	67	59	1	3	3	1	2	2
All elections	100	100	100	6	25	34	6	25	34

Note: Electoral context = percentage of House elections involving incumbent Republicans, open seats, or incumbent Democrats; Republican victory rates = percentage of each type of election won by Republicans; Republican yields = electoral context times Republican victory rates.

Sources: Calculated from *Congressional Quarterly's Guide to U.S. Elections,* 3d ed. (Washington, D.C., 1994); and *Congressional Quarterly Weekly Report,* various issues.

quent Republican "yields" from each type of election. For example, Republican incumbents appeared in 30 percent of the 1982–1991 southern House elections. They were reelected 93 percent of the time. Multiplying the Republican incumbents' share of elections by their victory rate produces a Republican yield from their incumbents of 28 percent of all House elections during the 1980s.

Though steadily diminishing across time, Democratic incumbency fundamentally constrained and deterred Republican growth. Democratic incumbents outnumbered Republican incumbents by 17 to 1 in the 1950s and by better than 3 to 1 in the 1960s and 1970s. Even in the 1980s there were still twice as many Democratic as Republican incumbents in southern House races. The Republicans' slight improvement in their share of southern House seats during the 1980s was due entirely to higher yields from their larger group of officeholders.

THE PARTY BATTLE IN FOUR SOUTHERN ARENAS

Although the regional story of the southern party battle in the 1980s involved continued Democratic success in dominating and blocking the Republicans, the nature of the partisan fight varied considerably from white New South districts, the arena most advantageous to the Republicans, to the biracial Old South districts, the setting traditionally most resistant to GOP competition. Republicans won 49 percent of the elections in white New South districts and were almost as successful in white Old South districts (46 percent). Their victory rate fell to 34 percent in biracial New South districts and plummeted to 5 percent in biracial Old South districts. Figure 6.3 plots the shifting distribution of winning Republicans, conservative Democrats, moderate Democrats, and national Democrats in each arena over five decades. Because they contain many middle-class whites and relatively small black populations, the white New South districts have been the primary targets of the southern Republicans. In this expanding arena the party battle has been mainly a fight between conservative alternatives. By the 1980s (see "White New South Districts") the Republicans had opened a substantial lead over the conservative Democrats, and in the following decade the white New South districts—expanded to almost two-fifths of the southern seats—became the paramount Republican stronghold.

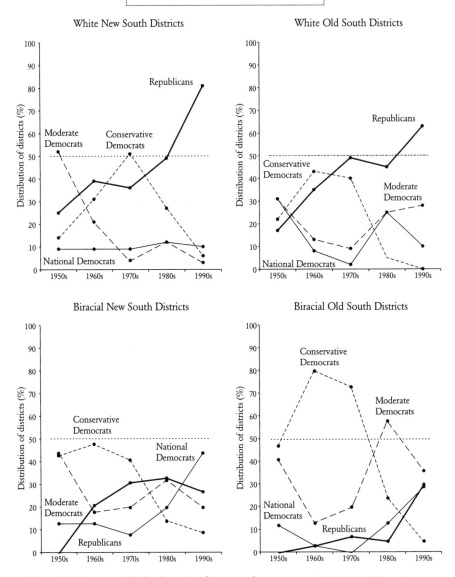

Figure 6.3 Party and ideology in four southern arenas, 1950s–1990s. *Sources:* Same as Figure 6.1.

White Old South districts have constituted a second Republican target. Lacking the large white middle classes found in the white New South settings, Republican strength was historically based on the mountain Republicanism of the Blue Ridge and the Ozarks. With increasing urbanization, white Old South districts account for less than a tenth of the regional delegation. Republicans replaced conservative Democrats as the single largest force in the 1970s, but the subsequent rise of moderate Democrats and national Democrats contained the Republicans in the 1980s. Republicans broke through to majority status in the next decade.

In contrast to the two arenas with very low black populations, Republicans have remained a distinct minority in biracial New South districts. From the 1960s through the 1980s part of the southern Democrats' persistent advantage was that biracial New South districts far outnumbered white New South districts. After the 1990 redistricting the two opposing New South arenas were roughly equal in size. In biracial New South districts (and especially those with black populations exceeding 30 percent) Republican candidates have seldom been able to muster the substantial white majorities needed to offset overwhelming black support for Democrats. Partly because this arena contains many majority or near-majority black (and Texas Hispanic) districts, it is the main source of national Democrats in the southern delegation.

The fourth arena—the biracial Old South districts—has persistently resisted Republican penetration. For three decades conservative white Democrats suffocated Republican challenges, and during the 1980s moderate Democrats replaced conservative Democrats as the dominant political tendency. From the 1950s through the 1980s Republicans never captured even a tenth of these House elections. In the 1990s biracial Old South districts contained only 15 percent of the House seats, and the party battle involved a three-way fight among moderate Democrats, national Democrats (primarily blacks), and Republicans. In all four arenas conservative Democrats have almost disappeared.

PERIPHERAL SOUTH PATTERNS

Through the 1980s Republicans continued to be more successful in the Peripheral South (winning 36 percent of congressional elections) than in the Deep South (27 percent). Peripheral South Republicanism flourished primarily in the overwhelmingly white districts. Thirty-eight of the South's forty-three white districts were located in the Peripheral South. During the 1980s Republicans won a small majority of the elections in white districts but less than a quarter of the contests in biracial districts. Republicans won 53 percent of the elections in white New South districts and 55 percent in white Old South districts. Their victory rate dropped to 31 percent in biracial New South districts and was zero in the biracial Old South districts.

In order to illustrate the party battle for control of the Peripheral South delegation, Figure 6.4 isolates selected districts in each of the four demographic arenas. By charting Democratic party unity scores over time, it is possible to compare Democratic and Republican approaches to winning and holding congressional seats. Consider first the white New South districts. Republican success in the metropolitan Peripheral South has been mainly a process of winning and holding newly created big-city/suburban white districts in Texas, Florida, and (less commonly) Virginia. During the 1980s Republicans won three-fifths of the elections in metropolitan white New South districts, their best performance in any single demographic setting. Texas' Seventh Congressional District, which includes the west side of Houston, exemplifies this process. Since its creation in 1966 it has been one of the nation's safest Republican seats. Texas' Seventh gave George Bush his start in national politics, and Bush's successor, Bill Archer, then used it to become the ranking Republican and ultimately the chairman of the Ways and Means Committee. Florida's Twentieth, the Miami district held in various configurations by Dante Fascell and (in the 1990s) by Peter Deutsch, stands in sharp partisan and ideological contrast to Texas' Seventh. Miami-area Democrats have long been paradigmatic big-city liberals.

Peripheral South Republicans also won over two-fifths of the races in mixed urban-rural white New South settings. Texas' Nineteenth, a West Texas district containing Lubbock and many rural counties, illustrates secular realignment. George Mahon, the powerful chairman of the House Appropriations Committee, became less inclined to vote with the Democratic leadership over time, and he was followed by conservative Democrat Kent Hance. Republican Larry Combest easily won an open-seat election in 1984 and soon made the district secure.

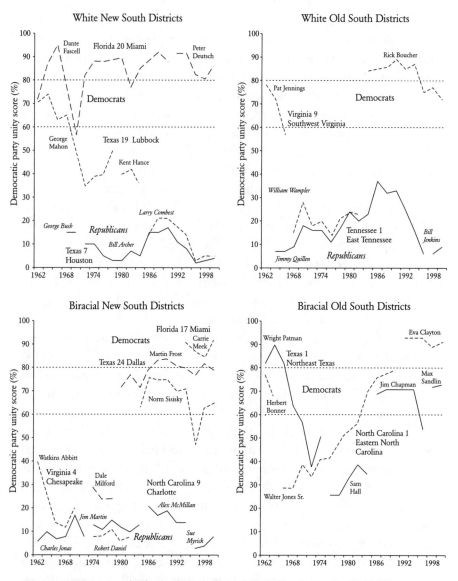

Figure 6.4 Party and ideology in selected Peripheral South districts. *Sources:* Same as Figure 6.1.

White Old South districts provide a contrast between the Republicans' traditional stronghold in East Tennessee (the First) with the intermittently competitive Ninth District of western Virginia. Tennessee's First District, represented for three decades by Jimmy Quillen, is the prime example of mountain Republicanism. Unlike the highly ideological metropolitan Republicans, Quillen was a practical conservative who was often inclined toward accommodation with the Democrats. His retirement opened the way for Bill Jenkins, who was far more conservative in his early voting record than Quillen had been during the 1980s. Virginia's Ninth District, containing Democratic coal miners as well as mountain Republicans, has swung back and forth between the parties. Despite lowering his party unity scores, Democrat Pat Jennings was defeated in 1966 by William Wampler, the same Republican Jennings had originally beaten in 1954. In 1982 Rick Boucher narrowly defeated Wampler to regain the seat for the Democrats. Through the 1994 elections Boucher regularly voted as a national Democrat, but in later Congresses he shifted into the moderate range.

The complexity of the South's largest metropolitan areas offers opportunities for Democrats as well as Republicans, especially in biracial New South districts in which larger black (and/or Texas Hispanic) electorates make it easier for Democrats to assemble majority coalitions. In 1972 television weatherman Dale Milford won a newly created Dallas seat as a very conservative Democrat. His conservatism put him at risk less from Republicans than from moderate to liberal Dallas Democrats. Organizing a coalition of whites, blacks, and Hispanics, Martin Frost defeated Milford in the 1978 Democratic primary. The enormous gap between Milford's and Frost's party unity scores exemplifies the important transition from Democratic conservatives to Democratic moderates. Moreover, as Frost secured his district and began to rise within the Democratic leadership (Democratic caucus chairman) and through the committee system (second-ranking Democrat on the Rules Committee), his party unity scores have hovered around the 80 percent benchmark for national Democrats. In 1992 the creation of additional big-city districts with black majorities expanded Democratic liberalism. Carrie Meek's Miami district (Florida's Seventeenth) is as safely Democratic as Texas' Seventh is securely Republican. The ideological and partisan gap between conservative Republicans and liberal Democrats is especially wide in southern metropolitan districts.

North Carolina's Ninth and Virginia's Fourth represent contrasting partisan outcomes in the Peripheral South's biracial New South districts that have mixtures of urban and rural population. The Ninth District of North Carolina, with Charlotte as its core, has sent Republicans to Congress continually since 1952. Despite repeated attempts by North Carolina Democrats to redistrict him into oblivion, Charles Raper Jonas held the district for two decades. When Jonas retired the district passed to (future governor) James Martin, and Alex McMillan, in turn, succeeded Martin. In 1992 black neighborhoods in Charlotte were removed in order to create an adjacent majority-black district. With its black population reduced to less than 10 percent, the Ninth District became a much safer Republican seat. In 1994 former Charlotte mayor Sue Myrick became the fourth Republican to hold the district.

Virginia's Fourth, a biracial Old South district in the 1950s and 1960s, was redrawn as a biracial New South district in the 1970s. Watkins Abbitt, a stalwart of the Byrd organization, had voted as an extremely conservative Democrat. When Abbitt retired in 1972 he was replaced by a slightly more conservative Republican, Robert Daniel. Daniel served five terms but was always vulnerable to any moderate Democrat who could effectively organize a biracial coalition. In 1982 the district's black population was increased to 40 percent. Provided that blacks turned out in rough proportion to their population and cast a unified Democratic vote, a Democratic candidate needed no more than 25 to 30 percent of the white vote in order to carry the district. Faced with a well-funded Democratic opponent and substantial black opposition, a Republican like Daniel needed to attract 70 to 75 percent of the white vote. In 1982 businessman Norman Sisisky demonstrated the power of organized biracial politics when he defeated Daniel by 54 to 46 percent. Operating primarily as a moderate Democrat, Sisisky proceeded to make the Fourth District safely Democratic once again.

During the 1980s Peripheral South Republicans failed to achieve any breakthroughs in the biracial Old South districts. The dominant partisan traditions in both Tennessee's First and Texas' First date back to the Civil War and Reconstruction. Just as Quillen and his predecessor

B. Carroll Reece had personified southern mountain Republicanism in the House of Representatives, so Wright Patman of Texarkana symbolized rural and small-town white Democracy. Patman had easily held Texas' First District ever since he was first elected in 1930. Before federal intervention Patman voted as a New Deal Democrat on practically every issue except civil rights. His declining party unity scores after federal intervention were in contrast to his earlier inclinations to support the leadership of Democrats such as his fellow Texan Sam Rayburn. His successor, Sam Hall, was far more conservative than Patman had ever been. Biracial Democratic politics in Texas' First began only with the election of Jim Chapman in 1985. Chapman's moderate party unity scores put him squarely in accord with other Democratic newcomers in similar districts, and Max Sandlin has continued the patterns of biracial politics and moderate party loyalty established by Chapman. North Carolina's First District, in the eastern part of the state, illustrates both continuity and change. Herbert Bonner, a moderate Democrat who retired in 1966, was replaced by the more conservative Walter Jones, whose party unity scores did not sharply increase until the early 1980s. In the 1990 redistricting the First became a new black-majority district won by Eva Clayton. North Carolina's First is the rural counterpart to newly created metropolitan majority-black districts such as Florida's Seventeenth.

DEEP SOUTH PATTERNS

In the Peripheral South almost half of the House elections during the 1980s—and two-thirds of the Republican victories—occurred in districts in which blacks were less than 15 percent of the population. Herein lies the crucial demographic difference between the subregions. Because of their larger black populations, the Deep South states have contained few white districts. Only a seventh of their congressional elections occurred in overwhelmingly white districts, and Republican candidates won less than a tenth of their white district opportunities. Over 90 percent of the Republicans' Deep South victories came in biracial districts. Deep South Republicans were relatively successful only in biracial New South districts, where they won almost two-fifths of the elections.

Figure 6.5 documents the changing party battle in selected Deep South districts. White New South districts have been rare, especially metropolitan white New South districts comparable to Texas' Seventh or Twenty-sixth. Alabama's Fifth (Huntsville) exemplifies the mixed urban-rural white New South district that has remained Democratic. With a strong Democratic heritage reinforced by the New Deal and TVA, Robert Jones was one of the staunchest New Deal Democrats before federal intervention. When Jones retired, he was replaced by Ronnie Flippo, whose party unity scores moved from initial conservatism to moderation. Flippo's biracial politics continued under Bud Cramer, who was first elected in 1990. After nearly losing in the 1994 Republican surge, Cramer dropped his party unity scores into the high 50s and gradually reestablished his incumbency advantage.

In the 1990s the creation of winnable districts for black Democrats produced Republican opportunities in neighboring districts. Newt Gingrich's 1992 move into a newly created metropolitan white New South district in the Atlanta suburbs (Georgia's Sixth) ironically provided him with a much safer seat than the mixed urban-rural biracial New South district he had previously represented. Similarly, Republican Spencer Bachus defeated Democratic incumbent Ben Erdreich in 1992 after Erdreich's Birmingham district (Alabama's Sixth) lost black voters to the adjoining Seventh.

The chart for white Old South districts is highly instructive. The party unity patterns for Tom Bevill (Alabama's Fourth) and Ed Jenkins (Georgia's Ninth) resemble the changes previously observed in the voting behavior of Jamie Whitten. Originally elected as conservative Democrats, Bevill and Jenkins voted as such for many Congresses. Over time Bevill, with a seat on the Appropriations Committee and eventually the chairmanship of the public works subcommittee, shifted decisively into the moderate range. When he retired in 1996, however, Robert Aderholt became one of the first Deep South Republicans to win a white Old South district.

Georgia's Ninth District, in the rural northern part of the state, provides a roughly similar example of sustained Democratic dominance in a white Old South setting finally reversed by a party switch after the Republican breakthrough in 1994. Like many other Democratic veterans,

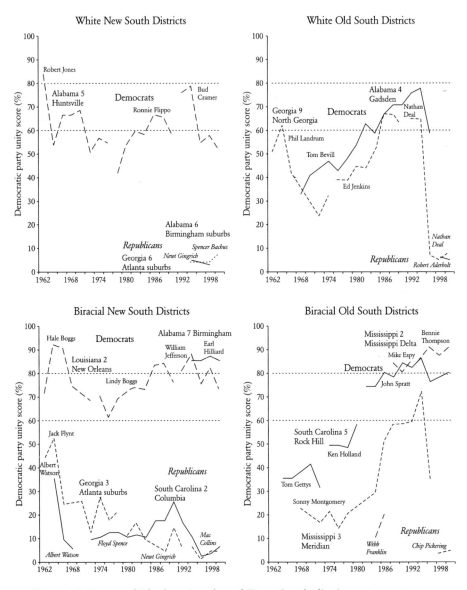

Figure 6.5 Party and ideology in selected Deep South districts. *Sources:* Same as Figure 6.1.

Phil Landrum moved sharply to the right in the aftermath of federal intervention. Jenkins, his successor, eventually rejoined the House Democrats as Bevill and Whitten had done. In the 1990s, however, Nathan Deal successfully switched parties and gave the Republicans another rural Deep South district.

In the Deep South both parties have prospered in the biracial New South districts. Louisiana's Second (central-city New Orleans) illustrates continuous Democratic success. Hale Boggs survived stormy campaigns in the 1960s as he pioneered biracial politics in the Louisiana delegation. At his death in 1972 he was serving his first term as Democratic majority leader. Boggs's widow, Lindy Boggs, a skillful politician herself, continued his biracial politics until she retired in 1990. William Jefferson then became the first black Democrat in the Louisiana delegation when he won the intraparty battle to replace Boggs. In the 1990s a newly created black-majority district anchored in Birmingham (Alabama's Seventh) provided a safe seat for Earl Hilliard.

Through the 1980s biracial New South districts with smaller urban majorities were the primary site of Deep South Republicanism. Three-quarters of the Deep South Republican victories occurred in mixed urban-rural districts whose black populations ranged from 15 to 35 percent. Such districts could generate the comparatively larger white majorities the Republicans needed to offset strong opposition from most black Democrats and minorities of white Democrats.

South Carolina's Second (Columbia) and Georgia's Third (Atlanta suburbs) Congressional Districts illustrate Republican success in the mixed urban-rural biracial New South constituencies. Republicans first won the Columbia district under the leadership of Albert Watson, a segregationist Democrat turned segregationist Republican. When Watson vacated his seat in 1970, Floyd Spence kept the seat in Republican hands. During the 1980s the district's black population was 35 percent, and that figure encouraged Democrats to challenge Spence. In 1986 and 1988 Spence's majorities dropped below 55 percent. With no black support, Spence survived only by winning 75 percent or more of the white vote. Redistricting in the 1990s reduced the black population of the Second District by ten percentage points in order to help create the new black-majority Sixth District subsequently won by James Clyburn. As a result Spence—after 1994 the chairman of the House Armed Services Committee—emerged with a considerably safer district.

Georgia's Third District is the site of the story—told in full by Richard F. Fenno Jr. in *Congress at the Grassroots*—of Jack Flynt's inability to maintain his incumbency advantage when his rural Georgia district was converted into a mixed urban-rural district on the outskirts of Atlanta. Newt Gingrich ultimately drove the veteran conservative Democrat into retirement, and, after the district was redrawn following the 1990 Census to eliminate Gingrich (who foiled the attempt by moving into the new and much safer Sixth District), the Republicans under Mac Collins retained the reshaped Third District.[8]

Mississippi's Third and Second and South Carolina's Fifth Districts illustrate important trends in the biracial Old South constituencies of the Deep South. Like Bevill and Whitten, Sonny Montgomery (Mississippi's Third) went to Congress originally as a hard-core Democratic conservative. For two decades his voting record was resolutely conservative. Although no Republican could defeat him, Montgomery never reaped the full benefits of his congressional seniority. Chairing the Veterans' Affairs Committee throughout the 1980s, Montgomery ultimately increased his party loyalty in order to retain his chairmanship. In the old days, when seniority automatically controlled committee chairmanships, he would have automatically shifted his chairmanship from Veterans' Affairs to Armed Services after the 1992 election. Instead, Ron Dellums of Berkeley, California, not Sonny Montgomery of Meridian, Mississippi, became the new chairman of the Armed Services Committee. When Montgomery finally retired in 1996, his district easily passed (61 to 36 percent) to a young, conservative Republican, Chip Pickering.

Democrats still retain considerable electoral advantages in biracial Old South districts. Mississippi's Second, the Delta district established in 1982 as a rural black-majority district, has become a thoroughly safe seat for black Democrats. Mike Espy and Bennie Thompson have given blacks their first representation in the Mississippi delegation. Finally, South Carolina's Fifth illustrates the profound transformation of a district once controlled by racially conservative white Democrats. John Spratt's election in 1982 provided the decisive ideological breakthrough. With the decline of conservative white Democratic voters,

Spratt can afford to vote as a national Democrat and still hold his district.

THE NEW REPUBLICAN PREDICAMENT

During the 1980s southern Democrats used increased black participation to minimize Republican gains in congressional elections. As many older conservative Democrats ended their House careers, younger white Democrats skillfully exploited the Republicans' most obvious weakness—their inability to compete for black votes, which was the legacy of Goldwater and Reagan Republicanism—by forming durable biracial coalitions. The fundamental Democratic advantage was clear. As long as 90 to 95 percent of blacks voted Democratic, no Democratic candidate ever needed to win a majority of the white vote in order to be elected. The Democratic white target was thus always less than 50 percent, and usually a good deal less. Unlike many of their predecessors, the new, "moderate" Democrats understood that their long-term survival required them to pay attention to the central demands of their black constituents as well as their white constituents. "Moderation" became the principal ideological style among white Democrats in the 1980s because it allowed them to act positively on behalf of all the main elements of their electoral coalitions. Few white Democratic candidates could survive Democratic primaries as full-fledged conservatives, and few white Democrats could win general elections if they were generally perceived as undiluted liberals. Practical politics pushed white Democrats in the direction of mixing things up ideologically.

Southern Republicans, however, were exclusively wedded to conservatism. Their approach succeeded primarily in the districts they had previously won and occasionally in newly created metropolitan districts in Texas and Florida that contained many middle- and upper-income whites. In the Peripheral South, Republicans were elected to Congress primarily in districts in which whites constituted 85 to 95 percent of the population. Deep South Republicans generally represented districts with smaller white majorities, and this reality meant that the Republicans had difficulty winning new districts when they faced Democrats who knew how to organize biracial coalitions.

During the 1980s, then, Democratic incumbents dominated the Republican challenge with moderate ideology and safe seats. "The Democratic Domination" (see the lower right panel in Figure 6.2) suggests the profound impact of increased black participation on the ideology of most southern House Democrats. Although traces of Democratic conservatism remained, the central image of "the Democratic Domination" is the emergence of moderate Democrats. Beginning in 1982 and continuing through 1990 moderates displaced nominals as the single largest category of southern House Democrats (see the trend lines in Figure 3.1).

Democratic adjustment prevented the Republicans from taking immediate advantage of Reagan's presidential victories. Figure 6.6 presents southern Republican victory rates in House elections since 1950. With Reagan at the top of the ticket Republicans won 36 percent of southern House seats in 1980, the highest share they had yet achieved. Two years later, with the nation in recession, the Republicans dropped back to 29 percent in the first election involving the districts established after the 1980 Census. Reagan's 1984 coattails helped bring the Republicans back up to 37 percent of the delegation, but 1984 was their peak performance for the decade. From 1986 through 1990 the southern Republicans managed to control only a third of the southern seats. Democratic biracial politics effectively contained the southern Republicans well short of a regional majority.

PRESIDENTIAL FOUNDATIONS OF
CONGRESSIONAL REPUBLICANISM

And yet Republican prospects were not quite as bleak as they might seem. In the presidential elections of 1984 and 1988 the Republicans made unprecedented advances in the South. Republicans carried most congressional districts, often achieving consecutive landslide majorities of 60 percent or greater. Ronald Reagan consistently ran ahead of George Bush, but the overall image of the Republican presidential votes in Figure 6.7 is one of impressive grassroots strength. Many presidential landslide or near-landslide Republican districts—districts with black dots signify Republican winners in the 1990 House elections—already contained Republican incumbents. In the Peripheral South the most presidentially Republican districts (Texas' Seventh, with Bill Archer;

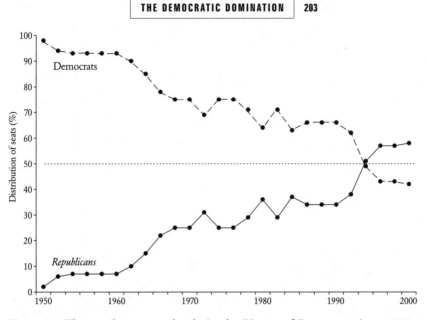

Figure 6.6 The southern party battle in the House of Representatives, 1950–2000. *Sources:* Same as Figure 6.1.

Texas' Third, with Sam Johnson; and Texas' Twenty-first, with Lamar Smith) were all held by Republicans. Likewise, Robert Livingston (Louisiana's First, in suburban New Orleans) occupied the most presidentially Republican district in the Deep South.

While Peripheral South Republicans controlled more presidential landslide Republican districts than did Democrats, in the Deep South the reverse was true. Southern Democrats who served in House districts in which Republican presidential candidates could win landslide or near-landslide votes—X's designate winning Democrats in 1990—were potentially vulnerable to carefully planned Republican challenges. Republican presidential success in the 1980s was expanding the grassroots base needed to improve Republican competitiveness in congressional elections.

There were very few presidentially Democratic constituencies. Consecutive Republican defeats in 1984 and 1988 were limited to a small number of southern districts. These included most majority- or near-majority-black districts (Houston, Memphis, Atlanta, and New Orleans), two Hispanic-majority seats in Texas (San Antonio and southern Texas), and William Lehman's Miami district. In 1990, twenty-five years

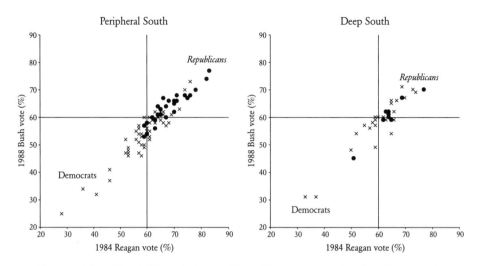

Figure 6.7 Presidential foundations of Republican congressional realignment in the 1990s. *Sources:* Calculated from Michael Barone and Grant Ujifusa, *The Almanac of American Politics* (Washington, D.C.: National Journal), various years.

after the Voting Rights Act, there were only 5 black Democrats out of 116 southern representatives. Texas, Tennessee, Georgia, Mississippi, and Louisiana each sent a single black Democrat to Congress; the other six states sent none. Many African-American Democratic politicians were acutely dissatisfied with their transparent congressional underrepresentation. They wanted realistic opportunities to win House elections.

White Republicans, energized by their unprecedented presidential success and confident that drawing new black-majority districts would make their party highly competitive in many other situations, were eager to join forces with black Democrats. Reapportionment and redistricting after the 1990 Census thus promised to have exceptionally wide-ranging ramifications for the southern congressional delegation. What would be the political consequences for the South of creating many additional black-majority districts? Given the unrealized Republican potential in many districts based on improved presidential Republicanism, reapportionment and redistricting might well accelerate a southern congressional realignment significantly benefiting white Republicans as well as black Democrats.

7

REAGAN'S REALIGNMENT OF
WHITE SOUTHERNERS

In the South the Reagan realignment of the 1980s was a momentous achievement. By transforming the region's white electorate, Ronald Reagan's presidency made possible the Republicans' congressional breakthrough in the 1990s. The secular realignment of southern white voters, chiefly involving conservative men and women, occurred in two distinct stages. Greater white support for Republican *presidential candidates* commenced in 1964, but the more fundamental Republican advantage in *partisan identification* emerged two decades later. The extended lag between the presidential and partisan realignments allowed Democrats to dominate southern elections to Congress long after federal intervention had ended racial segregation and started to destabilize the one-party system.

The Great White Switch in presidential voting appeared immediately after Congress passed and Democratic president Lyndon Johnson signed the 1964 Civil Rights Act. Republican Barry Goldwater easily defeated Johnson among white southerners. Since 1964 more whites have voted Republican than Democratic in every single presidential election. Similar changes in southern party affiliation, however, did not immediately accompany the white switch in presidential voting. Partisan realignments require political leaders whose performance in office expands the party's base of reliable supporters. Not until Reagan's presidency did more southern whites begin to think of themselves as Republicans than as Democrats. Reagan was the first Republican presidential candidate to poll back-to-back landslide majorities from white southerners; and his vice president, George Bush, captured the presidency in 1988 by running on the strategy that Reagan had mastered: attracting substantial majorities from conservative and moderate whites, while implicitly conceding the votes of blacks and liberal whites.

Important as his electoral victories were, Reagan's presidency had a far more crucial impact upon many southern whites. His optimistic conservatism and successful performance in office made the Republican party respectable and useful for millions of southern whites. Many of them, for the first time in their lives, began to think of themselves as Republicans.[1] The Great White Switch in partisan identification created a much more competitive playing field for two-party politics, one that ultimately encouraged, expanded, and intensified Republican campaign activity for Senate and House seats.

The Republican approach to top-down party building in the South was modeled upon its successful strategy in presidential elections: realign white conservatives as a reliable source of Republican support and neutralize white moderates as a consistent foundation of Democratic strength. Reagan attracted a majority of white conservatives into the Republican party and persuaded many other conservatives to think of themselves as "independents" rather than as Democrats. The Republican president had a different impact on southern white moderates. He eroded their traditional attachment to the Democratic party and increased their Republican ties, thereby neutralizing a huge, longstanding Democratic advantage among this critically important segment of the southern electorate.

By *realigning* white conservatives and *dealigning* white moderates, Reagan produced a *partial* realignment of the southern white electorate. The Republican party became more competitive with the Democratic party but still fell far short of attracting the three-fifths share of whites necessary to assure dominance in the South's biracial electorate. Republican candidates can prevail if they combine their partisan base with sufficient strength among white moderate independents and conservative Democrats, but Democratic candidates can still win whenever they fully mobilize blacks and attract around two-fifths of the white vote. Analyzing what has—and what has not—changed in the southern electorate helps explain the Republican surge in congressional and senatorial elections during the 1990s as well as the persistence of truly competitive two-party politics in the twenty-first century.

PRESIDENTIAL REPUBLICANISM AND THE
PARTIAL REALIGNMENT

During the first half of the twentieth century most white southerners, Democrats by birth and experience, despised and loathed the Republican party. Figure 7.1 ("Southern Presidential Voting") shows the Democrats' supremacy during the New Deal. The first important departure from southern Democratic solidarity in presidential elections occurred in 1948 after Democratic president Harry Truman reversed the party's historical priorities and began to advocate civil rights legislation.[2] Many racial conservatives interpreted Truman's civil rights policies as a sign that their ultimate concern—the preservation of a racially segregated South—ranked below the priorities of satisfying blacks and organized labor in the national Democratic party. Ultraconservative white Democrats bolted and organized a makeshift regional political device—the States' Rights Party, commonly known as the Dixiecrats—in an unsuccessful effort to win enough southern electoral college votes to deny the White House to the Democrats. Almost three-fourths of southern white voters had backed President Franklin D. Roosevelt in 1944, but only 50 percent of them voted Democratic in 1948. The Democrats' white losses were permanent. Not since 1944 has a Democratic presidential candidate drawn a landslide majority from southern whites.

In 1948 Democratic losses among southern whites did not produce Republican gains. For the southerners most concerned about preserving white supremacy, New Yorker Thomas Dewey, the Republican candidate, was no better than Truman. The "leaders" of the southern Republican party were "neither politically influential nor politically important people" at this time.[3] Dewey made no effort to campaign in the South and polled only 26 percent of the 1948 presidential vote.

Matters changed in 1952, when Republican leaders believed that a candidate-centered strategy focused on General Dwight Eisenhower's extraordinary appeal—"Ike" was the personification of a genial, non-threatening Republican—could attract conservative Democrats and in-

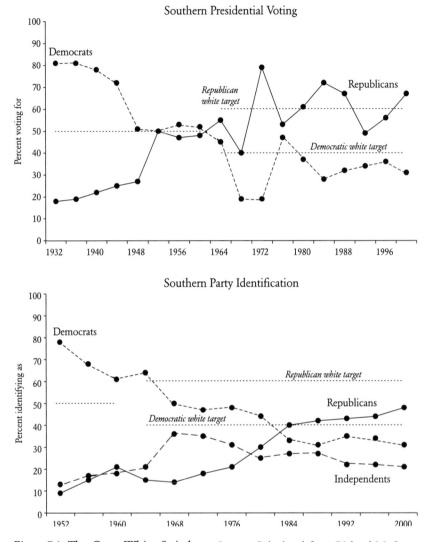

Figure 7.1 The Great White Switches. *Sources:* Calculated from Richard M. Scammon, ed., *America at the Polls* (Pittsburgh: University of Pittsburgh Press, 1965); National Election Study presidential-year election studies; CBS News/New York Times exit polls; and Voter News Service exit polls.

dependents and carry several southern states. Eisenhower was "a Texas native who accepted the Republican party's timid stance on civil rights" but who also came to his feet before a South Carolina audience when the band struck up "Dixie." The Eisenhower campaign "attracted strong support from the rising urban and suburban middle class," and the struggling minority party began to establish a precarious beachhead in the region's metropolitan areas.[4] The Republican presidential vote of southern whites rose to 50 percent in 1952.

Even without trying to convert southern whites into full-fledged Republicans, the Republicans scored modest gains in party identification during Eisenhower's presidency (see "Southern Party Identification" in Figure 7.1). Democrats declined from an overwhelming 78 percent in 1952 to a still robust 60 percent in 1960 among white southerners, while the percentage of whites willing to identify themselves as Republicans rose from 9 to 21 percent. A nearly nine-to-one advantage in party identification had fallen to a three-to-one edge.

Limited success in presidential elections offered little immediate help in building a southern Republican party. Most of the region's whites had no desire to replace their Democratic senators and representatives with Republicans. Quite the contrary. It was precisely the congressional Democrats, armed with leadership roles and committee chairmanships in the majority party, upon whom white voters depended to preserve traditional southern race relations as well as to continue the practical benefits of the New Deal.

Over the next four presidential elections the Republican vote fluctuated wildly, depending in part on the choices offered to southern voters. In 1964 Goldwater received 55 percent of the southern white vote, the best a Republican presidential candidate had ever done. Whereas Eisenhower and Richard Nixon (in 1960) had won substantial shares of the small black vote, Goldwater's prominence instantly transformed the southern Republican party into an organization uninterested in winning black support. "By abandoning civil rights in the name of states' rights," Numan V. Bartley and Hugh D. Graham concluded, "the Goldwater Republicans presumably sought . . . a general polarization of southern voters along racial lines."[5] The national Republican party repudiated its Lincoln heritage and rejected the aspirations of southern blacks for freedom and equality. By nominating Johnson, a

Texan who had challenged Congress to pass civil rights legislation, the national Democratic party embraced the civil rights movement. Blacks, north and south, overwhelmingly rejected the Republicans and shifted toward the Democrats.

With black voters permanently alienated, Republican candidates in the South have needed a massive landslide among white voters—approximately 60 percent is a useful rule of thumb—to prevail in contests involving two candidates. At a time when Republicans claimed the loyalties of merely one-fifth of southern whites, they needed three times that share of the white vote in order to defeat the Democrats' biracial strategy. Southern Democrats, provided they could unify around an acceptable candidate, now needed only two-fifths of the white vote to prevail. Figure 7.1 shows the Republicans' white target vote beginning in 1964 as a benchmark for measuring Republican performance. Goldwater carried the five Deep South states, where white hostility still prevented the vast majority of blacks from registering and voting, but he lost all six Peripheral South states, where many blacks could vote. In the first test of political strength after passage of civil rights legislation, the new Democratic biracial strategy prevailed over the new Republican white strategy.

Richard Nixon's second run for the presidency in 1968 featured a skillfully crafted southern strategy to gradually realign whites into the Republican party.[6] Those white southerners primarily opposed to racial change found their champion in George C. Wallace, the segregationist ex-governor of Alabama. Forfeiting those votes to Wallace, Nixon positioned himself to southern voters as opposed to segregation but favoring only voluntary integration. Nixon won 40 percent of the white vote (the rest was split between Wallace and liberal Democrat Hubert Humphrey), far short of the share necessary to carry all the southern states.

According to Dewey W. Grantham, President Nixon "saw in the South an unmatched opportunity to strengthen his political base and that of his party." Through a deliberate and calculated southern strategy, Nixon sought in 1972 to add the Wallace vote to his 1968 supporters. "Conceding the loss of black votes and those of white liberals, the new president reached out for the backing of white southerners, suburbanites, and ethnic workers troubled by the threat of racial equality and social disorder," Grantham observed. "He combined law and order appeals with economic conservatism."[7] Nixon's southern strategy worked perfectly against liberal Democrat George McGovern. The Republican polled four-fifths of the southern white vote, a feat not seen since the heyday of Franklin Roosevelt. Nixon's strategy had the potential to produce shifts in partisanship, but the Watergate scandal and his 1974 resignation in disgrace to avoid impeachment made the Republican party unattractive to southern whites.

During this volatile era the Democratic party continued to lose white support, but most of the defecting Democrats identified themselves as independents rather than as Republicans. The share of southern whites identifying with the Republican party in 1976—21 percent—was the same as in 1960, while independents had increased from 18 to 31 percent. In 1976 Georgia's Jimmy Carter ran for president as a Democratic outsider. Winning the nomination and the presidency as a new, "centrist" Democrat, Carter carried ten of the eleven southern states and appeared to blunt the Republican advance in the South. Four years later a landslide majority of white southerners judged Carter a political failure. In his place came Reagan, another former governor, whose message of confident conservatism resonated in a time of high unemployment and high inflation, of Americans held hostage by a foreign nation for more than a year. Reagan successfully executed the Republican southern strategy of mobilizing landslide white support.

REAGAN'S SOUTHERN ACHIEVEMENT

"The situation was ripe for the culmination of the Republican southern strategy," emphasized Bartley. The California Republican turned out to be the most popular president among southern whites since Franklin Roosevelt. Utilizing "anecdote over analysis," acting from "ideological principles when possible" but willing to "compromise when necessary," as Charles W. Dunn and J. David Woodward characterized his style, Reagan appealed to the emotions, aspirations, and interests of the region's conservative and moderate white voters. According to journalist Lou Cannon, who had covered Reagan's entire political career, "the ideological core of Reaganism" encompassed three priorities: "lower tax rates, a stronger military force and reduced government spending." These objectives resonated powerfully among conservative and moderate whites in the South. Deliberately avoiding any explanation of how his priorities might be simultaneously achieved, Reagan instead promoted "values that have a base in the collective subconscious of every American," according to Dunn and Woodward. Reagan "promised a new era of national renewal emphasizing traditional values—the dignity of work, love for family and neighborhood, faith in God, belief in peace through strength and a commitment to protect freedom as a legacy unique to America."[8]

In 1980 the Democratic and Republicans parties also differed in many important respects over the proper role of the federal government. "The Democratic party platform favored affirmative action, federally funded abortions, and busing, and it endorsed the Equal Rights Amendment to the point of denying party support to candidates who opposed the amendment and encouraging boycotts of states that refused to ratify it," Bartley noted, whereas "Reagan's Republican platform disavowed busing and abortion, ignored the Equal Rights Amendment, demanded prayer be allowed in the schools, and advocated family values." Throughout the campaign he emphasized "a visceral hatred of burgeoning federalism," of the ever-growing presence of federal laws, rules, and regulations in domestic affairs. "I would take the lead in getting the government off the *backs* of the people of the United States and turning you loose," promised Reagan. As a former Democrat who had switched to the Republican party late in his life, Reagan knew how to appeal to a southern white electorate that contained many born-and-bred Democrats. "Now I know what it's like to pull that Republican lever for the first time because I used to be a Democrat myself," Reagan would say. "But I can tell you—it only hurts for a minute." San Antonio Democrat Henry Cisneros acknowledged Reagan's appeal among southern blue-collar workers, a traditionally Democratic constituency: "Carter's hole card was that Reagan would be seen as a horrible alternative. But so far, he doesn't look so horrible. He goes out and talks to working people in language they can understand."[9]

Even to many Democrats President Carter was a tough sell. The 1980 election took place during "a recession, double-digit inflation and interest rates, and high unemployment, along with the Democratic party's usual morass of foreign policy problems." Reagan repeatedly lampooned Carter's performance in office and turned the contest into a referendum on the unpopular incumbent. He told a Dallas audience that Carter was "like the guy who can name you 50 parts of a car–he just can't drive it or fix it." He ridiculed the Georgian as a failed Democrat: "'When I look at what he has done in the last four years, you can see why he spent so little time in the [presidential] debate talking about his record,' Reagan told an enthusiastic crowd of about 10,000 in Houston's Tranquility Park. 'He has grown fond of referring to Franklin Roosevelt, Harry Truman and John Kennedy. There's one Democratic president he doesn't talk about, and that's Jimmy Carter.'" Toward the end of the campaign, Reagan's central theme was, in his words, "Jimmy Carter's demonstrated inability to govern our nation."[10]

Carter had been helped in 1976 by the votes of some white southerners on the basis of regional pride, but this support had now gone soft. At a Reagan rally in Lowndes County, Mississippi, reporter Martin Schram asked a "clean-cut and well-dressed plant manager" how he had voted in 1976. "Carter–I ain't going to lie about it," replied the thirty-year-old white man. "I voted for him because he was a good old southern boy. But he just didn't have it." By October Reagan operatives were trying to induce "wholesale defections among the white conservatives who voted for Mr. Carter on the basis of sectional loyalty." After the election Representative Carroll A. Campbell Jr., of South Carolina, who along with Lee Atwater had directed Reagan's efforts in the South, summed up the change. "It appeared to me that the regional pride issue had kind of paled," Campbell observed. "People felt that their national pride had been hurt, and in the end it's their national pride that counts the most."[11]

The "main issue of the campaign" was the president's "handling of the economy." In Mississippi Reagan claimed that Carter had "betrayed the people with an inflation rate that they hope they might get back down to 10 percent after it had risen to 18 percent earlier this year." His attack continued in Norfolk, Virginia. "A recession is when your neighbor loses his job," Reagan told a large crowd, "a depression is when you lose yours, and recovery will be when Jimmy Carter loses his." Campaigning in Greenville, South Carolina, and St. Petersburg, Florida, Reagan asserted that "nowhere has his inability to handle the job of the Presidency been more apparent than in his handling of the American economy" and further charged that "Mr. Carter has not answered for the economic misery he's caused." Southern white voters responded favorably to Reagan's emphasis on economic matters. Only 18 percent believed their family financial situation had improved in the year before the election, while 38 percent thought their economic situation had worsened. Reagan's victory was enthusiastically welcomed in the southern business community. "People were looking for new leadership," said the head of a Charlotte, North Carolina, realty company. "Inflation was rampant, interest rates were high, the economy was running out of control and people were just fed up with it."[12]

Reagan also attacked Carter's foreign policy. Its weakness was dramatically symbolized by the Americans held hostage in Iran during 1980. In addition, nearly three-fourths of southern white voters believed, with Reagan, that the United States should be more forceful in its dealings with the Soviet Union. According to Texas governor William Clements, a Republican poll found that "88 percent of the Texas voters wanted the United States to be in a position of military superiority" over the Soviet Union, and "they know Carter hasn't kept us there."[13]

Reagan especially sought to mobilize and win the votes of white religious conservatives—a new force in Republican politics. John C. Green, Lyman A. Kellstedt, Corwin E. Smidt, and James L. Guth argue convincingly for the inclusion of "religion" as a "standard feature of analysis of southern politics."[14] The southern white conservative religious movement is composed primarily of evangelical Protestants and sizable numbers of conservative Catholics, who believe that secular forces are undermining their way of life and who seek to advance their beliefs, values, and interests through partisan politics.

In 1976 many conservative Christians had voted for Carter, a devout, "born-again" Baptist, but his performance in office disappointed many of them. They were eager to embrace Reagan, who, as Dunn and Woodward noted, "attended church only on the rarest of occasions and certainly never Sunday School and absolutely never with a Bible in his hand."[15] Yet on the issues of primary concern to the religious conservatives—opposition to abortion and support for prayer in public schools—the Republican platform and candidate were much closer to their own views than were Carter and the Democratic party.

Reagan appeared at Liberty Baptist College in Lynchburg, Virginia, to address the National Religious Broadcasters Association. "I would be absolutely opposed to a state-mandated prayer," he told the group, "but I have always thought that a voluntary, nonsectarian prayer was perfectly proper, and I don't think we should have expelled God from the classroom." He also met with the influential Rev. Jerry Falwell, the head of the Moral Majority, who worked hard for Reagan's victory. "One of his [Falwell's] commandments to his fellow ministers," the *Washington Post* reported, was to "get them saved, baptized and registered." At a Reagan rally in Mississippi, a fundamentalist minister prayed for Reagan's election while "Reagan prayed with him, carefully humble but appreciative." During the campaign, the *New York Times* reported, "Thousands of fundamentalist Protestant churches became political centers for Mr. Reagan and other Republican candidates, as politicized evangelical groups moved into the political arena."[16]

By becoming an integral part of the southern Republican electoral coalition, the religious right helped the party solve its problem of attracting landslide majorities of white voters. As Warren Tompkins, an experienced party strategist in South Carolina, later explained, "Until the religious conservative movement broke its behavioral Democratic patterns and started voting in large part in Republican primaries and for Republican candidates, we weren't winning elections in the South."[17]

Reagan's version of core American values did not, to say the least, emphasize the civil rights of minorities. Reagan was one of the few prominent northern Republicans who had opposed both the Civil Rights Act and the Voting Rights Act. He told David Broder in 1966 that "he was 'in complete sympathy with the goals and purposes' of the 1964 and 1965 civil rights acts, but opposed their enactment because they had 'legislative flaws and faults and parts of them were, in my view, unconstitutional.'" There are, of course, abundant reasons to doubt Reagan's "complete sympathy" with the goals of the civil rights movement. Reagan "may not have been antiblack, possibly didn't have any hostility at all toward people of color, but to him, those people were simply none of government's business and none of his business of politics," Richard Reeves believed. "When Reagan talked of civil rights, a rare thing for him, and of governing and the role of government, he seemed to be describing America in the late 1920s." As Dorothy Gilliam concluded, "Reagan's strategy is basically a negative one: to avoid arousing blacks to vote against him, to neutralize the black vote."[18]

Indeed, Reagan made inroads among southern racial conservatives on the basis of his objections to the civil rights acts. "Reagan avidly courted the support of white southerners during the mid-1960s," observed Cannon, "and he consistently refused during his abortive campaign for the presidency in 1968 to criticize George Wallace's segregationist advocacies." In turn, southern Republican leaders perceived Reagan as a valuable ally. According to Lewis Chester, Godfrey Hodgson, and Bruce Page, "the [white] South was his natural constituency." Reagan, they explained, "was, quite literally, adored by the party's rank and file and by many of its chieftains everywhere below the Mason-Dixon line. Thurmond himself had been a Reagan fan ever since the Goldwater campaign. 'I love the man,' he would say. 'He's the best hope we've got.'"[19]

Reagan made his case against civil rights legislation not in the pugnacious, arm-waving, and belligerent style of Wallace but in a polished and low-key manner. "In his years in the California governorship and in his three presidential campaigns, Reagan showed that he could use coded language with the best of them, lambasting welfare queens, busing, and affirmative action as the need arose," observed Dan T. Carter. "But even when he lashed out against the 'liberals,' he always sounded like an avuncular uncle reluctantly scolding because he saw no alternative."[20]

Reagan began his postconvention presidential campaign in Mississippi. At the urging of Mississippi representative Trent Lott, he visited the Neshoba County Fair, in the small town of Philadelphia, "a community where three civil rights workers were slain with the complicity of local police officials in 1964." Rejecting his pollster's emphatic advice to cancel his scheduled appearance in a town that symbolized murderous white racism, the Republican candidate "was greeted by thunderous applause and chants of 'We want Reagan' from about 10,000 fairgoers." Just as Goldwater had drawn virtually all-white audiences in the Deep South in 1964, so Reagan was greeted by a "crowd almost entirely made up of whites." He did not let them down. "I believe in states' rights," Reagan said. "I believe in people doing as much as they can at the private level." The Republican presidential candidate promised that, if elected, "he would reorder priorities and 'restore to states and local governments the power that properly belongs to them.'" As Cannon observed, "The visual statement on television the next day was a sea of white faces at the Neshoba Fair with Reagan's words floating above them."[21] The Mississippi event powerfully communicated Reagan's sympathies and electoral targets in the rural Deep South.

Soon after, on the op-ed page of the *Washington Post,* veteran civil rights leader and former Georgia representative Andrew Young explained "why code words like 'states' rights' and symbolic places like Philadelphia, Miss., leave me cold." He recalled Martin Luther King Jr. "standing on the Neshoba County Courthouse steps in 1966, describing how the bodies of the slain civil rights workers had been found buried in a dam two years earlier. He said, 'the murderers of Goodman, Chaney and Schwerner are no doubt within the range of my voice.' And from the white mob guarding the courthouse door, someone called out, 'Ya, damn right. We're right here behind you.'" Young continued: "Remembering that day in Mississippi, I'm obsessed with a chilling question: what 'states' rights' would candidate Reagan revive?" Because "these code words have been the electoral language of Wallace, Goldwater, and the Nixon southern strategy," he emphasized, "one must ask: Is Reagan saying that he intends to do everything he can to turn the clock back to the Mississippi justice of 1964? Do the powers of the state and local governments include the right to end the voting rights of black citizens?"[22]

The Reagan campaign, of course, vehemently denied any such motivations or intentions, but a message of white racial solidarity had been sent. Presumably many southerners, white and black, did not need a scorecard to distinguish the opposing sides. Three months later Reagan carried Mississippi with an estimated 62 percent of the white vote and virtually none of the black vote. Reagan's popularity among whites, Carter argues, "allowed him to forgo the grubby manipulation of racial appeals." A master in applying "racism-free conservative principles to each case at hand," Reagan reinforced the reputation of the southern Republican party as a respectable version of the newest "white people's party" for many conservatives and some moderate whites.[23]

On the key question—whose side are you on?—there was never any doubt about how Reagan was perceived. Goldwater and Wallace supporters could connect with Reagan's emphasis on states' rights and sympathies with racial conservatives. Wallace himself endorsed Carter in 1980, just as he had done in 1976. Yet many of Wallace's "former supporters," the *New York Times* reported, were active in Reagan's campaign "across the South." As Charles Snider, Wallace's national campaign chairman in 1972, put it, "We're looking for a conservative individual for President, and we don't care what party he runs on."[24]

As president, Reagan would reluctantly sign the twenty-five-year extension of the Voting Rights Act in 1982, oppose but finally accept a federal holiday honoring Dr. Martin Luther King Jr., try to preserve tax-exempt status for private schools that practiced racial discrimination in admissions, shift the government's position on affirmative action questions, and veto the Civil Rights Restoration Act of 1988. "Ronald Reagan, the most popular president among white Americans since Franklin D. Roosevelt," concludes Michael Dawson, "was for African Americans the most despised president since early in the century." At the close of his political career, "by a three-to-one majority" blacks "agreed with the statement that the president was a racist."[25]

And yet Reagan's appeal to conservative southern whites went far beyond his ability to utter racial codewords in a calm manner. After the election some southern Democrats believed that "the ideology that Mr. Reagan held out to the nation this year [was] tailor-made for the Southern majority on matters concerning the family, religion and military strength."[26] Reagan's priorities appealed to southern conservatives on many grounds. Those who wanted a smaller federal government and less burdensome taxation could find promise in Reagan; voters concerned with weakness abroad might see Reagan as someone who could restore American stature. The newly activated religious right, concerned about abortion, school prayer, and family values, found Reagan considerably more supportive and sympathetic than the "born-again" Jimmy Carter; and members of the business community, disillusioned with the state of the economy and Carter's ineffectual leadership, enthusiastically followed Reagan. The Republican presidential candidate emphasized these themes while campaigning in the South before virtually all-white audiences.

Southern white voters rewarded Reagan—and his immediate successor, George Bush—with three consecutive landslide majorities. In 1980 Reagan won 61 percent of the southern white vote. He executed the Republican strategy of sweeping the conservative whites while also winning a majority of the moderate whites. He even attracted support from a sizable minority of white liberals. For reasons that are abundantly clear, he won very little support from blacks. Reagan's defeat of Carter's biracial coalition was a turning point in modern southern politics—conservative and moderate whites preferred a former California governor over a sitting president from the South.

It is one thing to win an election; it is quite another to remain strong while governing. "Reagan's policies at home and abroad were popular among white southerners and received considerable support from southern Democrats in Congress," writes Grantham. "This regional response involved more than racial considerations. White southerners generally liked Reagan's emphasis on lower taxes, economic growth, reduction of federal regulatory activities, resistance to redistributive welfare programs, opposition to a 'predatory' Soviet Union, and insistence upon the importance of patriotism and traditional values and institutions." Although he delivered more rhetoric than legislation, Reagan's "symbolic and timely identification with the key positions of religious conservatives, such as opposition to abortion and support for school prayer, enabled him to win their support, but without producing very many substantive results." By capturing the allegiance of the religious right, Reagan dramatically expanded the conservative base of the Republican party. In 1984 Reagan's vote soared to 72 percent among southern whites.[27] Running against Walter Mondale, a liberal Democrat who announced his intention to raise taxes to balance the budget, the incumbent president countered with the argument that cutting taxes was the best way to (eventually) balance the budget. Reagan captured 88 percent of conservative southern whites and 63 percent of moderate southern whites.

As his presidency ended Reagan was extraordinarily popular among whites. Southern whites respected Reagan, who embodied many qualities they found admirable in a national leader. In 1988 huge majorities of southern whites perceived Reagan as a "strong leader" who was "decent," "moral," "knowledgeable," and "honest." Two-thirds felt "inspired" by him, and slightly smaller majorities said Reagan made them feel "proud" and "hopeful." Over half believed that he "cared" for them. "The Democrats left the South a long time ago," a 57-year old North Carolina AT & T supervisor told a reporter for the *Raleigh News and Observer* in 1988. Although he was a registered Democrat in

Alamance County, he had not supported a Democratic presidential candidate since voting for Lyndon Johnson in 1964. He was high on the Republicans. "I think Reagan restored confidence in the country," because
he "made you proud to be an American, whether you agree with his policies or not."[28]

The GOP's critical test of landslide white strength was the 1988 election of Vice President Bush, who campaigned as a Reagan protégé. Most
importantly for the Republicans, voters such as the North Carolina supervisor perceived a crucial connection between Reagan and Bush: "I
think he's trained Bush pretty well."[29] Using television advertising,
phone banks, and direct mail linking Massachusetts liberal Democrat
Michael Dukakis with a wide variety of liberal policies, Bush carried
every state in the South. During the 1980s, Republican presidential candidates averaged 67 percent of the southern white vote while holding
their Democratic opponents to 32 percent. Never before in southern
history had Republican presidential candidates done so well among
whites in three consecutive elections.

Southern presidential elections during the 1990s, however, have
demonstrated that landslide Republican victories cannot be taken for
granted. Bush's retreat from his unequivocal promise not to raise taxes
produced a challenge within his own party for the 1992 nomination. In
addition to the weaknesses of Bush and Robert Dole as effective campaigners, the Republican share of the white vote declined from its earlier
peaks because a third-party candidate, Ross Perot, disrupted the coalition and because Democratic nominee Bill Clinton campaigned as a
moderate, centrist politician who mixed liberal positions on some issues
with conservative positions on others.

Even so, Bush and Dole still ran ahead of Clinton among white
southerners. The Republicans won fourteen of the twenty-two presidential contests in the southern states in 1992 and 1996. Indeed, had the
Republicans won only half of the Perot vote in the two elections, their
candidates would have averaged about three-fifths of the white vote—
their regional target. Clinton managed to split the South (winning four
of the eleven states in each election, much as Eisenhower had done in
1952) but failed to revive Democratic fortunes among southern whites.
The Arkansas Democrat's share of the white vote (35 percent) was only
three points higher than Mondale and Dukakis had averaged during the

Republican heyday. Over the five elections from 1980 to 1996, Democratic presidential candidates averaged 87 percent of the southern black vote while Republicans averaged only 11 percent. In the 2000 presidential election, George W. Bush returned his party to the level of landslide white support common during the 1980s by carrying 67 percent of the southern white vote. Despite his message of "compassionate conservatism," he won merely 8 percent of the vote cast by southern African-American voters. By contrast, Al Gore attracted the support of less than one-third (31 percent) of southern whites but won 91 percent among southern blacks.

In the 1980–1988 presidential elections Reagan and Bush averaged 84 percent of the conservative white vote and 59 percent of the moderate white vote, groups that together accounted for over four-fifths of southern white voters. Republican losses, as in 1976, or very narrow victories, as in 1992 and 1996, have occurred when the Republican candidates failed to draw impressive support from moderate whites. The different patterns of support for Republican presidential candidates among white conservatives, white moderates, white liberals, and blacks suggest a strategy for exploring the partial partisan realignment of the southern electorate. Liberal whites have continued to support Democratic presidential candidates and have remained, for the most part, Democrats. Blacks reentered the southern electorate largely as Democrats in the 1960s, and they have accounted for increasingly large segments of the region's Democrats. Because these groups have remained pillars of support for the Democratic party, we shall set them aside. To understand the rise of the Republicans as a competitive political party in the region it is crucial to examine the political behavior of conservatives and moderates, the two groups of white voters who have shown the most support for Republican presidential candidates.

THE REALIGNMENT OF SOUTHERN WHITE CONSERVATIVES

The Republican party's primary realignment targets have been, of course, those white southerners who think of themselves as conservatives.[30] Their realignment has given the Republican party its largest base of reliable support. The erosion of southern Democratic conservatism started during the New Deal and accelerated when the national Democratic party began to champion civil rights. By 1968, merely half of southern white conservatives still thought of themselves as Democrats (see the top half of Figure 7.2). Defections from the region's traditional majority party, however, failed to produce commensurate gains for the southern Republican party: only 24 percent of southern white conservatives were Republicans. President Nixon's southern strategy during his first term enticed more conservative whites to leave the Democratic party, but his resignation in disgrace severely embarrassed and discredited the Republicans. For most southern conservatives the Republican party had not yet become an attractive or useful institution, one through which they could effectively advance their political interests. In 1976 only 30 percent of conservative white southerners were Republicans.

Reagan's first major impact on southern partisanship was to realign conservative whites. "Reagan's popularity," Broder observed in 1986, "has created a real opportunity for political realignment of the region."[31] During the Reagan presidency identification with the Republican party soared among conservative southern whites, most of whom shared his values, concerns, and priorities.[32] Reagan's appearances on the ballot, as well as Bush's 1988 campaign, were associated with sizable increases in Republican identification among southern white conservatives. Only 40 percent of southern white conservatives were Republicans in 1980 when Reagan defeated Carter. Eight years later, 60 percent of the region's conservative whites thought of themselves as Republicans—a 50 percent increase in identification. The massive realignment of conservative southern whites into the Republican party occurred exactly when, in theory, it should have happened—during the administration of the most popular conservative Republican president in the second half of the twentieth century. Southern conservatives had finally experienced a Republican president with whom they could proudly identify. Reagan was warmly approved by 86 percent of southern white conservatives in the 1980–1988 period.

Among many white conservatives repeated votes for Republican presidential candidates, reinforced by successful governing, presumably severed their attachments of interest or sentiment with the Democratic party. Through his principal issues, performance in office, and persuasive leadership style, Reagan effectively "sold" conservative white south-

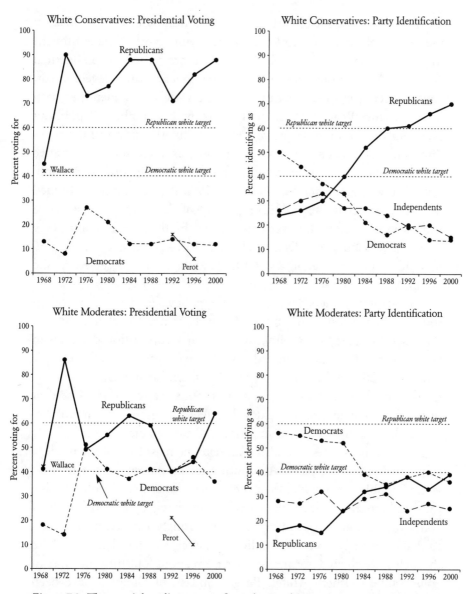

Figure 7.2 The partial realignment of southern whites. *Sources:* Calculated from Comparative State Elections Project; National Election Study presidential-year election studies; CBS News/New York Times exit polls; and Voter News Service exit polls.

erners on the Republican party as the institution best suited to advance their political interests. Most conservative white voters finally brought their partisanship in line with their voting preferences in presidential elections. Even more important for Republican party development, larger percentages of southern white conservatives have identified with the GOP since Reagan left office. In 1992, with incumbent Republican president Bush on the defensive because of the slowdown in the economy and his broken promise to oppose tax increases, conservative southern whites were still three times more likely to identify as Republicans than as Democrats. Even with the 1996 Republican ticket headed by the lackluster Robert Dole, 66 percent of the region's conservative white voters called themselves Republicans. By the 2000 elections, they preferred Republicans to Democrats by 70 to 14 percent, a margin of 56 percentage points—the biggest GOP advantage ever observed in the South.

Conservative leaders have long set the policy agendas of the modern southern Republican party. Robert Steed, Laurence Moreland, and Tod Baker's 1984 survey of Republican state party convention delegates in six southern states documented conservative saturation of the party leadership. Ninety-four percent of the southern Republican party activists described themselves as some sort of "conservative." Only 4 percent of the party convention delegates described themselves as "middle-of-the-road," and merely 2 percent as some sort of "liberal."[33]

Conservative whites now also dominate the mass base of the modern southern Republican party. Accounting for 64 percent of the region's white Republicans in 1996, their preferences about public policy define the southern Republican party's center of gravity. The worldview of conservative southern Republicanism is strongly colored by partisanship and ideology. Every Republican presidential candidate from 1972 through 1996 elicited warm responses from about four-fifths or more of conservative southern whites. Reagan and Newt Gingrich have been their political heroes. Ninety-eight percent of the region's conservative Republican voters held a favorable impression of Reagan in 1988, and 85 percent of them were favorably inclined toward Gingrich in 1996. They loathed President Bill Clinton, 83 percent regarding him with either hostility or indifference. Many conservative Republicans see the modern Democratic party as an alien institution led by politicians reso-lutely unsympathetic to their beliefs, values, and priorities.[34]

The policy preferences of conservative southern Republicans merit exploration.[35] Their worldview starts with a highly developed sense of personal responsibility for one's own economic well-being. The vast ma-jority think that individuals themselves—acting alone or as part of a fam-ily—should be mainly responsible for finding employment and provid-ing a good standard of living for themselves and their families. When they are asked whether "the government in Washington should see to it that every person has a job and a good standard of living" or if "the gov-ernment should just let every person get ahead on their own," the im-portance of individualism becomes clear. Eighty-one percent of the re-gion's conservative Republicans place responsibility for "getting ahead" on the individuals themselves, while only 7 percent believe that it is pri-marily the responsibility of the federal government to see that individu-als have "a job and a good standard of living." Conservative whites ac-cept the need for welfare programs to handle temporary losses of income, but they believe that long-term welfare programs violate the in-dividualistic philosophy, are unfair to taxpayers, and are harmful—in the long run—to the recipients. Not surprisingly, 97 percent of the conserva-tive Republicans supported the welfare reform program that passed in 1996.

Most conservative Republicans oppose the growing size and cost of the federal government's activities. The overarching appeal of the mod-ern Republican party for many conservative southern whites is grounded in its rhetorical insistence upon minimizing the scope of the federal government to regulate the activities of law-abiding individuals and businesses. Goldwater, Nixon, Reagan, Gingrich, and countless other Republican politicians have called for downsizing the federal gov-ernment, reducing income tax rates, and allowing citizens more choice in decisionmaking, while portraying Democratic politicians as funda-mentally opposed to these objectives. As Republican Mike Huckabee put it in an interview with a *Washington Times* reporter in 1995: "Arkan-sans may not be aware of each item in the House Republicans 'Contract with America,'" he says, "but they understand that it promises less gov-ernment."[36] Most conservative southern Republicans believe that they bear an excessive burden of taxation. In 1996 74 percent of conservative Republicans thought that they paid "more than the right amount in taxes," and these whites presumably constituted a receptive audience for the Republican message of reducing income tax rates. Most believed that the government has taken on too many problems better left to individuals themselves to resolve, and that much of their tax money is wasted. Two-thirds preferred to cut government services rather than to increase taxes to finance more spending. Only 40 percent of conservative Republicans wanted to increase spending on public education.

It is one thing to support a smaller role for the federal government, but it is another thing entirely to reject the need for a strong government to handle the economy. Yet that was the position of two-thirds of conservative southern Republicans when asked whether "a strong government" was needed to handle a complex economy or whether the "free market could handle the economy without governmental interference." Reliance on the free market extended to international trade: 65 percent did not want to limit imported goods. On economic issues, therefore, southern Republicans view themselves as overtaxed to support many governmental activities they believe are unnecessary and unwarranted.

Conservative Republicans have definite views about governmental priorities. In 1996 one-third believed that handling the breakdown in family values was the most important priority of the new administration. Twenty-six percent wanted to reduce the size of the federal government, and another 15 percent thought that reducing taxes on the middle class should be the most important priority of the federal government. Few conservative Republicans believed that the priorities of the federal government should be keeping the economy healthy (14 percent) or improving education, health care, Medicare, and Social Security (13 percent). They wanted a considerably smaller federal presence in their lives.

While accepting integration as their preferred form of race relations, conservative southern Republicans resisted governmental efforts to promote racial change.[37] Sixty percent were warm toward blacks as a group, and nearly 90 percent were enthusiastic about Colin Powell, the nation's most distinguished African-American military leader. However, a large majority was hostile or indifferent to Jesse Jackson, the civil rights leader, and only one in sixteen conservative southern Republicans supported policies designed solely to "help" blacks. According to the 1996 National Election Study survey, substantial majorities of the conservative white Republicans believed it was not the responsibility of the federal government to see that blacks are treated fairly in employment. They thought that too much effort had already been made to push equality in the nation, and they overwhelmingly rejected preferences for "women and minorities" in hiring decisions. Most southern Republicans oppose governmentally mandated change on nearly all of the controversial issues separating the races. It is hardly surprising that few blacks identify with the modern southern Republican party.

Many conservative southern whites were originally attracted into the Republican party because of its conservatism on economic and racial issues, but during the 1980s Reagan brought into the party large numbers of conservatives associated with the religious right. "The religious right provides voters for the [Republican] party," Glenn H. Utter and John W. Storey have observed, "while the party supports evangelicals on issues such as abortion, pornography, prayer in the schools, and 'family values.'"[38] These Republicans have different priorities and have sometimes exhibited a dogmatic and uncompromising style of debate about matters of right and wrong behavior that can bitterly divide local and state Republican parties.

To gauge the importance of religious conservatism in the Republican party, we have classified conservative white voters according to their self-placement on a 1996 exit poll question, "Do you consider yourself part of the religious right political movement?" Forty-five percent of white conservative Republican voters said they were part of the religious right movement. Among the issues that religious right leaders have emphasized, the most controversial, divisive, and intractable policy question has been whether a woman should have the legal right to an abortion. The abortion issue represents the greatest philosophical contradiction among southern conservative Republicans, who ordinarily seek to minimize governmental interference with private decisions. A majority of conservative southern Republicans believe that abortions should be either always illegal (30 percent) or mostly illegal (40 percent). When the relatively secular conservatives are separated from those who identify with the religious right, the nightmarish intraparty politics of

the abortion issue becomes clear: 89 percent of the religious right conservatives want abortions to be either entirely or mostly illegal, while a
slight majority of the secular conservatives prefer that abortions be always or mostly legal.

Finally, more than half of the conservative southern Republicans
sampled in the 1996 poll rejected the notion of tolerating moral standards that differed from their own, while less than a third were willing to
be tolerant of other moral standards. Presumably such rigidity increases
when the basis for one's moral beliefs rests upon interpretations of revealed truth. From the perspective of sincerely believing conservative
Christians, standing up for one's beliefs in the political arena makes perfect sense: "Let me tell you the craziest statement a person can make:
We need to keep religion out of politics," asserted one southern Christian Coalition supporter in 1996. "If a person is trying to live for the
Lord, then their life should be dominated in all areas by that principle,
politics included."[39] Not all religious right conservatives would express
themselves so bluntly, but such beliefs have probably motivated many
like-minded individuals to view the southern Republican party as their
political instrument. However, it is just this sort of view, expressed in
dogmatic and uncompromising language, that has prevented many
other white southerners from embracing the Republican party.

Not all southern Republicans—an understatement—have welcomed
the religious right into the party. "I just feel like all these preachers don't
have any business getting involved in this stuff," commented one Georgia Republican. "I'm still one of those types who believe that church
and state ought to be separated." Another Republican was skeptical
about the impact of the religious right. "I think they [the Christian Co-
alition] are like organized labor," he commented. "They are thought to
have a whole lot more strength than they do. Their role has been over-
stated. The perception of their power has given them power."[40] The entry of religious right activists into the Republican party has generated
countless battles over local, state, and national priorities.

In the metropolitan South the realignment of conservative southern
whites has been especially pronounced. Seventy-one percent of metropolitan white conservative voters were Republicans while only 10 percent were Democrats. Moreover, the bulk of urban conservative Republicans—61 percent—were not part of the religious right political

movement. Rural conservative whites in 1996 had also realigned into the Republican party, but the GOP advantage, 59 to 19 percent, was considerably smaller than in the metropolitan areas. The religious right contributed mightily to the conservative realignment in the region's rural areas, accounting for 57 percent of conservative white Republicans.

In one policy area after another, conservative whites set the tone of the southern Republican party. Conservative white Republicans, however, do not constitute a majority of voters in any southern state. There are some congressional districts—chiefly suburban or mixed-suburban rural districts with large white majorities—where conservative Republicans do represent voting majorities. However, in all states and most congressional districts, conservative Republicans are a minority of the active electorate. It is useful to keep their unique worldview in mind as we consider the partisan tendencies of southern white moderates, a crucial component of the southern electorate. The challenge for southern Republicans, saturated with a conservative base and conservative leaders, is to develop support among the much larger number of southern voters who do not completely share their worldview.

THE DEALIGNMENT OF MODERATE SOUTHERN WHITES

Important as the conservative realignment has been, conservatives make up only a sizable minority of the region's electorate—43 percent of southern white voters and 34 percent of all southern voters in 1996. Even the complete political mobilization of white conservatives would still leave Republican candidates far short of the three-fifths share of the white vote necessary to win two-candidate statewide elections in the South. The Republican party's continuing imperative, therefore, has been to increase its strength among moderate white southerners, who also make up 43 percent of the region's white voters and (rounding up) 35 percent of the entire active electorate. To become a genuine majority in the southern electorate, Republicans would need to realign moderate whites while retaining the loyalties of conservative whites. Attracting moderate whites into the Republican party—and keeping them there—has proven much more difficult than realigning white conservatives.

Over the past three decades, moderate white southerners have been favorably disposed toward most Republican and southern Democratic nominees for president. Moderates liked Nixon (1972), Ford (1976), Reagan (1980, 1984, and 1988), and Bush (1988 and 1992), as well as such centrist *southern* Democrats as Carter (1976 and 1980) and Clinton (1992 and 1996). However, the two most visible national Republican leaders in 1996, Gingrich and Dole, were in no position to attract southern white moderates into the Republican party. Indeed, their prominence as party leaders may well have repelled or weakened the attachments of southern white moderates to the GOP.

Reagan accelerated the partisan dealignment of moderate whites (see the bottom half of Figure 7.2). He neutralized the southern Democratic party's longstanding advantage in party identification. In 1968 55 percent of moderate white southerners were Democrats while only 15 percent were Republicans. Majorities of the moderates remained Democrats during the next twelve years, and as late as 1980 only 24 percent were Republicans. Reagan's performance in office, however, pleased moderate white southerners, prompting many to break with the Democratic party. From 1980 to 1988 Democratic identification dropped from 52 to 35 percent, while Republican identification increased to 34 percent. As Reagan's presidency ended, the Democratic edge among southern white moderates had narrowed to a single percentage point—a tremendous achievement in a region where few white moderates had ever felt close to the Republican party. Nonetheless, Reagan did not convert most of the moderates into Republicans. In 1988 an immense gap remained between the 70 percent of moderate southern whites who were warmly disposed toward Reagan and the 34 percent who considered themselves Republicans.

Bush won 59 percent of the southern white moderate vote in 1988 but collapsed to 41 percent in 1992. Clinton followed with 39 percent, and Reform party candidate Ross Perot won 21 percent among southern white moderates. According to the 1992 exit polls, moderate white voters in the South continued to be evenly divided in partisanhip, with each party claiming the loyalty of 38 percent. President Bush's defeat left Senator Dole of Kansas and Representative Robert Michael of Illinois as the leaders of the national Republican party. Neither of these northern Republicans was remotely capable of envisioning, much less leading, a partisan realignment of white moderates in the South. The Republican party needed a national leader who could build upon Reagan's achievement of appealing simultaneously to conservative *and* moderate whites.

Filling this vacuum of national Republican leadership in the fall of 1994 was the dynamic and bold new leader of the House Republicans, Newt Gingrich.[41] Untested as a national leader, Gingrich represented an overwhelmingly white and largely middle-to-upper-income suburban district in Atlanta, Georgia. Gingrich had arrived in Washington in 1979, when Democrats still dominated southern congressional elections. Ambitious to transform the House Republicans into a majority party, he rapidly became the main leader of programmatic conservatives who wanted to wrest control of the party from the older moderate Republicans. In 1989 Gingrich was elected minority whip, and in 1993 he signaled his intention to lead the Republicans after the 1994 elections, a move that hastened Michael's retirement from Congress.

A key part of his national strategy required Republicans to eliminate the immense surplus of southern seats that House Democrats had enjoyed throughout the twentieth century. This ambitious goal was feasible if and when the Republican presidential preferences of southern whites could be transferred to Republican congressional candidates. In 1994 Gingrich and his aides devised the strategy, recruited many of the candidates, raised much of the money, and suggested aggressive tactics for congressional candidates to build upon the opportunities that had been created in the southern electorate during the previous decade. Angry and dissatisfied southern conservatives, 86 percent of whom disliked President Clinton, turned out in large numbers in 1994. According to exit polls, conservatives made up 47 percent of southern white voters, a substantial increase from their share of 38 percent in the 1992 elections. Eighty-four percent of southern white conservatives and 48 percent of southern white moderates voted for Republican congressional candidates, enough to yield a Republican majority of southern House seats. As a result of these gains, combined with those in the rest of the nation, Gingrich led the Republicans back into power in the House of Representatives for the first time in forty years. For better or for worse, the new Speaker emerged as the nation's most conspicuous Republican.

Gingrich was a hero among conservative white southerners, but his relentlessly partisan agenda, erratic judgment, and belligerent style alienated many southern white moderates. Gingrich recast the party in the image of the far more strident and aggressive conservatism of Barry Goldwater, and his ascendance gave Republican conservatism a sharpness that was markedly different in tone from Reagan's approach. The new Speaker was a polarizing politician who thought and acted in terms of either/or dichotomies: win/lose, good/evil, allies/enemies. His slashing debate style, eagerness to volunteer advice and opinions, and volatile public temperament bewildered, embarrassed, and irritated large segments of the public. Many blacks, as well as liberal and moderate whites, viewed Gingrich and his fellow Republicans as a mean-spirited collection of ideological zealots who were willing to shut down the government and take away accustomed benefits and services. "They're coming for the children," said Georgia congressman John Lewis in the debate over welfare reform. "They're coming for the poor. They're coming for the sick, the elderly, and the disabled." The message of some embarrassed House Republicans—"Tell Newt to shut up!"—resonated loudly outside Washington.[42]

Following the Republicans' unexpected congressional victory in 1994, Gingrich temporarily dislodged President Clinton as America's most important elected political leader. However, the new Speaker overreached when he tried to set the agenda in areas where the president's interpretation of the national interest conflicted with the views of the House Republican leadership. Completely inexperienced in the craft of legislating and concentrating their efforts upon an unrealistic and unachievable agenda, the House Republicans were unable to govern.[43] In the American system of "separated institutions *sharing* powers," it is against the grain of political reality for the Speaker of the House of Representatives rather than the president to establish the policy agenda of the national government.[44] It is especially difficult to do so with narrow House and Senate majorities and without the presidency. Only if Speaker Gingrich had somehow been able to assemble bipartisan two-thirds majorities in both the House and Senate to override presidential vetoes would it have been possible for him to defeat a president of the United States.

In the fall of 1995 President Clinton, not Speaker Gingrich and the House Republicans, won the political battle for the center of American politics. David Maraniss and Michael Weisskopf observed that Gingrich "was often astute at anticipating the consequences of various courses of action, but less adept at shaping events. On the shutdown [of the federal government], his missteps had so weakened him in the public eye and within his own rank-and-file that he was not in a good position to overcome members of his leadership team who pushed hardest to close the government, a policy that Gingrich privately opposed." Clinton then skillfully used his veto power to block Republican budget proposals, which twice led to the partial shutdown of the government. However the Republicans interpreted their electoral "mandate," it had not been to close the federal government. President Reagan's sunny, optimistic yet practical conservatism had been replaced by "a Newt Gingrich shut-down-the-government scowling conservatism," as commentator Larry Kudlow later put it.[45] Blessed with the unpopular Gingrich as his principal rival, Clinton reemerged as the champion of necessary government programs and services, the reasonable defender of "strong government" against the uncompromising, extremist Republican budget-cutters.

Gingrich's persona as well as his policies and actions repelled many southern white moderates. Seventy percent had viewed Reagan warmly in 1988, and 79 percent approved Clinton in 1996. By contrast, 64 percent of southern white moderate voters disliked Gingrich. The self-described "conservative revolutionary" was viewed unfavorably by 80 percent of the region's moderate white Democrats, 74 percent of moderate white independents, and even 35 percent of moderate white Republicans. Gingrich's unfavorable evaluations in 1996 placed him in close company with such politicians as Jesse Jackson, Edward Kennedy, George McGovern, the disgraced Richard Nixon (1976), Pat Buchanan, Pat Robertson, and Ross Perot, public figures who elicited more loathing and ridicule than admiration and respect from southern white moderates.

By displaying strong presidential leadership, Clinton had become useful to the many southern white moderates who wanted a forceful check against Gingrich-style Republicanism. Yet Clinton, too, had a major weakness among these voters: 63 percent viewed him as dishonest and untrustworthy. In the 1996 presidential election, President Clinton ran only one point ahead of Dole, 46 to 45 percent, among southern white moderates. If the southern Republican House Speaker could not draw more moderate whites into the Republican party, neither could the Democratic president from Arkansas lead many of them back into the Democratic party. Between 1992 and 1996 more southern white moderates abandoned the Republicans (5 percent) than joined the Democrats (2 percent). In 1996, according to the exit polls, Democrats had reopened a lead in partisan identification, 40 to 33 percent, among the region's white moderates. In the 2000 presidential campaign the Republican party's image among moderate white southerners was being reshaped by the "compassionate conservatism" of Texas governor George W. Bush. White moderates voted for Bush over Democrat Al Gore by the decisive margin of 64 to 36 percent, and slightly more of them (39 versus 36 percent) called themselves Republicans than Democrats. Neither party was close to a majority among this crucial group of voters.

The political worldview of southern white moderates contrasts sharply with that of the region's conservative white Republicans. Moderate southern whites are characterized by conservative *and* liberal tendencies; they are not polarized by party and ideology. As a group, 69 percent in 1996 were warm toward Democrats while only 49 percent liked Republicans; 57 percent were warm toward conservatives but only 41 percent were favorably disposed toward liberals. Their mixed ideological preferences make them an especially difficult group for conservative Republicans to realign. No policy matter better illustrates their divergent opinions than a question about government spending and services. When asked to place themselves on a scale anchored by the options of "the government should provide fewer services, even in areas such as health and education, in order to reduce spending," or the government should "provide many more services even if it means an increase in spending," moderate southern whites split into three equal subsets: 34 percent wanted fewer services, 33 percent wanted more, and 33 percent were in the middle.

Majorities of southern white moderates hold conservative views in some important areas. Most assume primary responsibility for providing a good standard of living for themselves and their families. Three-fifths of the moderates prefer less government, and a majority believe they pay too much in taxes. Majorities of white moderates support welfare reform and government efforts to prevent crime. Nearly four-fifths approve of the death penalty. Sixty-five percent of southern white moderates approve of a designated moment of silent prayer in public schools, while only 9 percent think prayer should never be allowed in public schools. About three of every five white moderates believe there should be no special programs to help blacks, and nine of every ten oppose preferential hiring practices. More than three of every five believe that equality is being pushed too much.

However, moderate southern whites do take liberal positions on other important issues. Sixty-three percent believe that a strong government is necessary to handle the economy. Three-fifths think that taking care of the economy and attending to Social Security, Medicare, public education, and health care should be the top priorities of the federal government, and more than three-fourths want to increase spending on public education. Nearly seven out of ten are favorably disposed toward the women's movement, and a smaller majority believe it is important to protect the environment even if more governmental regulation of behavior by private companies and individuals were required. Sixty percent want abortions to be always or mostly legal. Finally, 56 percent of southern white moderates are willing to tolerate moral standards different from their own. Thirty-six percent of the moderates hold qualified views about tolerance, and only 20 percent say they could not put up with different moral standards.

Because such ideological crosscurrents run through southern white moderates, a Republican party led by religious and secular conservatives is not an attractive institution for a majority of this group. In 1996 only one-third of white moderates identified as Republicans. These moderates, as would be expected, took conservative positions on more issues than did the rest of the moderates, but their views were not uniformly conservative. Large majorities of moderate Republicans believed a strong government is needed to handle the economy, were pro-choice on abortion, supported new laws to protect the environment, and favored increased spending for public schools. A plurality supported toleration of different moral standards. However, the moderates are clearly junior partners in the modern southern Republican party.

To attract more moderates into the party, Republican politicians and officeholders would need to emphasize matters they usually ignore or deemphasize. A more sympathetic understanding of issues that appeal to women and environmental groups, more nuanced positions on abortion, a greater sensitivity to the practical side of governing, and above all, perhaps, a greater concern for improving public education might help the Republicans with these groups. Republican success depends upon mixing their issue appeals–taking more liberal positions on some issues of relevance to moderate Republicans to broaden the base of their party while continuing to emphasize issues that motivate their conservative supporters. Just as successful southern Democrats have learned to campaign as centrists, mixing liberal and conservative positions under the constraints of public opinion, so, too, successful Republican politicians will need to learn to temper their conservatism with the practicalities of politics. This segment of the electorate will probably continue to be divided in partisanship unless events or political personalities emerge who can attract them into a new majority configuration of support.

The Republican party's attraction for moderate whites has differed sharply along metropolitan versus rural lines. Only in the metropolitan South have white moderates been neutralized as a Democratic asset. According to the 1996 exit polls, 37 percent of the white moderates who lived in metropolitan areas identified as Republicans, compared with 34 percent who called themselves Democrats. However, in the rural and small-town South, the Democratic party continued to hold a nearly two-to-one advantage over the Republican party, 50 to 26 percent, among white moderates.

Separating the party into its metropolitan and rural wings reveals the dilemmas as well as the opportunities confronting southern Republicans. In the metropolitan South Republican growth has been based on realigning the conservatives and dealigning the moderates. More than seven of every ten urban white conservatives are now Republicans, and most of them are *not* part of the religious right. However, Republicans cannot become a majority party in the metropolitan South by appealing only to conservatives. Among metropolitan whites in 1996 there were fewer conservatives than moderates (39 versus 44 percent), and moderate white Republicans only slightly outnumbered moderate white Democrats. For metropolitan white voters who identified themselves as Republicans, moderates and liberals made up 42 percent, secular conservatives accounted for 36 percent, and conservatives belonging to the religious right amounted to only 23 percent. In the metropolitan South the winning Republican formula is a party led by secular conservatives sensitive to the concerns of both religious conservatives and moderates. If the party is to expand in southern cities and suburbs, its growth potential lies in realigning white moderates.

Republican penetration of the rural South has followed a quite different path. It has been based primarily upon mobilizing conservatives, especially those associated with the religious right. "These southern rural folks are basically conservative, religious and believe in family values," South Carolinian Richard Quinn told Thomas Edsall of the *Washington Post* in 1988. "They really should be in the Republican party."[46] Nearly half (48 percent) of rural southern white voters in 1996 were conservatives, but fewer than three-fifths called themselves Republicans. In the rural South a majority (57 percent) of conservative white Republicans were members of the religious right political movement. However, in rural areas the Republicans have made little headway with moderate whites. In 1996 half remained Democrats, and only a quarter had become Republicans, a distribution similar to the pattern of the entire South before Reagan's presidency. Many rural southern Republicans practice an ultraconservative religious and cultural style of politics that severely diminishes the party's appeal to moderate whites everywhere. It is impossible for the Republicans to become a majority party if their candidates espouse the views of voters in the most traditional parts of the South and ignore the mix of issues that appeal to voters in the growing metropolitan areas.

A COMPETITIVE REPUBLICAN MINORITY

Repeated votes for Republican presidential candidates in the 1980s induced millions of southern whites to redefine their basic partisanship. Reagan's presidency changed the southern party system by making the Republican party socially respectable and practically useful for two-thirds of the white conservatives and one-third of the white moderates. As a consequence of the realignment of white conservatives and the dealignment of white moderates, Republicans outnumbered Democrats, 44 to 33 percent, among the region's white voters and made up 37 percent of all southern voters in 1996. The plurality party of the South's racial majority now has enough reliable partisans to support genuinely competitive Republican candidates for most Senate and many House seats.

United by their belief in personal responsibility for providing a good standard of living for themselves and their families, most white southern Republicans want less government in general. They want to earn decent salaries, keep most of what they make, and then spend, save, or invest their money according to their own priorities. Most believe they pay too much in taxes. They prefer fewer services from the federal government if additional taxes would be necessary to finance new or expanded programs. A majority even rejects the need for a strong government to handle the economy and is willing to rely upon impersonal market forces. Republicans accept integration as the preferred form of race relations, a change of immense importance from their support for strict segregation of the races during the 1960s. At the same time, large majorities of white southern Republicans take very conservative positions about *governmental* efforts to provide aid to racial minorities. Most do not believe that governmental programs should be specifically targeted to help blacks, overwhelmingly oppose preferential hiring practices for blacks, and take the view that there has been too much of a push toward equality in the country.

Controversies about abortion, tolerance of differing moral standards, and protection of the environment continue to divide southern white Republicans, who otherwise have much in common. The abortion issue especially splits the Republicans: 56 percent want abortion to be either always or mostly illegal, while 44 percent prefer abortion to be either mostly or always legal. Nearly half of the region's white Republicans are intolerant of moral standards that differ from their own conceptions of right and wrong. A plurality of southern white Republicans rejects more regulations to protect the environment.

Southern Republican candidates for the Senate and House of Representatives still face the problem of generating sufficient support from whites who do not think of themselves as members of the party. Republican positions resonate with majorities of the remaining whites about personal responsibility for earning a good standard of living, a preference for less government (at least in the abstract), a perception of paying more than the right amount in taxes, and resistance to further governmental efforts to produce more equality in society. However, there are clear political liabilities if Republican leaders try to govern exclusively from the right. The Republican party is hurt by its separation from majorities of the remaining southern whites in its preference for market forces to handle the economy, its reluctance to regulate the activities of businesses and private individuals to protect the environment, its strong opposition to legalized abortions, and its intolerance of different standards of morality.

The Republicans generally offer less government than majorities of the remaining white and black southerners want whenever their leaders express hostility or indifference toward governmental programs, such as Social Security, Medicare, and unemployment insurance, that try to respond to the dislocations and negative consequences of market forces operating in the economy. While most southerners do not think government should be primarily responsible for their standard of living, and while they do not support public welfare beyond a minimal period and for only a small number of children, most also do not want to abandon the security of a "strong government" to handle the economy. In addition, Republicans are skeptical about increased regulations to protect the environment. Most southerners who are not Republicans do not believe that market forces will automatically "solve" the problems generated through economic development. When Republicans fail to intervene, Democrats can portray Republicans as indifferent to and uncaring about the problems faced by individual citizens as a consequence of market-driven dislocations.

In other policy areas, Republican politicians appear to be offering too much government to satisfy the preferences of southern voters who are not members of the party. The pro-life position of most Republicans on the abortion issue attracts only a sizable minority among other southerners. The religious right's "growing strength . . . in a region that has become the party's new base of power," conclude Dan Balz and Ronald Brownstein, "not only guarantees greater attention by the party to divisive issues like school prayer and abortion, but threatens to make secular conservatives and moderates think twice about their longer-term allegiance with the GOP."[47] In addition, rejection of toleration by many Republicans injects moralistic and dogmatic tones into public debate that alienate many other southerners. Conservative Republicans present themselves as adherents of personal freedom who wish to live their lives as much as possible without interference from the federal government. But their entire agenda is so relentlessly conservative across economic, racial, and cultural matters that the Republicans often appear to be trying to impose their own moral standards, values, and priorities upon other groups in the society who do not share them.

Southern Republicans have probably gone about as far as they can with a purely conservative agenda and an overwhelmingly ideological approach to governing. Although Republicans have realigned majorities of white conservatives in rural as well as metropolitan areas, they only split the urban white moderates and continue to trail the Democrats among rural white moderates. As a governing party the Republicans' central deficiency has been the absence of a national leader with the persona and leadership skills to reinvigorate and extend the Reagan realignment. Their ideological conservatism needs to be tempered with pragmatism. What the Republicans need are leaders and programs that unite conservatives while attracting moderates.

If the Republicans wish to become the South's majority party, their leaders will probably need to demonstrate greater interest and competence in governing. Applying conservative principles of accountability to public institutions and to services valued by urban and rural moderates is a plausible strategy to broaden the party's appeal beyond its conservative base. Majorities of voters in the South, as elsewhere in the nation, expect senators and representatives to pay attention to the practical side of government as the provider of necessary services and as an adjuster of the dislocations of demographic and economic change. Republicans need more pragmatic conservative problemsolvers, politicians more along the lines of Georgia representative Mac Collins. Holding a mixed suburban and rural district, Collins blends rural conservatism with a businessman's desire to make practical decisions: "As I told President Clinton when we met for the first time and [I] looked him in the face, 'We have different philosophies. Let's get that out of the way right now and talk!' I like to talk things out. I believe in dialogue."[48]

8

A NEW PARTY SYSTEM
IN THE SOUTH

Two intensely competitive political parties now structure southern politics. Although the partial Reagan realignment has produced enough Republicans to sustain competitive two-party politics, in 1996 self-identified Democrats still outnumbered Republicans by 43 to 37 percent among all southern voters. Yet despite their apparent disadvantage in party identification, southern Republicans won more House and Senate elections from 1992 to 2000 than did Democrats. To better understand the Republicans' congressional surge in the 1990s, it is necessary to characterize the region's new partisan balance more realistically. Relying exclusively on party identification to determine the competitive equilibrium *exaggerates* Democratic strength and *underestimates* Republican strength. Our approach is to group southern voters according to their partisanship *and* their ideology, observe their voting behavior in presidential elections, and then regroup them into "core Republicans," "core Democrats," and "swing voters."[1]

Adding ideology enhances Republican strength because all three types of Republicans (conservatives, moderates, and liberals) are supplemented by conservative independents. At the same time, conservative Democrats have not dependably supported Democratic presidential candidates. Using information about ideological identification as well as party identification captures the strategic dynamics of the conservative realignment by treating *conservative independents* as a reliable GOP pillar and by understanding *conservative Democrats* as swing voters rather than as a Democratic bulwark. The revised partisan balance gave Republicans a *slight plurality advantage* over Democrats in 1996. It helps explain why Republicans experienced greater success in congressional elections during the 1990s but also demonstrates their failure to develop a solid Republican majority *in the electorate*. Future Republican success is not inevitable, and Democrats can assuredly still win many elections.

This chapter probes the transformed southern party system by examining the relative strength of core Republicans and core Democrats among key sectors of the electorate. Race remains the starting point for understanding the modern South. Whites account for nearly four-fifths of the region's electorate, but blacks constitute one-sixth and Hispanics one-twentieth of the voters. Yet southern politics involves more than racial divisions. Three in ten white voters identify with the religious right political movement. Nowhere else in the United States are political conflicts regularly patterned by the simultaneous presence of a large racial minority and a large conservative religious minority. Important as racial and religious groups are in producing a distinctive southern politics, the region shares two other partisan cleavages with the rest of the nation—differences falling along the fault lines of gender and income. Race, religion, gender, and economic class profoundly shape and channel partisan divisions in the modern South. By 1996 the Republicans had expanded their original grassroots base among whites in cities, suburbs, and mountain enclaves to penetrate and neutralize the traditional Democratic advantage in the southern countryside.

CORE VOTING GROUPS IN THE SOUTHERN ELECTORATE

Once the region's only viable party, the Democrats lost their majority status in the 1980s but have continued to win many elections as a competitive minority party. Republicans, formerly a hopeless minority, have also begun to win elections even though they have been unable to attract a majority of the region's voters. Neither party can win simply by appealing to its most reliable supporters. Strategically, each party needs to mobilize its core supporters and carry swing voters. Depending upon many short-term factors—the attractiveness of the candidates, relative financial support, issues of the moment, and campaign and turnout strategies—each party can construct winning coalitions in statewide and congressional elections.

The relative electoral strength of the two southern parties has been estimated in a two-step process. White, black, and Hispanic voters were first separately classified according to their partisan orientation (Democrat, independent, or Republican) and political ideology (liberal, moderate, or conservative) in the 1996 Voter News Service General Election Exit Poll. This cross-tabulation generates nine groups of voters, ranging from liberal Democrats to conservative Republicans. Because there are few liberal independents or liberal Republicans, the original nine categories have been reduced to seven. Liberal independents have been combined with moderate independents, and liberal Republicans have been grouped with moderate Republicans. Next, each of the seven groups that averaged a two-to-one lead for either the Republican or Democratic presidential candidates between 1976 and 1996 is considered a core element of its respective party. Any group failing to do so is treated as a swing vote.

Among whites core Republicans include all Republicans plus conservative independents, core Democrats consist of liberal and moderate Democrats, and the swing vote is made up of conservative Democrats and moderate plus liberal independents. Reagan's presidency dramatically transformed *white partisanship* (see Figure 8.1). Between 1968 and 1996 core Republicans expanded from 31 to 53 percent of the southern white electorate. Republican candidates can now rely upon a substantial base of party activists, financial supporters, and straight-ticket voters. Core Democrats have declined to 27 percent of southern white voters. Largely because of the deaths of older conservative Democrats and the realignment of young and middle-aged conservative Democrats, the white swing vote fell from 33 percent in 1968 to 20 percent in 1996. The collapse of conservative Democrats in the white southern electorate— dropping from 23 percent in 1968 to merely 6 percent in 1996—is one of the region's most important secular trends. Few consistently conservative candidates for statewide office or for congressional seats have continued to campaign as Democrats. The partial realignment of the white electorate toward the Republicans fell short of the party's 60 percent share of white voters necessary for victory. At the same time, the percentage of reliable white Democratic supporters has dropped considerably below the white Democratic target of 40 percent.

Among the region's black voters, core Democrats are comprised of all Democrats plus liberal and moderate independents, core Republicans are limited to self-identified Republicans, and swing voters are the minuscule group of conservative independents. Within the small but growing group of Hispanic voters, core Republicans consist of all Republicans, core Democrats include all Democrats, and independents are swing voters. According to the 1996 exit poll, 44 percent of southern voters were core Republicans, 38 percent were core Democrats, and the rest of the electorate—18 percent—were swing voters. Winning seriously contested statewide elections requires unifying core partisans while attracting swing voters.

THE RACIAL CHASM TRUMPS THE CLASS GAP

Southern whites and blacks have been in virtually continuous conflict since the introduction of slavery in the seventeenth century. "The legacy of slavery, segregation, and white supremacy," Numan V. Bartley and Hugh D. Graham have argued, "leaves little doubt about the basic ethnocultural division in southern society." For centuries whites repressed black achievement and denied blacks any independent political voice. Undiluted white racism, a racism so ingrained that preserving "the supremacy of white over black" seemed the most transparent "outcome" of southern politics, was the heart of the old order. "Whatever phase of the southern political process one seeks to understand," V. O. Key asserted in 1949, "sooner or later the trail of inquiry leads to the Negro."[2] The civil rights movement and federal intervention in the 1960s began to restore political rights that had been ruthlessly stripped from black men after Reconstruction and never extended to black women.

Without question the racial divide remains the most important partisan cleavage in the South. Blacks are by far the most united of the three racial/ethnic groups. Favoring Democrats over Republicans by 87 to 10 percent, the extraordinary Democratic cohesion of southern blacks resembles in magnitude and intensity the traditional Democratic attachments of southern whites. White southerners, by contrast, are now far more likely (53 to 27 percent) to be classified as core Republicans than

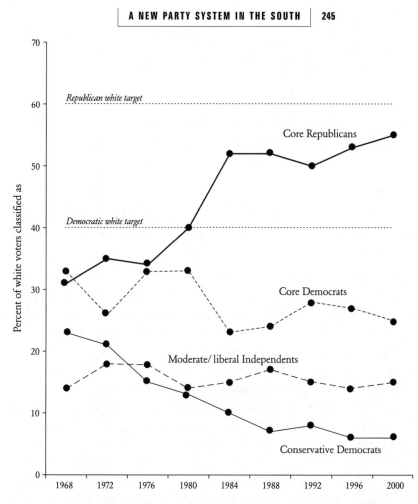

Figure 8.1 The partisan transformation of southern white voters, 1968–2000.
Sources: Calculated from Comparative State Elections Project; National Election Study presidential-year election studies; CBS News/New York Times exit polls; and Voter News Service exit polls.

as core Democrats. Hispanic voters occupy a middle position. A much smaller Democratic edge (53 to 26 percent) appears among Hispanics than among blacks. The association between core partisanship and race/ethnicity is strong (see Table 8.1).

One of Key's working assumptions, as he put it in *Southern Politics in State and Nation,* was that "Politics generally comes down, over the long run, to a conflict between those who have and those who have less."[3] As the poorest region in the United States, the South has always seemed

Table 8.1 Race trumps class: core partisanship by race/ethnicity and economic class among all southern voters in 1996 (%)

	Race/ethnicity			Income			
	Black	Hispanic	White	Low	Middle	High	All
Core Republicans	10	26	53	32	45	61	44
Swing voters	3	21	20	17	19	15	18
Core Democrats	87	53	27	51	36	24	38
Overall share	16	5	79	35	46	19	100
		gamma = .75			gamma = .31		

Source: Calculated from the 1996 Voter News Service General Election Exit Poll.

to rank extraordinarily high in its potential for a successful populist politics that would heavily tax the few haves (persons and business corporations) in order to redistribute goods and services to the great many have-nots and have-littles. Nonetheless, economic development and industrialization have complicated the expected pattern of conflict between southern income groups by creating a large middle class composed of individuals who are neither poor nor wealthy.[4]

Table 8.1 also compares the percentages of core Republicans, swing voters, and core Democrats among three groups of voters: those with family incomes of less than $30,000, those with family incomes of $30,000 to $74,000; and those with family incomes of $75,000 and higher. Across the entire southern electorate Democratic and Republican strength differed sharply between the lowest and highest income groups. Core Democrats strongly outnumbered core Republicans, 51 to 32 percent, among low-income southern voters, whereas core Republicans swamped core Democrats (61 to 24 percent) among the region's affluent voters. Among the crucial middle-income group of voters, there were slightly more core Republicans (45 to 36 percent) than core Democrats. Core partisanship roughly paralleled differences in income.

However, race and ethnicity overshadow economic class once the association between partisanship and income is examined separately for whites, blacks, and Hispanics. As would be expected in a pattern of economic class polarization, large majorities of low-income blacks (93 percent) and Hispanics (65 percent) were core Democrats. Contrary to theoretical expectations, however, core Republicans (42 percent) slightly outnumbered core Democrats (35 percent) among working-class whites. While majorities of middle-income blacks (83 percent) and Hispanics (56 percent) were core Democrats, among middle-income southern whites core Republicans (57 percent) substantially dominated core Democrats (27 percent). Huge majorities of upper-income whites (64 percent) and Hispanics (69 percent) were core Republicans, as a model of class polarization would predict, but southern blacks with high incomes remained overwhelmingly Democratic (81 percent).

Although Republicanism increased with income among southern whites, core Republicans outnumbered core Democrats in each income category. The picture of Republican support from lower-income whites as well as wealthy whites is much more a pattern of white solidarity than of economic class conflict. The observed structure is not the New Deal model of partisan cleavage pitting a large majority of economically marginal Democrats against a tiny minority of wealthy Republicans. Instead, it represents an effort to unite as Republicans "the men and women who drive pickup trucks to work at the Red River Army Depot or haul lumber for the John Cunningham Co." in Bowie County, Texas, with the "Texas Commerce Bank and Tenneco executives who drive Mercedes and BMWs from their River Oaks homes" in Houston, Texas.[5] Partisan attachments in the South continue to be embedded in a social fabric that works against redistributive class politics from the affluent and those who aspire to affluence to the have-littles and have-nots.

Blacks have been far and away the most politically cohesive group in modern America. "African-American politics, including political behavior, is *different*," Michael Dawson has emphasized. "It has been shaped by historical forces that produced a different pattern of political behavior from the pattern found among white citizens." He argues that the "critical component" in understanding the political unity of blacks has been the "legacy of a social identity in which racial and economic oppression have been intertwined for generations." Enslavement, second-class citizenship, and persisting racism—patterns of extended discrimination not experienced to the same degree or duration by other ethnic or racial groups in the United States—have united most African Americans in a common political effort: "What is perceived as good for the group still plays a dominant role in shaping African-American partisanship, political choice, and public opinion." Accordingly, Dawson argues,

"Most students of black politics generally, and of black political behavior specifically, argue that one should expect continued political homogeneity among African Americans. This position is based on the belief that the primary imperative in black politics is to advance the political interests of African Americans as a racial group."[6]

Among southern blacks in 1996 attachment to the Democratic party united liberals (89 percent), moderates (84 percent), and conservatives (66 percent). A plurality of southern blacks believed that the government, rather than individuals themselves, should be primarily responsible for providing jobs and good standards of living. Most blacks believed that a strong government was necessary to handle the economy, wanted more rather than less government, supported increases in governmental services even if more taxes were necessary to finance the programs, and favored health insurance provided by the federal government. Majorities of southern blacks supported affirmative action programs, did not believe that affirmative action on behalf of women and minorities discriminated against white men, and thought equal rights had not been pushed too much.

The use of a "southern strategy" by Republican presidential candidates to attract conservative southern whites into the party, as well as positions on racial issues taken by many southern Republican politicians, have continued to make the GOP a fundamentally unattractive and hostile institution to many southern blacks. Eighty-two percent of southern blacks viewed Gingrich unfavorably in 1996. By contrast, Democratic presidential candidates and officeholders have been favorably evaluated. At the same time that Gingrich was perceived unfavorably, 85 percent of southern black voters found President Clinton honest and trustworthy. Because of the historical experiences of blacks in the United States, the preferences of blacks on salient policy questions, and the electoral strategies of the rival parties, nearly all calculations of self *and* group interests have positioned most blacks far closer to the Democrats than to the Republicans. The result is a level of partisan unity among African-American voters unmatched by the region's smaller group of Hispanic voters and its larger group of white voters.

In 1996 black women (90 percent) made up the region's most pro-Democratic group, and black men (83 percent) were not far behind. The most interesting gender difference was the disproportionately female composition (58 percent) of the active black electorate. The absence of men at the polls was especially pronounced among low-income blacks. Men accounted for only 36 percent of low-income black voters. Middle- and upper-income southern black voters, according to the 1996 exit poll, were divided evenly between men and women.

Income differences among the region's African-American voters produced only slight variations in the size of the Democratic advantage. Low-income black voters favored Democrats over Republicans, 93 to 6 percent. Democrats outnumbered Republicans, 83 to 13 percent, among middle-income southern black voters. And even among the 7 percent of southern black voters who reported incomes of $75,000 and higher, Democrats still enjoyed a huge advantage (81 percent) over Republicans (19 percent). "Within the confines of mainstream American politics," Dawson concludes, "individual economic status plays a small role in shaping African-American political choice."[7]

Although Hispanic voters also favored Democrats over Republicans, there was a striking difference in the magnitude of the Democratic advantage between women and men. Core Democrats constituted a majority among female Hispanic voters, 60 to 22 percent, but only a plurality among male Hispanic voters, 43 to 32 percent. Low- and middle-income Hispanic voters were heavily Democratic, while those with higher incomes favored Republicans over Democrats, 69 to 16 percent. Majorities of liberal (65 percent) and moderate (56 percent) Hispanics were Democrats, while a plurality (47 percent) of conservative Hispanics were Republicans.

Although the Hispanic population is growing in every southern state, many Hispanics are not citizens, and even fewer are registered voters. Hispanic voters are likely to increase greatly in the twenty-first century, and politicians of both major parties are making considerable efforts to win their support. The "Hispanic" label is often misleading, because it groups together Spanish-speaking people of different national origins and experiences. In 1996 Texas Hispanics were primarily from Mexico and were lopsidedly Democratic in core partisanship (70 to 14 percent). A very different situation prevailed in Florida, where many Hispanics were refugees or descendants of refugees from Castro's Cuba. They were more likely to be core Republicans (51 percent) than core Democrats (33 percent).

If modern southern politics were polarized *solely* along racial lines (with Hispanics in the middle), whites would be as solidly Republican as blacks are cohesively Democratic. They are not. The classification of only a small majority of southern whites as core Republicans undercuts a purely racial explanation of partisanship in the South. Southern whites in 1996 varied in their policy preferences. Nearly three-fifths supported the individualistic culture of personal responsibility, but more than one-fifth thought the government should be mainly responsible for providing a good standard of living, and another fifth had mixed attitudes about where responsibility lay. Two-thirds preferred less government in general, while one-third wanted more government. Over three-fifths believed they paid too much in taxes, but more than a third thought they paid about the right amount. Because southern whites vary in their philosophy of government, it is important to determine which whites have remained reliable Democrats and which ones have become consistent Republicans.

The South is the most religiously conservative region of a formally religious nation. According to the exit polls, 87 percent of white voters are Christians. The partisan realignment of the religious right has helped southern Republicans solve their problem of attracting landslide majorities of white voters. Thirty percent of southern white voters in 1996 identified with "the religious right political movement," a considerably larger fraction than white voters elsewhere in the nation (18 percent). Sixty-six percent of religious right whites in the South are core Republicans, while only 17 percent are core Democrats. The few policy questions asked in the 1996 exit poll merely hint at the breadth of their conservatism. Seven of every ten religious right whites wanted less government in general, although 71 percent also wanted the federal government to make abortions always illegal or mostly illegal. A large majority believed that not enough money had been cut in the 1996 welfare reform act. Nearly three-fifths owned a gun. Two-thirds of the southern religious right white voters had a favorable impression of Gingrich, who championed many of their causes.

Because the religious right political movement supplied nearly two-fifths of core Republican voters, many Republican candidates in the South have emphasized religious and social issues to win their support.

Voters' guides comparing Republican and Democratic candidates on issues salient to religious right voters have often been distributed in or around evangelical churches prior to election day. Republican candidates generally adopt conservative positions on such controversial policy matters as taxpayer funding for abortions, parental notification and consent for abortions by minors, vouchers for public or private schools, government regulation of private and home-school education, and benefits for homosexual partners of government employees.[8]

Republican strength in the South extends far beyond the religious right. The vast majority of white southern voters—70 percent in 1996—do not identify with this political movement. Most of these whites are Christians, and among these (relatively) secular white voters, there are considerably more core Republicans (47 percent) than core Democrats (31 percent). Herein lies the central Republican dilemma in building electoral majorities. Conspicuous reliance upon the white religious right by Republican politicians frequently carries the risk of being viewed as "extremists" among those core Republicans, swing voters, and core Democrats who reject and resent many aspects of the religious right's political agenda as unwanted intrusions into their personal lives.

Gender also structures the core partisanship of white southerners. Core Republicans outnumbered core Democrats among white men *and* white women, but there was a large difference in the size of the Republican advantage. A majority (57 percent) of southern white men were core Republicans, while a plurality (49 percent) of southern white women were core Republicans. Only 23 percent of southern white men were core Democrats, compared with 31 percent of southern white women.

"Drawn initially to the anti-government, free-market message of Ronald Reagan 20 years ago," observed Thomas Edsall, "white men have been shifting their loyalties from a Democratic Party that supports a strong regulatory state, affirmative action, expanded protection for women's rights and a social safety net to a Republican party well to the right on all these issues." Compared with the rest of the population, white men "are one of the strongest anti-tax constituencies. They are more distrustful of regulations, from gun control to environmental protection. And they tend to see an activist federal government as a threat to personal freedom." As Celinda Lake put it, "They don't want anything from government except to be left alone. White men think the best role of government is to do nothing, and 'Leave us alone.'"[9]

Edsall's observations about white men apply with special force in the South, "the region that has undergone the most dramatic partisan shift among white voters."[10] Conservatism was their main ideological tendency. Nearly half of the region's white male voters (48 percent) thought of themselves as conservatives, while 40 percent were moderates and only 12 percent were liberals. Seventy-three percent wanted less government, 63 percent owned a gun, and more than half believed that too little had been cut from the welfare program. They split over abortion, with 52 percent wanting abortions to be mostly or always legal. Fifty-nine percent approved of Gingrich. According to the 1996 National Election Study survey, substantial majorities of southern white men took personal responsibility for providing a good standard of living for themselves and their families, thought they paid too much in taxes, and wanted fewer services in order to reduce governmental spending. They split almost evenly on the question of whether a strong government was needed to handle the economy (51 percent) or whether the free market should handle the economy without governmental intervention (49 percent). Large majorities of southern white men opposed preferences for women and minorities in hiring, believed that affirmative action discriminated against white men, thought the government should not have programs specifically designed to help blacks, and believed that equality was being pushed too much.[11]

Among the southern white men who identified with the religious right, core Republicans (71 percent) overwhelmed core Democrats (13 percent). Core Republicans also greatly outnumbered core Democrats, 53 to 24 percent, among the region's relatively secular white men. Majorities of both groups of southern white men wanted less government, thought too little had been cut from the welfare program, and owned a gun. A large majority of the religious right men approved of Gingrich, but barely half of the secular white men looked with favor on the Republican Speaker of the House of Representatives. Abortion policy produced the biggest difference between the two groups: more than four-fifths of the religious right white men opposed abortion, a view held by little more than a third of the relatively secular white men.

Whereas conservatives were the largest ideological group among southern white men, moderates (45 percent) outnumbered conservatives (38 percent) among southern white women. A majority of southern white women took personal responsibility for their standard of living, while only one-fourth believed this was a governmental responsibility. They held mixed views about the proper role of government and the burden of taxation. Majorities said they wanted less government and felt they paid more than the right amount in taxes. In addition, most southern white women opposed preferences for minorities and women in hiring, thought that affirmative action discriminated against white men, opposed specific governmental programs for blacks, and believed that equality was being pushed too much. However, only 43 percent of southern white women approved of Gingrich. Sixty-five percent supported a strong government to handle the economy, and 55 percent believed government had become bigger because the problems had become more numerous. Fifty-eight percent wanted most or all abortions to be legal, a plurality believed the welfare cuts had been "about right," and only 36 percent reported owning a handgun.

Conservative religion primarily accounts for the Republican advantage among the South's white women. Among the 34 percent of white female voters who identified with the religious right political movement, core Republicans (63 percent) far outnumbered core Democrats (20 percent). Large majorities of these women opposed abortion and generally preferred less government. Most approved of Gingrich and thought welfare had not been cut enough. More than two of every five owned a handgun.

The South's relatively secular white women, 57 percent of whom were moderates, were very different: core Republicans (41 percent) barely outnumbered core Democrats (38 percent). Fifty-nine percent of the relatively secular southern women held a favorable impression of Hillary Clinton, while 64 percent disliked Gingrich. A plurality thought the cuts in welfare were about right; only 38 percent thought not enough had been cut. Only 34 percent of these women reported owning a handgun. Fifty-seven percent wanted less government. The Republican party's antichoice position weakened its appeal among many of these women. Seventy percent wanted abortions to be legal, and among this group, core Democrats led core Republicans, 47 to 38 percent. Among the 30 percent who preferred abortions to be illegal, core Republicans dominated by 54 to 29 percent.

Attention to the social and economic groups that make up important segments of the electorate reveals the complexity and competitiveness of modern southern politics. Figure 8.2 displays the social bases of core southern partisanship for the entire South and for low-income, medium-income, and high-income voters. "The Southern X" in the upper left corner plots the percentage of core Republicans and core Democrats among blacks, Hispanics, secular white women, secular white men, and religious right whites to produce the big "X" of modern southern politics. In 1996 core Republicans fell far behind core Democrats among southern blacks and southern Hispanics, barely exceeded core Democrats among secular white women, and greatly outnumbered core Democrats among secular southern white men and religious right southern whites. Other "X"s appear, in a systematic fashion, within the high-income, middle-income, and low-income groups. Among relatively affluent southerners the "X" separates religious right whites, secular white men, secular white women, and Hispanics from black southerners. For middle-income voters the "X" distinguishes religious right whites and secular white men from blacks and Hispanics. And among low-income voters the "X" divides religious right whites from blacks, Hispanics, and secular white women. In short, Figure 8.2 provides a visual understanding of the social and economic foundations of modern southern politics.

Cohesive black support for Democratic candidates has increased the Republican party's imperative for landslide white majorities. Core Republicans were still well shy of the party's 60 percent target among the region's racial majority. The GOP attracted majorities from every income segment of religious right southern white voters, middle- and upper-income secular white men, upper-income secular white women, and upper-income Hispanics. Yet only among middle- and high-income religious right voters and among secular men with high incomes did core Republicans constitute three-fifths or more of southern white voters. Core Democrats were 13 percentage points below the party's target of 40 percent among white voters. Core Democrats did not constitute a majority of the voters in any of the nine white subgroups and reached

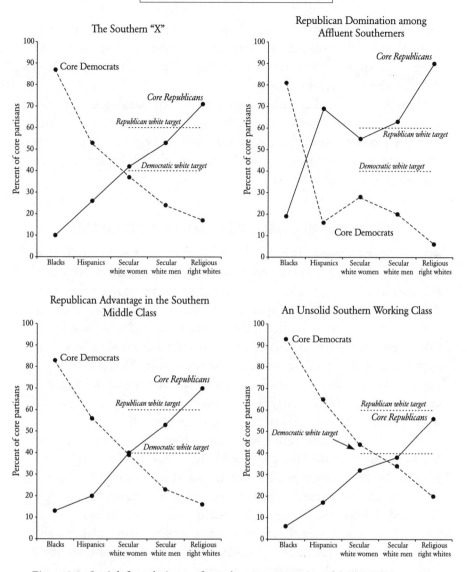

Figure 8.2 Social foundations of southern core partisanship in 1996. *Sources:* Same as Figure 8.1.

their electoral target only among low- and middle-income secular women. Democratic weakness was especially apparent among all income
levels of religious right whites and middle- and high-income levels of
the relatively secular white men.

With the social and economic bases of core partisanship in the modern South clearly delineated, it is now possible to analyze more realistically the growth of southern Republicanism as it began among affluent
whites, spread to middle-income whites, and finally has partially penetrated to low-income white voters.

REPUBLICAN DOMINATION AMONG AFFLUENT SOUTHERNERS

Modern Republicanism came to the South from the top down. In 1948
Texan Jesse Jones, a lifelong conservative Democrat, former New Deal
administrator, and one of the wealthiest businessmen in the South, used
the editorial page of his newspaper, the *Houston Chronicle,* to complain
that "our party, as we inherited it from our fathers, and as we would still
like to have it, has left us." The editorial urged voters to elect New York
Republican Thomas E. Dewey to the White House.[12] Jones's defection
from the Democratic presidential ticket was an early signal of interest in
the national Republican party as a legitimate and respectable institution
for the exercise of political influence by affluent southern whites.

The exodus of conservative southerners from the Democratic party
had been building since the 1930s. Although President Roosevelt's programs were enormously popular among the vast majority of southerners, many upper-income whites were becoming disenchanted. "The New
Deal and the Fair Deal," Alexander Heard argued, "added up to a program of national political action so distasteful to many planters and
businessmen—who formerly had made the Democratic party their home
and their servant—that conservative Democrats began to desert to the
Republicans before there were any Dixiecrats." Their disagreements with
the national Democratic party, he believed, "did not arise alone from
worries about civil rights for Negroes; they disagreed on labor legislation, economic controls, taxation, Federal jurisdiction, and many another domestic issue."[13]

After World War II the rapid expansion of the upper middle class began to transform southern society. "The new industrialization," Heard

concluded, "contributed to a class of business, commercial, and industrial managers, some of them from outside the region, who inclined toward the national policies of the Republican party."[14] Mass defections at
the top of southern social structure in favor of the Republicans began in
earnest in 1952 in response to Dwight Eisenhower's nomination as the
Republican presidential candidate. More than seven-tenths of upper-
income urban whites voted for Eisenhower.[15] It was a Republicanism
based largely on the economic self-interest of successful white southerners who were increasingly subject to high income taxes and federal regulations.

Affluent southern whites have long voted their economic interests in
presidential elections. GOP strength among upper-middle-class southern whites is crucial in several respects. These individuals provide economic, cultural, and social leadership, set the general contours of acceptable behavior, and are assuredly the main source of campaign
finance. "Compared with the national upper middle class, the white
southern segment was more provincial, more religious, and more conservative," Bartley has stressed. "In the South, however, its members
were in the vanguard of social and ideological change. As the prime
beneficiaries of the postwar suburban boom, they were the most at-
tuned to rapid economic development and entrepreneurial individualism."[16]

Making and keeping money has strongly motivated many affluent
southerners and others who aspired to wealth. As voters subject to the
highest brackets of the federal income tax, their natural home is a political party at least rhetorically committed to reducing government spending and cutting tax burdens. If a reported family income of $75,000 or
higher is used to distinguish affluent southerners, 19 percent of the region's vote was cast by the upper middle class in 1996. Whites accounted for nine of every ten high-income voters (see "Republican
Domination among Affluent Southerners" in Figure 8.2). Most upper-
income whites classified themselves as moderates (46 percent) or conservatives (43 percent), while only 10 percent thought of themselves as liberals. Core Republicans (64 percent) outnumbered core Democrats (21
percent) among these wealthy whites.

Republican emphasis on cutting taxes resonates strongly with this
segment of southern society. In 1996 seven of every ten wealthy whites

believed they paid more in taxes than was right, and 65 percent of the region's affluent individuals reported that their taxes had gone up during the Clinton administration. Their preferences in other important policy areas frequently pointed in conservative directions. Seven-tenths of upper-income whites favored less government over more government, thought that citizens themselves rather than the government bore the main responsibility of finding employment and providing a good standard of living for their families, and wanted welfare programs limited in time and reduced in benefits. Although most told interviewers that integration was their preferred form of race relations, more than nine of every ten opposed affirmative action that involved preferential hiring and promotion, and seven of every ten thought that the federal government should not have special programs to help blacks. A small majority thought that society had gone too far in pushing equal rights. While few thought public schools should be permitted to offer a Christian prayer, a majority favored letting public school students pray silently. Republican appeals involving individual effort, reducing the size of government, cutting taxes, and limiting welfare benefits were directed at majorities of affluent southern whites.

Wealthy white southerners did not always adopt conservative positions. Most expressed permissive views about abortion, wanted increased spending on public education, and supported additional regulations to protect the environment. A small majority conceded the need for a strong government to handle complex economic problems, and a plurality were willing to tolerate moral standards that were different from their own. A majority (54 percent) did not own a gun. Strident and uncompromising opposition to abortion, as well as the appearance of writing off investments in public education, a lack of concern about the environment, and a too-narrow view of the role of government weakened support for the Republican party among a minority of affluent southern whites.

The most lopsidedly pro-Republican voters were the few affluent whites who identified with the religious right: 90 percent were core Republicans, while only 6 percent were core Democrats. However, the vast majority of wealthy southern whites did *not* belong to the religious right, and many "country club Republicans" did not share the religious right's political agenda. Wealthy southern whites who rejected the religious right still had multiple reasons—opposition to high income taxes, personal responsibility for economic well-being, desire for less government, and opposition to affirmative action, to cite only a few—to prefer the Republican party. Fifty-nine percent were core Republicans, while only 23 percent were core Democrats.

Among the South's relatively secular affluent white voters, core Republicanism was more likely among men, 63 to 20 percent, than among women, 55 to 27 percent. Majorities of these wealthy white men had a favorable impression of Gingrich. They wanted less government and thought too little had been cut from welfare. Half of them reported gun ownership. However, nearly seven of every ten secular affluent men wanted abortions to be mostly or always legal—a huge break with the pro-life position of a majority of core Republicans. Majorities of the affluent secular white women disliked Gingrich. Large majorities wanted less government and thought too little had been cut in the welfare reform legislation. On the liberal side, 88 percent of these wealthy white women wanted abortion to be mostly or always legal, and only 32 percent reported owning a gun.

Most affluent southerners affiliated with the more fiscally conservative political party. Economic self-interest brought relatively wealthy whites and Hispanics to the Republican party, while high-income blacks did not behave according to an economic class interpretation of politics. Many of the well-to-do whites were drawn to the Republican party despite the influence of the religious right. Important as affluent voters are in explaining the rise of the Republican party in the South, Republican candidates cannot succeed simply by winning the votes of the most economically successful southerners. The party's candidates must also attract votes from the middle and working classes to develop their landslide white majorities.

REPUBLICAN ADVANTAGE IN THE SOUTHERN MIDDLE CLASS

The social structure of the pre–World War II South resembled a pyramid whose main characteristics were "a small, land-owning and commercial elite at the top; a relatively small middle class of professionals,

managers, and public officials; a large segment including the small farmers, tenant farmers, and the urban poor; and finally, the whole of this
structure resting upon the bulk of the Negro population bound to agriculture."[17] Most of the population—the "have-nots"—consisted of poor
whites and even poorer blacks situated at the bottom of the social structure, while most of the "haves" were located in two small groups of
whites at the top of the society. The "old South" lacked a substantial
middle class. However, the growth of industry and services and the rise
of metropolitan areas in the last half of the twentieth century radically
altered the region's social structure. For the first time there appeared in
the South a sizable middle class, a large group of people who had es-
caped poverty but who were far from rich.

How would the partisan tendencies of the southern middle class be
expressed? Although the southern middle class was "susceptible to the
blandishments of both a liberal and a conservative party," Heard theo-
rized that this large group "would offer the Republican party a potential
source of votes in those states where it could achieve some kind of competitive equality." Journalist Samuel Lubell emphasized in 1950 that
"the first fruits of Southern industrialism have been a rising urban middle class that is almost Republican in its political thinking." According
to Louis Harris, the "up-coming white-collar groups—on the make—are
the most natural and most enthusiastic source of Republican votes below the Mason-Dixon line. If a two-party system is to be begun, they are
the most likely candidates to begin it." Many southern white-collar voters in the expanding cities and suburbs were recent migrants from rural
and small-town areas. These new urban residents "feel, no doubt, that
they will grow beyond their present income status, and with advancement will come new wealth, new responsibilities, and new social status."
Some undoubtedly "felt a new-found sense of pride and respectability
in voting Republican." Harris believed that, "given the right circumstances, the middle-income voters of the South can demonstrate a
definite and decisive upward social orientation in their voting." The region's "middle-income group behaved much more like the upper-
income people than like those in the lower-income brackets" in the
1952 presidential election. Many of these southern voters no longer
connected "the Democratic Party with their economic well-being. In

fact, by the end of the campaign, well over four out of ten of these southern white-collar people were complaining about high taxes."[18]

These interpretations of the southern middle class's Republican presidential support in the early 1950s are applicable to this segment's partisanship in the last decade of the twentieth century. As the South's economy expanded in subsequent decades, and as many southerners began to earn incomes subject to direct taxation, the Republican advocacy of limited government and lower taxes began to resonate with the region's middle class (see "Republican Advantage in the Southern Middle Class" in Figure 8.2). Respondents in 1996 who reported family incomes of $30,000 to less than $75,000 accounted for 46 percent of the region's voters. Neither party attracted a majority of the southern middle class, but core Republicans held a plurality advantage, 45 to 36 percent, over core Democrats. Blacks accounted for 15 percent of the region's middle-income voters, and Hispanics for another 4 percent. These middle-class minority voters favored the Democrats over the Republicans. However, because whites made up over four-fifths of middle-income voters in the South, their political views dominated this segment of the region's electorate.

Core Republicans outnumbered core Democrats by nearly two to one (53 to 27 percent) among middle-income whites. Most of these whites thought of themselves as conservatives (44 percent) or moderates (43 percent). A majority was favorably disposed toward Gingrich. Most middle-income whites accepted personal responsibility for their standard of living. While more than two-thirds of these voters wanted less government, they split evenly on the need for a strong government to handle the economy. A large majority believed they paid too much in taxes, and most preferred fewer government services to paying more taxes for additional services. More gun ownership was reported by middle-income white voters (55 percent) than among whites with either lower or higher incomes. Majorities of the white middle class did not believe the federal government had the responsibility of seeing that blacks received fair treatment in employment, opposed special help for blacks and preferential hiring, and thought equal rights were being pushed too much. They split on abortion, with 52 percent wanting abortions to be mostly or always legal. Majorities wanted to increase spending on public education and favored more regulations if necessary to protect the environment. Nearly half were willing to tolerate moral standards different from their own.

Among middle-class white southerners enthusiasm for the Republican party varied considerably by religion and gender. Adherents of the religious right movement accounted for 30 percent of the white middle class, and they were decisively Republican, 68 to 17 percent. Almost three-fourths of the middle-income religious right whites wanted less government, while nearly four of every five wanted abortions to be mostly or always illegal. The vast majority thought too little had been cut from the welfare program. Most of these voters owned a gun. Middle-income white men who did not identify with the religious right were split primarily between moderates (46 percent) and conservatives (42 percent). Fifty-two percent of these men were core Republicans, while only 24 percent were core Democrats. Most liked Gingrich, owned a gun, wanted less government, and believed that too little had been cut from the welfare program. However, they also believed that abortions should be mostly or always legal.

Middle-income white women who rejected the religious right had a different pattern of partisanship. Core Democrats (41 percent) barely exceeded core Republicans (39 percent). Hard-line conservative Republicanism offered little to these women, three-fourths of whom thought of themselves as moderates or liberals. They were less conservative than their middle-income male counterparts. A plurality thought that enough had been cut from welfare, more than three-fifths did not own guns, and most disliked Gingrich. Although a majority favored less government, these views did not produce a Republican advantage. More salient for partisanship were their positions on abortion. Core Democrats led core Republicans, 52 to 38 percent, among the 71 percent of relatively secular middle-class women in the South who were pro-abortion. By contrast, core Republicans outnumbered core Democrats, 54 to 18 percent, among the much smaller group who were antiabortion.

The southern middle class, as Heard conjectured a half-century ago, has both conservative and liberal tendencies. Core Republicans outnumbered core Democrats, but the GOP advantage fell far short of domination. For Republican strategists, the failure to create a reliable majority base in the region's middle class has meant that the party has needed to generate strength among southerners with relatively modest incomes, among voters who have virtually no economic interests in common with the most affluent voters in the region.

THE UNSOLID SOUTHERN WORKING CLASS

Thirty-five percent of the region's vote in 1996 was cast by respondents who reported family incomes of less than $30,000. If mobilized as a cohesive bloc, such a group could presumably anchor political efforts to advance the interests of low-income southerners. The reality is a politically divided southern working class. Low-income southern voters in 1996 displayed little working-class solidarity in their partisan preferences. While core Democrats (51 percent) did outnumber core Republicans (32 percent) among all low-income voters, Democratic cohesiveness disappeared once they were sorted into the different social groups (see "An Unsolid Southern Working Class" in Figure 8.2). Blacks accounted for 24 percent of the region's low-income voters, and they displayed extraordinarily high attachments to the Democratic party, as did nearly two-thirds of low-income Hispanics. However, only 35 percent of the low-income white voters were core Democrats, while 42 percent were classified as core Republicans—a remarkable departure from a pattern of economic class conflict.

A majority of low-income white voters took personal responsibility for their standard of living. Fifty-five percent preferred less government, but 70 percent also thought that a strong government was needed to handle the economy. A majority thought they paid the right amount in taxes, and a plurality believed that governmental services should be expanded even if more taxes were required. They split on abortion, with 51 percent agreeing that abortions should be mostly or always illegal. Few thought that too much had been cut from welfare programs. Forty-one percent of low-income white voters said they owned a gun. Most believed that the environment should be protected even if more regulations were required, and three-fourths thought more money should be spent on public schools. A majority believed in tolerating other moral standards. Three-fifths had an unfavorable view of Gingrich.

Majorities of working-class southern whites rejected special governmental help for blacks, opposed preferential treatment for "women and minorities," and thought equal rights were being pushed too much. Robert Botsch's interviews with fifteen young working-class southern men (ten whites, five blacks) in a small North Carolina town ("Furntex") during the 1970s analyzed their racial attitudes. His thoughtful and insightful analysis illuminates their political worldview. "Not a single white man in the group was found to be totally without any prejudice in the areas examined," he reported—a generalization that would probably have rung true if similar interviews had been conducted with middle-income and affluent southern whites in the 1970s and the 1990s. Botsch found "negative racial stereotypes of blacks, some concern over government actions that might force integrated housing, ambivalence over the results of integrating the schools, concern that whites could be relegated to minority status in schools and neighborhoods, a small amount of concern about blacks joining and perhaps even taking over white churches, disapproval of interracial sexual contacts and marriage, and a very strong concern that the national government has changed the rules in life's game giving blacks an unfair advantage in gaining jobs, promotions, housing subsidies, and welfare benefits."[19] Under these conditions, organizing a successful and durable biracial coalition on populist themes has been virtually impossible.

Southern Democrats have also been hurt by the weakness of the labor union movement. Despite the presence of unions in some important industries and occupations, the region continues to be hostile toward organized labor. Heard emphasized in 1952 the need for labor unions to educate southern workers in the organized pursuit of their economic self-interest. More than "any other factor," he believed, "successes in organizing southern laborers and stimulating them to political action" were necessary for the emergence of a liberal Democratic party. In addition, he argued, "a liberal Democratic politics in the South depends also on the assumption that lower economic groups, white and black, will vote in increasingly large proportions, with a fair degree of political unity, in response to sustained exertions in political education."[20] In 1996, however, only 11 percent of low-income white voters reported living in a family with a union member. Most of the southern working class, white, black, and Hispanic, is unorganized and politically inert.

Conservative religious convictions explain much of the Republican party's support among working-class whites. In 1996 low-income white voters were nearly four times more likely to identify with the religious right political movement than to live in a union household. Two of every five working-class white voters considered themselves part of the religious right. Among these workers Republicanism thrived. Fifty-six percent were core Republicans, while merely 20 percent of low-income whites were core Democrats. They were mainly fundamentalist in their Christian faith, concerned about the decline of morality in society, and strongly influenced by conservative Christian ministers, who, decades ago, would have either been Democrats or uninvolved in politics. Most of them owned guns, preferred less government, wanted abortions to be entirely or mainly illegal, and believed welfare reform had not gone far enough. The beliefs, values, and interests of individuals associated with conservative religion helped to wedge apart from the Democrats more than one-fourth of the entire southern working class.

Core Republicans slightly outnumbered core Democrats, 38 to 34 percent, among working-class white men who were not part of the religious right. Nearly two-thirds believed in less government, half owned guns, 44 percent believed that too little had been cut from welfare, and few lived in a family in which someone belonged to a labor union. The vast majority of these white men favored legalized abortions, a view that separated them from the working-class white men who belonged to the religious right. The ability of Republican candidates to split the relatively secular segment of the southern working class represented a tremendous penetration of the "good-ole-boy" vote, which in previous generations had been an essential element of the southern Democratic party.

Working-class women who rejected the religious right were the least Republican segment of the white working class. A plurality (44 percent) of these women were core Democrats, while only 32 percent were core Republicans. Only 24 percent of them were conservatives. Majorities wanted *more* government and opposed restrictions on abortion. Only a minority owned guns.

Far from being unified, southern working-class voters were deeply split by race, ethnicity, religion, and gender. Blacks, Hispanics, and secular white women made up the Democratic sectors of the low-income South, relatively secular white men were divided in their partisanship, and religious right voters were heavily Republican.

THE REPUBLICAN PRESENCE IN CITY AND COUNTRYSIDE

According to the 1996 exit poll, Republican support among whites was extensive in the South's metropolitan *and* rural areas. Apart from the rural highlands of the Peripheral South, southern Republicanism for decades had been primarily limited to the region's cities and suburbs. Among metropolitan white voters there were twice as many core Republicans (54 percent) as core Democrats (27 percent). This large and growing grassroots base provides ample strength for metropolitan Republican candidates to raise money and seek votes for congressional and senatorial elections. The Republican presence was also remarkable in the countryside. Fifty-one percent of rural whites were core Republicans, while only 28 percent were core Democrats. The neutralization of the accustomed Democratic advantage in the rural and small-town South has enabled the Republicans to become highly competitive in Senate elections and in congressional districts with relatively low black populations.

Republican growth in the metropolitan South has been based chiefly on votes from the expanding middle- and upper-income classes. Among metropolitan white voters, affluent and middle-income whites made up more than four-fifths of the core Republicans. Reagan's appeal to the religious right political movement mobilized many conservative Christians in evangelical and fundamentalist churches, but in the cities and suburbs the religious right has largely supplemented income-based Republicanism. In the metropolitan South secular conservatives made up 39 percent of core Republicans, moderates and liberals constituted another 35 percent, and religious right conservatives were only 25 percent. Successful Republican candidates in metropolitan areas have to balance an ideologically diverse party and generally must heed the concerns and issues of large numbers of secular conservatives and moderates.

In the rural South affluent and middle-income whites accounted for less than two-thirds of white core Republicans. The Reagan realignment, based on racial, economic, cultural and religious conservatism, had a powerful impact on core partisanship in the rural Bible Belt.[21] Larger percentages of rural white voters than of urban whites were conservatives and supporters of the religious right political movement. Conservative white voters identifying with the religious right political movement made up 40 percent of white core Republicans in the rural South. Another 36 percent of the white core Republicans were secular conservatives, and only 24 percent were moderates and liberals. Republican politicians in the rural South generally paid greater attention to the religious right than did their metropolitan counterparts. Rural conservatism long supported Democratic members of the South's congressional delegations, but white rural conservatives have shifted to the Republicans as their new instrument of political influence.

Republican success at the ballot box now turns on the multitude of short-term factors that shift from election to election and office to office—the relative appeal of the rival candidates' messages, the shrewdness of their strategies and tactics, the relative financial resources, and the concerns or attentiveness of the electorate. In addition, no enduring Republican penetration of southern politics is possible unless Republican officeholders are able to govern successfully. Performance in office can either solidify Republican strength in the electorate or give the Democrats opportunities to regain power. What made the 1990s different was the development of the partial Reagan realignment during the previous decade. Three straight Republican presidential victories set the stage for invigorated Republican campaign efforts for the Senate and the House of Representatives. If grassroots presidential Republicanism could be converted into grassroots senatorial and congressional Republicanism, the South's impact on national politics would be immense.

9

THE PERIPHERAL SOUTH
BREAKTHROUGH

Although southern Democrats have always been highly visible in the U.S. Senate, during the second half of the twentieth century they did not ordinarily lead their party. Only Lyndon Johnson of Texas served as the official leader of the Senate's Democrats (1953–1961). In 1994, however, another southerner appeared certain to become the party's top Senate leader. James Sasser, an influential Tennessee Democrat, was on the verge of this achievement provided that he could win reelection for a fourth term in office. It was not to be. Bill Frist, a previously unknown but well-funded Republican challenger, relentlessly attacked the veteran Democratic senator for failing to represent Tennessee's values, interests, and beliefs. "Sasser says one thing in Tennessee and then votes a different way in Washington," Frist charged. "People are simply tired of his double-talk." Sasser was a "bleeding heart liberal," an "out-of-touch career politician," and the "personification of an arrogant, imperial Congress," the Republican told audiences. "The Frist campaign," observed the *Memphis Commercial Appeal*, "boils down to the chant he now leads at rallies, 'Eighteen years is long enough.'"[1]

Frist's blunt accusations produced enthusiastic responses from many Tennessee voters, responses that left the incumbent Democrat utterly bewildered. "I don't think they've really thought it through," Sasser said. "Historically in the South we have sent people to the Congress and to the Senate long enough to build up seniority so they can wield influence on behalf of the state."[2] In the strongly pro-Republican national tide of 1994, however, the election was not even close. By an astonishing margin of 56 to 42 percent, Tennessee voters refused to send the presumptive leader of the Senate Democrats back to Washington and elected instead a Republican with no officeholding experience at all. It was the worst defeat an incumbent Democratic senator had ever suffered in the modern South.

Sasser's humiliation exemplified the new era of aggressive Republican campaigning across the South. After the 1994 elections, Republicans held a majority of the South's Senate seats for the first time since Reconstruction. From 1992 through 2000 GOP candidates won twenty-two of the thirty-seven Senate elections in the nation's largest region. They unseated four incumbent Democrats and persuaded a popular conservative Democrat to switch parties. In contrast to their weakness in previous decades, Republican incumbents won all but one of their reelection campaigns. Open-seat Senate elections, however, remained problematic battlegrounds, with the GOP prevailing in merely four of nine contests.

As the twentieth century came to an end, Republicans from the South were important and influential members of the Senate. Trent Lott, a veteran Mississippi politician, served as the GOP's majority leader. Chairing Senate committees were such influential southern Republicans as North Carolina's Jesse Helms (Foreign Relations), Virginia's John Warner (Armed Services), Texas' Phil Gramm (Banking, Housing and Urban Affairs), Tennessee's Fred Thompson (Governmental Affairs), and Richard Shelby (Intelligence). Strom Thurmond of South Carolina, though well past his prime, was the Senate's oldest and longest-serving member. Many of the region's most prominent Republicans, men such as Thurmond, Helms, Lott, Gramm, and Shelby, were conservatives who had been born and raised as Democrats but who had come to view the Republican party as their appropriate ideological home.

The Republican ascent began in 1992 with the defeats of two experienced Democratic incumbents. Republican Lauch Faircloth upset North Carolina Democrat Terry Sanford while Republican Paul Coverdell unseated a heavily favored Wyche Fowler in Georgia. The following year, when Texas Democrat Lloyd Bentsen left the Senate to become Treasury secretary in the Clinton administration, Republican Kay Bailey Hutchison easily won a special election. In 1994 Republicans picked up both Tennessee Senate seats. In addition to Frist's upset of Sasser, Thompson won the vacancy created by Al Gore's elevation to the vice presidency. When the Republicans won the Senate in 1994, Alabama Democrat Richard Shelby immediately switched to the Republicans. The election of Alabama's Jeff Sessions and Arkansas's Tim Hutchinson in 1996 gave the Republicans fifteen southern senators. However, the GOP lost ground in 1998 when Democrat John Edwards unseated Faircloth. Two years later Coverdell's unexpected death further reduced the southern Republicans, although they continued to outnumber Democrats in the region's senatorial delegation.

Important as the GOP's southern advance has been, it is crucial to view these gains in historical context. The rise of Republican senators from the South has never been a steady upward march. Gradual advances and sudden surges have always been eventually throttled back by Democratic counterattacks (see Figure 9.1). Although the Republican share of the southern delegation increased steadily from 1961 to 1972, the minority party shrank in the middle and late 1970s. A 1980 surge, followed by a one-seat gain in 1982, brought the Republicans to exactly half of the delegation during President Ronald Reagan's first term in office. Yet another GOP decline began in 1984 and deepened in 1986, when all four Republicans from the "class of 1980" failed to return. After the 1990 elections the South sent only seven Republicans to the Senate. In the last decade of the twentieth century, the southern Republicans expanded to fifteen senators in 1996 before receding to thirteen in 2000. The modern advance of southern Republicanism has thus involved growth and decline, surge and contraction. During each expansionist period Republicans have only partially consolidated their peak gains.

Republican growth in the South gradually destroyed one of the great "constants" of American politics, the Democratic party's monopoly of all Senate seats in the eleven southern states from the first decade of the century through the 1960 elections. Because southern voters always provided Senate Democrats with a head start of 22 seats, Democratic control of the Senate required only that northern Democrats hold 27 seats before the admission of Alaska and Hawaii and 29 seats afterward. The party's solid base in the South, combined with the spread of Democratic strength in the North and West during the 1930s, virtually assured

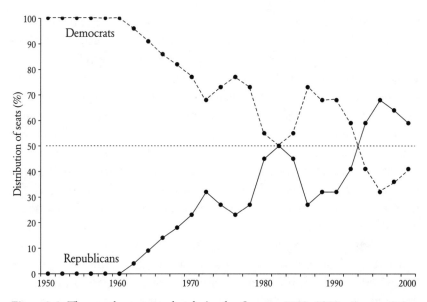

Figure 9.1 The southern party battle in the Senate, 1950–2000. *Sources:* Calculated from *Congressional Quarterly's Guide to U.S. Elections,* 3d ed. (Washington, D.C., 1994); and *Congressional Quarterly Weekly Report,* various issues.

Democratic control of the Senate for the next half-century. Completely shut out in the South, Republicans needed to win huge majorities of the remaining Senate seats (49 of 74 northern seats in the 96-member Senate, 51 of 78 northern seats in the 100-member Senate) to control the institution. Rarely were they successful. From 1932 to 1978 the Democrats organized the Senate in twenty-two of twenty-four Congresses.

The election of Texas Republican John Tower in 1961 broke the Democrats' monopoly of southern Senate seats, although the majority party still enjoyed a large 20-seat surplus (21 Democratic seats minus one Republican seat). From 1961 until the 1980 elections, the South continued to send far more Democrats than Republicans to the Senate, although the average size of the southern Democratic surplus dropped from 22 to 14 seats. A very important change had occurred in the customary regional structure of Senate elections. The Democratic party's southern surplus had now become a variable rather than a constant.

Additional Republican Senate gains in the 1980 elections produced a southern delegation composed of ten Republicans, eleven Democrats, and one conservative independent, Virginian Harry Byrd Jr., who still voted with the Democrats to organize the Senate. The Republicans essentially split the region's Senate delegation and reduced the Democrats' southern surplus to only two seats. A single southern GOP gain in 1982 brought their number to eleven and thereby completely neutralized the southern Democrats' customary edge. A subsequent Republican loss in 1984 revived a two-seat Democratic advantage in the South, but the Republicans' northern majorities were large enough to maintain control of the Senate. From 1981 to 1987 the collapse of the Democrats' customary southern advantage, coupled with substantial Republican majorities of Senate seats in the rest of the nation, undermined the Democratic party's near-automatic control of the Senate. Republicans held the Senate by carrying a majority of northern Senate seats and breaking even in the South.

The revival of substantial Democratic strength in the South in the 1986–1990 elections, however, combined with either partisan deadlock or a slight Democratic advantage in the rest of the nation, enabled the Democratic party to regain and hold the Senate. During these six years the Senate Democrats relied mainly on their southern wing to deliver the seats necessary to organize the institution. Democrats continued to control the Senate, fifty-seven to forty-three, after the 1992 elections, but the pattern of regional support had changed. The Democratic party's advantage in northern states had surged to twelve seats while its edge in the southern states had plunged to only two seats. Democratic control of the Senate now owed far more to northern than to southern surpluses.

Just as neutralizing the Democrats' southern surplus helped the Republicans control the Senate during the early 1980s, so, too, the emergence of a large southern Republican surplus helped the GOP win the Senate from 1995 to 2001 and share control from January to May 2001. The turning point came in the 1994 elections. For the first time in twelve decades, the Republican party emerged with a net advantage (a surplus of four seats) in the southern delegation. Combined with huge Republican gains in northern Senate seats, the GOP reclaimed control of the Senate. Indeed, in three consecutive Senate elections (1994, 1996, and 1998) the Republicans achieved southern as well as northern majorities. The 2000 elections produced yet another variation in the patterns of regional surpluses and deficits: Democrats reclaimed a majority of the northern Senate seats, 41 to 37, but lagged behind in the South, 9 to 13. The 50–50 partisan deadlock in the Senate at the onset of the twenty-first century resulted from a 4-seat southern Republican surplus that offset a 4-seat northern Republican deficit, a regional pattern unique in American history.

Until the Republicans overcame the Democrats' southern juggernaut, they were not a truly national political party and were not genuinely competitive in the struggle to win the U.S. Senate. By itself, of course, controlling a majority of the South's 22 Senate seats does not guarantee a Republican Senate. By no means. Each party is capable of winning or losing majorities of Senate seats in both the South and the North. Regional surpluses and deficits will fluctuate from election to election. At the minimum, though, the decline of a substantial Democratic advantage in the South has effectively eroded the *automatic* national majorities of the Democratic party and restored national two-party competition for the Senate. At the maximum, the rise of Republican strength in the South enabled the GOP to organize the Senate in seven of eleven Congresses from 1980 through 2000.

Within the South the Republicans' dramatic officeholding gains reflected the partisan transformation of the electorate as well as the increased ability of aggressive, energetic, and well-financed Republican candidates to seriously contest Senate elections. Reagan's presidency drew many conservative whites into the Republican party while neutralizing the longstanding preferences of most moderate white southerners for Democratic senators. Republican candidates for the Senate could now also draw upon large financial resources unavailable in previous decades. All in all, the 1990s was a decade of unprecedented Republican competitiveness. Southern Republicans secured at least two-fifths of the statewide vote (our benchmark for serious competition) in nearly 90 percent of the Senate elections.

Important as they have been, these Republican gains in officeholding have not signaled the emergence of a new majority party in the South. Both major parties have developed plausible routes to victory. For Democrats winning requires mobilizing African-American voters to the maximum extent possible and combining their votes with a substantial minority of white voters. Republican success lies in mobilizing conservatives (those identifying with the religious right as well as those who do not) while appealing to enough moderates to generate landslide white majorities. Because neither southern Republicans nor southern Democrats can claim grassroots partisan majorities, Senate elections can easily move back and forth between the parties. No southern state is safely Democratic or reliably Republican in Senate elections. Southern Republicans have finally become an aggressive, competitive minority party, but they are still just that—a minority in the electorate.

The new partisan foundations of the southern states appear in Figure 9.2. In the 1996 state exit polls respondents were asked about their party identification and their political ideology. As in the previous chapter, white voters, black voters, and all voters in each southern state have been classified as core Democrats and core Republicans. The left-hand chart shows the relative size of core partisans among white, black, and all voters in the six Peripheral South states, while the right-hand chart presents similar information for the five Deep South states. The two charts represent the partisan bottom lines for competitive politics in the modern South. They reveal consistently overwhelming Democratic strength among black voters, strong Republican leads among white voters, and the minority status of both political parties. Among all voters core Republicans outnumber core Democrats in every state except Louisiana and Arkansas. Partisan cleavages between white and black voters are much sharper in the Deep South states (those with the highest black populations) than in the Peripheral South states.

Over the past four decades the southern Democrats have been transformed from a comfortable majority party into a competitive minority party. No longer can Democratic candidates for the Senate triumph by appealing only to Democrats. In the Peripheral South Democratic candidates must draw from black Democrats and moderate to liberal white Democrats, but they must also supplement their base with the votes of swing whites. In the Deep South Democratic candidates draw considerably more support from black Democrats than from moderate to liberal white Democrats, but they, too, must appeal to white voters who do not think of themselves as Democrats.

Reagan's eight years in the White House made the Republican party respectable to many former Democrats and independents. Republican parties, once tiny, became highly competitive entities. In many rural areas and small towns as well as in suburbs and large cities, white voters

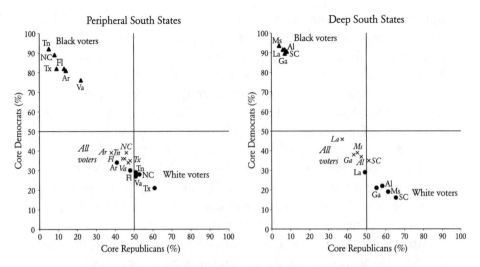

Figure 9.2 Foundations of the Republican breakthrough in the Senate: competitive core partisanship in 1996 in every southern state. *Source:* Voter News Service General Election Exit Poll, 1996.

are now much more likely to think of themselves as Republicans than as Democrats. Core Republicans are proportionally more numerous in the Deep South than in the Peripheral South. Republican Senate candidates can now build upon sizable Republican electorates, but they need to supplement their reliable bases with many white swing voters. These developments in the southern electorate during the 1980s set the stage for the rapid Republican advance in officeholding that then occurred in the 1992–1996 wave of Senate elections.

THE PARTY BATTLE IN THE PERIPHERAL SOUTH

To understand southern Republican competitiveness during the 1990s, elections for the Senate will be analyzed first in the Peripheral South (the rest of this chapter) and then in the Deep South (the next chapter). Most of the earliest southern Republican Senate victories occurred in the Peripheral South states, where the active electorates were more socially diverse and where Republican candidates needed smaller shares of the white vote than in the Deep South. After the 1982 elections, for example, Republicans accounted for a majority (seven) of the twelve Peripheral South senators. Not all of these senators were successful in office, however, and by 1990 only four Peripheral South Republicans—Jesse Helms of North Carolina, John Warner of Virginia, Phil Gramm of Texas, and Connie Mack of Florida—remained in the Senate.

Republican candidates won 65 percent of the Senate elections held in the Peripheral South from 1992 to 2000. GOP challengers unseated three veteran Democrats, incumbent Republicans won all but one contest, and Republican candidates won three of the five open-seat elections. After the 1996 elections nine of the twelve Peripheral South senators were Republicans. Despite the defeat of one GOP incumbent in 1998, the Republicans still made up eight of the Peripheral South's senators in 2001, a net advantage of four seats.

Attention to sharply contested campaigns—especially those in which the Republicans gained or lost ground—illustrates the importance of short-term factors in determining winners and losers in the subregion's competitive politics. Table 9.1, which draws on exit polls for most Senate elections during the 1990s, reports the vote won by Republican candidates by race, party identification, and (where possible) several combinations of party and ideology.

Republican gains in the Peripheral South recommenced in 1992. All three of the subregion's Senate elections that year involved Democratic incumbents: Dale Bumpers (Arkansas), Bob Graham (Florida), and Terry Sanford (North Carolina). Bumpers and Graham easily dominated their challengers, but Sanford was upset by Faircloth, a longtime conservative Democrat who had switched to the Republicans in 1991. Once political allies, Sanford and Faircloth had a falling out in 1986 over the Democratic Senate nomination. At that time Faircloth deferred to Sanford, but six years later the new Republican challenged the sitting Democrat.

Sanford was an experienced Democratic officeholder who had been North Carolina's governor in the early 1960s and was well known as the president of Duke University. He had originally won his Senate seat with 52 percent of the vote. In the Senate he behaved as a national Democrat, compiling much higher party unity scores (see Figure 3.3) than any other Tar Heel Democrat who had served in the Senate during the preceding three decades. Sanford's voting record reflected his moderate to liberal political philosophy as well as the dominance of blacks and moderate to liberal whites in the North Carolina Democratic party.

Faircloth's campaign was directed by Senator Helms's Congressional Club, a political organization that had long specialized in "battering Democrats as folks who are soft on crime and racial quotas . . . [and] friendly to welfare recipients and homosexuals." Although Sanford's liberal votes in the Senate provided ample ammunition for a conservative Republican challenger to polarize the election along liberal-conservative lines, David S. Broder found that the "racially coded issues that have worked so well here in the past have either been blunted—or left unused—in most of the top races this year," apparently because of greater concern among voters about the state of the economy. A month before the election, two polls put Sanford in the lead—45 to 39 percent and 48 to 34 percent—but short of a majority and with many voters undecided.[3]

The campaign's turning point came when heart surgery hospitalized Sanford for two crucial weeks in mid-October. "Terry and I have been friends for a long time, and I wish him a full and speedy recovery," noted Faircloth, even as other "Republicans said that the Senator's illness would not prevent attacks on his record." After a "pale" Sanford left the hospital to resume campaigning, the two rivals exchanged insults and admonitions. Faircloth made Sanford's health an issue by continuing to express his concern. "I would think a 75-year-old man who had been through heart surgery ought to go home and go to bed," suggested the Republican candidate. At a press conference one day after leaving the hospital, "Sanford defended his health and made a counter attack against Faircloth, citing the challenger's use of a hearing aid and bifocals." Sanford thought Faircloth's behavior was disgraceful. As he told reporters, "I would think a 64-year-old man who has been lying like Lauch Faircloth ought to go home and hide his head."[4]

The incumbent Democrat's well-publicized illness apparently raised doubts about his future vigor and effectiveness in office. Faircloth upset Sanford, 50 to 46 percent, and won by a margin of over 103,000 votes. Faircloth's vote followed Helms's pattern of support. He attracted 60 percent of the white vote but won only 7 percent from North Carolina blacks. The Republican challenger carried Republicans and conservative

Table 9.1 Republican support in southern Senate elections, 1992–2000 (%)

Candidate	All	Black	White	Whites							
				Dem.	Ind.	Rep.	Core Dem.	Cons. Dem.	M/L Ind.	Cons. Ind.	All Reps.
Republican winners											
Elections with Republican incumbents											
Hutchison Tex. 94	61	23	71	25	71	93	23	43	61	84	93
Mack Fla. 94	71	19	77	49	80	97	43	71	75	90	97
Lott Miss. 94	69										
Gramm Tex. 96	55	20	73	22	69	93	16	49	58	83	93
Helms N.C. 96	53	10	64	33	59	87	26	65	44	87	87
Thompson Tenn. 96	61	22	68	28	72	96	25	49	65	87	96
Warner Va. 96	52	20	58	20	60	88	19	24	54	74	88
Cochran Miss. 96	71	32	87	62	88	99	55	77	86	91	99
Thurmond S.C. 96	53	21	67	27	59	89	21	48	50	70	89
Shelby Ala. 98	63	15	74	40	81	99	36	57	70	91	99
Coverdell Ga. 98	52	9	72	29	67	94	25	52	56	87	94
Lott Miss. 00	67	11	88								
Frist Tenn. 00	66	21	74								
Hutchison Tex. 00	66	22	75								
Republican loser											
Faircloth N.C. 98	47	8	58	21	45	89	13	64	32	80	89
Open-seat elections											
Republican winners											
Hutchison Tex. 93	67										
Thompson Tenn. 94	60	14	67	27	73	95	24	37	68	80	95
Sessions Ala. 96	52	13	66	23	67	92	19	34	50	85	92
Hutchinson Ark. 96	53	16	57	26	64	95	25	32	51	82	95

Open-seat elections

Elections with Democratic incumbents

Open-seat elections											
Republican losers											
Millner Ga. 96	48	12	62	22	54	88	20	32	42	77	88
Jenkins La. 96	50	9	68	46	71	89	32	69	54	91	89
Boozman Ark. 98	42	26	46	14	52	88	12	30	39	77	
McCollum Fla. 00	47	8	53								
Mattingly Ga. 00	39	7	50								
Republican winners											
Faircloth N.C. 92	50	7	60	29	53	91	22	49	36	83	91
Coverdell Ga. 92	51	10	57	17	47	81					
Frist Tenn. 94	56	10	63	21	72	93	18	31	88	87	93
Allen Va. 00	52	16	60								
Elections with Democratic incumbents											
Republican losers											
Huckabee Ark. 92	40	7	43	18	49	72					
Hartnett S.C. 92	47	7	60	24	53	77					
Grant Fla. 92	35	7	37	11	35	61					
Sellers Ala. 92	33	3	39	14	33	63					
North Va. 94	43	5	50	9	44	76	7	17	30	74	76
Inglis S.C. 98	46	5	60	19	49	87	13	39	38	70	87
Crist Fla. 98	38	7	42	9	39	68	12	31	31	63	68
Donelon La. 98	32	7	45	17	45	75	13	28	33	56	75

Note: M/L = moderate/liberal.

Source: Calculated from Voter News Service exit polls, 1992–2000.

white independents by huge margins. He won large majorities among white men and white women, every white income group above $15,000, and every white age group younger than sixty. Sanford's share of the white vote declined slightly, from 43 to 40 percent, with an important dropoff concentrated among conservative Democrats. He was left with sizable white majorities only from moderate to liberal Democrats and independents.

The Republican advance in the Peripheral South continued the next year in a Texas special election to fill the vacancy when Democrat Lloyd Bentsen became the Clinton administration's Treasury secretary. Backed by "much of the Texas Republican establishment," state treasurer Kay Bailey Hutchison defeated Democrat Robert Krueger, whom Governor Ann Richards had appointed to fill the vacancy. Hutchison's main issue was "reducing the deficit, not by raising taxes, but by cutting spending," a position that resonated powerfully across the state and even penetrated Democratic working-class areas. A *USA Today* reporter who interviewed white working-class voters in the Dallas suburbs found disdain for Democrat Krueger—"He's going to get right up there with Clinton. Whatever Clinton wants, he'll do it. That's why I'm voting against him."—as well as a willingness to take a chance with Hutchison: "We just feel like the U.S. government needs help in cutting spending."[5]

Hutchison effectively put Krueger on the defensive in a televised debate by highlighting his performance as the interim senator. "Bob," she told her opponent, "you didn't vote for the [Clinton] budget, but you didn't have the guts to join with us Republicans and vote against it. You're the only member of the U.S. Senate that voted for nothing." The Texas Republican was also a "cautious supporter of abortion rights" who "made explicit appeals for women's votes" with a television commercial that called for a "future better for our sons and open for our daughters." Hutchison "crushed" her Democratic opponent, 67 to 33 percent. "She beat Kruger by nearly 20 percentage points in usually Democratic South Texas and by 30 points in East Texas," reported Thomas Edsall. "In the Panhandle, she led by 60 percentage points."[6] The first female Republican to be elected to the Senate from a southern state, Hutchison drew the largest share of the vote ever won by a Texas Republican in a statewide race in the twentieth century.

Peripheral South Republicans also did well in 1994. Hutchison and Florida's Connie Mack, the two incumbent Republican senators, easily won reelection. After a very narrow victory in 1988, Mack made his seat so secure that no serious Democratic politician was willing to challenge him. He spent $5.7 million while his Democratic opponent, Hugh Rodham, a brother of Hillary Clinton, could raise only $617,000. Mack routed Rodham, 71 to 29 percent. Hutchison also coasted to reelection. She outspent her opponent, Richard Fisher, $6.6 million to $3.4 million, and defeated him in a landslide, 61 to 38 percent. In addition, the Republicans won an open-seat election and captured one of two seats defended by incumbent Democrats in 1994.

When Senator Al Gore became vice president in 1993, Tennessee Democratic governor Ned McWherter appointed Democrat Harlan Mathews as the interim senator. Mathews did not seek election for the remainder of the term, and the open-seat contest in 1994 matched Democratic representative Jim Cooper against Thompson, a Nashville lawyer and movie actor who was closely allied with former senator Howard H. Baker. Cooper was the early frontrunner, but he distanced himself from the Clinton administration, ran as a conservative Democrat even though most white conservatives had already abandoned the Democratic party, and was unable to attract enthusiastic support from blacks and organized labor.[7]

Thompson recovered from an unimpressive start by recruiting new advisers and switching campaign tactics. After winning the Republican primary nomination against an opponent associated with the religious right, "Thompson parked his Lincoln, shed his lawyer attire, donned blue jeans, cowboy boots, and a western-style khaki shirt, and rolled out what would become the symbol of his campaign: a red extended-cab pickup truck," observed Philip Ashford and Richard Locker. "The costume and the prop remained in place for the duration of the race and made their reprise in his successful 1996 reelection campaign." Thompson crisscrossed the state and introduced himself to Tennessee voters "as that friendly Fred fellow in a pickup truck." As a campaigner, "Thompson was more of a celebrity than a political candidate. He would pull the truck, trailed by its caravan of supporters, into a Wal-Mart parking lot, and women would swoon." After meeting and greeting his followers, the candidate "climbed into the truckbed and proclaimed, 'What this country needs is a good housecleaning in Congress.'" His platform "called for twelve-year term limits for Congress, pay cuts for its members, cutting congressional sessions down to half a year, and allowing members to hold jobs at home." After the Republican candidate rose in the polls, Cooper went "negative on Thompson," in *Knoxville News-Sentinel* reporter Tom Humphrey's assessment, "just as the independent populace [was] getting sick of televised attack ads."[8]

"We started out about a year ago and a lot of people didn't think much about our chances," Thompson told his supporters in early November. "We had a 2-to-1 name identification deficit. But we knew there was something going on different in this country this year, something more fundamental," he continued. "People didn't wake up yesterday morning and decide they loved Republicans when they never did before. People just didn't decide they didn't like the policies of Bill Clinton; they've been thinking that for a long time. It's more fundamental than that: People feel alienated from their government. People feel like they're not being represented." Thompson easily demolished Cooper, 60 to 39 percent. The Republican candidate carried eighty-three of the state's ninety-five counties, including all four urban areas and all counties in East and West Tennessee. His few losses came in sparsely populated rural counties in traditionally Democratic Middle Tennessee. It was a decisive victory. "I think they yelled at the top of their lungs," the newly elected senator said about the state's voters.[9]

In 1994 Democratic incumbents were also on the defensive in the South. Luckily for the party, only two southern Democratic senators had to defend their seats. "It's a year in which all of the things we thought were etched in stone no longer apply," observed Tennessee Democratic Chairman Jane Eskind. As she told the *Washington Post*'s Guy Gugliotta, "The power of incumbency, past popularity, ability and the record—none of it seemed to matter."[10] Indeed, no Democratic incumbent had seemed more secure than Tennessee's Sasser. After unseating Bill Brock in 1976, he had twice easily won reelection against weak and poorly financed opponents. However, as Figure 3.2 shows, Sasser became a national Democrat during the 1980s and thereby cast many votes that could be convincingly portrayed as too liberal for most Tennessee voters. "Sasser's responsibilities in Washington," Ashford and

Locker observed, "had transformed him into that least loved of all southern political figures, the national Democrat. The mix that seems to work for Democrats in Tennessee is cultural conservatism with a leftward tilt on pocketbook issues; Sasser was merely seen as a tool of Democrats in Washington."[11] It was a voting record that offered Frist and his campaign advisers multiple opportunities for effective attacks.

After months of televised attacks, "Frist managed to convince Tennesseans that Sasser was too liberal for the state by citing every one of Sasser's 7,000 votes that Tennesseans might disagree with and saying Sasser 'votes with Ted Kennedy 86 percent of the time.'" Effective grassroots organization supplemented the television ads. Sasser had voted to ban assault weapons, and the National Rifle Association campaigned strongly against him. Tennessee's religious right political movement strongly backed the Nashville heart surgeon. Eventually Frist carried Tennessee "gun owners 2–1 over Sasser and white Christian conservatives 3–1." According to the *Memphis Commercial Appeal,* "The Frist campaign was as organized as any military unit, sending out more than 3 million pieces of direct mail targeted to gun owners, abortion opponents, conservative Christians, health care providers, tobacco farmers and any other group that might be dissatisfied with Sasser in the past or fearful of the policy choices he might make in the future."[12]

More than a day late and a dollar short (he was outspent, $7 to $5 million), Sasser tried to fight back in three ways: he stressed the value of his seniority, emphasized specific conservative positions he had taken, and launched his own personal assaults against Frist. None of these tactics worked in the climate of hostility toward Democrats that existed in 1994. However, even after three terms as a senator, "Sasser laments that, outside of community leaders, most voters are 'not aware of my efforts' despite constant visits back home and six field offices across the state."[13]

Sasser complained that Frist was trying to "demonize me as someone foreign to the culture of the state," and he countered with ads showing his support for school prayer and welfare reform. Sasser also called attention to his opponent's wealth and social status. "Bill Frist can't see beyond the high walls of his country club," Sasser told Tennesseans. "From his lounge chair, he has a view of the swimming pool and the rolling fairways, and all he can think about is the tax break he wants to give to his rich country club friends and to the for-profit health corporation that has made him and his family multimillionaires at our expense." Sasser told voters that the "major choice in this campaign" was "whether we go back to the failed policies of the 1980s with tax cuts for the wealthy, or whether we continue to make progress for the everyday working people."[14]

The exit polls "showed that about half the voters surveyed said Sasser agreed too much with Clinton."[15] Frist won by more than 211,000 votes in a very high-turnout election. He carried 63 percent of whites and 10 percent of blacks. According to the exit polls, 48 percent of the white voters were conservatives, 39 percent were moderates, and 13 percent were liberals. Over half of the white voters (53 percent) were core Republicans, while merely 23 percent were moderate or liberal Democrats. Frist secured very broad support among Tennessee whites. He captured 93 percent of the Republicans, 87 percent of the conservative independents, and 88 percent of the moderate to liberal independents. Frist's assaults upon Sasser's record as a national Democrat left the incumbent Democrat with majorities only from blacks and white Democrats. Among whites Frist carried men and women, low-, middle-, and high-income voters, and every age group. He won 73 percent of whites in Shelby County (Memphis and suburbs), 66 percent of whites in the traditionally Republican east, and 58 percent of whites in the traditionally Democratic central and western parts of the state.

Virginia's Charles Robb barely survived the Republican tide in 1994. Though weakened by revelations about his personal life, Robb was fortunate to draw the controversial Republican Ollie North as his main opponent. "North stirred more emotions, pro and con, than any other candidate in the 1994 cycle," reported *The Almanac of American Politics 2000.* "His believers saw him as a man who struggled to save the West from effete liberals, his detractors saw him as a man who lied to even his own associates in government as well as to Congress and broke the law."[16] Senator Warner conspicuously opposed North, whom he refused to accept as a fellow Republican. North so divided the Virginia Republican party that one prominent Republican, Marshall Coleman, entered the race as an independent candidate and attracted 11 percent of the vote. Facing a divided GOP, Robb prevailed with a plurality of 46 percent, 3 points ahead of North.

The Republicans again moved ahead in the Peripheral South in 1996 when Arkansas representative Tim Hutchinson defeated Democratic attorney general Winston Bryant for the seat previously held by veteran Democrat David Pryor. Arkansas had the weakest Republican party in the Peripheral South. In 1996 only 28 percent of the state's white voters identified themselves as Republicans. Even with the addition of conservative independents, merely 41 percent of whites were core Republicans. However, well-financed Republican candidates could be competitive in statewide elections because core Democratic voters amounted to only 39 percent of the active electorate.

Hutchinson was originally reluctant to compete for the seat. He was little known outside his northwest Arkansas congressional district, and his Democratic opponent had previously won seven statewide campaigns. As he explained to *Washington Times* reporter Nancy E. Roman, when Trent Lott asked him to run "I said, 'This is Arkansas, where Bill Clinton is at the top of the ticket, my own poll has me 11 points down, and you want me to give up a safe seat for that?'" Hutchinson eventually accepted the challenge even though no Republican had ever been elected to the Senate by Arkansas voters. "Arkansas voters vote for the person they feel good about," he later explained. "We've always been a conservative state that believes that government is too big and too intrusive and that the price tag's too high, too." Hutchinson was helped by Republican governor Mike Huckabee, whose statewide organization encompassed every county in the state, as well as by large amounts of out-of-state money that paid for extensive television advertising.[17]

A Baptist minister who was the co-owner of a Christian radio station, Hutchinson was a leader in the state's religious right political movement. However, he did not make social conservatism the focus of his campaign. Art English observed that Hutchinson did "a good job in terms of crafting his image as more of a centrist independent candidate," and Hal Bass concluded that Hutchinson "showed he wasn't the extremist that the Democratic Party ads portrayed him to be." Democratic consultant Skip Rutherford acknowledged that Hutchinson "appealed to a broad spectrum" of voters because he ran "not as a Republican, but as an Arkansan. He played on the state pride."[18]

Hutchinson excelled in one-on-one politics. In his appearances he would make "a short speech" and then devote his remaining time to "what he likes best about the campaign . . . retail politicking–meeting and greeting anyone who comes within arm's length." As he told a reporter, "We've been doing this kind of thing for 4½ months and the people of Arkansas respond to that. They want to meet their politicians. That's part of the reason we've moved so far so fast." Hutchinson used positive and negative appeals to undecided voters. "When I think about what will push the undecided [voters], I think it's not just my message and what I bring to the race, but it's also his [Bryant's] record." Republican advertising accused Bryant of "wasteful spending in 10 years as lieutenant governor and incompetence as attorney general."[19]

The Democratic candidate countered by trying to "portray Hutchinson as an extremist in 'lock step' with House Speaker Newt Gingrich, R-Ga., with whom, Bryant liked to note, Hutchinson voted 96 percent of the time." Hutchinson put "Newt Gingrich first and Arkansas last," Bryant charged. The Democratic attorney general also "accused Hutchinson of joining other Republicans in trying to slash funding for Medicare, child nutrition, Head Start, college tuition loans, benefits for veterans and other government programs to give a tax break to the rich." Hutchinson responded by telling voters, "We're not heartless and mean people. Help us get that message out."[20]

Because blacks accounted for only 9 percent of Arkansas voters, Hutchinson could win with less than three-fifths of the white vote. He carried 57 percent of whites and 16 percent of blacks, enough to generate 53 percent among the entire electorate. Hutchinson won 70 percent from Arkansas whites aligned with the religious right, but trailed his Democratic opponent with only 48 percent of the more secular whites. Republican strength was greatest among young and middle-aged whites. The Republican candidate won 95 percent from white Republicans, 82 percent from conservative white independents, and 51 percent from moderate to liberal white independents. Bryant was left with white majorities only from blacks and white Democrats.

Hutchinson won 63 percent of whites from the party's solid base in northwestern Arkansas, where, in the words of Governor Huckabee, "you can throw a rock into a crowd and come up with a Republican." Votes from the GOP rural base were supplemented, as Jay Barth pointed out, by the "rise of the suburbs around Little Rock as a Republican stronghold." The Republican candidate won 61 percent from Little Rock/Pine Bluff whites. In addition, Hutchinson ran well "in the First and Fourth Congressional Districts, traditionally heavy Democratic areas," where, as the candidate said, "we got a great response . . . and we just felt if they got to know me, that we'd do ok." He won 51 percent of white voters in eastern Arkansas and dropped only to 49 percent of white voters in the southern part of the state. By sweeping his areas of strength and holding down his Democratic opponent's leads in the customary Democratic strongholds, Hutchinson became Arkansas's first Republican senator since 1879. At the same time that President Bill Clinton was reelected in Arkansas by a majority of 150,000 votes, Hutchinson managed to win by 45,000 votes against an experienced Democratic officeholder. "For a Republican in Arkansas, that's a landslide," said the newly elected senator. "There is a pattern of Republican Party identity and loyalty trickling down in Arkansas politics," Bass observed. "We are lagging behind the rest of the South, but we are coming along slowly but surely."[21]

Helms, Gramm, Thompson, and Warner, the four Peripheral South Republican senators who ran for reelection in 1996, were all victorious. Helms won a rematch with Gantt by 53 to 46 percent. He carried 64 percent of the white vote and, if the exit polls are to be believed, 10 percent of the black vote. Helms's racial, economic, and cultural conservatism attracted large majorities from a wide assortment of North Carolina white voters. The Republican incumbent won 89 percent from white conservatives and 52 percent of white voters who called themselves moderates. He polled 68 percent from white men and 59 percent from white women, attracted three-fifths or more from every age group of whites, and carried every income category. The veteran senator won 78 percent from the white voters who identified with the religious right, but also 54 percent from those who did not. Helms continued to be the most conspicuous example of a successful rightwing Republican politician, but his representational style was *not* a model that could be successfully imitated.

Although incumbent Republican senator Phil Gramm's statewide vote fell to 55 percent in 1996 after his presidential campaign collapsed, he continued to draw nearly seven of every ten Anglo voters, as he had done in 1984 and 1990, and he attracted 20 percent of the black vote, much higher than a typical southern Republican. A poorer showing among Hispanic voters accounted for Gramm's reduced margin. In 1990 Gramm had won 48 percent of the Texas Hispanic vote. Six years later, against Democrat Victor Morales, a Hispanic high school civics teacher, he fell to 21 percent. Gramm's breadth of support among Anglo Texans (almost three-fourths of the state's electorate) carried him to victory. He swept conservative whites and enjoyed a smaller majority among moderate whites. The Republican senator won majorities in all twelve subsets of whites stratified by sex, income, and identification with the religious right. Gramm carried two-thirds or more of the white vote in the Dallas and Houston metropolitan areas, as well as East, South, and West Texas. Buoyed by this extraordinary support in the majority group, he remained an influential incumbent, a politician whose career illustrated the successful integration of a conservative southern Democrat into the Republican party.

As an incumbent senator Tennessee's Thompson behaved as a practical conservative. Enjoying a financial advantage of $3.5 million to $800,000 in 1996, he easily dominated the Senate race against Democrat Houston Gordon. The freshman Republican carried seventy-eight of the state's ninety-five counties. According to the exit poll, he won 68 percent from whites and 22 percent from blacks. Thompson was supported by 95 percent of core Republicans and 54 percent of the white swing voters, leaving his Democratic opponent with majorities only among African Americans and white core Democrats. Thompson's base among white voters was quite broad. It ranged from 73 percent among 18-to-29-year-olds to 61 percent among those 60 and older, from 70 percent among white men to 67 percent among white women, and from 60 percent among whites earning less than $30,000 to over 80 percent from whites earning $75,000 and higher. Thompson carried 75 percent of Tennessee whites who belonged to the religious right, but he also won 64 percent from the larger group of relatively secular white Tennesseans.

Virginia's John Warner, the only Republican incumbent who was narrowly reelected during the 1990s, seriously "underestimated" the challenge of multimillionaire Democrat Mark Warner. The veteran Republican had alienated many conservative Republicans when he refused to support North in 1994, and he had to fight hard to secure his renomination. Warner's preferred style of campaigning was to claim credit for keeping federal dollars flowing to Virginia. For example, appearing at the Suffolk Peanut Fest with a "ballcap embroidered with the name and number of the U.S.S. *Virginia*" on his head, Warner shook hands and told voters, "That's my campaign—jobs for Virginia. Keep what we've got and get as many as we can from the other states."[22]

It had been nearly two decades since Warner had faced a genuine challenge. Margaret Edds and Thomas R. Morris characterized the senator's reelection campaign as a "lackluster" effort. "A joint appearance at a Labor Day parade in Buena Vista seemed to set the tone for the ensuing campaign," they observed. "The younger Warner jogged the parade route, pouring sweat as he bounded from one outstretched hand to another" while the older incumbent "glided down the street on the back of a power-red convertible." The Democratic challenger "spent over $10 million of his own fortune" in the race. "'He's going to establish a record of having spent more of his personal funds than anyone else in the history of Virginia,'" the incumbent Republican complained. "Trying to buy an election, John Warner said, is not 'the Virginia way,'" the *Washington Post* reported. Much of the younger Warner's money went into negative advertising, but Warner "let most of the Democratic attacks against his voting record go unanswered, and limped to victory on Election Day" with 52 percent of the vote.[23]

Warner won 58 percent of whites and 20 percent of blacks. He carried 63 percent of white men but attracted only 54 percent among white women. He won 76 percent among white religious right voters but only 55 percent among the more secular whites. Warner did not unify the GOP as in the past, winning only 88 percent of Virginia's Republicans. He dropped to 74 percent among conservative independents and managed only 54 percent from white swing voters. "Exit surveys suggested that a sizable number of Democrats crossed over to vote for John Warner but not as many as analysts predicted," said the *Washington Post*. Warner's narrow victory indicated that even apparently secure Republican incumbents needed to run aggressive campaigns against determined and financially potent Democratic opponents.[24]

As the 1998 elections approached, the Republicans had secured nine of the twelve Senate seats in the Peripheral South—their strongest showing in the twentieth century. Only three Senate seats were at stake in the subregion in 1998. In Florida Graham again easily turned aside a weak Republican challenger. The two contests of interest involved a sitting Republican in North Carolina and an open-seat contest in Arkansas.

Although several southern Republican senators in the 1980s had been unable to turn their incumbency into a political asset, during the 1990s only one newly elected Republican—Faircloth of North Carolina—failed to be reelected. Faircloth was anything but a practical conservative. He had criticized President Bill Clinton during the Whitewater hearings, "backed a balanced budget amendment, became one of the Senate's most conservative voices on welfare reform issues and made it a point never to vote for a tax increase." Just as John East had done in the early 1980s, Faircloth looked to Senator Helms for his voting cues. Though a member of the Banking and Appropriations Committees, only late in his term did he begin to emphasize constituent service and attend to state interests. Faircloth did not run as though he were a secure incumbent. Negative television ads against his likely Democratic opponent, newcomer John Edwards, began during the spring primaries. "Edwards is absolutely a Clinton clone," Faircloth emphasized in the closing days of the campaign. "I think that man that did the sheep clone in Scotland must have gotten to him." Faircloth declined invitations to debate.[25]

Edwards was a forty-five-year-old multimillionaire trial lawyer who had a compelling way with juries. "Edwards' strengths," Kevin Sack reported, were "his youth, energy, eloquence, boyish good looks and a blue-eyed earnestness that leaps through the television screen." Although he had never run for public office he "easily captured the Democratic nomination against a relatively weak field by mounting an expensive television advertising campaign and by winning endorsements of key Democratic Party constituent groups including teachers, trial lawyers, organized labor and black civic organizations." Edwards "hardly ever mentioned Faircloth's name and criticized him only indirectly—implying that Faircloth is in the pocket of special-interest groups in Washington. But he did spend a lot of time defending himself from Faircloth attacks." At a rally in Moore County, where he grew up, Edwards dismissed the charge of liberalism. "I just love listening to these politicians call me a liberal. Don't you all love that? The reality is, I believe in the same things all small-town North Carolinians believe in." Yet the *Raleigh*

News and Observer also noted that "if Edwards mainly stayed on the high road, his Democratic allies have been on the attack. The party has run a series of TV ads criticizing Faircloth for cutting Medicare, for missing votes in Congress, and for a feed spill on Faircloth's cattle farm." Edwards' "overriding theme," according to the *Raleigh News and Observer,* "was that he was an independent voice, not tied to traditional politics and independent of special interests."[26]

Edwards defeated Faircloth, 51 to 47 percent, winning by more than 83,000 votes. Faircloth's share of the white vote, according to the exit polls, had dropped only slightly (from 60 to 58 percent). However, blacks constituted 20 percent of the North Carolina electorate in 1998 (versus 15 percent in 1992), and they rejected the Republican senator by 92 to 8 percent. Faircloth won 89 percent from white Republicans, 80 percent from conservative white independents, and 64 percent from conservative white Democrats. But he attracted less than a third from moderate to liberal white independents and merely 13 percent from moderate to liberal white Democrats. He failed to adequately unify North Carolina Republicans and did not rouse the Jessecrats to the same degree as the senior senator. Faircloth received 65 percent from white men but fell to only 51 percent among white women. He won 75 percent among whites identified with the religious right, but only split the secular white vote. There has been no reliable market for junior senators in the Helms mold to represent North Carolina in the Senate.

Open seats in the Peripheral South have remained highly competitive with the outcomes dependent upon the qualities of the candidates, their issues, strategies, and relative financial resources. The retirement of national Democrat Dale Bumpers created another Republican opportunity in 1998. The Republican candidate was Fay Boozman, an ultraconservative state senator whose campaign was devoted mainly to the issues of the religious right. His peak media attention—virtually all of it harmful to his campaign—came when "he said it is rare for women to get pregnant by rape, because fear triggers a hormonal change that blocks conception." Former Democratic representative Blanche Lambert Lincoln ran a centrist campaign and won an easy victory, 55 to 42 percent. She won majorities from both whites and blacks. Boozman carried the core Republicans but lost the white swing vote—as always crucial to Republican success in a state such as Arkansas—and had no appeal among core Democrats. Boozman was by far the Republicans' weakest Senate candidate in southern open-seat elections during the 1990s. He lost every white income group. Boozman carried two-thirds of the religious right vote but only a third of the much larger group of relatively secular voters. He split the white male vote with Lincoln—a sure sign of weakness for a Republican candidate—and lost overwhelmingly among white women. It was the easy triumph of a centrist Democrat over a rightwing Republican who had no appeal beyond the small base of the Arkansas Republican party.[27]

In 2000 Republicans won three of the four Senate elections in the Peripheral South. They easily reelected two incumbents and defeated the weakest incumbent Democrat in the nation, but lost the only open-seat contest in the subregion. In Texas an incumbent Republican senator drew no serious Democratic opposition for the first time in the history of the state. Hutchison was reelected with two-thirds of the vote. The female Republican won 76 percent from white men, 75 percent from white women, 52 percent from Hispanics, and 22 percent from African Americans. She united Republicans (95 percent) and independents (69), and appealed to moderates (64) as well as conservatives (89). Six years after he had ended Sasser's career, Tennessee's Frist breezed to reelection. Deterring a challenge from any well-known Democrat, the freshman Republican united white men and women to win 74 percent of the white vote and attracted a fifth of the African-American vote. Much like Hutchison, Frist won majorities from independents and Republicans, moderates and conservatives.

In Virginia, former Republican governor George Allen narrowly defeated Robb, 52 to 48 percent. Allen beat Robb by 30 percentage points among white men (65 to 35) and by 10 points among white women (55 to 45). Robb was left with landslide support only from Virginia blacks (84 to 16). Allen won 91 percent of Republicans and 58 percent of independent voters. The Republican candidate attracted 84 percent from conservative voters but trailed Robb by 8 points among the state's moderates. Allen ran behind Robb in Virginia's large cities, 47 to 53 percent, but moved narrowly ahead in the suburbs (52 to 48 percent) and won decisively in the rural areas (59 to 40 percent).

Florida was the sole exception to Republican success in the Peripheral South in the 2000 elections. Republican senator Connie Mack's unforced retirement created a truly competitive battle between two experienced politicians. Democrat Bill Nelson was far more the consensus choice of his party for the seat than Bill McCollum was among Republicans. Nelson, who had already achieved statewide office as insurance commissioner, enjoyed a lead in the polls throughout the campaign. Although Nelson lost decisively among white men (40 to 58 percent), he had overwhelming support among blacks (88 to 8 percent), and he divided the votes of white females (48 to 49 percent) and Hispanics (47 to 53 percent). The Democratic candidate's broad-based appeal won majorities from moderates and liberals, leaving McCollum with a substantial majority only from conservatives.

In the 1990s as in previous decades, the Peripheral South was the chief center of Republican strength in senate politics. Every Peripheral South state elected at least one Republican senator, and from 1994 to 2000 the GOP controlled either three-fourths or two-thirds of the Peripheral South's twelve senate seats. Probably the fundamental reason for the Republicans' greater success in the Peripheral South than in the Deep South lies in the differing racial composition of the subregions. Because blacks are smaller percentages of the electorates in Peripheral South states, the white majorities required for Republican victories are (except for North Carolina) smaller than the regional white target of 60 percent. Persistent Republican difficulty in attracting significant black support has been slightly less damaging to their statewide prospects in the Peripheral South than in the Deep South.

10

THE DEEP SOUTH CHALLENGE

On a Saturday afternoon in late November 1992 Republican Senate candidate Paul Coverdell, a politician more at ease among affluent Atlantans than among beer-drinking college football fans, found himself campaigning against incumbent Democratic senator Wyche Fowler at Georgia Southern University in Statesboro, Georgia. *Atlanta Constitution* reporter Mark Sherman described the reception awarded the hardworking (and soon successful) candidate: "'You have a beautiful day for a game,' says Mr. Coverdell, in blue blazer and khakis, about as complicated as his sports talk will get. 'We sent Wyche a message Nov. 3 and we're going to finish the job on Nov. 24.' Around him, men are wearing warmup suits and baseball caps, some guzzling beer. But unlike a few months ago, when the Republican could have walked through this crowd unnoticed, people call out to him. 'You got all these votes,' one man says motioning to three people atop a pickup truck. 'We just don't vote for no damn Democrats,' says another."[1]

Such declarations of partisan preferences, spontaneous, blunt, and pungent, were commonplace among white conservatives across the Deep South in the 1990s. Beyond any doubt, the Reagan realignment of the 1980s had taken root among the most conservative voters in the most conservative part of the United States. Whites in the Deep South now generally looked to Republican politicians to represent their interests and beliefs. If white conservatives, a minority of the subregion's voters, could be combined with sufficient white moderates, Deep South

Republican candidates were well positioned to win elections to the U.S. Senate.

The Deep South had long been hostile territory for Republican politicians. From 1961 through 1990 Republican Senate candidates had made little headway. Before the 1992 elections, there were only three Republican senators from the Deep South: Thad Cochran and Trent Lott, both of Mississippi; and Strom Thurmond of South Carolina. From 1992 through 2000, however, Republicans made important gains. They swept all six contests when their incumbents sought reelection, attracted one party switcher, and defeated one of six Democratic incumbents. By 1999 Republicans held six of the ten Deep South Senate seats—their best showing since Reconstruction. Senator Coverdell's unanticipated death in the following year was a major setback. Georgia governor Roy Barnes appointed his Democratic predecessor, Zell Miller, to serve as the interim senator, and Miller then easily defeated former Republican senator Mack Mattingly in 2000 for a four-year term. After the 2000 elections the Republicans held half of the ten Deep South Senate seats.

GOP weakness persisted, however, in open-seat contests, where the Deep South Republicans won only one of four elections. When neither party could take advantage of incumbency, the higher black populations in the Deep South states generally established an important Democratic advantage. If Democratic candidates could defeat Republicans by nine to one or nineteen to one among black voters, Republican nominees required well over three-fifths of the white vote while Democrats needed less than two-fifths of the white vote in order to achieve statewide majorities. Democrats could still win Senate seats in the Deep South by appealing to African Americans and sufficiently large numbers of moderate and liberal whites. Most of the surviving Democratic senators from the Deep South behaved in the 1990s as national or moderate Democrats.

THE PARTY BATTLE IN THE DEEP SOUTH

In 1992 all four of the subregion's Senate elections involved efforts by veteran Democrats to return to Washington. Two Democratic incumbents encountered no serious Republican challengers. Louisiana's John

Breaux, a centrist who attracted majority support from whites and blacks, faced only token Republican opposition and was reelected with 73 percent of the vote. Alabama's Richard Shelby, the last of the truly conservative southern Democrats, spent $2.8 million and was reelected with 65 percent of the vote. Shelby won large majorities from both black (97 percent) and white (61 percent) voters. His Republican opponent, Richard Sellers, raised only $150,000, failed to unify the Alabama Republican party, and lost most of the white independents and Democrats. It was a far different story for the other two Deep South Democrats. Veteran senator Ernest Hollings of South Carolina and freshman senator Wyche Fowler of Georgia faced serious Republican challenges. Hollings narrowly prevailed against a second-tier opponent, while Fowler became the Deep South's first Democratic senator to be unseated since 1980.

During most of his Senate career Hollings had been able to attract majorities of white and black voters in South Carolina. In four reelection races before 1992 he had averaged 66 percent of the vote. In 1986 the veteran Democrat had defeated Republican Henry McMaster by more than 200,000 votes by combining 98 percent of blacks with 58 percent of whites. The 1992 election was very different. It occurred in the midst of growing Republican strength in South Carolina. Reagan's realignment of white conservatives and Republican governor Carroll Campbell's extensive party-building efforts had generated a pronounced Republican advantage among white voters. In the 1992 exit poll 52 percent of South Carolina whites identified themselves as Republicans and 26 percent as independents, while only 23 percent still called themselves Democrats.

The South Carolina campaign became a dogfight in which "two caustic Charlestonians flail[ed] away at each other in unusually harsh terms." The Republican candidate was former representative Tommy Hartnett. "If you want to change the Senate, change the senator," Hartnett told South Carolina voters. "Everybody's facing the same knock," Hollings complained to the *Washington Post*. "I've never seen a cancer like the incumbency cancer. Everybody in Congress is at fault and they're making me part of it." Hollings responded by brazenly seeking to "reinvent himself as an anti-Congress outsider." He ran a television advertisement "criticizing 'those boys in Washington.'" Hartnett was not persuaded. "How high does one have to be in the Senate to be one of 'those guys' in Washington?" the Republican challenger asked. "He [Sen. Hollings] is the epitome of the Washington establishment. If he's not, then who is?" The campaign "deteriorated into a bitter brawl over Congressional perks and issues that appeal to old prejudices, from job quotas for blacks and homosexuals to drug testing for welfare recipients." Hollings fought back with television "attacks on Mr. Hartnett's integrity."[2]

Blacks made up 21 percent of the electorate, according to the exit poll, and 93 percent supported Hollings. For the first time in a reelection contest, Hollings failed to carry a majority of white voters. Instead, Hartnett drew 60 percent of whites. The Republican challenger beat the veteran Democrat among white men and white women, whites of every age group, and whites with incomes of $15,000 and higher. Yet Hartnett's white landslide was not large enough to overcome Senator Hollings' combination of overwhelming black support and the continuing support of a large minority of whites. Hollings outspent Hartnett by a ratio of nearly 5 to 1, and the Republican candidate won only 77 percent of the state's white Republicans. Indeed, Hartnett "openly complained that Gov. Carroll Campbell and other senior Republicans in the state have not done enough to raise money and otherwise support him." The final result was a narrow Hollings victory, 50 to 47 percent. "Despite anti-incumbent fever," the *New York Times* pointed out, Hollings' "seniority still counts among many South Carolinians who feel that an insider will best serve their interests." Hollings' weakest performance since his original Senate election in 1966 signified growing Republican competitiveness in Deep South Senate elections.[3]

The 1992 Republican breakthrough in the Deep South took place in Georgia, where Republican challenger Coverdell unseated Fowler. The heavily favored freshman Democrat won a plurality of the vote, 49 to 48 percent, in the regularly scheduled November election, but Georgia law (since changed) required a candidate for statewide office to win a majority of the vote. In the second election, held three weeks later, Coverdell won a slim majority of 51 percent. It was a stunning triumph for Georgia Republicans.

A moderate to liberal white Democrat who had represented a majority black House district in Atlanta, Fowler was elected to the Senate in 1986 with 51 percent of the vote. He had unseated Mack Mattingly, a first-term Republican senator, by campaigning in each of Georgia's 159 counties. Described by the chair of the state Democratic party as "the best personal hands-on, look-'em-in-the-eye, out-in-the-street campaigner I have ever known," Fowler charmed thousands of Georgia voters to win a highly contested Democratic primary and then the general election. Despite Fowler's masterly campaigning, Richard F. Fenno has emphasized, the defeat of an incumbent usually owes more to the incumbent's failures than to the challenger's skills. The task for Fowler, as for any first-term senator, was to leverage his accomplishments and connections into a plausible case for reelection. Yet after six years in office Fowler remained "a blank slate." According to the candidate's own polls and focus groups, Georgians did not credit Fowler with specific, tangible achievements. "I could never develop a base," he later lamented to Fenno. "All our polls and interviews showed that people did not know what I had done."[4]

It was thus an open question whether Fowler could make a successful transition from challenger to incumbent. White Republicans and independents were increasing in the Georgia electorate while white Democrats were declining. When Fowler was elected in 1986, core Republicans had outnumbered core Democrats, 45 to 25 percent, among the state's white voters. Fowler had compensated for his lack of white support by winning 81 percent from African Americans. In 1992 the core Republicans had grown to 52 percent of white voters while core Democrats still accounted for only one-fourth of Georgia's white voters. Georgia Republicans might decline to challenge Sam Nunn, the state's senior Democratic senator, but they would not give Fowler a similar pass. Three-fifths of the state's white voters had rejected Fowler in 1986, and there was little in his voting record to think he had made much headway among conservatives. Nor had he consolidated his original base of support among liberal and moderate whites. His vote in favor of Clarence Thomas for the Supreme Court had alienated liberal women, and gays and lesbians believed Fowler had not supported legislation vital to their interests. Having "ticked off all those supporters of mine," as he acknowledged to Fenno, Fowler believed that his ceiling in the popular vote was about 53 percent—an expectation that held little room for miscalculation.[5]

Though facing the challenge of running as an incumbent, Fowler failed to develop an incumbency-relevant theme or message. The Democrat's passivity was apparent in his first meeting with Fenno: "I'm the incumbent, so the campaign will be attack, attack, attack me," the senator said. "We will figure out how to deal with that when we hear what my opponent says." Instead of setting the agenda of the campaign by emphasizing how he had represented the state during his first term—what he had accomplished for Georgians or how he had defended Georgia values in public policies—the incumbent Democrat let his Republican opponent control the campaign. "He was waiting for an opponent," Fenno observed about Fowler before the campaign, "and his plan was to counterpunch, not initiate." It was the wrong strategy for an incumbent. Fowler's "initial failure to adopt a sustaining campaign theme or message was the biggest failure of the campaign," Fenno concluded. "It undermined almost every campaign effort that followed."[6]

Instead, Coverdell defined the campaign. A native of the Midwest, Coverdell began to work in his parents' insurance business in Atlanta in his early twenties. He was elected as a Republican to the Georgia Senate in 1970, where he behaved as a moderate conservative and built ties with white and black Democratic politicians. After joining the Bush administration as director of the Peace Corps, he returned to Georgia in 1991 to campaign for the Senate. Coverdell recruited Tom Perdue, a conservative Democrat turned Republican, as his campaign manager, and Whit Ayres, who had been involved in expanding the Republican party in South Carolina, as his pollster. According to Atlanta journalist Dick Williams, this team devised a strategy to unseat Fowler that centered upon "making Sen. Wyche Fowler into Walter Mondale and Michael Dukakis" by hammering two themes: "'To change Congress,' says Mr. Ayres, 'you have to change the people in it. And Wyche Fowler was out of step and out of touch with Georgia.'"[7]

A Georgia advertising firm produced a series of stinging negative ads that trashed Fowler's reputation for honesty and trustworthiness. A grandmother sang about her unhappiness with Fowler's association with liberal Democrats in an unpolished television ad that caught fire with many voters. Other television ads provided "devastating" attacks on

Fowler's character. "One suggested Fowler led a 'double life' in Washington and Georgia, tapping the strong anti-Washington sentiment among many voters," observed the *Washington Post*. "Another used Fowler's words during a child-support custody dispute with his former wife to suggest that he bounced checks at the House Bank while he served in the House, which Fowler denies." The line of attack that most irritated Fowler concerned statements he had made under oath in court proceedings that were supposedly sealed. Many of Coverdell's ads went unanswered because Fowler chose to conserve his financial resources until later in the campaign. "Mr. Coverdell's hard-hitting, largely negative ads raised questions about Mr. Fowler's integrity and turned the election into a referendum on the senator," concluded reporter Mark Sherman. "The challenger did not appear on the screen once during the general election or runoff campaigns to offer his views."[8]

According to the 1992 exit poll, Fowler failed to increase his support among Georgia whites. His share of the white vote remained at 40 percent. Nor was he able to unify Georgia Democrats. According to the 1986 and 1992 exit polls, Fowler's share of the black vote increased from 81 to 86 percent. However, blacks declined from 25 percent of voters in the off year of 1986 to 19 percent in the presidential year of 1992. During the same period his share of the white Democratic vote dropped from 75 to 71 percent. Majorities of white independents and Republicans voted for Coverdell. The Republican challenger won white majorities among men and women, every age group, every income group from $30,000 and higher, and every educational category above high school dropouts.

By forcing a runoff, Coverdell completely changed the momentum of the campaign. "While the runoff gave Coverdell a new lease on life," wrote Helen Dewar, "it hit the Fowler campaign like a three-week stay of execution." Veteran Georgia journalist Jim Wooten observed: "Mr. Fowler sounded on the morning after [the first election] like a man who'd lost his bearings. For good reason, too. He's sailing in uncharted waters with a broken compass."[9]

During the next three weeks, both candidates sought to mobilize the "core constituencies within their own parties." The GOP candidate's "natural base" of support was among the members "of the North Fulton GOP breakfast club that gathered Saturday to hear Housing and Urban

Development Secretary Jack Kemp stump for Mr. Coverdell or the residents of St. Simons Island who turned out for an afternoon rally. Overwhelmingly white and well-to-do, these are the people Mr. Coverdell represented in the state Senate and can relate to most easily." Affluent suburbanites may have been the candidate's natural constituents, but these voters—commonly labeled "country club Republicans"—were too few in number to carry a Georgia GOP candidate to success in a statewide election.[10]

Coverdell energetically worked to attract support from other groups necessary for a successful statewide Republican coalition. He worked football games and fundamentalist churches. The day after campaigning among tailgating football fans in southern Georgia, Coverdell appeared at several "fundamentalist churches. Those worshippers are not his natural constituents either. Nor is Mr. Coverdell their ideal candidate—he says he supports a woman's right to an abortion, although he opposes the Freedom of Choice Act. But they prefer him to Sen. Wyche Fowler, polls indicate." As another religious right leader put it, "Paul Coverdell does not take a pro-life stance, but he's miles closer than Wyche Fowler on pro-family, pro-life issues."[11]

Fowler was now frantically trying to "put back together the coalition that sent him to the Senate six years ago—primarily black, female and liberal voters." The Democratic incumbent had to meet with leaders of groups whom he had disappointed. Victory required a large turnout from African Americans as well as increased support among white women and rural white Democrats. "I need your help, Lord knows, I need your help," Fowler told "black ministers and other key supporters." In an interview with Dewar, Fowler explained why he expected blacks to return to the polls in large numbers in the runoff. "Blacks look at who can best promote the policies that we all share. I like to think they know my record over the years . . . I may be white, but my soul is black. I wear my biracial support very proudly on my sleeve."[12]

In addition to courting African-American leaders and voters, Fowler met with groups of moderate to liberal Georgia women who had been disappointed in his voting record—specifically his support of Thomas for the Supreme Court—and had a "closed-door meeting with gay and lesbian leaders" to enlist their support. It did not work. Without a theme that could resonate with Georgians, he was defeated by slightly more than 16,000 votes. Fowler's entire 1992 campaign had dismayed his supporters. "Privately, leading Georgia Democrats were virtually unanimous in their criticism of Fowler's conduct of the race," David Von Drehle reported. "His campaign, they said, was at various times lackadaisical, imperious and derivative. The senator cancelled rallies and—in the eyes of some observers—sleepwalked through speeches even in the last week of the runoff campaign. 'I've never seen him like this,' one experienced Atlanta Democrat said. "I never saw the fire in him.'"[13]

Coverdell attracted middle- and upper-income metropolitan whites, but he also ran well in rural and small-town counties with large white populations in the northern and southeastern parts of the state. According to Ayres, "The Coverdell campaign showed [that] traditional Republicans and religious conservatives could submerge their differences in the common cause of defeating a liberal Democrat. Religious conservatives, who had generally supported other candidates in the primary, became an important component of Mr. Coverdell's winning coalition." Newt Gingrich, Georgia's most important GOP leader, emphasized his party's achievement. "The Republican Party for the first time was able to field genuinely seasoned candidates with local volunteers in every county that mattered," Gingrich said. "The result was that they were genuinely competitive for the first time in the 20th century."[14]

The Republicans' Deep South advance solidified in 1994 when freshman Republican senator Trent Lott of Mississippi showed that he knew how to use incumbency as a political resource. "Self-assured, quick witted, and highly conservative," Lott was a natural leader. Elected to the House as a Republican in 1972, "his ability to keep friends while taking hard-line positions brought him election as Republican whip" in 1980. He left the House's second-highest leadership position to run for the Senate in 1988. Lott emphasized his commitment to exercising power on behalf of his constituents by telling voters, "I want to be a Senator who will be there when the votes count." Anticipating that Democrats would attack him as a "country club Republican" who cared nothing about the needs of average Mississippians, Lott presented himself as "the proud son of a union shipyard worker, a self-described 'populist' and champion of Social Security, broader highways, better education and other largess from Washington that helps the average

Mississippian, black or white." His opponent, Congressman John Dowdy, complained: "He's not running as a conservative Republican. He's running as a middle-of-the-road Democrat. He's got the conservative vote locked up, and he's aiming for the moderate white who doesn't know how he voted in Washington." In turn, Lott charged that Dowdy had missed important votes in the House of Representatives: "We don't need a good old boy from Mississippi standing in the back row of the U.S. Senate just shuffling around."[15]

Once elected to the Senate, Lott knew what to do to make himself electorally secure in Mississippi. He behaved as a practical conservative who combined a very conservative voting record with service on two committees–Armed Services and Commerce–that enabled him to give close attention to the state's share of federal funds. According to one assessment, although Lott "has been more of a political operator than a legislative initiator, he is vigilant in protecting Mississippi interests, particularly the state's military-related businesses." In 1994 he spent $2.5 million on his reelection campaign against a former state senator who was able to raise only $345,000. Lott crushed his token Democratic opponent, 69 to 31 percent, and ran up a majority of nearly 229,000 votes. The incumbent Republican carried seventy-six of the state's eighty-two counties and failed to win only six sparsely populated majority-black rural counties. It was a tremendous demonstration of grassroots support for a Republican senator in Mississippi.[16]

Lott's overpowering strength at home in 1994 coincided with GOP gains that gave the Republicans control of the Senate. Lott immediately sought a greater leadership role among the Senate Republicans. Two years earlier he had wielded internal influence to gain election as secretary of the Republican Conference, the party's number-four leadership position. Now he moved even more aggressively. Ignoring the opposition of Senate majority leader Robert Dole, he challenged Wyoming senator Alan K. Simpson for whip, the party's second most important leadership position. Supported by "younger conservatives elected in 1992 and 1994 who thought Simpson too moderate on some issues and insufficiently partisan," he won by a single vote. In the process Lott "leapfrogged over his more senior Mississippi colleague, Thad Cochran, who held the number-three leadership position. Lott's comment was typically unsentimental: 'There comes a time in life, in politics as in baseball, when you seize the moment or it's gone forever. I ran and he didn't.'"[17]

When Dole resigned from the Senate in 1996 to run for the presidency, Lott easily defeated Cochran, forty-four to eight, to become majority leader. As leader of the Senate Republicans, Lott was superbly positioned to maintain and enhance Mississippi's interests. Interviewed about the federal contracts he helped to bring to the Ingalls shipyards at Pascagoula, Lott showed that his understanding of Republican principles included doing well with federal dollars at home: "'It's one of the most important shipyards in the country,' Mr. Lott said of Ingalls Shipbuilding, 'and if I were not supportive of my hometown, that shipyard and the workers in that shipyard, I wouldn't deserve to be in Congress, now would I?'"[18]

The 1994 Republican Senate gain in the Deep South came not from an election but from a veteran senator who chose to change parties. One week after the Republicans gained control of the Senate Richard Shelby of Alabama switched to the GOP, the first crossover since Thurmond in 1964. Shelby had long behaved as a nominal Democrat, and he gladly joined the new majority party of the Senate. "This is a great day," he announced. "You don't know how free I feel." Always a conservative, he had felt increasingly alienated from the national Democratic party. "Shelby is the great-grandson of a farmer turned Confederate captain, a man, like most of his forebears, who thought that truth and right reposed in the Democratic party," wrote David Shribman. "Hardly anybody Shelby knows nowadays believes that anymore. 'I don't know anyone I'm kin to who are now Democrats,' he says. 'They have been moving to the Republican party step by step.'"[19]

Later that year Shelby analyzed the frustrations of conservative Democrats. "As a conservative Democrat in the Democratic Party, you're in the minority . . . because you don't basically agree with them," he said. "I do not believe that there is any future for any conservative Southern Democrat in the Democratic Party . . . they're marginalized, they're being used, and they're not going to really function within the makeup of the House or Senate." Shelby felt no such frustrations in the Republican party. "He's got a smile on his face," observed Senator Lott. "I think he really is excited and feels liberated as a Republican. He feels good about it, and we certainly feel good about having him."[20] Shelby's defection meant that Republicans made up half of the Deep South Senate delegation.

In 1996 both Republican incumbents—Mississippi's Thad Cochran and South Carolina's Strom Thurmond—were reelected. Cochran won 71 percent of the vote, even higher than Lott's share two years earlier. He had long represented the state as a pragmatic conservative. "His voting record," Michael Barone and Grant Ujifusa have observed, "is tempered with respect for Mississippi interests."[21] Cochran leveraged service on the Agriculture and Appropriations Committees and a reputation for effective constituency relations into strong political support at home. Since his initial reelection victory in 1984 Cochran has always coasted to reelection. His remarkably broad grassroots support deterred serious challengers. Against a token Democratic opponent in 1996 Cochran won 87 percent of the white vote and nearly a third of the black vote. He carried 98 percent of white core Republicans, 82 percent of white swing voters, and 55 percent of white core Democrats.

Thurmond's reelection was rather different. "Forget term limits; forget anti-incumbency; forget citizen legislators. Forget the need for new blood, new faces, new ideas or any other 'new' things Republicans are trying to promote elsewhere in the country," observed Guy Gugliotta. "This is South Carolina, and Sen. Strom Thurmond (R–S.C.) is doing fine. He may be 93, hard of hearing, slow of foot and prone to lose his place when paragraphs get too long, but he delivers the goods for his state in a way that most politicians can only dream of." Thurmond, "the oldest person ever to serve in Congress," had represented South Carolina in the Senate since 1954.[22] After switching to the Republican party in 1964, he had been reelected five times with an average vote of 62 percent.

In 1996, however, Thurmond faced opposition within his own party as well as a challenge from a multimillionaire Democratic opponent. A Republican state senator openly made Thurmond's age the main issue in the primary election. Thurmond won by more than two to one, carrying forty-five of the state's forty-six counties. The general election became a contest between "a well-known incumbent and a little-known challenger." Democrats united around Elliott Springs Close, a forty-three-year-old heir to a textile fortune who spent $1.9 million, much of it his own money, seeking to unseat Thurmond. The main issue was whether advanced age had undermined Thurmond's ability to represent South Carolina effectively. To handle this delicate matter, the Thurmond campaign "designed a strategy of carefully chosen appearances, limited exposure to the media and a blanket refusal to debate" his Democratic opponent. Thurmond spent $2.9 million, much of it on television advertising emphasizing "He's earned our respect. He deserves our support."[23]

The veteran campaigner framed the choice for voters as "experience against money. I've got the experience, he's got the money, and we're going to beat him." When a reporter questioned the senator about his age, Thurmond responded, "Wouldn't you call that discrimination? Why should they discriminate against age when they don't discriminate for sex, race, or religion? Why even raise the question?" To many South Carolinians, Thurmond was "just a regular guy who, through longevity and prolonged public service, has achieved mythic status," Gugliotta concluded. "He has done favors for 70 years for at least four generations of South Carolinians, and people never forget it."[24]

"The root problem for the Close campaign," observed an *Atlanta Constitution* reporter, "is simply that Thurmond is a living legend." The Democratic candidate, who had himself voted for Thurmond in the past, appeared to be "almost apologetic about his uphill fight to deny the state's 93-year-old 'living legend' an eighth term in office." The campaign's strategy was to "speak of the popular Thurmond with reverence, but remind folks that he is the oldest senator in history and may not be able to carry out his duties anymore." Democrats complained about "the protective wall of campaign and staff aides that manage Thurmond's every move." Thurmond's supporters "see a politician who has given his life to public service for the good of South Carolina. They see in him their very heritage." As a Greenville voter explained, "Strom is to South Carolina what F.D.R. was to the nation, and no one can imagine him not being Senator, including Senator Thurmond. Everyone thinks Strom is supposed to die with his boots on." Longtime Thurmond supporters came "forward to tell him how he has touched their lives 'This is my last race,' Thurmond tells them in his Southern drawl."[25]

At the start of the general election campaign, Close "said he did not think that Mr. Thurmond's age 'should be an issue or a factor.'" Throughout the campaign, however, the challenger tried to raise doubts about "Thurmond's fitness to take South Carolina 'into the 21st century.'" As the campaign wound down with Thurmond still ahead in the polls, Close "abandoned his pledge" about age and ran TV ads that ended with "a lingering look at a cadaverous photograph of Mr. Thurmond that accentuates his liver spots and the bewilderment in his beady, blue eyes."[26]

The state's senior senator eventually won with merely 53 percent of the vote, far below his usual share. He polled two-thirds of whites and one-fifth of blacks. Many whites voted for Thurmond with reservations. "I believe Strom's done a good job over the years, (but) he's just too old. But Elliott Close doesn't have any experience at all," said one frustrated Thurmond voter. Included among the senator's black supporters was "an 81-year-old woman who showed up . . . to thank Mr. Thurmond for the condolence letter he sent when her husband died in 1993. It mattered little that it was a form letter, no different from thousands of others sent to survivors over the years by Mr. Thurmond's staff. Nor did it matter that Mr. Thurmond was once one of the South's staunchest segregationists," observed Kevin Sack. "'He sent me this fine letter when my husband died,' Mrs. Hunter said, clutching a wrinkled page. 'You can't pay attention to everything you hear. People say, you know, he didn't like black people. But he knows I'm 100 percent black and he sure did pay me respect. You have to praise the bridge that carries you across.'"[27]

Thurmond won 85 percent of white core Republicans, 49 percent of white swing voters, and 21 percent of white core Democrats. He carried white men and white women; low, middle, and high white income groups; religious right and secular white voters. Indeed, he won three-fifths or more of the vote among white men and white women of every income level who identified with the religious right, as well as every income level among relatively secular white men. His slippage occurred among white women who were not associated with the religious right.

While he carried majorities of every income group among secular white women, his support failed to reach landslide proportions.

In addition to reelecting their incumbents in 1996, the Republicans picked up one open seat and came very close to victory in two other open-seat contests in the Deep South. Alabama produced the single Republican open-seat gain. For eighteen years Howell Heflin, a conservative to moderate Democrat, had been unbeatable. His retirement in 1996 created an open-seat opportunity for the Republicans. In a hard-fought campaign, Republican attorney general Jeff Sessions defeated Democratic state senator Roger Bedford, 52 to 45 percent. Sessions was a conservative lawyer who had served as U.S. attorney in Mobile during the Reagan and Bush administrations. A social conservative, he disliked the direction he believed the country was taking. "I grew up in public schools, church, the Boy Scouts. The nation I see today is being led by a government that is hostile to the deepest convictions most of us grew up with." Sessions tied his Democratic opponent to Washington liberals, usually "the kiss of political death in Alabama."[28]

Sessions and Bedford emphasized their differences in a debate before the Birmingham Chamber of Commerce. Sessions "told the audience that if elected he would join 'our neighbor' Majority Leader Trent Lott of Mississippi in writing legislation. 'If you elected him [Bedford], he'll be working with liberal senator Ted Kennedy and Senate Minority Leader Tom Daschle, who voted against the balanced budget, against welfare reform and for enhanced rights for homosexuals.'" On another occasion Sessions pressed his attack. "My opponent says he's a conservative Democrat, but it's interesting that he sneaked Tom Daschle of South Dakota into Alabama recently to help raise money," Sessions asserted. "Why, Tom Daschle . . . is one of the most liberal people in Washington! He's as liberal as Ted Kennedy!"[29]

Republican control of Congress, however, gave the Democrats talking points and their own figure of scorn—Newt Gingrich—to hang around the necks of Republican candidates. Dewar reported that "Bedford has tried to paint Sessions as an 'extremist' too far to the right even for this bastion of conservatism" by linking him to the "extremist agenda of Newt Gingrich" and raising questions "about the impact of the GOP's agenda on government programs on which people of Alabama have come to depend." And so in the Chamber of Commerce debate, Bedford's rebuttal was, "I don't know about all his [Daschle's] voting record, but I'd rather have Tom Daschle than Newt Gingrich, who voted to cut Medicare."[30]

Bedford's campaign manager got to the heart of the Alabama battle: "It boils down to which campaign can best use the 'fear factor.' They'll tie us to organized labor, blacks, teachers and trial lawyers. Our job is to convince Alabamans that if [Sessions] is elected, he'll go to Washington and vote right in step with the extreme Newt Gingrich agenda." Two months later, Nancy E. Roman found that among many [white] Alabama voters "the party label that used to be synonymous with victory—Democrat—has lost its power to persuade. When asked whom they'll support for the Senate next month, many voters here responded with a question: 'Who's the Republican?'"[31]

According to the exit poll, Sessions beat Bedford by two to one among white voters. The Republican candidate won 92 percent from white Republicans, 85 percent from conservative white independents, and 50 percent from white moderate to liberal independents. Bedford was left with majorities from only blacks and white Democrats. Seventy-one percent of white men voted for the Republican Senate candidate, as did 62 percent of white women. Forty-five percent of Alabama white voters identified with the religious right, and Sessions won three-fourths of this group. His appeal went far beyond the religious conservatives; he took 59 percent from all other white voters. He carried whites at every level of income. The breadth of the Republican candidate's appeal among whites was impressive. When Alabama white voters were simultaneously classified by income, gender, and association with the religious right, Sessions won eleven of twelve subgroups, leaving his Democratic opponent with a majority only among low-income secular white women.

Democrats narrowly prevailed in two other open-seat elections in the Deep South. Sam Nunn's retirement in Georgia attracted a consensus Democratic candidate. Secretary of State Max Cleland, a triple amputee veteran of the Vietnam War, longtime officeholder, and genuine hero to many Georgians, was a "political celebrity whose personal history matters more than his views on any given issue." Cleland told the *Atlanta Constitution* that he had "a level of trust out there that I feel like I've earned. It's not so much issue-based as it is personality-based." Cleland ran on his inspirational personal story. "One of Cleland's commercials, entitled 'Help,' shows the candidate shaving himself, putting on a tie, getting himself into his car and driving," reported the *Washington Post.* "The voice-over: 'There was a time I could have given up . . . and let Uncle Sam take care of me. But I was raised to believe you can't expect help . . . if you don't help yourself.'"[32]

Although Republican candidate Guy Millner had never held public office, he had nearly upset Democratic governor Zell Miller in 1994. He won the Republican nomination in a bitterly contested runoff in which abortion became the central issue. Millner, a multimillionaire businessman supported by the Christian right, defeated moderate conservative Johnny Isakson, a veteran party leader, 53 to 47 percent. "In the July primary, Isakson took the unconventional step of running on an abortion rights platform, designed to attract moderate Republicans and independent women voters," observed Ken Foskett. "In the runoff primary, he went a step further and took on religious conservatives within the Republican Party, a group that some analysts believe makes up as much as 40 percent of the GOP primary electorate," and he called the supporters of the most conservative losing candidate "extremists." The scenario of a divisive Republican primary fight over abortion—identified by Paige Schneider as a set of circumstances usually associated with subsequent defeat in the general election—left Millner trailing Cleland in the months leading up to the fall election. "Isakson was better positioned ideologically to go head-to-head with Cleland," said Charles Bullock. "A moderate is in better shape to pick up independents and even peel away some Democrats."[33]

"Georgians are conservative, but I don't think they're radical right," Cleland said. In his view, "People are looking for someone who is a moderate, who is not an extremist, who doesn't pursue some ideological agenda, who doesn't go off half-cocked in terms of the issues." Millner's nomination, he argued, demonstrated that "the extremists are in charge of that party." Cleland portrayed himself as "independent, thoughtful, bipartisan and moderate, not ideological," a politician who represented "the sensible center." Bullock observed that "Cleland's TV is soft, positive, about jobs, about working and families, because that's the American way. There's nothing specific. No policy linkage. Just a nice fuzzy message."[34]

To close the gap Millner spent $9.9 million, both on positive adver-
tising to market his business success and civic involvement and on negative advertising to attack Cleland's performance in office. Millner accused the former secretary of state of using his political influence to free
a convicted murderer who was the son of a prominent Democrat and of
firing a black female employee who had criticized the operation of the
secretary of state's office. And in contrast to his previous effort, Millner
campaigned aggressively across the state.

Cleland barely won, 49 to 48 percent, with a margin of only 30,000
votes. The Democrat took 88 percent of blacks but only 38 percent of
whites. Millner won 91 percent of conservative white Republicans, but
dropped to 82 percent among moderate to liberal white Republicans—
"I'll vote for him, but I'm not enthusiastic about him," said one female
Isakson supporter—and fell to 77 percent among conservative white independents. The Republican candidate lost decisively, 58 to 42 percent,
among white swing voters.[35]

The voting patterns of Georgia whites varied by gender, religion, and
income. Millner won 58 percent of the male vote and swamped
Cleland, 68 to 32 percent, among white men. He carried more than
three-fourths of the white men who identified with the religious right, as
well as nearly two-thirds of the relatively secular white men. The Republican candidate won majorities of secular and religious right white men
of every income level. By contrast, Cleland triumphed with 58 percent
of Georgia's female voters. "Quite frankly, you're one of the reasons I'm
leading in the polls," the Democratic candidate told "a group of female
supporters" during the campaign. "And I know what side my bread is
buttered on." According to William Booth, Cleland emphasized "his
opposition to assault weapons, his support for abortion rights and small
businesses—particularly those run by women." As a group, women
seemed to be "unenthusiastic about the GOP's harder edges, particularly its stands on abortion, social spending and education."[36]

Although women helped to put Cleland in the Senate, white and
black women voted very differently. Nearly nine of every ten black
women voted for the Democrat, whereas a much smaller majority of
white women (56 percent) supported the Republican. White women associated with the religious right voted strongly (79 percent) for Millner,
while only 43 percent of the relatively secular white women did so.

Millner won majorities in every income category among religious right white women, but among the relatively secular white women he carried only those with incomes of $75,000 or more. Despite greatly outspending Cleland, Millner could not defeat a Vietnam War hero who, in his own words, had been "campaigning all over this state for 25 years."[37]

The Republicans came even closer to winning an open Senate seat in Louisiana. In the contest to replace veteran Democratic senator J. Bennett Johnson, former state treasurer Mary Landrieu defeated Republican Woody Jenkins by 5,700 votes. Supported by President Clinton, who campaigned for her, and by Senator Johnston, who told Louisianans that "John Breaux needs a partner, not an opponent," Landrieu put together a biracial coalition to defeat the ultraconservative state senator who had switched to the GOP two years earlier. It was a difficult struggle for Landrieu because she "had to overcome lingering resentment among black voters over her failure to support an African-American candidate in the 1995 gubernatorial runoff and differences with her fellow Catholics on the abortion issue," according to reporter Jack Wardlow. "She was still able to edge out Jenkins, whom she had branded an 'extremist,' with a strong turnout from black voters and her home base in New Orleans."[38]

Landrieu ran as a centrist Democrat who could "work with both parties" and "bring some balance and fairness and moderateness on issues important to the people of Louisiana—education, health care and crime." Throughout the campaign she emphasized "the need for a balanced budget, reduction of the national debt, a tax policy that targets help to business and families through education and child care tax credits, support for welfare reform, community policing and a better run health care system." Landrieu described her opponent as a person "who has shown no ability over 25 years (as a legislator) to do anything but tear down, not build up, or reach compromise."[39]

Jenkins was a state senator who sought to organize conservatives throughout Louisiana. "You have to understand what we're trying to do," he told reporters. "We're not trying to be elected to the Senate. We're trying to revolutionize Louisiana politics." To mobilize social conservatives he emphasized "ending abortions, promoting home schooling, opposing homosexuality and promoting religion in public life and prayer in public schools." As Jenkins told Louisianans, "We'll stand up for balanced budgets, lower taxes, traditional family values and a strong defense. We won't touch Social Security or Medicare or veterans' benefits. We'll stand up for our free enterprise system. We'll fight crime." Toward the end of the campaign, reporter Marsha Shuler observed: "Instead of defining who they are, Jenkins and Landrieu are trying to define and label each other. Some of the kinder labels are Landrieu as 'a liberal' and Jenkins as 'an extremist.'" A joint appearance in Baton Rouge "featured name calling and charge/countercharge ad nauseam," all delivered "in the name of setting the record straight."[40]

Landrieu prevailed by an exceptionally narrow margin. Jenkins carried thirty-nine of the state's sixty-four parishes and demonstrated strength in both northern and southern Louisiana. Except in the two parishes in which Landrieu polled large margins—Orleans (New Orleans) and Caddo (Shreveport)—Jenkins led, 53 to 47 percent, and ran 105,494 votes ahead of Landrieu. Lopsided Democratic support in New Orleans and Shreveport, combined with Jenkins' weak showing in his home parish, East Baton Rouge, gave the victory to Landrieu. She carried Orleans Parish by 100,395 votes and Caddo Parish by 10,887. The Louisiana Senate election was strongly polarized between white and black voters. Jenkins routed Landrieu, 68 to 32 percent, among the state's white voters. According to the exit poll, Jenkins won large majorities of whites in the New Orleans area, the Cajun south, and the Protestant north. Supported eventually by the endorsements and organizations of Louisiana's most influential black politicians—New Orleans mayor Marc Morial was especially important—Landrieu won 91 percent of the black vote. When Landrieu's black support was combined with nearly a third of the white vote, her biracial coalition narrowly prevailed.[41]

Jenkins swept the religious conservatives. Thirty-nine percent of Louisiana white voters belonged to the religious right in 1996, and 80 percent of them voted for Jenkins. Among these white voters, the Republican candidate won majorities of every gender and income subgroup. Jenkins was also supported by 63 percent of the relatively secular whites, a large majority but short of the huge white landslide needed for victory in Louisiana. Even among the whites who did not identify with the religious right, the ultraconservative Jenkins won majorities from every income level of white men and from middle- and upper-income white women. Landrieu, the female Democratic candidate, lost Louisiana white women (66 to 34 percent), religious right white women (82 to 18), and relatively secular white women (55 to 45). Among subgroups of white women she carried *only* secular females with low incomes.

Once in office Landrieu (unlike Breaux) has compiled Democratic party unity scores hovering around 80 percent, making her the most liberal Democratic senator in recent Louisiana history. Like the other freshmen Democrats elected to the Senate in the 1990s—Cleland in Georgia, Lincoln in Arkansas, and Edwards in North Carolina—Landrieu has chosen to vote as a national Democrat.

In the 1998 elections the Deep South Republicans maintained the status quo. Shelby and Coverdell were reelected as Republican incumbents, and two Democratic incumbents, Breaux and Hollings, also kept their seats. Breaux coasted to reelection. Easily defeating Jim Donelon, Breaux interpreted his victory as the triumph of "mainstream moderate politics over extremism." Nor did Democrat-turned-Republican Shelby face credible opposition.[42]

Approaching his first reelection campaign as a Republican, Shelby told a reporter that his "poll numbers are better than they've ever been" and that "Most people wondered why I didn't do it before." Shelby did not behave as an ideological purist. He used his seniority on the Senate Appropriations Committee to maximize federal dollars flowing into Alabama. While crediting his new party for holding down federal spending—"Republicans led the charge to limit overall government spending by setting caps"—Shelby honored his southern Democrat roots by aggressively seeking federal money. "I have and will continue to do everything in my power to see that those moneys find their way to Alabama rather than going to some other state," he said. The Republican senator refused to "apologize for working to see that Alabama receives its fair share."[43]

Shelby amassed over $5 million in campaign funds. Although the Alabama state Democratic chairman charged that Shelby was "slapping thousands and thousands of Alabamans in the face who supported him as a Democrat," no prominent Alabama Democrat stepped forth to contest the party-switcher in 1998. Shelby's opponent was a sixty-three-year-old retired ironworker and former county commissioner from a small rural county who had to "mortgage his truck to raise the $7,000 needed to qualify for the race." Running as a practical conservative, Shelby was reelected with 63 percent of the vote.[44] Shelby's support from white and black Alabamans changed in each of his Senate campaigns. As a Democrat trying to unseat a Republican, Shelby first won election to the Senate in 1986 with 91 percent of the black vote and only 37 percent of the votes cast by Alabama whites. As a Democrat running for reelection in 1990, Shelby drew majorities from whites and blacks. And as a Republican incumbent in 1998, he drew few black votes but a landslide majority from whites.

Coverdell became the first Republican senator from Georgia to win *reelection* when he defeated former state Democratic chair Michael Coles, 52 to 45 percent, in 1998. The freshman Republican was an experienced former state senator—"He and I were Republicans when being Republicans wasn't cool," according to veteran Georgia GOP leader Johnny Isakson—who positioned himself as a pragmatic, problem-solving conservative politician in the Senate. Coverdell had run for the Senate in 1992 as an "outsider, a 'change agent' as he called himself, vowing to reform Congress and relentlessly attacking the voting record of his incumbent opponent, Wyche Fowler." He became one of Lott's protégés and quickly won the respect of fellow senators for his work ethic. He was very useful to other senators. "One of the reasons he is in the leadership is that he is so low key when it comes to claiming credit," commented Texas Republican Phil Gramm. "As a result, people like to put Paul in leadership positions because he makes other people look good."[45]

Although he was an "uninspiring speaker" and indeed a person "uncomfortable with much of the back-slapping and glad-handing that goes with the office," Coverdell nevertheless cultivated a large and devoted following among Georgia Republicans. The Reagan realignment of white conservatives had generated sufficient numbers of straight-ticket Republicans to serve as a reliable political base. While Coverdell was not well known throughout Georgia for specific, tangible achievements during his first term, he was well organized at the grassroots, had not alienated any elements of his original supporters, and possessed adequate financial resources for media advertising. "Coverdell has been a steady senator who has avoided controversy and scandal," journalist Bill Shipp observed in 1997. "While Georgia's own Speaker Newt Gingrich bounced from one headline-making gaffe to another, Coverdell kept his head down and minded his business." Moreover, Georgia Republicans were optimistic that the incumbent senator would be able to overcome Democratic media attacks. According to Randy Evans, Coverdell "has systematically developed an organizational political infrastructure that has to be the envy of politicians everywhere. From local business leaders to small media outlets to political operatives to religious leaders, Coverdell has developed a network across all of Georgia's 159 counties. As a result, isolated attacks in major media markets are unlikely to have any significant effect on the Coverdell base."[46]

As an incumbent senator who was widely perceived as a rising behind-the-scenes Republican leader, Coverdell was well positioned to raise millions of dollars for reelection. In the past Coverdell had lacked "the money to promote his image and message." However, as Coverdell media adviser Ayres told the *Washington Post*, "That's not going to be a problem this year." His reelection slogan, "Coverdell Works," tried to capitalize upon his rise "to the center of the Southern Republican leadership that controls Congress." Media advertising and direct mail highlighted the senator's efforts to pass education savings accounts, to control abuses of power by the Internal Revenue Service, and to stop the flow of illegal drugs into the country. Democratic efforts to label him an extremist did not resonate with the vast majority of Georgia's white voters.[47]

Coverdell faced an inexperienced Democratic challenger who was unknown to most voters. Veteran Democratic politicians, including popular governor Zell Miller, declined to run against the freshman Republican. Almost by default, the party's eventual nominee was Michael Coles, a "multimillionaire cookie magnate from the north Atlanta suburbs," who had no officeholding experience and was campaigning statewide for the first time. Coverdell was not intimidated by his Democratic opponent. "I represent Georgia's views and attitudes better than he does," he told the *Washington Post*. "I am on the Reagan-Bush team, and he is on the Kennedy-Clinton team."[48]

Coverdell outspent Coles, $6.9 million to $5.3 million, and ran one percentage point higher than in the 1992 runoff. The returns indicated that the Republican incumbent had consolidated rather than expanded his previous base of support. According to the exit poll, Coverdell took about seven of every ten white voters but only about 10 percent of black voters. He won 93 percent of white core Republicans, 55 percent of white swing voters, and 21 percent of white core Democrats. He won two-thirds or more of the vote from whites in low-, medium-, and high-income categories. Coverdell ran as strongly among white women as among white men and showed the strength Republicans need to generate among both religious right whites (more than four-fifths) and relatively secular whites (nearly two-thirds). He carried the Atlanta suburbs, much of northern Georgia, and many counties in southeastern and south-central Georgia. The reelection of a Republican senator in a Deep South state that had long been a Democratic stronghold illustrated the GOP formula for victory: sweep the white conservatives and carry majorities of the white moderates.

Republicans mounted another serious but ultimately losing effort against Democratic senator Fritz Hollings. The election took place in a state where the Republicans had enjoyed enormous gains during the 1990s. So pervasive was Republican growth in South Carolina that Hollings publicly acknowledged the partisan transformation even as he campaigned for another term in office. "Basically, the whole state's gone Republican," he said. "If I had an 'R' by my name, I'd just go on back to Charleston and forget about a campaign. Wouldn't have to do it." James Rosen observed that Senator Hollings "is comfortable among the political action committees, interest groups, lobbyists and deal-makers of Washington. His notion of Senate service is to pull every lever, tap all cunning and scrap as hard as he can to bring federal largess to the people of South Carolina."[49]

His Republican opponent was thirty-nine-year-old representative Bob Inglis, whose "Coke-bottle glasses, toothy grin, preppy neckties and loafers cement[ed] his image as an earnest conservative." Inglis, a term-limit proponent, was giving up his safe Greenville House seat to campaign statewide. "Hollings and Inglis represent totally different philosophies of government, totally different ideologies, and totally different concepts of what a United States Senator should do," said John Cavanaugh. "Inglis is the reformer who wants to change the old system, while Hollings is the traditional Southern Democrat who believes the only way a small rural state like South Carolina can survive is with the help of the federal government."[50]

Hollings took credit for channeling massive amounts of federal dollars into the state for more than three decades. "I voted against all the budgets," Hollings told South Carolinians, "but once they pass, you can bet your boots Old Fritz will be there." He flailed his opponent for not pursuing money for the state as a member of the House of Representatives. "'What have you done over the past six years in Washington other than whine and complain and sleep on the floor?' Hollings demanded, mocking Inglis' six-year practice of sleeping on an air mattress in his Cannon House office." Inglis rejected the view that representatives and senators should furnish "pork" for their constituents. As a representative, he had "voted against federal financing for an interstate highway connector in his own House district and a bridge in Charleston." In a more prosperous era, Inglis believed that South Carolina no longer benefited from the Hollings approach.[51]

Inglis rejected "the compromise-filled game of going along to get along on Capitol Hill" and put "on the main door of his office . . . a plain white sheet of paper with bold, black lettering that reads: NOTICE TO ALL PACS: YOU DIDN'T GIVE ME A DIME AND I DON'T OWE YOU A THING. BOB INGLIS." Inglis explained his philosophy of representation to a visiting journalist: "In 1966, we sent Senators to Washington to get whatever they could because we were desperately poor. Today, in the age of free-enterprise opportunity, we no longer want government guarantees. The state's changed out from under him [Hollings]. The Senator is selling day-old bread, and we're not going to buy it." Inglis threw practicality to the winds by deliberately forsaking the role of service provider. While Inglis opposed bringing federal funds into the state, David Woodward pointed out: "If you look at the history of South Carolina, that's what's helped us."[52]

Personal hostilities reinforced the candidates' differences in representational philosophy. Hollings complained that Inglis had called him "arrogant, evil, corrupt," and a "Hollywood pervert." Never one to hide his feelings or restrain his tongue, the veteran Democrat lashed Inglis with unceasing sarcasm and invective. At various times during the campaign he referred to his opponent as a "hypocrite," a "choir boy," and a "goddamn skunk." He later apologized "for using the Lord's name in vain" but not for calling Inglis a skunk. "Fritz Hollings is not as beloved a figure as Strom," observed Lee Bandy. "He's arrogant, pushy and a know-it-all. Voters always cuss him and complain about him, but they always vote for him in the end." Inglis was incensed by Hollings' personal attacks. "We deserve a Senator who does not belittle us or humiliate us," Inglis told his followers. "We should expect a Senator not to cuss us and treat us like a bunch of hicks."[53]

Inglis called for President Clinton to resign for his involvement with Monica Lewinsky. "I can't imagine Jimmy Carter or Ronald Reagan or George Bush or even Richard Nixon not crawling to a helicopter and leaving no forwarding address if they had done what Bill Clinton had done," he said to "wild applause" in Rock Hill.[54] Hollings also denounced Clinton's personal conduct, but he took no position on impeachment because, he said, he wanted to maintain his impartiality for the pending Senate trial.

Hollings survived in 1998. The incumbent Democrat combined 90 percent of an unusually high black turnout with 39 percent of whites to win 53 percent of the total vote. Inglis won only 83 percent from white core Republicans, fell to 38 percent among white swing voters, and polled only 13 percent among white core Democrats. He could not unite the state's Republican voters behind his impractical vision of the responsibilities of a senator, and his appeal dropped precipitously among white voters who were not core Republicans. He won three-fourths of the white religious right voters, but dropped to 54 percent among the more secular whites. He carried white men and white women. Inglis won 69 percent among whites aged 18 to 44, 59 percent among those 45 to 59, but only half of the white South Carolinians aged 60 and older. Inglis found it impossible to apply to the entire state the philosophy he had used as a representative. Instead, his principled opposition to maximizing federal dollars, institutions, and services at home severely crippled his statewide effort.

In 2000 the parties split the two Senate races in the Deep South. Senate Majority Leader Trent Lott of Mississippi did not face serious, well-financed opposition. Lott's two-thirds majority of the total vote was based on extraordinary racial polarization. He carried the white vote 88 to 9 percent but lost the African-American vote 87 to 11 percent. No white gender gap surfaced in Mississippi. Lott won 91 percent of white men and 84 percent of white women. The conservative Republican senator appeared to be about as secure as conservative Democratic senators John Stennis and Jim Eastland had once been in Mississippi.

A very different voting pattern–far more favorable to the Democrats–appeared in Georgia. Governor Barnes's selection of former governor Zell Miller to fill the vacant Senate seat united the Democratic party while the Republican party returned to a one-term senator who had been out of office–and out of the public eye–for fourteen years. Miller had retired from public life after a successful governorship, enjoyed a huge financial advantage, and effectively used television advertising to emphasize that he would represent the state as an independent voice in the Senate. Miller won 90 percent from Democrats and 56 percent from independents. He won 86 percent from liberals but, far more importantly, attracted 70 percent from moderates. Miller's majority biracial coalition was based on 92 percent of the vote cast by African Americans and 51 percent of the vote from white women. Mattingly won a convincing majority (55 to 39 percent) only from white men.

For more than a century after the end of Reconstruction almost all the white conservatives in the Deep South's Senate delegation had called themselves Democrats. They may have been "Georgia Democrats" or "Mississippi Democrats" or "Louisiana Democrats," to be sure, but they still behaved as nominal adherents of the party of their fathers, grandfathers, and great-grandfathers. Reagan's realignment of conservative white southern voters during the 1980s undercut the principal base of electoral support for conservative Democratic politicians in Democratic primaries and general elections. During the 1990s white conservatives generally ceased to be interested in or concerned about the success of the Democratic party's candidates for the Senate.

Just as conservative white voters in the Deep South abandoned Democratic candidates and switched to the Republicans, so, too, the subregion's conservative senators now pursued national careers as Republicans. Shelby was the last truly conservative Democratic senator in the Deep South, and his switch to the Republicans after the 1994 elections completed the historic break of Deep South conservatives with the Democratic party that Thurmond had pioneered in 1964. The rise of conservative Republican senators in the Deep South did not, however, signify an end to Democratic success in the subregion. Biracial campaign strategies undergirded the careers of such prominent Deep South Democrats as Breaux, Hollings, Cleland, Landrieu, and Miller. During the last decade of the twentieth century, Republican candidates had neutralized the Democratic party's traditional advantage in the Deep South, a development that in no small measure had increased the strength of the Republican party in the Senate. As the new century began, both political parties had viable paths to the Senate from the Deep South, and the subregion remained a vital battleground in both parties' strategies to control the Senate.

SEIZING SENATORIAL OPPORTUNITIES

In the 1990s southern Republicans took considerably greater advantage of their improved opportunities in Senate elections. Table 10.1 reports the Republican opportunity structure for the 1992–2000 elections. For the first time the electoral context—the distribution of contests involving Republican incumbents, open seats, and Democratic incumbents—did not put the southern Republicans at a fundamental disadvantage. There were slightly more elections with Republican incumbents (41 percent) than with Democratic incumbents (35 percent). In the 1980s, by comparison, Democratic incumbents had outnumbered Republican incumbents by almost two to one. Moreover, the veteran Republicans in the 1990s were considerably more skilled and professional than their counterparts in the previous decade. Their reelection rate of 93 percent was considerably higher than that of their Democratic counterparts in the 1990s (69 percent), about the same as that of Democratic incumbents in the 1980s (95 percent), and much better than their own performance in the 1980s (75 percent).

As a result of improved reelection rates among a larger group of incumbents, Republicans controlled almost two-fifths of the southern Senate elections through their incumbents, a much stronger performance than before. Republicans also fared much better against Democratic incumbents, winning 31 percent of such elections. Ironically, they failed to win a majority of the open-seat contests. In the 1990s the Republicans performed much better in the Deep South than before, but their decisive Senate breakthrough came in the Peripheral South (see Table 10.1). Republicans won two-thirds of the Senate elections in the

Table 10.1 The Republican opportunity structure in southern Senate elections, 1992–2000

Elections involving	Electoral context			Republican victory rates			Republican yields		
	PS	DS	SO	PS	DS	SO	PS	DS	SO
Incumbent Reps.	43	38	41	89	100	93	38	38	38
Open seats	24	25	24	60	25	44	14	6	11
Incumbent Dems.	33	38	35	43	17	31	14	6	11
All elections	100	100	100	67	50	59	67	50	59

Note: Electoral context = percentage of Senate elections involving incumbent Republicans, open seats, or incumbent Democrats; Republican victory rates = percentage of each type of election won by Republicans; Republican yields = electoral context times Republican victory rates; PS = Peripheral South; DS = Deep South; SO = South.

Sources: Calculated from *Congressional Quarterly's Guide to U.S. Elections,* 3d ed. (Washington, D.C., 1994); and *Congressional Quarterly Weekly Report,* various issues.

Peripheral South, compared with half of the Deep South contests. With smaller black populations, Republicans in Peripheral South states did not need such overwhelming white majorities as they did in the Deep South. Moreover, Republicans came very close to winning two of their lost open-seat opportunities in the Deep South. Jenkins lost to Landrieu by less than 6,000 votes in the 1996 Louisiana contest, and Millner trailed Cleland by only one percent of the total vote in the 1996 Georgia election.

Reagan's southern realignment, combined with better-financed and more-aggressive candidates, enabled the Republicans to be far more competitive in Senate elections in the 1990s than earlier. Table 10.2 presents the average support for Republican Senate candidates in the 1990s in elections involving Democratic incumbents, open seats, and Republican incumbents. On average, Republican incumbents won seven-tenths of the white vote while Republican candidates in open-seat contests secured three-fifths of the white vote. Remarkably, Republicans even managed to split the white vote when they challenged Democratic incumbents. Presumably because of their constituency service, Republican incumbents also secured relatively strong black support.

Republican penetration of the white electorate becomes very clear when the results are presented by gender, income levels, and religion. Among important white subgroups the Republicans' vote increased steadily in most categories from Democratic incumbents through open seats to Republican incumbents. In eighteen of twenty-one subgroups Republicans averaged majority white votes. The three exceptions—white women, whites with incomes below $30,000, and secular whites—all involved elections with Democratic incumbents.

THE REVISED SENATE PARTY SYSTEM

Few developments in American politics are as momentous as the partisan and ideological reshaping of southern congressional politics. History provides the appropriate perspective for appreciating this immense transformation. Nothing contradicted American ideals more glaringly than the Jim Crow South. Southern racial discrimination mocked any notions of equal opportunity or fair play. There was no authentic life, liberty, or pursuit of happiness for black southerners subjected to the

Table 10.2 Average support for southern Republican Senate candidates, 1992–1998, by electoral context (%)

Population	Elections involving		
	Democratic incumbents	Open seats	Republican incumbents
Whites	51	60	70
Blacks	7	12	18
Whites only			
Men	54	65	72
Women	48	57	67
Under $30,000	46	58	65
$30,000–74,000	52	60	72
Over $75,000	55	65	73
Religious right	74	74	81
Secular	41	52	63

Sources: Calculated from Voter News Service exit polls, 1992–1998.

constraints of racial discrimination. Well into the second half of the twentieth century Democratic senators from the South used the filibuster to frustrate any serious legislative solution to racial discrimination in the public sector and thereby maintained the racial status quo. Most southern white voters considered themselves Democrats, while black southerners were either denied the right to vote or, at best, severely underrepresented in the electorate. Under these conditions, in the absence of any bipartisan northern determination to intervene, the South's twenty-two Democratic senators possessed an assured veto over the grand issue of southern race relations.

During the 1950s the South sent only Democrats to the Senate (see Figure 10.1). All but one of these Democrats was elected or reelected with landslide votes. Because northern Democrats had not yet mounted a full-fledged attack on southern racial practices, the safe-seat southern Democratic senators had some leeway in their voting behavior. It was still possible to vote as a moderate Democrat or (less frequently) as a national Democrat without inviting attack back home for being insufficiently conservative.

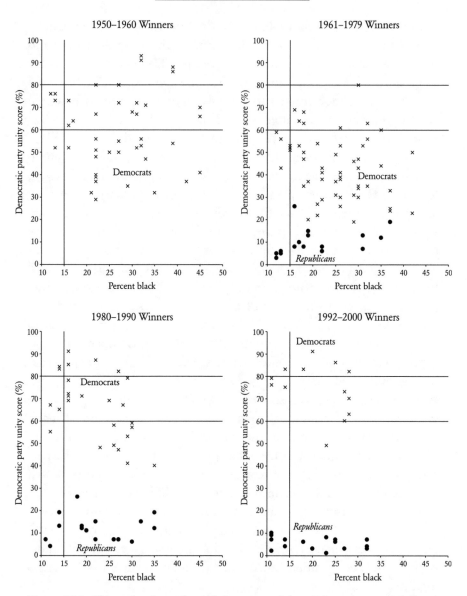

Figure 10.1 The reshaping of southern senatorial politics. *Sources:* Calculated from *Congressional Quarterly Weekly Reports,* various issues.

Beginning in the early 1960s and continuing through the 1970s, however, as the Civil Rights Act and the Voting Rights Act were passed and then implemented in the South, most southern Democratic senators became much more conservative in their party unity scores (see Figure 3.1). Generally, they reacted to federal intervention and to potential challenges from conservative Republicans by distancing themselves from their national party. Many veteran Democrats either ignored black voters or made only token efforts to win their support; and the Republican party, redefined as the party of Goldwater rather than of Lincoln, looked to white conservatives of every stripe for its primary support. By and large, southern Democratic senators could use incumbency, conservative ideology, and their power within the majority Democratic party to smother most challenges from conservative Republicans. "Wouldn't you say that was a thoroughly reactionary speech?" Jim Eastland is said to have inquired after one stump appearance. "I don't see how the Republicans can get to the right of that."[55] Eastland's go-to-the-right approach illustrates a common Democratic defense against Republican competition. During the 1960s and 1970s southern Democrats no longer automatically won landslide victories. The small band of Republican senators rarely did so.

In the 1980s conservatism was no longer the predominant Democratic ideology. Generational change resulted in the election of many New South Democrats who understood how to create biracial coalitions. As many Old South Democrats passed from the scene, the new reality of extensive black participation in Democratic primaries as well as in general elections made it much more difficult for conservative Democrats to thrive in Senate elections. Democratic senators increasingly positioned themselves as moderates or nationals. Although southern Democrats generally avoided describing themselves as liberals, most of those inclined to support their party leaders could do so without risking defeat.

The Republicans' advance in the 1990s produced an additional clarification of Senate politics. During this decade the ideological center of gravity among Senate Democrats shifted further away from the conservatism of the past. The single exception was Alabama's Shelby, who finally resolved his ideological mismatch vis-à-vis the Democrats by crossing the aisle and becoming a Republican. The wide gap in the

1990s between conservative Republican senators and liberal to moderate Democratic senators is a dramatic image—particularly in comparison with previous decades—of the reshaping of southern Senate politics. Neither the national Democrats nor many of the conservative Republicans were elected with landslide margins.

The Reagan realignment of southern white conservatives has important consequences for Democrats as well as for Republicans. By drawing many conservatives out of Democratic primaries and into Republican primaries, Democratic Senate candidates can now safely ignore the preferences of the most conservative whites. The reemergence of national Democratic senators from the South in the 1990s is a tacit recognition of the conservatives' irrelevance in securing Democratic nominations.

A final implication of the revised party system merits attention. Figure 10.1 portrays the unfolding Senate party battle in the context of racial composition. By the 1990s southern black populations ranged from slightly more than a tenth in Texas and Florida to slightly less than a third in Mississippi. The fundamental partisan transformation is clear. Although both parties can claim numerous safe House districts, *there are no safe southern states for either Democrats or Republicans.* Especially in open-seat situations each party is capable of winning elections to the Senate in every southern state. Strong incumbents can, of course, continue to deter serious opposition, but otherwise the racial composition and racial polarization characterizing the southern states give neither party a commanding advantage.

"Now we have a competitive, two-party environment," Tennessee Republican Lamar Alexander observed in 1994. "When we have the issue[s], we have the candidates and we have the money, we can win. But we can just as easily lose and we need to keep that in mind."[56] Hence the Republicans' southern breakthrough in the 1990s should not be mistaken for a permanent Republican advantage. Neither party can afford to take the South for granted. Whether or not the Republicans maintain their southern majority in the Senate, the Reagan realignment has allowed them to become genuinely competitive in statewide elections.

11

THE REPUBLICAN SURGE

Despite the enormous success of Ronald Reagan's and George Bush's presidential campaigns during the 1980s in the South, Democrats decisively dominated the region's delegation in the House of Representatives. In the 1990 congressional election 77 southern Democrats swamped 39 southern Republicans. Bleak and disappointing as these results were for the Republicans, they had reason to be optimistic about gains in the 1990s if their leaders and candidates could transfer the party's presidential strength into congressional campaigns. "You've got 35 or 40 Democrats sitting in 'Republican' seats, and that skews the House [of Representatives] a lot," Republican consultant John Morgan had told *Wall Street Journal* reporter David Shribman in 1986. "Politics in the next decade," he had predicted, "is going to be like the Battle of Stalingrad, county by county, a part of a state at a time." Nowhere did Morgan's observations have greater bearing than in the South, where "the power of [Democratic] tradition and incumbency" had long helped to prevent the penetration of Republican presidential strength into elections for Congress.[1]

A surge of victories during the 1990s propelled Republicans into a majority of southern congressional seats for the first time since Yankee troops had occupied the defeated region during Reconstruction. The GOP advance began in 1992 in a southern delegation that had now grown to 125 seats. Despite a politically damaged President Bush at the top of the ticket, 15 new Republicans were elected to Congress from the South. Six of the newcomers replaced retiring Republicans, but the other 9 captured newly established districts or won seats previously held by Democrats. Two years later, with the unpopular Democratic president Bill Clinton now providing an attractive sitting target and with an organized and focused Republican effort to capitalize on Democratic vulnerabilities, 20 new Republicans were elected from the South. Because 4 of these seats had previously been in Republican hands, the party's net gain in 1994 was 16 districts. Never before had southern House Republicans achieved such an immense expansion in successive elections. The GOP now held a slight edge, 64 to 61, in the South's congressional seats. Upon further reflection and assessment, 5 more southern Democrats converted to the Republican party. Additional net victories in 1996 gave the Republicans 57 percent of the largest regional delegation in the House of Representatives. After the 2000 elections, the southern congressional delegation consisted of 71 Republicans, 53 Democrats, and one independent, a conservative ex-Democrat who caucused with the GOP.

The Republicans' new southern success transformed and reinvigorated national politics. Southern advances helped the Republican party win and maintain control of the House of Representatives. In the 1994 election the region that had consistently provided House Democrats with large surpluses of seats ceased to be—*for the first time since 1874*—an assured asset for the national Democratic party. In their breakthrough election the southern Republicans neutralized the Democrats' traditional advantage in the South and opened up a slight 3-seat lead. Two years later the GOP widened its lead in the South to 71–54, even though House Republicans lost seats elsewhere in the nation. In the 1998 election the Republicans maintained their 17-seat southern surplus but slipped back into a 5-seat deficit in the North. The Republican setback severely weakened Newt Gingrich, the nation's most visible Republican leader. Faced with a possible revolt by House Republicans over his leadership, Gingrich resigned his seat. His immediate successor, Robert Livingston of suburban New Orleans, subsequently gave up his seat following embarrassing revelations about his personal life. At that point the House Republicans turned away from the South and selected Dennis Hastert of Illinois as the new Speaker. Under Hastert's leadership the Republicans maintained their southern advantage in the 2000 elections but continued to lose ground in the North. In 2001 the Republican party's fragile control of the House of Representatives thus rested entirely on the realignment of the region historically most hostile to the Republican party.

Why did these southern advances emerge in the early 1990s after more than a century of consistent Democratic domination? Our general explanation involves the complex reverberations of the grassroots Reagan realignment, congressional redistricting, Democratic vulnerability during the early Clinton presidency, and far more aggressive Republican efforts to fund and promote serious candidates than in the past. In the presidential elections of 1984 and 1988 huge majorities of southern whites—over seven-tenths in 1984 and two-thirds in 1988—voted for Ronald Reagan and George Bush.[2] As more and more white men and women became accustomed to voting Republican in presidential elections, and as a large majority of white conservatives and a significant minority of white moderates came to identify themselves as Republicans, a base of solid GOP grassroots support emerged that could be transferred to Republican House candidates. Reapportionment and redistricting after the 1990 Census then destabilized many districts and thereby better positioned southern Republican candidates to reap the benefits of the Reagan realignment. Before redistricting, 53 of 116 southern House districts—fewer than half of the region's seats—had been carried by Bush in 1988 with 60 percent or more of the vote. After redistricting, 65 of the South's 125 congressional seats—a clear majority—had given Bush a landslide vote in 1988. The initial political failure of Clinton's presidency then energized the southern Republicans in 1994 and propelled them to their greatest single-election advance ever. These new Republican victories, as will become clear, came primarily in districts in which the Republicans had already achieved presidential landslides.

Under normal circumstances congressional districts in which presidential candidates of a major party can win landslide victories are exceptionally safe arenas for congressional candidates of the same party. Neither in the North nor in the South were there any inconsistencies between Michael Dukakis' landslide districts in 1988 and Democratic House victories. Likewise, in northern states Republicans already held most of the Bush landslide districts. Southern Republicans confronted a different situation. After the 1990 House elections Democrats still controlled twenty-three of the fifty-three Bush landslide districts.

Presidentially landslide Republican yet still congressionally Democratic, these divided southern districts represented tremendous *unrealized Republican potential in House elections.* Understandably attracting the careful scrutiny of strategists and candidates, they became the Republicans' main southern targets in the 1990s. Southern Republican leaders aggressively sought to capitalize upon the growth of grassroots Republican sympathizers. Their basic strategy was to insert into many congressional campaigns the presidential model of Republican success: maximize cohesion among core Republican voters and win decisive majorities from moderate independents.

It was doable. And they did it.

DYNAMICS OF THE REPUBLICAN BREAKTHROUGH

In order for the Republicans to take advantage of the grassroots Reagan realignment, presidentially Republican districts held by Democrats would have to be destabilized. Sufficient disruption of congressional districts might induce some Democrats to retire as well as encourage Republicans to seriously challenge incumbent Democrats. As events unfolded, the reapportionment and redistricting following the 1990 Census produced in many southern states—Texas was the principal exception—the most disruptive redistricting since the 1960s, when all congressional districts had to be adjusted in order to equalize their populations.

Destabilization is evident, first of all, in the new racial foundations of southern congressional politics. Just as the Republican electoral base was expanding, congressional districts had to be redrawn for the 1992 elections. Republicans benefited from the specific legal and political obligations that southern state legislatures and governors faced in designing the new congressional districts. From time immemorial white Democrats in southern legislatures had controlled congressional redistricting. The southern white Democrats with the power to design district lines had never constructed more than a handful of House seats that black Democrats could realistically hope to win. A quarter of a century after the Voting Rights Act, blacks made up only 4 percent of the southern congressional delegation, far below their share of the region's population. After the 1990 House elections there were only five black

Democrats–John Lewis in Atlanta, Mike Espy in the Mississippi Delta, William Jefferson in New Orleans, Harold Ford in Memphis, and Craig Washington in Houston–in the entire southern delegation. All served in black-majority or (in the case of Texas' Eighteenth District) black-plus-Hispanic-majority districts. Because of racially polarized voting, civil rights groups argued, it was virtually impossible for more minorities to be elected unless new districts were created that contained substantial black majorities.

Southern Republicans were understandably eager to make common cause with black Democrats over congressional redistricting. They realized that concentrating blacks in a small number of districts necessarily meant creating additional districts made up primarily of white voters, many of whom were already accustomed to supporting Republican presidential candidates. The Bush administration's Department of Justice agreed to require legislatures to draw as many majority-minority districts as possible in order to maximize the election of black officeholders. Prospects of tangible political advantage encouraged black Democrats and white Republicans to unite, at the expense of particular white Democrats, over the politics of drawing the new district lines.[3]

Figure 11.1 shows how the Republicans finally realized much of their potential in southern congressional elections. In the four charts each symbol represents a congressional district. Black dots identify winning Republicans and X's winning Democrats. The story begins with the revised racial structure of southern congressional districts. "New Racial Foundations" compares the racial composition of southern congressional districts in the 1980s and the 1990s. Districts to the right of the diagonal contained smaller black populations in the 1990s, while districts to the left of the diagonal had larger black populations. Lines drawn at 15 percent black separate white districts, where the Republicans would be most likely to win, from biracial districts.

The alliance of black Democrats and white Republicans resulted in twelve newly drawn black-majority districts, all of which black Democrats easily captured in 1992. Ten southern states elected at least one black Democrat to the House of Representatives. Only Arkansas contained no majority-black district. The rationale for creating these districts lay in the history of racial discrimination and racially polarized voting in the South. Although blacks have occasionally been elected to

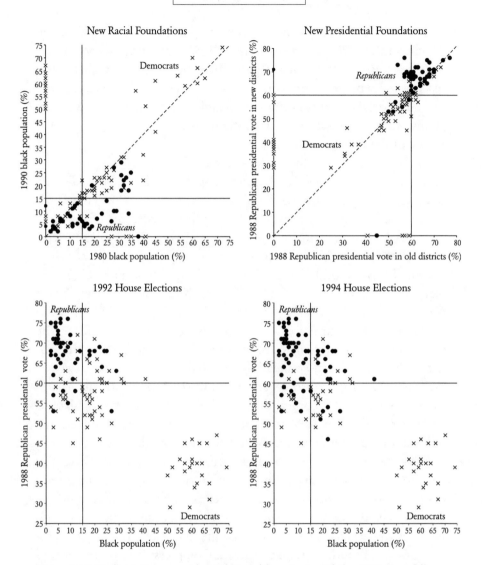

Figure 11.1 Redistricting, presidential Republicanism, and the 1994 Republican congressional breakthrough. *Sources:* Calculated from Michael Barone and Grant Ujifusa, *The Almanac of American Politics* (Washington, D.C.: National Journal), various years.

Congress from majority-white districts—for example, Andrew Young in Atlanta in the 1970s, as well as Sanford Bishop and Cynthia McKinney of Georgia in the 1990s—it has generally proved very difficult to elect blacks from white-majority constituencies. These districts, created with the aid of detailed census information and sophisticated computer programs, substantially expanded southern black representation in the House of Representatives.

In the Deep South the newly elected black Democrats were Earl Hilliard (Alabama's Seventh District), Sanford Bishop (Georgia's Second), Cynthia McKinney (Georgia's Eleventh), Cleo Fields (Louisiana's Fourth), and James Clyburn (South Carolina's Sixth). After the 1992 elections blacks were finally represented in every Deep South delegation. The freshmen black Democrats from Peripheral South states were Corrine Brown (Florida's Third District), Carrie Meek (Florida's Seventeenth), Alcee Hastings (Florida's Twenty-third), Eva Clayton (North Carolina's First), Mel Watt (North Carolina's Twelfth), Eddie Bernice Johnson (Texas' Thirtieth), and Robert Scott (Virginia's Third). The newly created majority-black districts appear in the upper left-hand corner of the "New Racial Foundations" scatterplot. When these newly established Democratic districts are added to the Democratic districts in the upper right-hand corner (districts with high minority populations before and after the 1990 reapportionment), the Democratic strongholds in the southern congressional delegation are obvious.

Devising districts in which black Democrats can build solid careers has provided representation for viewpoints and perspectives long present in the southern population but either excluded altogether or poorly expressed in the congressional delegation. Establishing new majority-minority districts had even more consequential outcomes for the explosive growth of southern Republicanism. Compressing large numbers of black voters, the vast majority of whom always voted Democratic, into a few districts radically reduced the number of black voters in many other districts. A persistent obstacle facing southern Republicans has been the large white vote needed to achieve district majorities if they received virtually no support from blacks. In the 1980s more than three-fifths of all southern districts had black populations of 15 percent or higher, which meant that Republican candidates who were completely unsuccessful among blacks needed white landslides in order to win bare majorities of the total vote. In the 1992 elections, however, nearly half (46 percent) of the southern districts had black populations of less than 15 percent. Many more Republicans could now run for Congress without having to attract such overwhelming percentages of the white vote.

Reapportionment and redistricting immediately gave many veteran Republicans much safer districts. In the Deep South states and in Virginia several districts with black populations previously ranging from 25 to 35 percent now contained far fewer blacks. As a result many Republican incumbents needed considerably smaller white majorities than before in order to win reelection. Republicans such as Floyd Spence (Columbia) and Arthur Ravenel (Charleston) in South Carolina, Bob Livingston (New Orleans), Jim McCrery (Shreveport), and Richard Baker (Baton Rouge) in Louisiana, Sonny Callahan (Mobile) in Alabama, and Herbert Bateman (Newport News) and Thomas Bliley (Richmond) in Virginia all benefited from the establishment of new black-majority districts. Likewise, drawing three new black-majority districts in Florida, three new black-and/or-Hispanic-majority districts in Texas, and two new black-majority districts in North Carolina produced safer districts for incumbent Republicans such as Bill McCollum (Orlando), Clay Shaw (Fort Lauderdale), Tom Lewis (West Palm Beach), Ileana Ros-Lehtinen (Miami), and Cliff Stearns (Ocala) in Florida, Jack Fields (Houston) and Joe Barton (Dallas) in Texas, and Alex McMillan (Charlotte) and Howard Coble (Greensboro) in North Carolina. In several instances Republican challengers capitalized upon the newly drawn districts either to win open seats previously held by Democrats (such as Jack Kingston in Savannah and Tillie Fowler in Jacksonville) or to defeat incumbent Democrats (such as Spencer Bachus in Birmingham and Mac Collins in the Atlanta suburbs).

Disrupting many southern districts had another major consequence. New racial foundations necessarily produced new presidential foundations. The number of Republican presidential landslide districts increased from fifty-three to sixty-five. "New Presidential Foundations" compares the old and new congressional districts according to their shares of the 1988 Republican presidential vote. Districts to the left of the diagonal became more presidentially Republican after redistricting; those situated to the right of the diagonal became less so. We are especially interested in the presidential landslide districts, the districts where

George Bush won at least 60 percent of the vote in 1988. Lines drawn at 60 percent separate the consistently landslide Republican districts in the upper right cell from the new landslide Republican districts in the upper left cell and the previously Republican landslide districts in the lower right cell. Many other reconfigured seats were only slightly below the landslide standard. The net political results were clear. While Democrats had immediately gained around a dozen exceptionally safe seats, Republicans had improved their own prospects in many other districts. By spreading rather than diluting the grassroots Reagan realignment, redistricting amounted to an unprecedented potential windfall for southern Republicans.

In the 1992 elections the Republicans' southern gains were concentrated in the sixty-five districts where Bush had won landslide victories. Fields, Ros-Lehtinen, Spence, and McCrery, all of whom had previously served in more competitive districts, now ran from landslide Republican districts, and Lincoln Diaz-Balart was unopposed in his newly created Miami district (Florida's Twenty-first). Redistricting enabled Spencer Bachus to defeat Ben Erdreich in a redrawn Birmingham seat (Alabama's Sixth), where the 1988 Bush vote increased from 57 to 76 percent, and helped Mac Collins defeat Richard Ray in a drastically revised Georgia Third after the Republican presidential base increased from 57 to 68 percent.

All other Democratic incumbents serving in redrawn Republican landslide districts survived in 1992. This group, which included Jamie Whitten and Sonny Montgomery in Mississippi, Roy Rowland in Georgia, Martin Lancaster and Tim Valentine in North Carolina, Norm Sisisky and Owen Pickett in Virginia, and Pete Peterson in Florida, would come under increasing pressure in the mid-1990s. All in all, in 1992 the Republicans won 42 of the 65 districts that Bush had carried by a landslide in 1988. Two years before they had won only 30 of 53 such districts.

"1992 House Elections" shows the initial impact of reapportionment and redistricting. This chart situates Democratic and Republican winners in 1992 according to the revised racial and presidential structure of their districts. The safest Democratic seats, those containing black majorities combined with robust opposition to Bush, are clustered in the lower right-hand corner. Democrats also won all but a handful of elections in the remaining districts where Bush had failed to win a landslide victory. Southern Republicans dominated the Democrats only in Republican presidential landslide districts with black populations of less than 15 percent. In 1990 they had won 64 percent of such favorable districts. Reapportionment and redistricting increased the number of presidentially Republican *and* very low-black seats from twenty-eight to forty-one. In 1992, despite Bush's own weak performance in his reelection campaign, the Republicans won thirty-three of these extremely advantageous districts for an unprecedented victory rate of 80 percent.

Revised racial foundations thus improved the southern Republicans' presidential foundations. The combined impact of lower black populations and greater presidential Republicanism produced a net Republican gain of nine seats from 1990 to 1992, and this impressive advance by no means exhausted Republican opportunities. The Republicans' congressional surge was based upon durable changes in white partisanship and much more aggressive party leadership in recruiting and financing GOP candidates. Gingrich's rise in the congressional Republican party gave southern Republicans an energetic and combative leader whose own career was a case study in the benefits of sustained, continuous contesting against sitting Democrats. Gingrich had originally succeeded the hard way, running as a Republican in a state that had been exceedingly hostile to his party for more than a century. He was convinced his conservative message would resonate among white suburbanites.

Republican challengers were more likely to secure serious financial backing in the 1990s than in the 1980s. Seldom had they won any elections in the 1980s without outspending their Democratic opponents, and seldom had they achieved rough financial parity. The financial situation changed in the 1990s for many Republican challengers. Throughout the decade the Republicans benefited from better finances and a much more aggressive leadership in recruiting, training, and aiding candidates. Important as these factors are, none of them would have probably mattered a great deal without the Reagan realignment of white conservatives and dealignment of white moderates.

All in all, the 1992 redistricting gave the southern Republicans an exceptionally promising playing field. Gingrich and Dick Armey, the aggressive southern congressional leaders, believed that Republicans could actually wrest control of the House of Representatives from the Democrats. To achieve that goal, however, the Republicans could not afford to let the Democrats continue to dominate the congressional delegation of the nation's largest region. Just as targeting the South had helped the Republican party win presidential elections in the 1980s, so, too, a major goal of winning control of Congress was all-out campaigning in the South. Encouraged by their initial success in 1992, Gingrich and Armey intensified their efforts to find, fund, and foster GOP congressional candidates ready to run in districts where Reagan and Bush had previously attracted landslide majorities.

In 1994 Gingrich seized upon adverse white reaction to the Clinton administration's efforts to expand the federal government's role in health care. Gingrich marketed his "Contract with America" as a referendum on the scope of legitimate activity by the federal government. In an election that placed many white Democratic incumbents squarely on the defensive, the Republicans achieved substantial southern gains. "1994 House Elections" completes the story of the Republicans' sequential efforts to convert the Reagan realignment into increased congressional Republicanism. Close comparison of the results for 1992 and 1994 shows far more Republican winners in the presidential landslide districts. In the presidentially Republican and white districts the Republicans won 39 of 41 elections for a victory rate of 95 percent. Ralph Hall (Texas' Fourth) and Bart Gordon (Tennessee's Sixth) were the only Democratic survivors. Hall, one of the few remaining conservative Democrats, did not have serious Republican opposition; Gordon, by inclination a national Democrat, was almost defeated in the Republican surge. After 1994 the Republicans controlled 55 of the 65 Bush landslide districts, a gain of 25 seats in four years. All but one of the remaining Republican victories occurred in districts that Bush had won with non-landslide majorities.

Between 1990 and 1994, then, a much tighter linkage developed between landslide presidential Republicanism and Republican congressional victories. There is a clear pattern in the location of congressional Republicanism. The Republicans' southern gains occurred exactly where they could be anticipated if the region were experiencing a genuine partisan realignment—mainly in the districts in which Reagan and Bush had polled huge majorities in the 1980s. In these constituencies substantial majorities of white voters had come to think of themselves as considerably closer to the Republicans than to the Democrats in basic political philosophy and inclination.

Targeting the Presidential Landslide Districts

The most profound consequence of reapportionment and redistricting in the South was the expansion of districts in which George Bush had won landslide majorities of 60 percent or more in 1988. Presidential voting characteristics of the newly drawn districts provide more analytic power than any other factor in understanding where the Republicans have targeted and achieved their greatest advances in southern congressional politics. We have used the 1988 presidential vote in each of the new districts as a benchmark indicator for potential Republican success in congressional elections.[4] Southern districts have been sorted into three categories on the basis of the vote polled by Republican candidate George Bush in 1988: districts in which Bush secured 60 percent or more of the vote ("Republican landslide districts"), those in which his support ranged from 50 to 59 percent ("Republican majority districts"), and those in which he drew less than 50 percent ("Republican minority districts"). The larger the Bush vote, we assume, the greater the potential for Republican congressional victories.

Running as "Ronald Reagan Jr." against a Democratic opponent successfully defined as a Massachusetts liberal, Bush carried 83 percent of the region's old congressional seats. This lopsided Republican presidential performance occurred when southern white voters were given a choice between a conservative Republican and a liberal northern Democrat. Dukakis took positions on many issues that experienced southern Democrats would have avoided like a plague. Moderate Democrats, those who mixed liberal and conservative positions, presumably would have run considerably better than Dukakis.[5] Realistic opportunities for Republican congressional candidates in the South existed in those districts in which Bush had run especially well. Forty-six percent of the old districts and 52 percent of the new districts had given Bush landslide victories in 1988.

Republican efforts in this breakthrough decade were realistically concentrated in their presidential landslide districts. By 1994 the Republicans had captured four-fifths of these districts, and by 1996 they had either won or competed seriously (defined as obtaining at least 40 percent of the vote) in over nine-tenths of them. Republicans also improved their performance in the presidential majority districts. In 1994 and 1996 they competed seriously in about three-fourths of the majority districts, and they sharply increased their victory rates among these secondary targets. Although they failed to win half of the presidential majority districts, their victory rates rose from 13 percent in 1992 to 43 percent in 1998. Southern Republicans more or less wrote off most of the congressional districts that Bush had failed to win in 1988. In these districts serious Republican competition was infrequent, and winning was virtually nil. Forfeits and nominal competition remained the central tendency.

Neutralizing Democratic Incumbency

Improved presidential foundations finally enabled the Republicans to neutralize the profound incumbency advantage that had traditionally been the most durable Democratic asset in southern congressional elections. The ratio of elections involving Democratic incumbents to those containing Republican incumbents is a straightforward and useful measure of district political power. The full-fledged two-party battle for control of the southern delegation emerged only after four decades during which the Republicans either forfeited or waged uphill struggles against experienced Democratic incumbents. As late as the 1980s the southern Democrats maintained an incumbency advantage of two to one over the southern Republicans.

In the 1990s a new pattern of two-party competition emerged as redistricting destabilized many veteran Democrats and thereby enabled the Republicans to reap the benefits of the grassroots Reagan realignment. For the first time in southern history the two major parties were roughly equal in the percentage of elections involving their own incumbents. Moreover, over the 1992–1998 elections the Republicans won almost half of the open-seat elections. Southern Republicans could not dominate the regional delegation simply by reelecting their veterans as southern Democrats had traditionally done, but they had finally ended the Democrats' incumbency advantage. Beginning from a position of severe disadvantage in the 1950s, Republicans could now use incumbency to solidify their own competitiveness vis-à-vis southern Democrats.

In the 1990s the southern Republicans leveraged their theoretically "promising situations"—the southern districts in which they could take advantage of one or both of their primary assets of Republican incumbency and Republican presidential landslide districts—into majority control of the southern delegation. Table 11.1 presents the Republicans' political opportunity matrix for the 1992–1998 House elections. During this critical period almost half of the southern elections represented "promising situations" for the Republicans. Promising situations included the three different types of elections—Republican incumbents in presidential landslide districts, Republican incumbents in presidential majority districts, and open-seat elections in presidential landslide districts—in which the Republicans could take advantage of presidential grassroots success, Republican incumbency, or both. Because they won 97 percent of their promising situations, their yield from this category represented victories in 46 percent of all the southern elections. In short, their base alone almost controlled a majority of the southern seats in 1992–1998. Ninety-one percent of all southern Republican victories occurred in promising districts.

In the general category of promising situations, the most common as well as the most valuable situation for Republicans was the congressional district in which incumbency and landslide presidential Republicanism were mutually reinforcing. Republican incumbents in presidential landslide districts accounted for a third of all southern House elections, far and away the largest single type of election among the nine different combinations of presidential Republicanism and incumbency. And Republicans won 99 percent of this large base. This single category gave the Republicans one-third of all southern House elections and two-thirds of all their victories. The other two types of promising Republican situations involved far fewer districts but also produced (especially among Republican incumbents in presidential majority districts) very high Republican victory rates.

The "less promising" Republican situations include three types of elections—Democratic incumbents in Republican presidential landslide districts, open seats in presidential majority districts, and Republican incumbents in Republican presidential defeat districts—in which the Republicans could not utilize any net asset. For example, in elections in-

Table 11.1 The Republican political opportunity matrix in southern House elections, 1992–1998

District situation	% of elections involving	Republican victory rates	Republican yields	% of all Republican victories	No. of elections
Rep. inc. in Rep. pres. landslide	34	99	34	67	171
Rep. inc. in Rep. pres. majority	7	97	7	14	36
Open seat in Rep. pres. landslide	6	81	5	10	32
Dem. inc. in Rep. pres. landslide	11	13	1	3	54
Open seat in Rep. pres. majority	4	50	2	4	20
Rep. inc. in Rep. pres. defeat	1	67	0	1	3
Dem. inc. in Rep. pres. majority	17	4	1	1	83
Open seat in Rep. pres. defeat	5	0	0	0	24
Dem. inc. in Rep. pres. defeat	16	1	0	0	80
Promising situations	48	97	46	91	239
Less promising situations	15	25	4	7	77
Unpromising situations	37	2	1	2	187
All elections	100	50	50	100	503

Note: Republican victory rates = percentage of each type of election won by Republicans; Republican yields = electoral setting times Republican victory rates.

Sources: Calculated from Michael Barone and Grant Ujifusa, *The Almanac of American Politics* (Washington, D.C.: National Journal), various years.

volving Democratic incumbents in presidential Republican districts the Republican asset of a presidential landslide was neutralized by the Republican liability of running against an incumbent Democrat. Republicans won 13 percent of these elections, a modest achievement but a much higher victory rate than they managed in other situations involving Democratic incumbents. By winning a quarter of all less promising elections the Republicans added another 4 percent of southern elections to their yield from their promising districts.

Settings in which Republicans would have to overcome their principal liabilities of Democratic incumbency, Republican presidential defeats, or both—the theoretically "unpromising situations"—almost never produced Republican victories. These Democratic strongholds, however, constituted less than two-fifths of the 1992–1998 southern House elections.

REPUBLICAN OPPORTUNITIES IN THE SOUTHERN SUBREGIONS

A Limited Republican Breakthrough in the Peripheral South

Although Republicans achieved substantial congressional gains in the Peripheral South, during the 1990s the party balance in the larger southern subregion shifted far less dramatically than it did in the Deep South. After a modest increase from 1990 to 1992, the Great Republican Surge in the Peripheral South occurred in the 1994 elections when the GOP added eleven representatives and increased its share of congressional seats to 52 percent. The 1996 elections produced no net gain, and in 1998 the Republicans added one more district (North Carolina's Eighth) when veteran Democrat Bill Hefner retired. In January 2000 Virgil Goode (Virginia's Fifth), previously one of the most conservative southern Democrats, left the Democratic party and declared himself an independent. After the 2000 House elections, the party balance was 47 Republicans, 41 Democrats, and one independent. Republicans held 53 percent of the Peripheral South seats, while the Democrats had dropped to 46 percent. In 1990 Democrats had outnumbered Republicans, 50 to 30, in the Peripheral South. Peripheral South Republicans neutralized the Democratic surplus but (as of January 2001) possessed only a 6-seat advantage in the subregional congressional delegation.

Congressional politics in the Peripheral South is much more complex than in the Deep South. Containing the megastates of Texas and Florida, the rapidly growing states of Virginia, North Carolina, and Tennessee, and the backwater of Arkansas, Republican success has varied widely in the Peripheral South. In the 2000 congressional elections Republicans dominated in Florida (15 to 8) and held small leads in North Carolina (7 to 5), Virginia (6 to 4 with one independent), and Tennessee (5 to 4). Republicans trailed Democrats in the big Texas delegation (13 to 17) and in Arkansas (1 to 3).

The potential for Republican gains during the 1990s was much weaker in the Peripheral South than in the Deep South. There were relatively fewer Republican presidential landslide districts in the Peripheral South (47 percent of 89 districts) than in the Deep South (64 percent of 36 districts), and Republican opportunities varied enormously in the Peripheral South. Prospects were especially strong in three states. Bush had won landslides in 14 of Florida's 23 districts, 8 of Virginia's 11 seats, and 5 of Tennessee's 9 districts. Elsewhere, however, the Republican potential was rather limited. Bush had achieved landslide victories in only 5 of North Carolina's 12 districts and one of Arkansas's 4 seats. North Carolina Democrats were past masters at the art of gerrymandering Republicans, and Democrats had controlled both houses of the General Assembly when the plans were passed. Arkansas was no surprise; by any standard, it was the weakest Republican state in the entire South.

Texas was an entirely different matter. The nation's second-largest state, which Reagan had carried with 64 percent and Bush with 56 percent, sent more Democrats to Congress than any other southern state. Before redistricting it was represented by nineteen Democrats and eight Republicans. Because of its rapid growth Texas gained three congressional seats after the 1990 Census. Holding the governorship and both chambers of the legislature, Texas Democrats completely controlled the redistricting process in 1991. As they had done in the past, Democrats protected their incumbents and consigned the Republicans to a few utterly safe seats. Since the "one person, one vote" ruling in the 1960s, Texas Democrats had packed most Republican voters into a small number of metropolitan/suburban districts, creating safe havens for a handful of Republican incumbents. Just as concentrating black voters into a few districts reduced the Democratic vote in neighboring districts, so also conceding Republican victories in a few seats benefited Democratic prospects in adjacent districts. Only nine of the thirty redrawn Texas districts had given Bush a landslide vote in 1988. Republican gains would have to be achieved without the assistance of a Republican presidential landslide electorate.

Michael Barone and Grant Ujifusa gave the Texas Democrats their coveted "Phil Burton Award for the decade—for its creatively drawn lines in unlikely places; for the convoluted boundaries of the districts which, snakelike, seem to be threatening to swallow each other; for the partisan effrontery which enabled the Democrats to protect all but one of their incumbents and to capture the state's three new seats as well; for the ingenuity with which white urban Democrats, long dependent on black votes, were given districts where Democratic rural counties were substituted for urban black neighborhoods." Likely Republican voters were concentrated into eight districts that had "voted at least 68% for Bush in 1988," a tactic that helped make Republican congressional candidates uncompetitive in many other districts.[6] Far from destabilizing the Texas delegation, reapportionment and redistricting enabled Texas Democrats to perpetuate their traditional advantage for another decade.

In the 1990s the Republicans' promising situations in the Peripheral South outnumbered their unpromising ones. The margin of the Republicans' advantage (46 percent to 41) was modest, but it gave the Peripheral South Republicans much greater opportunities than they had previously experienced. Republican success came from reelecting their incumbents in their presidential landslide and presidential majority districts, winning most open-seat elections in presidential landslide districts, and occasionally defeating Democratic incumbents in them. In 1992 the Republicans reelected all of their incumbents who served in presidential landslide districts.

Each district has its own distinctive characteristics, of course, but descriptions of some of these Republican presidential landslide districts taken from Barone and Ujifusa's *Almanac of American Politics* or *Congressional Quarterly's Politics in America* illustrate the flavor of Peripheral South Republicanism. Characterizations of Texas' Sixth District as a "generally white, financially secure, suburban Republican area" and of Texas' Seventh as a "collection of white, affluent, reliably Republican neighborhoods" apply as well to many metropolitan Republican strong-holds in Texas, Florida, and northern Virginia and to many mixed Republican strongholds in all six Peripheral South states. These districts contain the South's expanding white middle and upper classes, many of whom seriously consider Democratic candidates only if they are repelled by particular Republican nominees. For example, veteran Republican Bill Archer's Seventh District was created in 1966 as Houston's "silk stocking" district. "Thousands of oil and gas company executives, bankers, real estate brokers, developers, insurance company executives and retail employees live in the western and northwestern parts of the city," constituents who have (for the most part) made standing decisions to support Republican nominees. The adjacent Twenty-second District, represented by Tom DeLay, is a "heavily Republican district" in which one would be "hard pressed to find many national Democrats among the people who have come from other parts of Texas and the nation to live in these new, mostly affluent subdivisions. Even in local elections the historic Democratic leanings of the rural areas are usually over-whelmed by the strong Republican allegiance of the newcomers."[7] This pattern—Republican suburbs with few African Americans joined to rural counties in which the traditional Democratic political culture has been diluted if not displaced by Republican conservatism—is common across the Peripheral South.

Additional gains occurred among Republican incumbents serving in presidentially majority districts. The number of Peripheral South Republicans serving in such districts rose from three in 1992—Bill Young in St. Petersburg, Clay Shaw in Fort Lauderdale, and Charles Taylor in western North Carolina—to eight in 2001. Republican gains included Van Hilleary (rural Middle Tennessee) and four Texans (Mac Thornberry in Amarillo, Kay Granger in Fort Worth, Pete Sessions in Dallas, and Ron Paul in rural and small-town southeastern Texas). The only defeat among these Republican incumbents occurred in 1996. Having been upset by Fred Heineman in his North Carolina Fourth District in the Republican surge of 1994, David Price reclaimed his Raleigh-Durham seat with a decisive victory.

Much of the new Republican success in landslide districts occurred in seats for which no Democratic incumbent sought reelection. From 1992 through 1998 the Republicans won seventeen of the twenty open-seat contests in Bush landslide districts. Nine of these districts involved elections in which a Republican incumbent had retired. In each case voters sent another Republican to Washington. These elections, such as Sue Myrick's replacement of Alec McMillan in Charlotte, Kevin Brady's success in a suburban Houston seat following Jack Fields's retirement, Tim Hutchinson's succession of John Paul Hammerschmidt in northwest Arkansas, or Bill Jenkins' replacement of Jimmy Quillen in East Tennessee, illustrate genuine grassroots Republican strength. In such districts majorities of voters look first to the Republicans rather than to the Democrats for representation of their interests. Just as these districts tend to support Republican presidential candidates, so, too, they now line up behind Republican congressional candidates.

Important as the replacement of retiring Republicans has been in maintaining GOP congressional strength, the open-seat contests in newly created districts or in districts previously held by Democrats are even more interesting. In the 1990s the Republicans won eight out of eleven such opportunities in landslide districts. Their 1992 victories in new districts included Lincoln Diaz-Balart in Miami and Dan Miller in Sarasota, and their 1992 successes in seats previously held by Democrats included Tillie Fowler in Jacksonville and Robert Goodlatte in Roanoke. In 1994 four Democratic retirements in landslide districts led to Republican victories by Joe Scarborough in Pensacola, David Weldon in Florida's Space Coast, Zack Wamp in Chattanooga, and David Funderburk in eastern North Carolina. All save Funderburk soon made their districts relatively invulnerable to Democratic counterattack.

The transition from conservative Democrat Earl Hutto to conservative Republican Joe Scarborough in Florida's First District offers a prime example of the penetration of presidential voting patterns into congressional politics. Centered in Pensacola and including much of the "Redneck Riviera," Florida's First is filled with active-duty and retired military personnel. Traditionally it had sent conservative Democrats to Congress while voting for Republican presidential candidates. Bush had carried the district with 73 percent in 1988 and ran ahead of Bill Clinton, 51 to 26 percent, in 1992. Hutto's retirement in 1994 created an open seat that, after a bruising Republican primary, was won by Scarborough, a thirty-one-year-old conservative Pensacola lawyer who easily demolished his Democratic opponent, 62 to 38 percent.

All in all the Peripheral South Republicans won 97 percent of their promising opportunities for a 1992–1998 yield of 44 percent of all elections in the subregion. By capturing about a quarter of the elections in the less promising situations, they achieved a narrow majority of the Peripheral South seats in 1994. Peripheral South Republicans were less successful in unseating Democratic incumbents in presidential landslide districts than were their counterparts in the Deep South. In the heartland of conservatism Republican challengers defeated a fifth of the Democratic incumbents; in the Peripheral South they won only two of twenty-seven possible contests.

Many incumbent Democrats with liberal to moderate voting records came under strong ideological attack in 1994. In 1992 the Republicans had failed to win a newly drawn suburban district in northern Virginia. Bush had won 61 percent of the vote in the areas making up the new Eleventh District, but liberal Democrat Leslie Byrne, a state legislator, prevailed over a conservative Republican whom she effectively labeled as an "extremist." Yet although militant conservatism does not fit this district, liberal Democrats usually do not thrive either; they, too, can easily compile voting records that displease large segments of the electorate. An outspoken partisan Democrat who was closely allied with Clinton, Byrne voted with the Democratic party leadership on 90 percent of the party unity roll calls. She lasted one term. In 1994 Byrne was defeated, 53 to 45 percent, by Republican Tom Davis, a pragmatic conservative who "hammered Byrne for supporting the 1993 deficit-reduction bill that raised taxes."[8]

The other Republican victory against an incumbent Democrat occurred in a rural and small-town district. In 1994 the Republican revolution penetrated eastern North Carolina, long a stronghold of the Democratic party, and events there illustrated the generational shift of southern conservatives from the Democrats to the Republicans. In the Third District Walter B. Jones Jr., a former Democratic state legislator turned Republican, upset a four-term incumbent Democrat. Two years earlier, as a Democrat, Jones had failed to win the Democratic congressional nomination in the First District, a seat long held by his father, Walter B. Jones, but subsequently redrawn as a majority-black constituency. Jones was defeated in the Democratic primary by a black Democrat, Eva Clayton. The white conservatives' traditional route to power through the Democratic party was now blocked.

Still aspiring to a congressional seat, Jones abandoned the Democratic party and joined the Republicans. "The Democratic party in my 30s and 40s was a party of moderates to conservatives," he told reporter Jerelyn Eddings. "But I didn't see much room in the party for conservatives anymore . . . It came down to the question, 'Do I fit in?'" Such a question, once posed, answered itself. "'People are just tired of so much government,' [said] Jones, who runs an insurance business and a lighting-fixture company. 'When you're in business for yourself, you have to be conservative.'" The new Republican targeted the adjacent Third District, a "mostly white area of tobacco and hog farms in the Piedmont and fishing and resort communities on the coast that had voted Republican in presidential and U.S. Senate races." Unseating a veteran Democrat was unheard of in eastern North Carolina, but Jones had some advantages. "Reapportionment had given Jones's new district many of his father's old voters and considerable name recognition," observed Eddings. "Jones signed Newt Gingrich's conservative 'Contract with America,' linked his opponent, Martin Lancaster, to Bill Clinton and advocated term limits for members of Congress, an idea he readily admits his father did not endorse." He defeated Lancaster, 53 to 47 percent. Jones told Eddings that his father approved of his switch in partisanship. "The last time I saw him conscious," Jones recalled, "he said he understood my decision. He felt the party had become too liberal for him and me."[9] Two years later he easily dispatched his Democratic challenger, 63 to 37 percent, and North Carolina's Third District appeared to be safely Republican.

After the 1998 elections the Peripheral South Republicans had gone as far as they could with their promising situations. By winning all forty-five districts in the promising category, they controlled 51 percent of the Peripheral South seats. Democrats were equally successful in the thirty-eight districts with unpromising characteristics. As the 2000 Census approached, Republicans looked to Texas and (to a lesser extent) Virginia as the Peripheral South states most likely to create additional promising situations for congressional Republicanism in the next decade.

In 2001 Peripheral South voters were represented in Congress by 47 white Republicans (including 3 Hispanics), one white independent who usually voted with the Republicans, 32 white Democrats (including 5 Hispanics), and 9 African-American Democrats. Although whites were still more numerous than blacks among House Democrats from the Peripheral South, there were now far more Republicans than Democrats among the subregion's white representatives. It was a delegation much different from that of the previous decade, when 48 white Democrats (including 4 Hispanics) and 2 black Democrats had overwhelmed 30 white Republicans (including one Hispanic).

A Major Breakthrough in the Deep South

Republicans now dominate congressional elections in the Deep South, the most conservative part of America. An assured stronghold of white Democrats for more than a century, on the eve of the 1992 elections the Deep South was represented in Washington by 24 white Democrats, only 9 white Republicans, and merely 3 black Democrats. The number of majority-black districts in the Deep South increased to eight in 1992, and all were represented by African-American Democrats. Concentrating large numbers of the subregion's black voters in these districts reduced the number of black Democrats in adjacent congressional districts and created an even larger group of Deep South districts that were dominated by conservative whites, precisely the voters most interested in sending Republicans to Congress. These developments tremendously weakened the Deep South's white Democrats.

In January 2001 the racial and partisan composition of the Deep South congressional delegation bore little resemblance to that of the past. The subregion's voters now sent 24 white Republicans, 7 black Democrats, and only 5 white Democrats to represent their beliefs, interests, and values. Republicans had gone from an 18-seat deficit to a 12-seat surplus. The breadth of the transformation was impressive. Republicans outnumbered Democrats in four Deep South states: 8 to 3 in Georgia, 5 to 2 in both Alabama and Louisiana, and 4 to 2 in South Carolina. Only in the Mississippi delegation did Democrats have a 3 to 2 majority.

As a result of George Bush's performance in 1988, the Deep South offered many opportunities for Republican congressional gains. Presidential landslide districts abounded in South Carolina (5 of 6 districts) and Mississippi (4 of 5), were widespread in Georgia (7 of 11) and Alabama (4 of 7), and included fewer than half the districts only in Louisiana (3 of 7). Deep South Republicans could therefore draw upon their asset of grassroots presidential success in 23 of the subregion's 36 districts. In the Deep South there was no Texas, no large state where Democrats could guide reapportionment and redistricting to their overwhelming advantage. Consequently, more Deep South districts were destabilized through the creation of new majority-black seats.

Why did the Republicans achieve much larger majorities in the Deep South than in the Peripheral South? The answer does not lie in superior Republican victory rates in promising, less promising, and unpromising situations. In both subregions Republican candidates performed about the same in all three settings. Instead, Republicans had a stronger Deep South breakthrough because redistricting produced relatively more promising situations and fewer unpromising ones. In the 1992–1998 Deep South elections promising situations were twice as common as unpromising ones (52 versus 27 percent). By contrast, in the Peripheral South there was only a five-point difference between the percentage of promising and unpromising situations.

Republican incumbents in Republican presidential landslide districts have been the key to GOP success in the Deep South. In the 1990s they were undefeated in 36 percent of all House elections. All eight Deep South Republican incumbents who sought reelection in 1992 represented districts in which Bush had polled a landslide vote four years earlier. Seven of these incumbents were reelected in 1992: Newt Gingrich (suburban Atlanta), Robert Livingston (suburban New Orleans), Richard Baker (Baton Rouge), Jim McCrery (Shreveport), Sonny Callahan (Mobile), Floyd Spence (Columbia), and Arthur Ravenel Jr. (Charleston). Each man represented a district containing many middle-class suburban neighborhoods, areas in which the Republican party was thoroughly respectable. The only losing veteran Republican was Clyde Holloway, whose district had been abolished when Louisiana lost one House seat. Baker defeated him in Louisiana's new Sixth District.

Gingrich himself had a spirited contest for the Republican party nomination because his old district had been obliterated by Democrats in the Georgia General Assembly. Ironies abounded, for Gingrich had won by fewer than 1,000 votes in 1990 against Democrat David Worley. The newly created Sixth District now stretched over portions of Cobb, Fulton, and Gwinnett, the suburban heartland of north Georgia Republicanism. Bush had carried this district with 75 percent of the vote in 1988. Republican state legislator Herman Moore, challenging Gingrich as a carpetbagger in the Republican party primary, came within 1,000 votes of upsetting the rising national star. Having secured the Republican nomination, however, Gingrich easily won the general election with 58 percent of the vote.

Starting from their seven veterans in 1992, the Deep South Republicans expanded their doubly advantaged situations—running incumbents in presidential landslide districts—to eleven in 1994 and seventeen in 1996 and 1998 by winning most open-seat elections in landslide districts and (to be discussed shortly) by defeating five incumbent Democrats in the landslide districts. Three Republican open-seat victories in Bush landslide districts involved replacing retiring Republicans (Alabama's Second with Terry Everett in 1992, South Carolina's First with Mark Sanford in 1994, and South Carolina's Fourth with James DeMint in 1998).

Through 2000 the Republicans gained six presidential landslide seats that had been opened up by Democratic retirements. The process began with Jack Kingston's victory in Georgia's First District, the Savannah seat previously held by Lindsay Thomas. Three Democratic retirements in 1994 in landslide settings also resulted in Republican gains. Mississippi's First, a rural district that also included some white suburbs of Memphis, Tennessee, illustrates the high stakes of these open-seat contests. For fifty-three years the district had been held by the legendary Democrat (and eventual chairman of the House Appropriations Committee) Jamie Whitten. Whitten had moderated his extremely conservative racial views over the years in order to keep his leadership position on Appropriations. His retirement gave Republicans "a clear shot at capturing what was once a 'yellow dog' Democratic district (one where voters would vote for such a creature rather than vote Republican)," observed *Congressional Quarterly*. As veteran Mississippi reporter Bill Minor pointed out, "Northeast Mississippi used to be the strongest Democratic area in the state. If they elect a Republican it will show that identification with the Republican party is no longer a barrier in Mississippi politics." The eventual winner, by a huge margin of 63 to 37 percent, was Republican state senator Roger Wicker. Wicker adroitly capitalized on the realignment of white conservatives in the Deep South. "The next generation of conservative public officials is realizing that the Republican Party is where we ought to be. If he [presumably Whitten] were in office now, he would be a Republican."[10] Similar partisan transitions occurred in Georgia's Eighth and South Carolina's Third Districts; Republican Saxby Chambliss succeeded Georgia's Roy Rowland, and Republican Lindsay Graham followed South Carolina's Butler Derrick.

Democratic retirements in 1996 produced two more Republican open-seat gains in landslide districts. In Alabama's Third District the retirement of moderate Democrat Glen Browder culminated in a close victory (50 to 47 percent) for Republican Robert Riley. The more decisive change occurred in Mississippi. The retirement of fifteen-term conservative Democrat Sonny Montgomery led to an easy victory for Republican Chip Pickering in Mississippi's Third. "This mostly rural district," *USA Today* observed, "stretching from the suburbs of the state capital, Jackson, past chicken farms and forests to the Alabama border, gave Bush some of his biggest vote percentages: 58% in 1992 and 67% in 1988." Nonetheless, before "1985 the district had no Republican local or county officials, no Republican organization, no party recruitment efforts and no fund-raising drives," reported the *Wall Street Journal*. But even as the party began to establish a grassroots presence in the district, strategists were utterly realistic about the likelihood of upsetting a popular conservative Democratic incumbent. "'We're not ever going to beat Sonny Montgomery, but we're going to get the district when he retires,' says Joseph Gaylord, the executive director of the Republican campaign committee. 'We can beat the Democratic Party, but not him.'" Montgomery had never experienced a serious Republican challenge since being elected in 1966 as a Democrat who opposed civil rights legislation and the Great Society. "Sonny was different," said a forty-five-year-old Bell South manager in explaining the incumbent's longevity. "He wasn't a true Democrat." Now that the seat was vacant, he told a visiting reporter, "I'm not sure I could vote to send a Democrat to Washington."[11]

There was a not-so-subtle indicator of the relative popularity of the Democratic and Republican party labels in the district:

> Whenever he campaigns for Congress, John Eaves Jr. distributes cards that say he's "pro-life and pro-prayer," a "family man" who's "dedicated to Mississippi values."
> Nowhere do they say he's a Democrat.
> Eaves' opponent, Chip Pickering, hands out cards that cite his "pro-family, pro-life" views, too.
> But they also say he's a Republican, in red capital letters.[12]

The young (32) Republican candidate enthusiastically endorsed the national Republican party and attacked President Clinton and liberal Democrats. Speaking to the Meridian Exchange Club, Pickering said, "I'm proud to be on the Republican team, the team of Trent Lott and Bob Dole," while also emphasizing that "My opponent wants to distance himself from his team, the Clinton team, the liberal Democratic team." He predicted that a reelected Clinton would return to the governing style of his first two years in office, when "he gave us the biggest tax increase in history, gays in the military and tried to take over health care." The Republican candidate went on to stress that three liberal Democrats—Ron Dellums of California, Charles Rangel of New York, and John Conyers of Michigan—would become committee chairs if the Democrats regained control of Congress. "Although he doesn't mention it, all three are black," *USA Today* pointed out. "Later, Pickering says he didn't 'mean it in a racial way, but it's a fact they're liberal.'" By contrast, Clinton's unpopularity among white voters weighed heavily upon Democratic candidate Eaves's efforts: "Asked to assess Clinton, he replies: 'Well, I'm voting for him.' After a long pause, he adds, 'We agree on some issues and disagree on others.' And, after another pause, 'I'm not Bill Clinton.'"[13] The result was a landslide victory for Pickering. The young conservative Republican received 61 percent of the vote, probably drawing about three-fourths of the white vote.

Although there were few Deep South districts in which Republican incumbents ran in presidential majority settings, the Republicans won all of these promising situations as well. By the end of the decade, after several districts had been redrawn, they included Billy Tauzin, John

Cooksey, and Jim McCrery in Louisiana, Charlie Norwood and Chambliss in Georgia, and Robert Aderholt in Alabama.

By winning 96 percent of their numerous promising situations, the Deep South Republicans used their base to control half of the 1992–1998 congressional elections. They moved into a stronger majority position by capitalizing upon their secondary opportunities in the less promising situations, winning a quarter of the thirty-one elections in this category. The greater power and breadth of the presidential realignment in the Deep South are suggested by the Deep South Republicans' superior performance against Democratic incumbents in presidential landslide districts. Deep South Republicans won five of these difficult contests (compared with two Peripheral South victories), and their victory rate of 19 percent was almost three times greater than in the Peripheral South.

In the 1990s Deep South Republicans finally stopped conceding to incumbent Democrats who held Republican landslide seats. Instead, they began to challenge them aggressively. For more than a generation after the initial Republican surge in 1964, incumbent Democrats had easily dominated elections in the Deep South. This situation fundamentally changed when Republican candidates unseated three incumbent Democrats in 1992 and two more in 1994. These successes may well have encouraged some of the remaining veteran Democrats to retire before they experienced the humiliation of defeat.

In South Carolina's Fourth District imaginative and aggressive campaigning enabled conservative Republican Bob Inglis to reclaim a Greenville and Spartanburg district pioneered for the Republicans in 1978 by Carroll Campbell but subsequently won by moderate Democrat Liz Patterson when Campbell vacated the seat to run successfully for governor in 1986. In Alabama's Sixth District, redistricting shifted black voters in Birmingham into the new majority-black Seventh District and made Birmingham's white suburbs the nucleus of the revised Sixth. Despite his reputation as a moderate Democrat, incumbent Ben Erdreich was unseated by Spencer Bachus, a former state legislator and chairman of the Alabama Republican party. Representing one of the most secure Republican constituencies in the nation, Bachus has never faced a serious Democratic challenge.

In neighboring Georgia, Republican businessman and state senator Mac Collins defeated veteran conservative Democrat Richard Ray in the newly drawn Third District in 1992. Ray's old district had encompassed south-central Georgia, but the new district extended into the southern white suburbs of Atlanta to include many middle-class voters no longer firmly attached to the Democratic party. Collins, a good-old-boy trucking company owner, former Democrat, and now Republican state senator who had grown up in rural Butts County, "attacked Ray on the congressional pay raise and junketeering, called for less government spending and, in the words of one aide, 'ran a "stealth campaign"—lots of meet and greet and very little campaign dollars.'" Conservative white suburbanites strongly preferred the new conservative Republican to the old conservative Democrat. Carrying the district's metropolitan counties, which accounted for a substantial majority of the seat's voters, Collins defeated the incumbent Democrat by 55 to 45 percent. Armed with "his rural style and Atlanta area partisan appeal," the new Republican congressman quickly made himself unbeatable in a district that had given Bush 68 percent of the vote in 1988. "Collins' laid-back cowboy boots and blue jeans image," concluded the *Congressional Quarterly*, "fits the conservative district."[14]

The three Democratic incumbents who were beaten in 1992 equaled the entire total of defeated Deep South Democratic incumbents from 1966 through 1990. It was a dramatic indication of the new vulnerability of veteran Democrats in the Deep South, no matter how moderate or conservative their voting record, in districts where Republican presidential strength had created a large bloc of white voters willing to think of themselves as Republicans. In 1994 two more incumbent Democrats were beaten. Both defeats occurred in Georgia. Bob Barr's victory over veteran Democrat Buddy Darden in the Seventh District (Cobb County and northwest Georgia) and Charlie Norwood's drubbing of Don Johnson in the Tenth District (northeast Georgia) relied upon complaints that the Democrats were far too liberal and too aligned with the Clinton administration.

After the 2000 elections the Republicans controlled two-thirds of the subregion's districts and had a huge advantage—69 to 19 percent—over the Democrats in terms of promising versus unpromising situations. Republican incumbents in Republican presidential landslide districts—the ideal situation for the GOP—accounted for 47 percent of the Deep South districts.

Astonishing partisan and racial changes thus transformed the Deep South congressional delegation during the 1990s. From 1990 to 2000 black Democrats increased from 3 to 7, or 19 percent of the delegation. White Democrats plummeted from 24 (two-thirds of the delegation) to merely 5, or 14 percent. White Republicans soared from 9 to 24. White representatives from the Deep South were nearly five times more likely to be Republican than Democratic, a telling sign of realignment among conservative white voters.

Forging Republican Majorities in Both Subregions

By the end of the 1990s Republicans in both the Peripheral South and the Deep South had substantially realized their congressional potential based on the grassroots Reagan realignment. Figure 11.2 plots winning Republicans and winning Democrats in 1998 according to the racial and presidential structure of their districts. Lines drawn at 15 percent black and at 60 percent for the 1988 Republican presidential vote let us compare Peripheral South Republicans, Peripheral South Democrats, Deep South Republicans, and Deep South Democrats.

Peripheral South Republicans dominated House elections only in *white districts with presidential landslide bases.* In 1998 Republicans held thirty-two of thirty-four such districts and competed seriously against both Hall (Texas' Fourth District) and Gordon (Tennessee's Sixth), the Democratic survivors. A conservative Democrat throughout his career, Hall will probably retire before the 2002 elections. Gordon, whose Middle Tennessee district has been trending Republican with the growth of Nashville suburbs, adapted to increased Republican competition by moderating slightly his once-liberal voting record. Peripheral South Republicans have been competitive in two other environments: higher-black districts with presidential landslides, and white districts with Republican presidential majorities. In 1998 Republicans did not challenge Owen Pickett (Virginia's Second) or Virgil Goode (Virginia's Fifth), the two successful Democrats in biracial presidential landslide districts. Pickett, an experienced moderate from Virginia Beach, retired in 2000, and Edward Schrock's open-seat victory gave the Republicans another presidential landslide district. Goode, the former Democrat who now

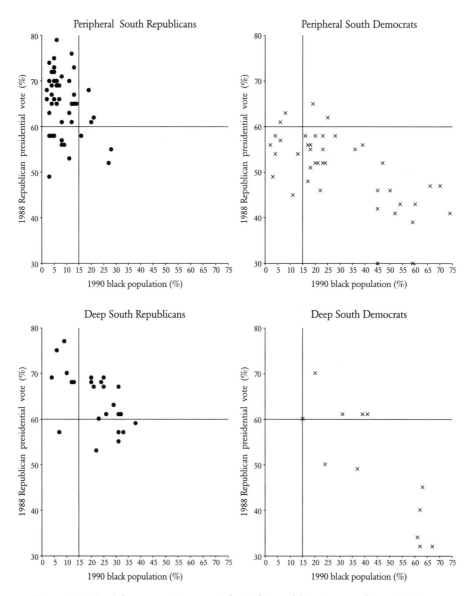

Figure 11.2 Racial composition, presidential Republicanism, and the 1998 southern congressional delegation. *Sources:* Same as Figure 11.1.

caucused with the Republicans, was easily reelected as an independent in 2000.

Peripheral South Republicans have fared poorly in districts of biracial populations without Republican presidential landslides (shown in the lower right-hand cell). In addition to the black Democrats previously discussed, this cell includes many white Democrats serving in Republican presidential majority districts with black populations in the range of 15–30 percent. Incumbent Democrats from the Peripheral South in this category included Texans Martin Frost, Chet Edwards, Ken Bentsen, and Max Sandlin; Tennesseans Bob Clement and John Tanner; North Carolinians David Price, Bob Etheridge, and Mike McIntyre; Floridians Jim Davis and Allen Boyd; and Arkansans Marion Berry and Vic Snyder. These Democrats ranged in ideology from very liberal (such as Price, Snyder, and Bentsen) to borderline liberal (Frost, Edwards, Etheridge, and Davis) to moderate (Tanner, Berry, and Sandlin) to conservative (only McIntyre in 1999). Their common denominator was an ability to construct effective biracial coalitions.

Deep South Republicans, unlike their Peripheral South counterparts, were not limited to the presidential landslide and very low-black settings. They controlled all seven of their opportunities in such districts, but in general they predominated over Democrats in all but two presidential landslide districts with black populations up to 30 percent. The remaining Democrats were Gene Taylor (Mississippi's Fifth District) and Bud Cramer (Alabama's Fifth). Taylor, who holds the Gulf Coast district previously secured by Republican Trent Lott, has survived by voting as a conservative Democrat. Cramer's Huntsville district has long been a Democratic stronghold. After he was nearly defeated in 1994, Cramer (even more than Gordon) dropped his Democratic party unity voting in an effort to defuse Republican attacks as too liberal for his district.

Probably the central explanation for the Deep South Republicans' considerable success in biracial districts is greater racial polarization in Deep South environments culminating in higher proportions of realigned whites. Acute racial cleavage had enabled some Deep South Republicans to hold districts with black populations in the 30–35 percent range since the mid-1960s. At the end of the 1990s Deep South Republicans held seven seats with black populations exceeding 30 percent. These included three presidential landslide districts (Chip Pickering in Mississippi's Third, Jack Kingston in Georgia's First, and Richard Baker in Louisiana's Sixth) and four presidential majority districts (Jim McCrery in Louisiana's Fourth, John Cooksey in Louisiana's Fifth, Saxby Chambliss in Georgia's Eighth, and Charlie Norwood in Georgia's Tenth).

Deep South Democrats continued to represent three Republican presidential landslide districts with black populations exceeding 30 percent. Winning Democrats faced more serious Republican competition in three situations. Sanford Bishop (Georgia's Second), the only black Democrat in a Republican landslide district, had originally been elected in a majority-black district. When his district was redrawn, he was able to use his incumbency and seat on the Agriculture Committee to retain a working biracial coalition in a majority-white district. Unlike other African-American Democrats, he has positioned himself as a moderate rather than a national Democrat. Ronnie Shows (Mississippi's Fourth) won the open seat in this district created by the retirement of Republican convert Mike Parker. Parker had left the Democratic party after the 1994 elections and had used his incumbency and name recognition to be reelected as a Republican in 1996. Once the seat became open in 1998, however, the district's black population of 41 percent made it extremely difficult for an unknown Republican to win. In 1999 Shows appeared to recognize the significance of white conservative sentiment; his party unity score was 56. John Spratt (South Carolina's Fifth) was the only veteran Democrat in a landslide district who has generally continued to vote as a national Democrat despite a very close call in 1994.

THE REAGAN REALIGNMENT
AND CONGRESSIONAL REPUBLICANISM

The emergence of the Republican party as the dominant force in southern presidential politics has gradually reshaped southern congressional politics. Grassroots presidential realignment has both created safer seats for incumbent Republicans and identified districts that might be aggressively targeted. Reagan's successful presidency was the central development that eventually established favorable conditions for the Republicans' southern breakthrough in the 1990s.

To overcome the southern Democrats' incumbency advantage in congressional elections, the Republicans needed to expand substantially the number of House districts in which they could unite a presidential landslide base with their own incumbents. By and large, Reagan's presidency made the Republican party respectable and preferable to many southern whites who had never before thought of themselves as Republicans. Figure 11.3 tracks the steady development of an emphatic linkage between landslide presidential Republicanism and Republican success in congressional elections. When the former California governor defeated President Jimmy Carter in the 1980 presidential elections, Reagan carried only a handful of southern districts by landslide proportions (see "Southern Districts in 1980"). Four years later ("Southern Districts in 1984") Reagan expanded the presidential landslide districts from 9 percent in 1980 to 62 percent in 1984.

A harder test of presidential Republicanism came in 1988. At the conclusion of Reagan's second term, Vice President George Bush capitalized upon the Reagan realignment to win every southern state. Lacking Reagan's charisma and rhetorical skills, Bush nonetheless achieved landslide votes in 46 percent of the southern districts. After the 1990 elections, however, congressional Republicans controlled only 57 percent of their landslide districts ("Southern Districts in 1990"). During the 1990s, reapportionment and redistricting, followed by President Clinton's early performance, enabled the Republicans to realize much of their potential in southern congressional elections. "Southern Districts in 1998" reveals the Republican dominance of their presidential landslide districts and their competitiveness in presidential majority districts. After the 1998 elections southern Republicans controlled 86 percent of the congressional districts in which the Reagan realignment generated landslide presidential votes in the 1980s.

Exit poll results underscore the impact of the Reagan realignment. By the mid-1990s Republicans were drawing upon similar social bases in southern congressional elections as in presidential politics. In the 1996 congressional election Republicans won substantial majorities from religious right whites (76 percent) and secular white men (69 percent) and a slim majority among secular white women (52 percent). They ran poorly among blacks (15 percent) and Hispanics (38 percent). Figure 11.4

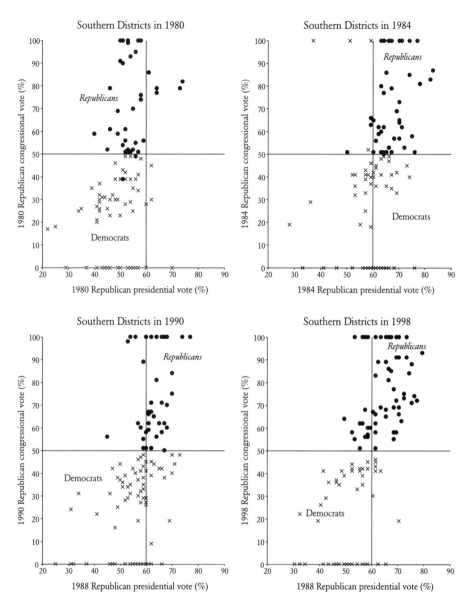

Figure 11.3 The Reagan realignment: presidential foundations of congressional Republicanism. *Sources:* Same as Figure 11.1.

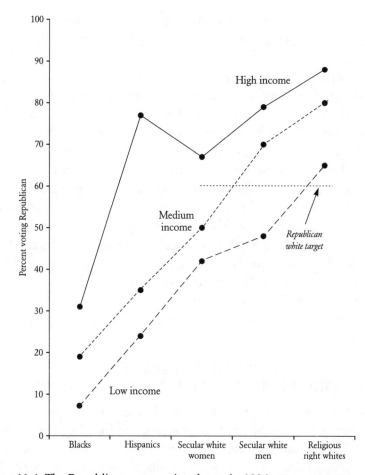

Figure 11.4 The Republican congressional vote in 1996. *Source:* Voter News Service General Election Exit Poll, 1996.

shows the Republican congressional vote in the South for 1996 according to income levels in each of the five social groups. Although the results apply to the entire region rather than to particular districts, they help us understand how the Republicans accomplished their southern breakthrough. In six of nine situations the Republicans bettered their white target of 60 percent: all income categories involving religious right whites, high-income and medium-income secular white men, and high-income secular white women. They broke even among medium-income secular white women (50 percent) and nearly did so (48 percent) among low-income secular white men. Among white groups Republicans were badly defeated (42 percent) only among low-income secular white women.

As the Reagan realignment pulled conservative white voters and politicians out of the Democratic party, the southern congressional delegation in the 1990s sorted itself more sharply by party and ideology. With the addition of liberal black Democrats in the southern delegation, national Democrats emerged in 1992 as the leading ideological force among the southern House Democrats (see the regional and subregional trend lines in Figure 3.1). Although many white Democrats lowered their party unity scores considerably after the 1994 Democratic losses, across the region and in both subregions national Democrats have outnumbered (or tied) any other ideological category. Most black Democrats have been consistently liberal in their party unity scores, and more Peripheral South white Democrats have voted as moderates than as liberals or conservatives. Conservatism has persisted only among white Democrats in the Deep South. In 1999 all but Spratt voted as nominals.

THE POLITICAL CONTEXT:
REPUBLICANS CAPITALIZE THEIR "PROMISING SITUATIONS"

At the end of the twentieth century the Republicans finally emerged as the majority party in the southern delegation to the House of Representatives. They did so by slowly overcoming immense Democratic advantages in controlling southern congressional politics. Democrats had historically dominated the delegation because there were so few Republicans in the electorate. Republicans could not expect to win many House seats without a major grassroots realignment of southern voters, and only the personalities, issues, and events connected to presidential politics could possibly produce such a realignment. Reagan's presidential performance, broadly considered, was the turning point in expanding grassroots presidential Republicanism. Despite the Republicans' success in presidential elections, in congressional politics Democratic incumbents remained a major obstacle to Republican growth through the 1980s. When the southern Republicans adopted the Goldwater strategy of writing off blacks, they compounded their problem in winning southern House seats by limiting their opportunities to those districts in which they could expect to secure substantial white majorities. As a practical matter, this meant that overwhelmingly white districts would constitute the main Republican targets. Biracial coalitions became the standard Democratic antidote to Republican competition. And if Democratic incumbency per se were not sufficient to deter Republican competition, the ability of veteran Democrats to win safe-seat victories would further discourage Republican challenges. Consequently, in a process that has played out since the early 1950s, the southern Republicans have struggled to overcome mutually reinforcing Democratic advantages in grassroots partisanship, incumbency, biracial coalitions, and safe seats.

In order to win a majority of southern districts, Republicans have needed to take advantage of landslide presidential Republicanism, protect their own incumbents, effectively target the overwhelmingly white districts, and then use safe-seat Republican incumbency to turn the tables and discourage Democratic challenges. Figure 11.5 provides a visual summary of the Republicans' southern breakthrough. It portrays the 1998 party battle in the southern House delegation. Dividing the southern districts into "Promising Situations," "Less Promising Situations," and "Unpromising Situations," it places the Republican assets of presidential realignment and incumbency in the context of district racial composition and safe-seat victories.

In 1998 southern Republicans dominated their promising situations, elections in which they could capitalize on their assets of Republican incumbency and/or Republican presidential landslides. The winning Republicans were heavily concentrated in the upper left-hand cell, the area representing very low-black districts and safe-seat victories. In 1998 the southern Republicans won sixty-nine of seventy promising situations. Their only loss came in Mississippi's Fourth District, where the retirement of Democrat-turned-Republican Mike Parker led to an open-seat election won by Democrat Ronnie Shows. With blacks constituting two-fifths of the electorate, Shows did not need much support from white Mississippians in order to reclaim the seat for the Democrats.

Outside their promising situations Republicans fared poorly. They won only two of ten elections in their less promising situations. In these contests Republicans had no net assets to deploy. Henry Bonilla (Texas' Twenty-third) used safe-seat Republican incumbency to keep a seat that

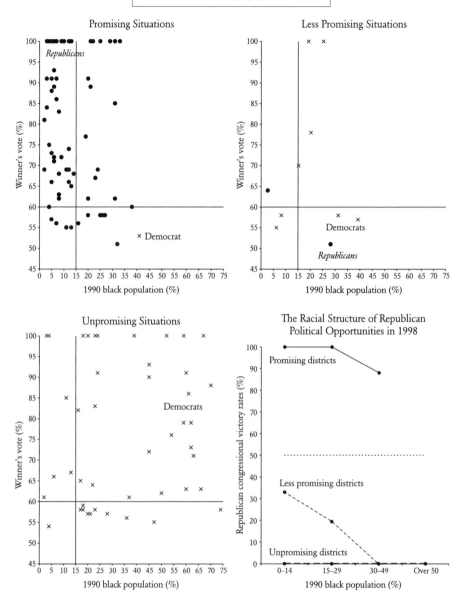

Figure 11.5 Republicans realize their opportunities: the southern House delegation in the 1998 elections. *Sources:* Same as Figure 11.1.

George Bush had lost in 1988, and Robin Hayes (North Carolina's Eighth) won a narrow open-seat victory to fill the vacancy created by the retirement of veteran Democrat Bill Hefner. Only by winning about two-thirds of the white vote could Hayes survive in a district that was 28 percent black.

Southern Democrats completely dominated the Republicans' forty-five unpromising situations. Confronted with their own powerful liabilities (Democratic incumbents and/or Republican presidential defeats), Republicans could not seriously compete in many of these districts, much less win any of them. A majority of the Democrats were in the highly advantageous upper right-hand cell of biracial populations and safe-seat victories. They were overwhelmingly incumbent Democrats serving in non-presidential landslide districts.

An exceedingly unfortunate but enduring legacy of Goldwater and Reagan Republicanism for the party's congressional candidates is their permanent need to win substantial majorities of the white vote. This underlying constraint on Republican growth needs to be addressed in terms of the assets (Republican incumbency and/or Republican presidential landslides) and the liabilities (Democratic incumbency and/or Republican presidential defeats) of southern Republicans in congressional elections.

"The Racial Structure of Republican Political Opportunities in 1998" plots Republican victory rates in promising, less promising, and unpromising situations according to the districts' racial composition. In promising districts, districts in which the Republicans could take advantage of presidential landslides and/or incumbency, they used their assets to win all of their opportunities in both the 0–14 percent black and 15–29 percent black districts and all but one of them in the 30–49 percent black districts. Only in Mississippi's Fourth District, an open-seat contest in a Republican landslide district with a sizable black population, did the Republicans lose.

At the other end of the continuum, in those unpromising districts where Republican liabilities of Democratic incumbents and/or Republican presidential defeats structured elections, Republicans could not win even in the seven in which blacks were less than 15 percent of the population. And in the intermediate area of less promising situations, racial composition structured Republican victory rates; with neither a net asset to deploy nor a net liability to overcome, the political advantage generally resided with the Democrats.

By the end of the 1990s, then, the impact of the Reagan realignment had been substantially realized in the Deep South and partially realized in the Peripheral South. Future Republican gains in the southern House elections would probably require another combination of politically successful Republican presidential governance—a new version of Ronald Reagan in the White House—along with another round of reapportionment and redistricting beneficial to Republicans. Texas, Florida, and (to a smaller extent) Virginia, for example, appeared to be ripe for increased congressional Republicanism. Unlike in the 1990s, however, in the other Peripheral South states and across the Deep South there were few obvious Republican targets that had not already been won. Indeed, many Democratic state legislators and/or governors in Georgia, North Carolina, and elsewhere were determined to halt and even reverse the GOP surge by creating many districts for the 2002–2010 elections that experienced and skillful Democratic politicians could win and hold. Whether Republicans could keep majorities of the South's seats in the House of Representatives against sophisticated Democratic counterattacks would surely be among the most important considerations in twenty-first-century American politics.

12

COMPETITIVE SOUTH, COMPETITIVE AMERICA

A newly competitive South means a newly competitive America. Once the Great Depression destroyed many Republican strongholds in the North and reinforced the Democratic party's commanding advantage in the South, Republicans could no longer expect to win many national majorities in Congress. From 1933 to 1995 the Democratic party enjoyed almost automatic control of the U.S. Senate and House of Representatives. Structurally, the Democrats' enormous surpluses of senators and representatives from the South—their dependable southern mega-majorities—became the tacit keystone to their assured domination of Congress. Provided that Democrats retained the lion's share of southern congressional districts and Senate seats, they needed to carry only about a third of the seats in the rest of the nation in order to secure Congress. As a practical matter most Democrats in Congress could plan their careers without having to worry a great deal about maintaining their national majorities. With Republicans unable to live down their image as the party of the Great Depression, the Solid Democratic South normally guaranteed Democratic Congresses. Only when unusual circumstances temporarily weakened Democrats in the North could the Republican party aspire to national victories.

In the watershed elections of 1994 the innovative feature of the Republicans' congressional victories was its national scope, its penetration of the South as well as the North. One hundred and twenty-two years had elapsed since the Republican party had simultaneously controlled majorities of House and Senate seats in the North and the South. Our concluding chapter emphasizes how dramatically the southern congressional delegation has changed since the early 1950s and assesses the national significance of rising southern Republicanism.

THE SOUTHERN REALIGNMENT

Exit polls for House elections from 1980 through 2000 clarify the underlying racial structure of the Republicans' southern congressional surge (see Figure 12.1). During these eleven elections Republicans never won more than tiny shares of the southern black vote ("Black Southerners"). Given their steady deficit of roughly nine to one among blacks, Republicans needed to secure about three-fifths of the much bigger white vote in order to win a majority of the total southern vote. From 1980 through 1992 they failed to reach their white target ("White Southerners"). In 1994, however, the Republicans surged to 64 percent of the southern white vote, an increase of 11 points over their previous showing. By achieving presidential-level white votes in the 1994–2000 congressional elections, the Republicans finally captured majorities of the entire southern House vote ("All Southerners"). Ultimately, "The Southern Republican Surge" reversed the relationship between the Republicans' House vote and their share of House seats. Before 1994 the Republicans' share of southern House seats trailed their share of the congressional vote by around ten percentage points. Beginning in 1996 the Republicans converted their deficit in seats into small surpluses.

Ronald Reagan's presidency legitimized the Republican party for many white southerners. His southern legacy was immense. Reagan substantially expanded grassroots Republicanism and inspired many potential Republican politicians to seek office. Over time the structure of the Republicans' congressional vote has closely paralleled their presidential success at the end of Reagan's second term (see the top two charts in Figure 12.2). Using the 1988 Republican presidential vote as a benchmark, the charts array blacks and five groups of whites from left to right according to their reported vote for George Bush. In 1988 sizable gaps existed between presidential and congressional Republicanism. By 1996, however, white Republicans and conservative independents were voting Republican in House elections by about the same overwhelming proportions that they had given Bush in 1988. Among Republicans and

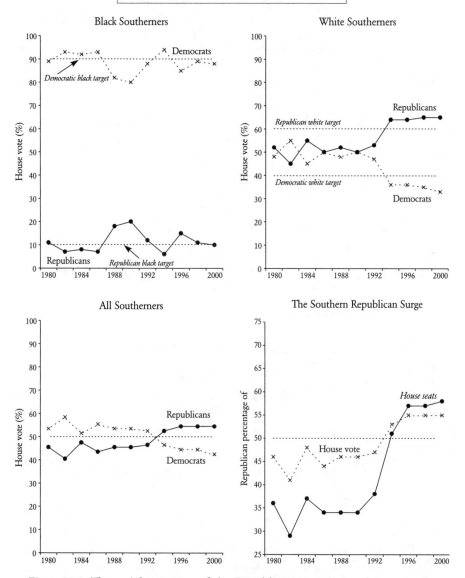

Figure 12.1 The racial structure of the Republican congressional surge in the South. *Sources:* Calculated from *Congressional Quarterly's Guide to U.S. Elections,* 3d ed. (Washington, D.C., 1994); *Congressional Quarterly Weekly Report,* various issues; and Voter News Service General Election exit polls, 1980–2000.

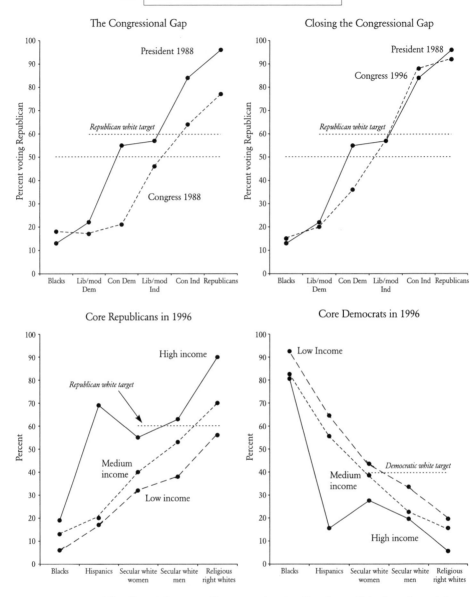

Figure 12.2 The Republican realignment in the South: political and social foundations. *Sources:* Calculated from the Voter News Service General Election exit polls, 1988 and 1996.

conservative independents the Republican party far exceeded its white target of 60 percent, and moderate and liberal independents provided smaller Republican majorities. Only among conservative Democrats was there no tight fit between their 1988 presidential vote and their 1996 congressional vote.

Distinctive social foundations divided the two major parties (see "Core Republicans in 1996" and "Core Democrats in 1996" in Figure 12.2). Race clearly trumped economic class in separating core Republicans from core Democrats. At the grassroots, religious right whites anchored the Republican party, just as black southerners did the Democratic party. Core Republicans increased and core Democrats declined across the spectrum of blacks, Hispanics, secular white women, secular white men, and religious right whites. Class differences *within* each social group were smaller—upper-income Hispanics were the sole exception—than the differences *separating* blacks, Hispanics, and whites.

Among white voters religion and gender also trumped economic class. At every income level the extraordinarily pro-Republican stances of religious right whites set them apart from all other white southerners. Low-income religious right whites, for instance, were almost as pro-Republican as high-income secular white men. In 1996 the Republican party thus symbolically united country clubs and fundamentalist churches, institutions that otherwise do not overlap. Secular white women, though more Democratic than other groups of whites, were considerably less so than blacks or low- and medium-income Hispanics.

Because the southern electorate is fluid and diverse, neither Democrats nor Republicans can win elections, as the Democrats easily did in the past, simply by uniting and turning out their core partisans. In 1996 Republicans exceeded their white target of 60 percent only among high-income religious right men and women, high-income secular men, and medium-income religious right men and women. Because Democrats can count on strong black support, their regional white target for core Democrats is 40 percent. In 1996, however, only secular white women with low incomes exceeded that target, and only secular white women with medium incomes approximated it. Religious right whites have by and large abandoned the Democratic party.

RESHAPING THE SOUTH'S CONGRESSIONAL PARTY SYSTEM

After World War II the social structure, economy, and, most significantly, racial practices of the Old South were fundamentally transformed.[1] Sustained federal intervention was the key to establishing a New South. Nothing was more important. Prodded and embarrassed by a civil rights movement that effectively dramatized massive racial injustice in the South, a Democratic president from Texas seized the political and moral high ground and promised the nation that "we shall overcome" on civil rights. Lyndon Johnson then confronted the southern Democratic senators who had always prevented national action. In a classic illustration of presidential leadership Johnson patiently assembled the overwhelming northern majorities of Democrats and Republicans he needed to defeat the southern Democrats' filibusters in the Senate. The 1964 Civil Rights Act outlawed racial segregation in the public sector, and the 1965 Voting Rights Act addressed racial discrimination in voter registration.

These complex political and socioeconomic developments have slowly culminated in a congressional delegation acutely divided by party, ideology, and race. The congressional delegations of the New South differ radically from those of the Old South. To help readers appreciate this monumental development in American politics, it is useful to compare southern House elections during the 1950s (the decade preceding federal intervention), the 1960s and 1970s (decades encompassing federal intervention and its aftermath), the 1980s (the decade when New South Democrats replaced Old South Democrats), and the 1990s (the decade of the Republicans' breakthrough).

Southern congressional politics was fundamentally reshaped between the 1950s and the 1990s (see Figure 12.3). The clusters of X's and dots, representing respectively Democratic and Republican winners in House elections, present collective portraits of southern politicians in action. They let us *see* hundreds of ambitious southern Democrats and Republicans before, during, and long after a critical juncture in American history. Figure 12.3 links the representatives' voting behavior to their constituencies. The electoral context of the South's revised congressional party battle becomes clear when the party unity scores of Republicans and Democrats are displayed in relation to the racial composition of their districts. As V. O. Key observed, "the struggles of [southern] politics take place within an institutional framework fixed by considerations of race relations, a framework on the order of a mold which gives shape and form to that which it contains."[2] In different ways they still do. The changing racial underpinnings of southern congressional politics provide insight into the long-term impact of substantially increased black participation on congressional voting behavior. For each era the vertical line drawn at 15 percent black separates winners in districts with very low black populations from winners in districts with higher black populations.

Once again, we use *Congressional Quarterly*'s Democratic party unity scores to approximate each representative's ideology. In the real political world those scores frequently serve as rough and ready practical indicators of ideological orientations. Horizontal lines drawn at 80 percent and 60 percent establish cutting points to distinguish national or liberal Democrats (scores of 80 or higher) from both moderate Democrats (scores of 60–79 percent) and nominal or conservative Democrats (scores of less than 60). Among Republican winners, Democratic party unity scores of 20 or lower identify national or conservative Republicans, and scores in the 21–39 percent range isolate moderate Republicans. Any Republican scoring higher than 40 can be viewed as a nominal or liberal Republican.

Given that incumbents won 85 to 90 percent of all the contests in each electoral era, these scatter plots generally separate incumbent Democrats from incumbent Republicans. In a competitive party system in which Democrats alone regularly secure overwhelming black support and in which the two parties divide sharply over ideology, House Democrats would disproportionately appear in the upper right cell (national Democrats serving in districts with higher black populations), while House Republicans would be heavily concentrated in the lower left cell (national Republicans representing districts with very low black populations). Figure 12.3 presents four powerful images of the changing southern party battle in the second half of the twentieth century: overwhelming Democratic strength during the 1950s, the conservative Democratic smother of the 1960s and 1970s, the moderate Democratic domination

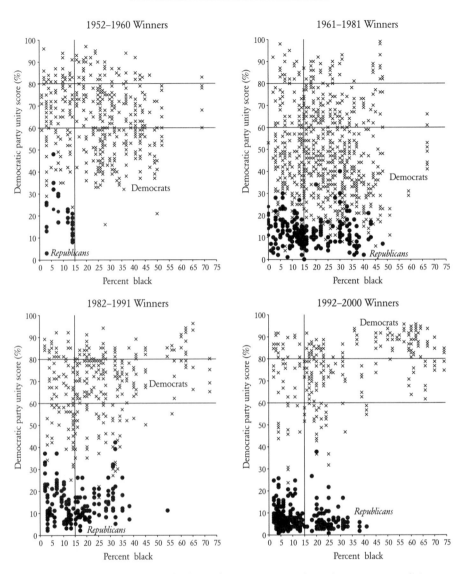

Figure 12.3 The racial and ideological restructuring of southern House politics.
Sources: Calculated from *Congressional Quarterly Weekly Report,* various issues.

of the 1980s, and, in the 1990s, a fairly sharp alignment of conservative Republicans versus liberal and moderate Democrats.

In the 1950s the status quo on southern race relations continued to prevail in Congress. With blacks severely underrepresented in most southern districts, higher black populations generally identify areas of more intense white racial conservatism. Democrats with safe seats dominated the delegation, but southern Democrats were more ideologically diverse than they would become once civil rights became a central issue. Because southern white control of race relations remained a given for most white Democratic politicians and voters, relatively high Democratic party unity scores were not yet the distinct political burden they would soon become. Forty-five percent of southern Democrats voted as moderates, another 15 percent voted with the party more than 80 percent of the time, and only 40 percent voted as nominal Democrats.

With Speaker Sam Rayburn of Texas leading the House Democrats, southern representatives who identified with the New Deal could vote as national or moderate Democrats and survive while conservative southern Democrats were free to vote as they pleased and still draw upon their seniority to lead powerful and prestigious committees.[3] The few southern Republicans, unlike the many Democrats, did not enjoy the luxury of representing safe congressional districts. Whereas 94 percent of the winning Democrats (and 99 percent of the Deep South Democrats) secured safe-seat victories of 60 percent or better, only a third of the Republican winners during the 1950s were able to do so.

In the 1960s and 1970s conservative Democratic incumbents with safe districts smothered most challenges from conservative Republicans. Three-fifths of the huge group of incumbent Democrats were safe-seat conservatives. White politicians who had entered the House as traditional southern Democrats by and large reacted to federal intervention by protesting much of the agenda of the national Democratic party.[4] And because conservative to moderate white Democratic voters remained the predominant grassroots presence in most southern congressional districts, Republicans could ordinarily make little headway against experienced southern Democrats.

Many conservative Democrats and some conservative Republicans succeeded in districts with substantial black populations. Veteran conservative Democrats could easily win Democratic primaries and general

elections without making more than superficial gestures and conces-
sions to newly mobilized black voters. Some Deep South Republicans
in higher-black districts were elected during the Goldwater surge, generally before black voters were effectively organized. They, too, could use
their incumbency advantages to sustain their careers despite having no
significant appeal to blacks. Across the region, however, Republicans
did best in Peripheral South districts in which blacks were less than 15
percent of the population and in which racial cleavages were generally
less pronounced. Needing much smaller white majorities, Republicans
won over two-fifths of the elections in very low-black districts during
the 1960s and 1970s.

Gradually, however, greater black participation significantly changed
the ideological dynamics of Democratic primaries and general elections.
By the 1980s moderate Democrats increasingly dominated or discouraged Republican opposition by developing majority biracial coalitions.
Many veteran white Democrats could use their local prestige and their
congressional seniority to deter serious opposition from rival Democrats in the nominating primary and from Republicans in general elections. Nonetheless, as the Old South Democrats began to retire, ambitious newcomers could not ignore increased black participation. In
many districts white Democrats campaigning in open-seat primaries and
elections, as well as a few veterans, came to appreciate the strategic advantage of forging biracial coalitions.[5] Voting as moderates would enable Democrats to establish and then market an ideologically mixed
voting record, one that supported black preferences on many issues but
also permitted enough conservative votes to insulate themselves against
Republican charges of liberalism.

Among southern Democrats the ideological center of gravity in the
1980s shifted dramatically toward moderation and a sprinkling of liberalism. Democrats retained significant incumbency advantages, and the
vast majority of Democratic veterans won safe-seat elections. As Democratic conservatism dissipated, many Democrats used their incumbency,
safe seats, and "moderation" to overcome the Republican threat despite
the increased appeal of presidential Republicanism. Conservative Republicans who had been unable to compete against conservative Democrats now found themselves equally unable to attract the extraordinary
white majorities required to defeat white Democrats skilled at devising

biracial coalitions. By the 1980s black Democrats were much better organized in many higher-black congressional districts, and most of the
winning white Democrats in such districts accordingly positioned themselves as moderate Democrats. The effectiveness of Democratic biracial
coalitions continued to restrict most winning Republicans to the very
low-black districts, where they won almost half the elections.

New dynamics structured southern congressional politics in the
1990s. The revised party system, in remarkable contrast to the three previous eras, sorted most House winners by party and ideology. Conservative Democrats, already a waning force, almost disappeared as the Republican party became the undisputed new home of southern
conservatism. At the same time the Democrats' ideological center of
gravity moved into the liberal or national range. The result was a
significant clarification of party and ideology. For the first time in the
southern delegation, conservative Republicans faced mainly liberal and
moderate Democrats. During the 1990s, again for the first time, more
Republican incumbents (86 percent) than Democratic incumbents (59
percent) achieved safe-seat reelections. The surviving southern Democrats were considerably more national than their predecessors, but they
were no longer in the majority. Redistricting in the 1990s increased the
number of majority-black districts and thereby created many safe seats
for liberal black Democrats, decreased the number of districts (previously white Democratic strongholds) in the 30–49 percent black range,
and substantially improved Republican prospects in the very low-black
districts.

The partisan transformation of the House delegation is rooted in the
region's changing demography. Districts with very low black populations, those with the highest potential for Republican penetration, increased from fewer than two-fifths of all southern districts in the 1980s
to 46 percent in the 1990s. The expansion of a southern middle class
barely discernible before World War II has been reflected in the growth
of urban districts. In the 1950s, before districts were required to have
equal populations, almost two-thirds of the southern seats contained rural majorities. Each subsequent decade has marked the steady expansion
of districts with urban majorities, and by the 1990s there were almost
four times as many urban (78 percent) as rural districts (22 percent). Secular demographic change eroded traditional one-party politics.

Figure 12.4 reveals the demographic foundations of congressional Republicanism. An obvious advantage of being the established majority party is the leverage it affords to deflect and delay adverse demographic and political trends by crafting district lines to maximum partisan benefit. Applied to the South, Democratic control of reapportionment and redistricting—Democratic governors working with Democratic state legislatures was the norm—allowed the traditional majority party to protect its vital partisan interests by drawing few districts that Republicans could win and hold. The top half of Figure 12.4 charts Republican victory rates according to district racial composition (on the left) and district urban-rural composition (on the right). Republicans have consistently had their greatest success in very low-black (0–14 percent) districts. By the 1980s they controlled around half of these districts, a much better showing than they managed in 15–29 percent black districts or in districts with black populations of 30 percent or greater.

Reapportionment and redistricting in the 1990s, however, clarified the racial structure of the party battle for southern seats. It produced Republican domination in the 0–14 percent black districts, Republican competitiveness in the 15–29 percent black districts, and Republican failure in districts with black populations of 30 percent or greater. By controlling over four-fifths of the seats in the very low-black category that now contained almost half of the southern districts, Republicans were far better positioned to exploit their incumbency than ever before. District racial composition separates Republican victory rates far better than urban-rural characteristics. From the 1950s through the 1980s Republicans were always relatively stronger in urban than in rural districts. In the 1990s the Reagan realignment and the retirement of veteran Democratic incumbents enabled Republicans to deepen their penetration of the urban South and substantially improve their performance in the rural South.

The bottom half of Figure 12.4 further reveals the demography of congressional Republicanism. It compares the Republicans' urban and rural victory rates in the two racial settings in which Republicans have either dominated (the very low-black districts) or become competitive (the 15–29 percent black districts). Although the mountain Republican tradition enabled the GOP to compete in a minority of rural as well as urban districts, the Reagan realignment took hold in the rural as well as

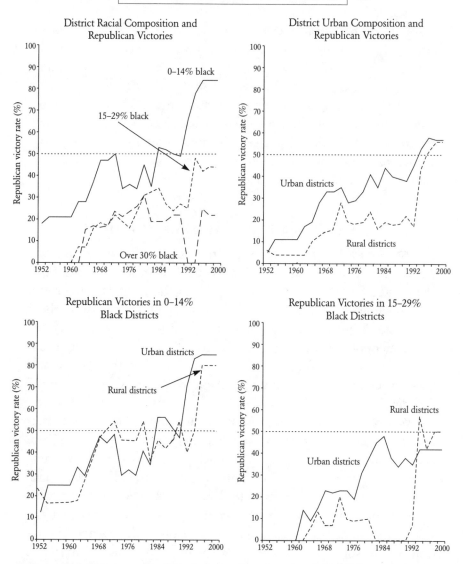

Figure 12.4 Demographic foundations of congressional Republicanism in the South, 1952–2000. *Sources:* Same as Figure 12.3.

the metropolitan South. In the very low-black districts Republicans dominated in rural as well as urban districts. In both settings they were vastly more successful in the 1990s than they had been in the 1980s. The common denominator of Republican success is the relatively smaller white majorities needed to win and then control these districts.

A different pattern characterizes the 15–29 percent black districts. Before the 1990s Republicans experienced moderate success in urban districts but performed very poorly in rural ones. Again the destabilization induced by redistricting and the early Clinton presidency, occurring in the wake of the Reagan realignment, enabled the GOP to remain moderately competitive in the urban districts and to become fairly competitive in the rural districts. Open-seat elections in the 15–29 percent black districts require considerably higher white majorities for Republican victories than in the very low-black districts.

THE NEWEST SOUTHERN CONGRESSIONAL POLITICS

In the 1990s the South's delegation to the House of Representatives was dramatically transformed. A white Republican majority, more black Democrats, far fewer white Democrats, and the complete absence of black Republicans—these developments distinguish the newest southern congressional politics. (In the Senate the principal change has been the replacement of white Democratic majorities by white Republican majorities.) The politicians who were elected to the House in the Republicans' breakthrough year of 1994 illustrate the racial and partisan anatomy of the southern delegation.

Any realistic understanding of southern campaigning must address its racial structure. Although explicit racial appeals have diminished, race profoundly shapes the ways in which politicians assemble winning coalitions. Our comparison of white Republicans, white Democrats, and black Democrats begins with the relationship between district racial composition and the total vote achieved by each winner.[6] Although the size of the black voting-age population clearly divides black winners from white winners, it fails to isolate white Republicans from white Democrats (see "Southern Beginnings" in Figure 12.5). The winner's share of the total vote separates politicians with comparatively safe seats, those in which the victor obtained 60 percent or more of the total vote, from those running in more competitive districts. In 1994 white Republicans and black Democrats generally achieved more comfortable majorities than white Democrats. Most of the Republicans with narrow victories were freshmen, whereas all the white Democrats who won with modest majorities were incumbents. Many incumbent white Republi-

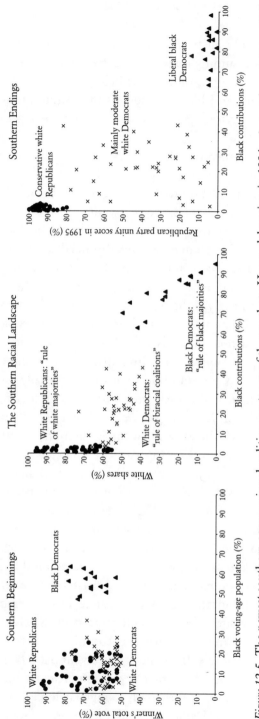

Figure 12.5 The newest southern congressional politics: anatomy of the southern House delegation in 1994. *Sources:* Same as Figure 12.3.

cans and practically all black Democrats inhabited districts in which their reelection—assuming no self-destructive behavior—was not realistically in doubt. Other considerations being equal, therefore, far more white Republicans and black Democrats than white Democrats could speak and vote as strong partisans without jeopardizing their political careers.

Our initial examination of racial composition and election results points to a larger and more intriguing political story. "Southern Beginnings" identifies electoral outcomes but conceals the underlying political dynamics. Using it as a point of departure, the next two scatter plots in Figure 12.5 unravel the partisan and racial realities that have culminated in the South's most diverse congressional delegation since the Reconstruction era. Edward Tufte's innovative work with graphics has demonstrated the value of "envisioning" complex political situations, and our goal is to analyze the political anatomy of the newest southern congressional delegation in terms of successive "visual explanations."[7]

Politicians and their strategists need reasonably accurate images of their supporters and opponents. In districts where whites plus blacks constitute practically the entire electorate, it is especially useful to know the relative *contributions* of blacks and whites to a politician's total vote. What percentage of X's vote comes from blacks? What percentage comes from whites? The answers to these questions identify the racial center of gravity for politicians in particular districts. Determining the size of the black (or white) contribution to a representative's vote has practical as well as theoretical importance. The larger the black (or white) contribution, the more likely the officeholder will be to take black (or white) opinion into account in campaigning and policy-making. On the other hand, in districts in which both blacks and whites contribute substantially to a winner's vote, the political implications of that situation will probably be clearly understood. The relative size of their black contributions ought to separate black Democrats, white Democrats, and white Republicans much more decisively than does the black percentage of the voting-age population.

Consider, for example, the radically divergent black contributions of Newt Gingrich (Georgia's Sixth District), soon to be the Republican Speaker of the House in the 104th Congress; John Lewis (Georgia's Fifth), a senior black Democrat; and John Spratt (South Carolina's

Fifth), a veteran white Democrat. Campaigning in a district in which blacks were only 6 percent of the voting-age population, Gingrich captured 64 percent of the total vote in 1994. If we assume that he received 10 percent of the black vote and round up to the nearest whole number, Gingrich's black contribution amounted to *one percent* of his total vote. In the neighboring Fifth District, Lewis was reelected with a larger majority (69 percent). If he received the entire black vote in a district in which blacks were 58 percent of the voting-age population, blacks accounted for 83 percent of his total vote. Spratt secured 52 percent of the vote in a district that was 28 percent black. Assuming that he obtained 90 percent of the black vote, blacks cast 44 percent of Spratt's total vote.

As well as having a realistic idea of the sizes of their white and black contributions, politicians need to know how well they fared in particular constituencies. In southern politics campaigners are acutely interested in their *shares* of the white vote and black vote. What percent of the white vote did X win? What percent of the black vote? Both questions are certainly important, but in general elections white shares are less predictable than black shares. Most politicians especially need strategic information about their white targets—the share of the white vote they must achieve (given their black contribution) in order to win a majority of the total vote. These white targets constitute the politicians' white necessities or white requirements, and they differ enormously for white Republicans, white Democrats, and black Democrats. Thus Gingrich needed only around 53 percent of the white vote to win, Spratt could hold his district with an estimated 35 percent of the white vote, and Lewis did not need a single white vote to keep his seat.

The South's racial landscape can be understood theoretically as the intersection of black contributions and white shares. Black contributions and white shares constitute the two most significant general characteristics of southern electoral politics. Borrowing Richard F. Fenno's valuable term, each represents a vital component of the "reelection constituency" of white Republicans, white Democrats, and black Democrats.[8] How much of X's vote came from blacks? How much of the white vote did X win? The answers to these two questions reveal the racial anatomy of the newest southern congressional politics.

Three distinctive paths to victory dominate the South's racial landscape in House elections. As "The Southern Racial Landscape" reveals, black Democrats, white Democrats, and white Republicans now cluster in separate and distinct political universes to a far greater extent than they did in "Southern Beginnings." White Republicans dominate the upper left corner of the scatter plot. Running in districts where blacks contribute almost nothing to their total votes, white Republicans have survived by securing landslide majorities of the white vote. Because they drew almost all of their votes from whites and won much higher shares of the white vote than the black vote, the victorious white Republicans both symbolized and perpetuated the *rule of white majorities*. Whether or not they resorted to overt racial appeals (and few did in 1994, at least not of the sort traditionally recognized as craven attempts to win white support), the white Republicans' thoroughgoing conservatism was ideally designed to attract substantial white majorities in districts in which most voters were whites. Their reelection constituencies were the modern incarnation of the oldest story in southern politics; securing white majorities in virtually all-white districts was the standard route to victory among white Democrats in the old southern politics.

Black Democrats cluster in a separate political world in the lower right corner, the space representing overwhelming black contributions in conjunction with much smaller shares of the white vote. Among black Democrats the fundamental reality was that their victories did not require white support. Provided that blacks turned out in the same proportion as their share of the voting-age population and voted cohesively, black Democrats did not need any white votes. Because most of their vote came from blacks and because they won much greater shares of the black vote than of the white vote, it seems fitting to describe these victories as based upon the *rule of black majorities*. By winning virtually all of the black vote in majority or near-majority black districts, black Democrats could use their black contributions as their base and increase their victory margins by attracting a minority of the white vote.

White Democrats occupy a third distinctive space. Their black contributions were much smaller than those of the black Democrats but in most cases considerably larger than those of the white Republicans. White shares separate white Republicans from white Democrats much more clearly than did their total votes. Few white Democrats (but most white Republicans) won three-fifths or more of the white vote. A majority of the white Democrats' total votes came from whites, but they won much higher shares of the black vote than of the white vote. Although black Democrats and white Republicans ran best among the race that generated most of their votes, white Democrats could not possibly succeed without doing well—in different ways—among both whites and blacks. Because the white Democrats ran in districts where whites were a sizable majority of the electorate, they needed large white contributions as well as landslide support among blacks. To a greater extent than the black Democrats and to a much greater extent than the white Republicans, white Democrats relied for their victories upon the *rule of biracial coalitions.*

Although white Republicans might welcome black support and black Democrats might encourage white support, in a strategic sense such support was generally incidental rather than essential to their political survival. White Democrats typically competed in more chancy environments. They needed to win huge black shares while also securing sizable fractions of the white vote. As "The Southern Racial Landscape" shows, white Democrats were more diverse than either white Republicans or black Democrats. They differed considerably among themselves in terms of the relative size of their black contributions as well as the extent of their appeal to whites. While black Democrats thrived by securing most black votes in majority-black districts and while white Republicans succeeded by obtaining white majorities in even more heavily white districts, white Democrats prevailed by combining lesser white shares with landslide black majorities in heavily white districts.

The racial landscape suggests why black Democrats and white Republicans typically possess safer districts—districts requiring less attention in anticipation of a serious general-election challenge—than do many white Democrats. Politicians who can get most of their votes from one race or the other, especially veterans who know their districts thoroughly and serve on important committees, have an inherently easier task than politicians who must first construct and then constantly revitalize biracial coalitions. White Democrats generally have to work harder to keep their seats than most black Democrats or white Republicans.

Because it provides a concrete image of their divergent reelection constituencies, "The Southern Racial Landscape" helps us understand why conflict between white Republicans and black Democrats is so common. The short-term imperatives involved in securing reelection generally reinforce and intensify, rather than bridge or moderate, the immense racial and partisan cleavages revealed in the figure. Only white Democrats are truly compelled to balance the interests of blacks and whites. Neither white Republicans nor black Democrats face much constituency or institutional pressure to see beyond the interests of the race that has elected them. On the basis of their different constituencies, it would be reasonable to expect these groups to vote in distinctive patterns. Is this the case?

When the heavily southern House Republican leadership of Speaker Gingrich and majority leader Dick Armey advanced its controversial "Contract with America" in the first session of the 104th Congress, white Republicans, white Democrats, and black Democrats responded in very distinctive ways. The policy consequences of the newest southern congressional politics become more apparent if we plot Republican party unity scores for 1995 against the black contribution to each winner's total vote in 1994. "Southern Endings" clearly distinguishes *conservative* white Republicans, usually *moderate* white Democrats, and *liberal* black Democrats. Highly partisan voting prevailed in the two groups with single-race reelection constituencies, while the white Democrats with biracial coalitions were much less partisan in their voting patterns.

White Republicans are even more tightly bunched in the extreme upper left corner of "Southern Endings" than they were in "The Southern Racial Landscape." Districts with microscopic black contributions—on the order of 1–3 percent—are closely associated with exceptionally high Republican party unity scores. Conservative white Republicans, who averaged 94 in their party unity, voted as though their seats were secure. Campaigning in districts in which they won large—frequently very large—white majorities and in which whites accounted for the vast majority of their entire votes, the southern white Republicans were well positioned to represent the interests, values, beliefs, and aspirations of their white supporters. For most white Republican officeholders, adopting highly conservative to moderately conservative positions on issue after issue involved no inordinate strains between their own inclinations, the preferences of their reelection constituents, and the demands of their party leaders. Many were generally free to be about as vigorously conservative as they wished without fear of effective challenge, much less defeat.

At the opposite end of the political spectrum, in the lower right corner of "Southern Endings," liberal black Democrats resolutely rejected the Republican agenda. Most of the districts that elected black Democrats were an innovation—a long-overdue innovation—in southern congressional representation. The creation of many new majority-black districts after the 1990 Census finally reversed longstanding institutional barriers against black officeholding. They represent exceptionally safe seats for incumbent black Democrats. Like white Republicans, black Democrats are free to be as partisan as they wish. As a practical matter the black-majority districts provide firm bases for southern liberalism in the House of Representatives. In 1995 the average Republican party unity score among black Democrats was 6, and the least partisan black Democrat, Sanford Bishop (Georgia's Second District), had a score of 15. Both black Democrats and white Republicans could represent their principal constituents by voting as strong partisans.

In stark contrast to both the white Republicans and the black Democrats, the white Democrats are scattered all over the chart. They averaged 37 in Republican party unity and ranged from strong Democratic partisans to virtual Republicans (several of whom later switched parties). Their relative moderation reflected the political complexities and diverse imperatives of their biracial coalitions. White Democrats with similar black contributions could nonetheless differ substantially in their personal responses to the Republican agenda. A few opposed the Contract with America about as completely as most black Democrats, and a smaller number had Republican party unity scores approaching those of the least loyal southern Republicans. Most white Democrats were fairly divided in their voting patterns.

Our comparison of the extraordinarily different reelection constituencies of the three groups suggests that while the district characteristics of the white Republicans and black Democrats probably encourage highly partisan voting behavior, many white Democrats cannot afford to be strong partisans even if they would like to. White Republicans and black Democrats who aspired to prestigious committee appointments and party leadership positions had a significant advantage in compari-

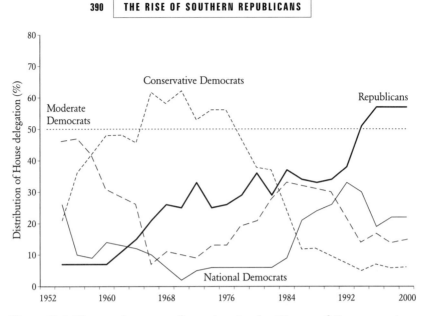

Figure 12.6 The southern transformation in the House of Representatives, 1952–2000. *Sources:* Calculated from *Congressional Quarterly's Guide to U.S. Elections,* 3d ed. (Washington, D.C., 1994); and *Congressional Quarterly Weekly Report,* various issues.

son with many white Democrats: the former could point to their records of party loyalty; the latter frequently could not.

In the second half of the twentieth century the South's congressional delegation has undergone momentous partisan and ideological changes. Figure 12.6 shows the percentage distribution of conservative Democrats, moderate Democrats, national Democrats, and Republicans in the House delegation since midcentury. In the early 1950s, before white southern control of race relations was truly challenged, Democratic conservatives did not dominate the southern delegation. However, as federal intervention approached and then became a reality, conservative Democrats became the largest single force in the southern delegation through the early 1980s. Although conservative Democrats have not completely disappeared, by the 1990s they represented less than a tenth of the southern delegation. With fewer and fewer conservative white voters participating in Democratic primaries and with high party unity scores a necessity for advancement within the House Democratic caucus, conservative politicians had no meaningful future as Democrats. By the mid-1980s the Republicans had emerged as a slightly larger force than the rising moderate Democrats. In the 1990s the Republicans became the new southern conservative majority, and national Democrats replaced moderate Democrats as the second strongest force in the southern delegation. When blacks and Texas Hispanics were added to liberal whites in (mainly) big-city districts, national Democrats finally had a permanent southern base. Aside from the early 1950s, the decade of the 1980s stands out as the only period in which conservatism—whether expressed by Democrats or by Republicans—was not the majority ideological tendency in the South's congressional delegation.

SECTIONAL CHANGES AND NATIONAL POLITICS

The ideological transformation of southern Democrats and the rise of southern Republicans were only the most dramatic examples of partisan and ideological change in the House of Representatives. Figure 12.7 charts ideological trend lines for northern Democrats, southern Democrats, northern Republicans, and southern Republicans, the four great sectional wings of the national parties. The results enable us to compare sectional cleavages within each party and partisan divisions within each section.

From 1954 through 1994 the Democratic party continuously controlled the House of Representatives. Although northern Democrats always outnumbered southern Democrats, the southerners' seniority advantage traditionally prevented northern Democrats from accumulating political power commensurate with their numbers. Very few northern Democrats ever voted as nominals, and sectional strains within the Democratic party were particularly strong in the aftermath of northern Democratic gains in 1958, 1964, and 1974. After the 1974 post-Watergate election northern Democrats outnumbered southern Democrats by 210 to 81. Northern Democrats promptly took charge of the House Democratic caucus and changed the party's rules to require secret ballots to select committee chairmen, a reform calculated to encourage greater party loyalty from southern conservatives who either chaired committees or hoped to do so.[9]

Although few northerners were ever nominal Democrats, before the 1980s "programmatic liberals" did not dominate the northern Democratic delegations.[10] Prior to Reagan's victory in 1980 moderates as well

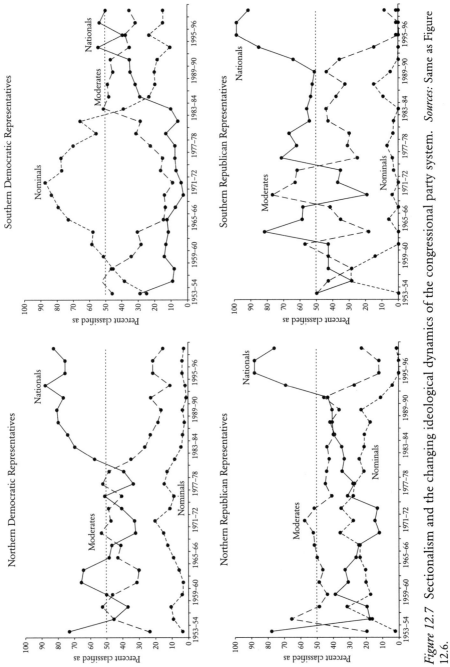

Figure 12.7 Sectionalism and the changing ideological dynamics of the congressional party system. *Sources:* Same as Figure 12.6.

as liberals were prominent among northern Democrats. Perceiving Reagan as the first Republican president who seriously threatened key components of the New Deal and Great Society, programmatic liberals from the North took firm control of the Speakership.[11] "Democrats, by virtue of the political threat Reagan posed and the impact of his policies on their constituencies, were constrained to develop and promote distinct alternatives and to unify against a common adversary," argued Democratic representative David E. Price of North Carolina. "They were aided in this by the continued, albeit incomplete, closing of the gap between the northern and southern wings of the congressional party."[12] Possessing the advantage of numbers, northern Democrats could control the House agenda and make party loyalty an unwritten requirement for key leadership positions and prestigious committee assignments.

Beginning in the early 1980s, the gap between liberal and moderate northern Democrats widened considerably. As the Democratic leaders in the House and substantial majorities of northern Democrats pressed their liberal agenda and began to scrutinize voting records carefully before making committee assignments, some southern Democrats faced a difficult situation. Advancement within the House caucus might require the sort of high party unity scores that, sooner or later, might well attract more serious Republican opposition back in the district. These cross-pressures between the demands of the district versus the demands of the Democratic House leadership meant that, at the least, many veteran Democrats would have to spend more time raising money and working their districts than they would have preferred.

Conflicts between northern and southern Democrats have certainly not disappeared, but during the 1990s they mainly involved matters of degree—there were fewer nationals and more moderates in the South—rather than the extraordinarily divisive ideological battles that characterized southern Democrats and northern Democrats from the late 1950s through the late 1970s.[13] Whereas most southern Democrats had traditionally viewed defending racial segregation as an imperative, nothing more disgusted, angered, and embarrassed liberal northern Democrats than involving the Democratic party in the preservation of southern racial discrimination. With the passage and enforcement of major civil rights laws, however, the segregationist southern Democrats lost their battle against federal intervention. Eventually the Old South Democrats departed. Their withdrawal resolved the most pressing and difficult strain within the congressional Democratic party. Few nominal southern Democrats remain, and none are overt racial conservatives in the manner of their predecessors. Even in the 1990s much lower percentages of southern Democrats voted as nationals than did northern Democrats.

In the 1950s northerners almost completely dominated the House Republican party, and four decades later they continued to outnumber southern Republicans by better than two to one. Trend lines for the northern Republicans reveal quite different ideological patterns from those prevailing among northern Democrats or southern Democrats. After they returned to the minority following their defeat in 1954, northern Republicans did not vote primarily as national partisans. Instead moderate partisanship became their central tendency. Tacitly accepting their destiny as a permanent minority party,[14] pluralities and occasionally majorities of northern Republicans voted with the Democrats on one-fifth to about two-fifths of the party unity roll calls. By accommodating the majority Democrats part of the time, they could sometimes cut deals aimed at securing benefits for their districts. The percentage of conservative northern Republicans gradually increased, but throughout the 1980s moderates and nationals were about evenly balanced in the northern wing of the party. About a fifth of them could even be classified as nominal Republicans.

For the northern Republicans the early Clinton presidency functioned as an ideological watershed. As northern programmatic liberal Democrats took firm control of the House of Representatives, northern Republicans eventually responded by voting as programmatic conservatives. And as southerners like Gingrich, Armey, and DeLay—programmatic conservatives par excellence—emerged as Republican leaders after the 1994 election, many northern Republicans came under intense pressure to increase their party unity scores, sometimes at the expense of risking their seats, in order to please their new party leaders. Unlike the southern leaders, many northern Republicans did not possess exceptionally safe seats. Hence Gingrich's insistence on strict party loyalty was bound to create for many northern Republicans painful cross-pressures between district realities and leadership demands similar to those previously confronted by many southern Democrats. After their losses in the 1998 House elections, Gingrich resigned his seat, and some of the northern Republicans returned to their previous pattern of moderate partisanship.

If moderate partisanship was the central tendency of northern Republicans before the 1990s, the much smaller group of southern Republicans was less inclined to follow that approach. As early as the mid-1970s programmatic conservatism was the main tendency of southern Republicans. Though lacking significant influence within their own party, Gingrich, Armey, and DeLay were not content to remain in the minority. They believed that countering the Democrats' hard-edged liberalism with an equally hard-edged conservatism could eventually bring the Republicans back into power in the House. In the mid-1990s, as the Republicans won narrow national victories, the percentage of national southern Republicans rose to the highest levels yet seen for any combination of party and section.

Within the House of Representatives the sharpest partisan and ideological divisions involve northern liberal Democrats and southern conservative Republicans. Gingrich (before his resignation), Armey, DeLay, and countless rank-and-file southern Republicans have little in common (and vice versa) with House Democratic leaders Dick Gephardt and David Bonier and many other northern Democrats. "Minimum high regard" appears to be the informal norm governing relationships between Democrats and Republicans. And because many of Congress' Democratic and Republican ideologues represent safe seats, they can afford to be exceptionally loyal on key roll-call votes. When the Republican party won the 1994 House elections and subsequently installed a southern leadership team whose common denominator was a suburban district dominated by conservative middle-class whites, they turned decisionmaking in their party over to aggressive conservatives who could press the Contract with America without risking their own reelection.

As Fenno has cogently argued, the House Republicans were completely without practical experience either in "interpreting" their victory or in knowing how to govern astutely.[15] Part of their misinterpretation may have been rooted in confusing the agendas favored in their very safe districts with those preferred in the entire nation. The Republicans' House leadership was far too southern, far too conservative, and, indeed, far too *southern conservative* to serve as a unifying force in the nation. Once the euphoria of the 1994 surge subsided, it was increasingly clear that the Republicans would have a difficult time maintaining their narrow majorities. In a fashion that would surely have flabbergasted Sam Rayburn, Gingrich proclaimed ideological victory and cashed in on his meteoric celebrity with book deals before he was even sworn in as Speaker of the House. There were abundant early-warning signs of immature leadership skills.

The immense sectional changes of the past five decades have reshaped the Republican and Democratic parties in the House of Representatives (see Figure 12.8). In both major parties the most significant trend has been the sharp rise of "national" partisans. As Price observed in 1992, "Party voting has reached levels since the early 1980s not seen since the party polarization of Harry Truman's presidency." Indeed, "individual members have become more and more inclined to stick with their party on such divided votes."[16] Among House Democrats the disappearance of southern conservatives and the expansion of northern liberals have resulted in a national party in which a substantial majority of all Democrats—generally ranging from two-thirds to three-fourths since the late 1980s—vote as liberals. Nearly four-fifths of all House Democrats (78 percent) voted as nationals in the 103rd Congress of 1993–94, the first years of the Clinton presidency.

For the Republicans, "national" partisanship reached truly extraordinary levels only in the 1990s. Seventy-three percent of the Republicans were nationals in the Congress immediately preceding their 1994 breakthrough, and during the two Congresses in which Gingrich was Speaker 91 percent of all the House Republicans had party unity scores of 80 or higher. In 1999, after Gingrich resigned from Congress, the percentage of Republican nationals dropped to 81 and the percentage of Democratic nationals climbed to 74.

When liberal Democrats and conservative Republicans are charted together (see "House 'National' Partisans") the sequencing of change is clear. Understood from partisan standpoints the rise of the nationals has been a process of successive responses to perceived provocations and outrages. Thus Reagan's election in 1980 galvanized northern liberal Democrats under Speaker of the House Tip O'Neill of Massachusetts to defend Democratic achievements going back to the New Deal. O'Neill

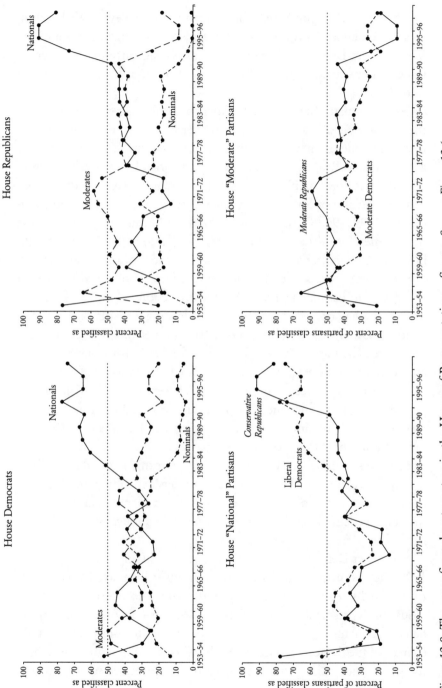

Figure 12.8 The reconfigured party system in the House of Representatives. *Sources:* Same as Figure 12.6.

and his successors, Jim Wright of Texas and Tom Foley of Washington, all saw tremendous advantages in tightening Democratic control of the House. More Democrats began to vote as liberals once the Democratic leadership insisted on greater party loyalty from Democrats who wanted to be insiders.

For their part, Republican backbenchers like Gingrich interpreted these developments as a challenge to overthrow a defeatist Republican leadership and then unify House Republicans under a conservative agenda. Just as Reagan's agenda "provoked" liberal Democrats, so President Bill Clinton (mainly with his health-care initiative) and the Democratic leadership of Speaker Tom Foley "provoked" the House Republicans in 1993–94. Gingrich, now the Republican whip, used these developments to drive Republican minority leader Bob Michel of Illinois into early retirement. As the incoming leader of the House Republicans, Gingrich then invented and marketed the Contract with America as a device to nationalize the 1994 House elections.

Once he had exceeded expectations by leading his party back into the majority, Gingrich seized his opportunity and personally selected every committee chair and subcommittee chair for the 104th Congress. It was an exercise of personal power never attempted by a modern Democratic Speaker. In the process Gingrich ignored seniority and deliberately passed over some experienced Republicans who had been, in his view, overly sympathetic and accommodating to the Democrats. Every Republican in the House of Representatives understood that the new Speaker was keeping an eagle eye on their performance, and all realized that Gingrich could make or break their careers depending on his assessment of their party loyalty. These practical considerations help explain the unprecedented acceleration of national Republicans during Gingrich's four years as Speaker of the House.

Even after Dennis Hastert of Illinois replaced Gingrich as Speaker in 1999, the vast majority of House Republicans still behaved as conservatives. Led by a southern majority leader and a southern whip in the House of Representatives, as well as by a southern majority leader in the Senate, congressional Republicans continued to draw Democratic charges of ideological extremism. Such criticism did not, of course, hurt the party among the nation's conservatives, who made up nearly one-third of all white voters in 2000. According to the Voter News Service Exit Poll, 84 percent of white conservatives supported Republican congressional candidates and 86 percent backed GOP senatorial candidates. Republican candidates enjoyed virtually the same levels of support among white conservatives throughout America.

In addition to their strength among white conservatives, Republican success in congressional elections also requires considerable support from moderates, who accounted for half of America's white voters in 2000. Nationally, white moderates favored Republicans over Democrats for the House of Representatives, 52 to 48 percent, and for the Senate, 54 to 46 percent. However, the South and the North displayed rather different patterns. In the South roughly three-fifths of moderate whites voted for Republican House (62 percent) and Senate (61 percent) candidates. Northern white moderates, however, split their votes between the major parties. Republican House candidates won only 49 percent of white moderates in the North, while GOP Senate candidates carried 50 percent of these voters.

In the 2000 election Republican presidential candidate George W. Bush attempted to soften the party's ideological image by defining himself as a "compassionate conservative." In effect, Bush let the noun reassure white conservatives and used the adjective to attract white moderates. His campaign strategy succeeded brilliantly with southern white voters. Bush carried 88 percent of the conservatives, 64 percent of the moderates, and even 29 percent of the liberals. It was far less effective among northern white voters; while he won 87 percent of the conservatives, Bush attracted only 47 percent of the moderates and plunged to 13 percent among liberals. The Republican party needs leaders who can unite conservatives without frightening moderates. Unless and until Republicans demonstrate more competence in practical governance, they will remain a minority in the electorate, and their hold on Congress will be tenuous.

BATTLEFIELD SECTIONALISM AND THE NATION

History offers the best perspective for assessing the impact of southern Republicans on the fortunes of the Republican party in Congress.

Battlefield sectionalism in congressional elections appears dramatically when Republican victory rates in the North and South are charted from 1854 through 2000 (see the top half of Figure 12.9). After the Civil War the enfranchisement of former slaves and disfranchisement of many ex-Confederates temporarily produced Republican ascendancy in the South. With the end of Reconstruction, however, the South became a persistent dilemma for the Republican party. An enormous sectional gap structured elections for Congress until the 1970s, and for *sixty* consecutive elections–from 1874 until 1994–Republicans were a minority of the southern delegation in the Senate and the House of Representatives.

Because of their overwhelming southern losses, the Republicans could control Congress only by winning sizable majorities of Senate seats and House districts in the North. To show the practical effect of writing off the South, the battlefield sectionalism charts include a line representing the Republicans' "northern target" for each election. The northern target identifies the minimum percentage of northern Senate or House seats the Republicans needed to win, given their performance in the South, in order to achieve a bare national majority. Hence the northern target lines separate the Republicans' national victories from their national defeats. As the Republicans' shares of southern seats plummeted in the late nineteenth century, a rule of thumb emerged for Republican success in congressional elections. Despite their poor performance in the South, Republicans could generally control Congress by winning approximately *two-thirds* of the North's seats. The fairly straight lines depicting the Republicans' northern necessities in Senate and House elections symbolize the durability of sectional divisions in American national politics.

Before the Great Depression the Republicans' southern problem was worrisome but often surmountable. Southern Democrats might be exceptionally unified in congressional elections, but northern Republicans had the critical advantage of far superior size. With three times as many northern as southern House seats and a slightly greater sectional advantage in the Senate, Republicans could frequently offset their southern losses with northern victories. From 1860 to 1930 the Republican party controlled the Senate in 86 percent of the Congresses and the House of Representatives in almost two-thirds of them. Lincoln's strategy of unit-

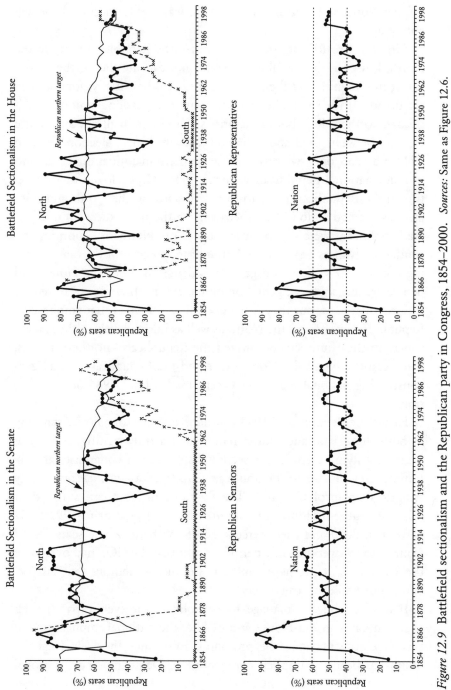

Figure 12.9 Battlefield sectionalism and the Republican party in Congress, 1854–2000. *Sources:* Same as Figure 12.6.

ing the North and writing off the South was highly successful for seventy years.

After the Great Depression undermined the Republican party in the North, however, the Republicans could not execute the northern two-thirds rule required by their Lincoln Strategy. Essentially, for the next six decades they shrank to a permanent congressional minority. Although northern Republican majorities reappeared in all but one House election between 1938 and 1956 and in every Senate election between 1942 and 1956, only twice were those northern majorities big enough to produce national Republican victories. Fresh House losses in 1958 returned the Republican party to minority status in the North and initiated a sustained period of southern *and* northern weakness. In the Senate Republicans were slightly more successful. Northern majorities and southern advances enabled the Republicans to control the Senate during the first six years of Reagan's presidency. In both the House and Senate gradual southern gains combined with northern losses to reduce the sectional gaps, but they generally did so on terms that emphasized Republican weakness in the North as well as in the South. Although advances in the South slowly lowered the Republicans' northern targets, Democratic gains in the North prevented the Republicans from again constituting national majorities except in the 1980–1984 Senate elections.

Hence the Republicans' 1994 southern advance to majority standing in both the Senate and House represented a truly significant innovation, a clarifying event in the sectional structure of congressional elections. Developments in the South have restored a *nationwide* two-party struggle to control Congress. The Republicans' southern surge—their share of southern House seats jumped from 38 percent in 1992 to 57 percent in 2000 and their percentage of southern Senate seats soared from 32 to 59 over the same period—meant that the GOP had overcome the Democrats' customary southern surplus, something that last occurred during Reconstruction.

If the Republicans manage to consolidate (or even expand) their southern gains in the House and Senate, the national implications of this development would be profound. Ever since the New Deal the South has been the implicit cornerstone of Democratic congressional majorities, and there is every reason to expect that the Democrats will vigorously attempt to reclaim majorities of southern seats in future elections. If the Democrats cannot reestablish an advantage in the South, however, their only route to power will be to increase their northern majorities.

Though impressive, GOP gains in the South are assuredly not precursors to the development of southern Republican juggernauts in Congress comparable to those historically enjoyed by southern Democrats. The South's immense size and growing diversity are more likely to result in competitive two-party politics than in a Solid Republican South. During the 1990s the population of the eleven southern states increased by 19 percent, nearly twice the rate of increase in the rest of the nation (11 percent). According to the 2000 Census, 84 million people lived in the South, more than in any other part of the United States.[17] Southern seats in the House of Representatives increased from 125 in the 1990s to 131 in the 2000s. Indeed, the South now supplies three of every ten House members. Increasing size has generated considerable social diversity. As the South has become more desirable as a place in which to live, work, and retire, it has attracted huge numbers of northern migrants as well as immigrants from around the world.

Such a complex society cannot be confined within the boundaries of a single political party. Both parties in the South now have many safe congressional seats, a condition that makes unlikely truly lopsided House delegations. White Republicans control a majority of the southern congressional delegation, but many white Democrats have survived on the basis of biracial coalitions, and a small number of African-American Democrats have established safe seats based on black majorities. At the same time, because of the partisan and social diversity permeating every southern state, neither party can consider any state "safe" in elections for the Senate. In 2001 there were more white Republicans than white Democrats, but no black Democrats, in the southern senatorial delegation.

In both Senate and House elections the rule of white majorities, the universal road to victory for white Republicans, has reappeared as a forceful tendency in southern politics. Lincoln's party, reinvented as the party of Reagan, relies heavily on conservative white majorities for its continued success. Whether or not Republicans can hold their majorities in Congress, for the foreseeable future they will be the main advocates of southern white conservatism.

Rising congressional Republicanism in the oldest regional stronghold of the Democratic party has reshaped the Republicans into a truly national party for the first time since Reconstruction. Not since Whigs fought Democrats in the 1830s and 1840s has American politics been based on a thoroughly nationalized two-party system. Because leaders in both parties can easily see ways to win or lose their House and Senate majorities, the national stakes of each election cycle are permanently high. A retirement here, an unexpected death there, to say nothing about short-term political trends helping one party or the other—all these factors contribute to the seesaw nature of the modern party battle. In its unmitigated ferocity contemporary congressional partisanship reflects the new reality that the results of national elections are no longer foregone Democratic victories or assured Republican triumphs.

Thus the South's political transformation holds extraordinary consequences for America. Old-fashioned sectional conflict has dissipated, but sectional considerations continue to pervade national politics through the conservative agenda pursued by Republican congressional leaders from the South. As it has been in presidential politics for some time, the South is now at the epicenter of Republican and Democratic strategies to control Congress. In order to comprehend national political dynamics, it is therefore more important than ever to understand the changing South.

NOTES
INDEX

NOTES

1. THE SOUTHERN TRANSFORMATION

1. *Houston Chronicle*, October 22, 1996.

2. Observed by one of the authors.

3. V. O. Key Jr., *Southern Politics in State and Nation* (New York: Knopf, 1949), p. 277.

4. Ibid., p. 665.

5. Earl Black, *Southern Governors and Civil Rights* (Cambridge, Mass.: Harvard University Press, 1976); Earl Black and Merle Black, *Politics and Society in the South* (Cambridge, Mass.: Harvard University Press, 1987); Earl Black and Merle Black, *The Vital South: How President Are Elected* (Cambridge, Mass.: Harvard University Press, 1992); Charles S. Bullock III, "Regional Realignment from an Officeholding Perspective," *Journal of Politics* 50 (August 1988): 553–574; Charles S. Bullock III and Mark J. Rozell, eds., *The New Politics of the Old South* (Lanham, Md.: Rowman & Littlefield, 1998); John C. Kuzenski, Laurence W. Moreland, and Robert P. Steed, eds., *Eye of the Storm: The South and Congress in an Era of Change* (Westport, Conn.: Praeger, 2001); Joseph A. Aistrup, *The Southern Strategy Revisited* (Lexington: University of Kentucky Press, 1996); Alexander P. Lamis, *The Two-Party South* (New York: Oxford University Press, 1984); Lamis, ed., *Southern Politics in the 1990s* (Baton Rouge: Louisiana State University Press, 1999); Robert P. Steed, Laurence W. Moreland, and Tod A. Baker, eds., *Southern Parties and Elections* (Tuscaloosa: University of Alabama Press, 1997); Jack Bass and Walter DeVries, *The Transformation of Southern Politics* (New York: Basic Books, 1976); Robert H. Swansbrough and David M. Brodsky, eds., *The South's New Politics* (Columbia: University of South Carolina Press, 1988); Richard K. Scher, *Politics in the New South* (New York: Paragon House, 1992); Dewey W. Grantham, *The Life and Death of the Solid South* (Lexington: University of Kentucky Press, 1988); and Kevin P. Phillips,

The Emerging Republican Majority (Garden City, N.Y.: Anchor, 1970), pp. 187–289.

6. *Knoxville News-Sentinel,* November 9, 1994.

7. We postpone to a later chapter consideration of Hispanics (important especially in Texas and Florida).

8. These calculations are based on census results reported in the *Atlanta Journal-Constitution,* December 28, 2000.

9. Dan Balz and Ronald Brownstein, *Storming the Gates* (Boston: Little, Brown, 1996), p. 210.

10. Ibid., p. 211.

11. Peter Applebome, *Dixie Rising* (New York: Times Books, 1996), pp. 27, 44–45.

12. In response to a complaint filed by Gingrich against Wright, the House Ethics Committee had charged the Speaker with "sixty-nine specific violations of House rules." The attack on Wright paid off for Gingrich among his fellow Republicans. According to Balz and Brownstein, "Gingrich's relentless and often singular pursuit of Wright convinced many of his colleagues that he was more than an intellectual gadfly, more than a disruptive ideologue. Some of them actually began to see him as a leader, someone who could carry them out of their long period of exile. When House Republicans caucused on the morning after Wright's resignation, Gingrich received a standing ovation"; *Storming the Gates,* pp. 125–126. For a detailed treatment of Wright's career, see John M. Barry, *The Ambition and the Power* (New York: Viking, 1989).

13. See Richard F. Fenno Jr., *Learning to Govern* (Washington, D.C.: Brookings Institution, 1997).

14. V. O. Key Jr. and Frank Munger, "Social Determinism and Electoral Decision: The Case of Indiana," in *American Voting Behavior,* ed. Eugene Burdick and Arthur J. Brodbeck (Glencoe, Ill.: Free Press, 1959), p. 286.

15. The sectional geography of congressional elections appears dramatically in Kenneth C. Martis, *The Historical Atlas of Political Parties in the United States Congress: 1789–1989* (New York: Macmillan, 1989).

16. Stephen Skowronek, *The Politics Presidents Make* (Cambridge, Mass.: Harvard University Press, 1993), pp. 288–324.

17. See James L. Sundquist, *Dynamics of the Party System,* rev. ed. (Washington, D.C.: Brookings Institution, 1983), pp. 198–268.

18. Key, *Southern Politics,* p. 669.

19. Richard Franklin Bensel, *The Political Economy of American Industrialization, 1877–1900* (New York: Cambridge University Press, 2000), pp. 50, 52. An intriguing county-level map of economic development appears on p. 51. See generally Bensel's *Sectionalism and American Political Development, 1880–1980* (Madison: University of Wisconsin Press, 1984), and *Yankee Leviathan: The Origins of Central State Authority in America, 1859–1877* (New York: Cambridge University Press, 1991).

20. Black and Black, *Politics and Society*, pp. 48–49. See generally pp. 3–72.

21. Neil R. Peirce, *The Megastates of America* (New York: Norton, 1972), pp. 450–563.

22. Michael Barone and Grant Ujifusa, *The Almanac of American Politics 1998* (Washington, D.C.: National Journal, 1997), p. 1333.

23. Quoted in Skowronek, *Politics Presidents Make*, p. 431.

24. The table builds on Black, *Southern Governors*, pp. 326–334; and Black and Black, *Politics and Society*, pp. 138–144.

25. *Congressional Record*, January 12, 1938, p. 381.

26. Nadine Cohodas, *Strom Thurmond and the Politics of Southern Change* (New York: Simon & Schuster, 1993), p. 318; and Jack Bass and Marilyn W. Thompson, *Ol' Strom* (Atlanta: Longstreet, 1998), p. 2. For illuminating analyses of the locale in which Thurmond was raised, see Orville Burton, *In My Father's House Are Many Mansions: Family and Community in Edgefield, South Carolina* (Chapel Hill: University of North Carolina Press, 1985); Francis Butler Simpkins, *Pitchfork Ben Tillman: South Carolinian* (Baton Rouge: Louisiana State University Press, 1944); and David Robinson, *Sly and Able: A Political Biography of James F. Byrnes* (New York: Norton, 1994).

27. Bobby Baker, *Wheeling and Dealing* (New York: Norton, 1978), p. 99.

28. Bass and Thompson, *Ol' Strom*, p. 2.

29. Cohodas, *Strom Thurmond*, p. 480.

30. Throughout this book *Congressional Quarterly*'s Democratic party unity scores are used to classify representatives and senators according to their ideology in a given Congress. Democrats with party unity scores of less than 60 are considered conservatives.

31. *Washington Post*, May 30, 1978.

2. CONFRONTING THE DEMOCRATIC JUGGERNAUT

1. J. Morgan Kousser, *The Shaping of Southern Politics* (New Haven: Yale University Press, 1974); Earl Black and Merle Black, *Politics and Society in the South* (Cambridge, Mass.: Harvard University Press, 1987), p. 237; *Washington Post*, December 8, 1994; *Webster's Seventh New Collegiate Dictionary* (Springfield, Mass: Merriam, 1967), p. 460.

2. Valuable studies of Congress in the 1950s include David R. Mayhew, *Party Loyalty among Congressmen* (Cambridge, Mass.: Harvard University Press, 1966); Donald R. Matthews, *U.S. Senators and Their World* (Chapel Hill: University of North Carolina Press, 1960); and William S. White, *Citadel: The Story of the U.S. Senate* (New York: Harper & Brothers, 1957).

3. C. Dwight Dorough, *Mr. Sam* (New York: Random House, 1962), p. 191.

4. Wayne Greenhaw, *Elephants in the Cotton Patch: Ronald Reagan and the New Republican South* (New York: Macmillan, 1982), p. 4.

5. D. B. Hardeman and Donald C. Brown, *Rayburn* (Austin: Texas Monthly Press, 1987), p. 154; Donald R. Matthews and James W. Prothro, *Negroes and the New Southern Politics* (New York: Harcourt, Brace and World, 1966), p. 382.

6. David Robertson, *Sly and Able: A Political Biography of James F. Byrnes* (New York: Norton, 1994), pp. 190, 192.

7. Alexander Heard, *A Two-Party South?* (Chapel Hill: University of North Carolina Press, 1952), p. 145; V. O. Key Jr., *Southern Politics in State and Nation* (New York: Knopf, 1949), p. 9.

8. Key, *Southern Politics,* pp. 3–12; and Kousser, *Shaping of Southern Politics,* pp. 238–265.

9. *Congressional Record,* January 21, 1907, p. 1440.

10. Ibid.

11. Ronald L. Heinemann, *Harry Byrd of Virginia* (Charlottesville: University Press of Virginia, 1996), p. 92.

12. Black and Black, *Politics and Society,* p. 10.

13. There are many valuable biographies of leading southern Democrats in Congress. In addition to books already cited, see Robert A. Caro's *The Path to Power* (New York: Knopf, 1982) and *Means of Ascent* (New York: Knopf, 1990); Ronnie Dugger, *The Politician* (New York: Norton, 1982); Robert Dallek, *Lone Star Rising* (New York: Oxford University Press, 1991); Gilbert C. Fite, *Richard B. Russell, Jr., Senator from Georgia* (Chapel Hill: University of North Carolina Press, 1991); Robertson, *Sly and Able;* Virginia Van der Veer Hamilton, *Lister Hill* (Chapel Hill: University of North Carolina Press, 1987); Bruce J. Dierenfield, *Keeper of the Rules: Congressman Howard W. Smith of Virginia* (Charlottesville: University Press of Virginia, 1986); T. Harry Williams, *Huey Long* (New York: Knopf, 1969); Randall Bennett Woods, *Fulbright* (New York: Cambridge University Press, 1995); and Stephen Kantrowitz, *Ben Tillman and the Reconstruction of White Supremacy* (Chapel Hill: University of North Carolina Press, 2000).

14. Hardeman and Bacon, *Rayburn,* p. 332.

15. Dorough, *Mr. Sam,* p. 179.

16. *Atlanta Journal,* October 26, 1972.

17. Hardeman and Bacon, *Rayburn,* pp. 35–474.

18. Paul H. Douglas, *In the Fullness of Time* (New York: Harcourt Brace Jovanovich, 1972), p. 227; Rowland W. Evans and Robert Novak, *Lyndon B. Johnson* (New York: New American Library, 1966), p. 31.

19. Caro, *Means of Ascent,* pp. 145–402; Dugger, *Politician,* pp. 307–341.

20. Merle Black and Earl Black, "The South in the Senate," in *The Disappearing South?,* ed. Robert P. Steed, Laurence W. Moreland, and Tod A. Baker (Tuscaloosa: University of Alabama Press, 1990), pp. 5–20.

21. See, for example, Carl Elliott Sr. and Michael D'Orso, *The Cost of Courage* (New York: Anchor, 1992).

22. David M. Potter, *The South and the Concurrent Majority* (Baton Rouge: Louisiana State University Press, 1972), p. 68.

23. *Congressional Record*, January 12, 1938, p. 381; Robertson, *Sly and Able*, p. 282; Fite, *Russell*, pp. 231, 233.

24. George W. Mowry, *Another Look at the Twentieth-Century South* (Baton Rouge: Louisiana State University Press, 1973), p. 66.

25. Hardeman and Bacon, *Rayburn*, p. 346.

26. Douglas, *Fullness of Time*, p. 203. See also James T. Patterson, *Congressional Conservatism and the New Deal* (Lexington: University of Kentucky Press, 1967); and Dierenfield, *Keeper of the Rules*.

27. Evans and Novak, *Johnson*, p. 30; Douglas, *Fullness of Time*, p. 203.

28. Caro, *Path to Power*, pp. 558–559.

29. Ira Katznelson, Kim Geiger, and Daniel Kryder, "Limiting Liberalism: The Southern Veto in Congress, 1933–1950," *Political Science Quarterly* 108 (Summer 1993): 285–286.

30. Bascomb Nolly Timmons, *Garner of Texas* (New York: Harper, 1948) p. 20; see also George Rothwell Brown, *Speaker of the House: The Romantic Story of John N. Garner* (New York: Brewer, Warren and Putnam, 1932).

31. For analyses of southern white support for many New Deal programs, see Frank Freidel, *F.D.R. and the South* (Baton Rouge: Louisiana State University Press, 1965); George B. Tindall, *The Emergence of the New South, 1913–1945* (Baton Rouge: Louisiana State University Press, 1967), pp. 607–649; James C. Cobb and Michael V. Namorato, eds., *The New Deal and the South* (Jackson: University Press of Mississippi, 1984); Dewey W. Grantham, *The South in Modern America* (New York: HarperCollins, 1994), pp. 116–138; and David Brady, *Critical Elections and Congressional Policy Making* (Stanford: Stanford University Press, 1988), pp. 84–114.

32. Jordan A. Schwarz, *The New Dealers* (New York: Knopf, 1993), p. 287.

33. Caro, *Path to Power*, pp. 471–472.

34. *Atlanta Journal*, November 1, 4, 1956.

35. Heard, *Two-Party South?*, p. 75.

36. Ibid., p. 97; James L. Sundquist, *Dynamics of the Party System*, rev. ed. (Washington, D.C.: Brookings Institution, 1983), pp. 271–272; and Key, *Southern Politics*, p. 292.

37. Key, *Southern Politics*, p. 296; *Atlanta Journal*, November 1, 1956.

38. Considerable Republican potential lay also in the Tennessee Third District, as well as in a band of Blue Ridge districts that spilled over into Virginia and North Carolina from east Tennessee. Virginia's Ninth District, located in the southwestern corner of the state, had been represented by Republican C. Bascomb Slemp during the first two decades of the twentieth century. Pockets of mountain Republicanism also appeared in western Virginia in the Sixth and Seventh Congressional Districts. Republican potential in North Carolina had

been diluted by Democratic state politicians who skillfully drew long and narrow districts, referred to as "bacon strips," that scattered Republican voters in the northwest among five congressional districts, which sloped downward in a southeasterly direction to include enough Democratic counties to neutralize the rural highland Republicans. The GOP had a smaller rural base in the Ozark Mountains of Arkansas. Much smaller groups of mountain Republicans were scattered across northern Alabama and Georgia, but these voters were swamped by much larger numbers of rural white Democrats and did not constitute a realistic base for GOP congressional gains in the Deep South.

39. Heard, *Two-Party South?*, pp. 102–103.

40. Key, *Southern Politics*, p. 674; Heard, *Two-Party South?*, pp. 133–134.

41. Earl Black and Merle Black, *The Vital South: How Presidents Are Elected* (Cambridge, Mass.: Harvard University Press, 1992), pp. 178–186.

42. Frank B. Atkinson, *The Dynamic Dominion* (Fairfax, Va.: George Mason University Press, 1992), pp. 50–51.

43. Ibid., p. 54.

44. *U.S. News and World Report,* November 14, 1952.

45. Atkinson, *Dynamic Dominion,* pp. 54–55; *Time,* November 17, 1952; *U.S. News and World Report,* November 14, 1952.

46. *Time,* November 15, 1954; *U.S. News and World Report,* November 12, 1954.

47. *Time,* November 10, 1958.

48. *U.S. News and World Report,* November 14, 1958, p. 101; *Time,* November 10, 1958.

49. Since the early 1950s the *Congressional Quarterly* has reported party unity scores for all senators and representatives. *Congressional Quarterly* defines a party unity roll-call vote as one in which a majority of Democrats oppose a majority of Republicans. Because *CQ*'s party unity scores provide a convenient means to compare the voting records of members of Congress, they circulate widely among professional participants and observers of American politics, from elected politicians, party leaders, and interest group officials to the national press corps. For decades attentive publics have used *CQ*'s party unity scores to size up particular politicians. Ranging from 0 (no party unity) to 100 (perfect party unity), the Democratic party unity scores represent the percentage of votes in which a Democrat supported the Democratic majority against the Republican majority. *CQ*'s party unity scores are used throughout this book to categorize southern Democrats into three possible groups: *national or liberal Democrats* (party unity scores of 80–100), *moderate Democrats* (party unity scores of 60–79), and *conservative or nominal Democrats* (party unity scores of less than 60).

50. Mayhew's *Party Loyalty* provides many examples of southern House Democrats in action during the 1950s and early 1960s.

51. *U.S. News and World Report,* November 16, 1956.

52. Ibid., November 16, 1956; November 21, 1960.

53. Numan V. Bartley, *The Rise of Massive Resistance* (Baton Rouge: Louisiana State University Press, 1969), p. 116.

54. Hardeman and Bacon, *Rayburn*, pp. 420–422.

3. THE PROMISING PERIPHERAL SOUTH

1. Chandler Davidson and Bernard Grofman, eds., *Quiet Revolution in the South* (Princeton: Princeton University Press, 1994).

2. John Brady, *Bad Boy: The Life and Times of Lee Atwater* (Reading, Mass.: Addison-Wesley, 1997), p. 70. Brady observed that Atwater "market[ed] himself as a Machiavellian political warrior, skillful at using ad hominem strategies and tactics, characterized by personal attacks, dirty tricks, and accentuating the negative"; ibid.

3. Richard F. Fenno Jr., *Senators on the Campaign Trail* (Norman: University of Oklahoma Press, 1996), p. 224.

4. Gilbert C. Fite, *Richard B. Russell, Jr., Senator from Georgia* (Chapel Hill: University of North Carolina Press, 1991), pp. 164–170, 224–270, 329–348.

5. Pat Watters and Reese Cleghorn, *Climbing Jacob's Ladder* (New York: Harcourt, Brace and World, 1967); Harvard Sitkoff, *The Struggle for Black Equality* (New York: Hill and Wang, 1981); John Lewis with Michael D'Orso, *Walking with the Wind* (New York: Simon & Schuster, 1998); David J. Garrow, *Bearing the Cross* (New York: Morrow, 1986); Taylor Branch, *Parting the Waters* (New York: Simon & Schuster, 1988); idem, *Pillar of Fire* (New York: Simon & Schuster, 1998).

6. *Congressional Record,* November 27, 1963, p. 22839; John A. Goldsmith, *Colleagues* (Washington, D.C.: Seven Locks, 1993), p. 103.

7. Robert Mann, *The Walls of Jericho* (New York: Harcourt Brace, 1996), p. 429.

8. Merle Miller, *Lyndon* (New York: Putnam, 1980), p. 371; David J. Garrow, *Protest at Selma* (New Haven: Yale University Press, 1978).

9. *Congressional Record,* March 15, 1965, pp. 5059–61.

10. Charles and Barbara Whalen, *The Longest Debate* (New York: New American Library, 1986); Mann, *Walls of Jericho;* Garrow, *Protest at Selma.*

11. Fite, *Russell,* p. 421.

12. Ibid.

13. Ibid.; W. Wayne Shannon effectively used the concept of "nominal Democrats" to discuss the southern revolt against the Democratic party in "Revolt in Washington: The South in Congress," in *The Changing Politics of the South,* ed. William C. Havard (Baton Rouge: Louisiana State University Press, 1972), pp. 637–687.

14. *Atlanta Journal,* September 19, 1972; November 2, 1972.

15. *Congressional Quarterly Weekly Report,* October 26, 1974, p. 2962.

16. Richard F. Fenno Jr., *When Incumbency Fails* (Washington, D.C.: CQ Press, 1992), p. 3.

17. Richard F. Fenno Jr., *Home Style: House Members in Their Districts* (Boston: Little, Brown, 1978), pp. 171–213.

18. *Time,* June 9, 1961. For discussions of Texas party politics, see V. O. Key Jr., *Southern Politics in State and Nation* (New York: Knopf, 1949), pp. 254–276; James R. Soukup, Clifton McCleskey, and Harry Holloway, *Party and Factional Division in Texas* (Austin: University of Texas Press, 1964); O. Douglas Weeks, "Texas: Land of Conservative Expansiveness," in Havard, *Changing Politics of the South,* pp. 201–230; Jack Bass and Walter DeVries, *The Transformation of Southern Politics* (New York: Basic Books, 1976), pp. 305–338; Arnold Vedlitz, James A. Dyer, and David B. Hill, "The Changing Texas Voter," in *The South's New Politics,* ed. Robert H. Swansbrough and David M. Brodsky (Columbia: University of South Carolina Press, 1988), pp. 38–53; Chandler M. Davidson, *Race and Class in Texas Politics* (Princeton: Princeton University Press, 1990); and James W. Lamare, J. L. Polinard, and Robert D. Wrinkle, "Texas: Lone Star(Wars) State," in *The New Politics of the Old South,* ed. Charles S. Bullock III and Mark J. Rozell (Lanham, Md.: Rowman & Littlefield, 1998), pp. 245–258.

19. John G. Tower, *Consequences* (Boston: Little, Brown, 1991), pp. 14–15.

20. Ibid., p. 165; *Time,* June 9, 1961; Soukup, McCleskey, and Holloway, *Party and Factional Division in Texas,* pp. 21–66; Numan Bartley and Hugh D. Graham, *Southern Politics and the Second Reconstruction* (Baltimore: Johns Hopkins University Press, 1975), pp. 96–97.

21. Tower, *Consequences,* p. 107; *Washington Post,* October 28, 1978.

22. Michael Barone and Grant Ujifusa, *The Almanac of American Politics 1984* (Washington, D.C.: National Journal, 1983), p. 1133; *New York Times,* October 28, 1984.

23. Here and elsewhere we have drawn upon exit polls to describe support patterns for particular candidates.

24. J. Lee Annis Jr., *Howard Baker* (Lanham, Md.: Madison Books, 1995), pp. 6–7. For Tennessee party politics, see Key, *Southern Politics,* pp. 58–81; Joseph Bruce Gorman, *Kefauver* (New York: Oxford University Press, 1971); Charles L. Fontenay, *Estes Kefauver* (Knoxville: University of Tennessee Press, 1980); Lee S. Greene and Jack E. Holmes, "Tennessee: A Politics of Peaceful Change," in Havard, *Changing Politics of the South,* pp. 165–200; Albert Gore Sr., *Let the Glory Out* (New York: Viking, 1972); Bass and DeVries, *Transformation,* pp. 284–304; Robert H. Swansbrough, *Political Change in Tennessee* (Knoxville: University of Tennessee, Bureau of Public Administration, 1985); William R. Majors, *Change and Continuity: Tennessee Politics since the Civil War* (Macon, Ga.: Mercer University Press, 1986); Robert M. Swansbrough and David M. Brodsky, "Tennessee: Weakening Party Loyalties and Growing Independence," in Swansbrough and Brodsky, *South's New Politics,* pp. 76–93; and David M. Brodsky, "Tennessee:

Genuine Two-Party Politics," in Bullock and Rozell, *New Politics of Old South*, pp. 167–183.

25. Annis, *Baker*, pp. 6–7, 31–37.

26. David Halberstam, "The End of a Populist," *Harper's*, January 1971, p. 39.

27. Gore, *Glory*, pp. 201–280; Halberstam, "Populist," pp. 38, 43.

28. Annis, *Baker*, p. 101.

29. Robert Sherrill, *Gothic Politics in the Deep South* (New York: Grossman, 1968), pp. 138–151; *Congressional Quarterly Weekly Report*, October 11, 1968, p. 2696; and Dewey W. Grantham Jr., *The Life and Death of the Solid South* (Lexington: University of Kentucky Press, 1988), p. 166. For discussions of Florida party politics, see Key, *Southern Politics*, pp. 82–105; Manning J. Dauer, "Florida: The Different State," in Havard, *Changing Politics of the South*, pp. 92–164; Bass and DeVries, *Transformation*, pp. 107–135; Suzanne L. Parker, "Shifting Party Tides in Florida: Where Have All the Democrats Gone?" in Swansbrough and Brodsky, *South's New Politics*, 22–37; and Michael J. Scicchitano and Richard K. Scher, "Florida: Political Change, 1950–1996," in Bullock and Rozell, *New Politics of the Old South*, pp. 227–244.

30. *San Diego Union-Tribune*, November 1, 1988; *St. Petersburg Times*, October 5, 1988; and *National Journal*, October 22, 1988.

31. *St. Petersburg Times*, November 11, 17, 1988.

32. Numan V. Bartley, *The Rise of Massive Resistance* (Baton Rouge: Louisiana State University Press, 1969), pp. 108–117; Ronald L. Heinemann, *Harry Byrd of Virginia* (Charlottesville: University Press of Virginia, 1996); J. Harvie Wilkinson III, *Harry Byrd and the Changing Face of Virginia Politics* (Charlottesville: University Press of Virginia, 1968); and Grantham, *Life & Death of Solid South*, pp. 125–148. For studies of Virginia state politics, see Key, *Southern Politics*, pp. 19–35; Ralph Eisenberg, "Virginia: The Emergence of Two-Party Politics," in Havard, *Changing Politics of the South*, pp. 39–91; Bass and DeVries, *Transformation*, pp. 339–368; Larry Sabato, *The Democratic Party Primary in Virginia* (Charlottesville: University Press of Virginia, 1977); John C. McGlennon, "Virginia's Changing Party Politics, 1976–1986," in Swansbrough and Brodsky, *South's New Politics*, pp. 56–75; Mark J. Rozell, "The New Politics of the Old Dominion," in Bullock and Rozell, *New Politics of the Old South*, pp. 123–139; and Frank Atkinson, *The Dynamic Dominion* (Fairfax, Va.: George Mason University Press, 1992).

33. *Washington Post*, September 30, 1982; September 20, 1987.

34. Bruce J. Dierenfield, *Keeper of the Rules: Congressman Howard W. Smith of Virginia* (Charlottesville: University Press of Virginia, 1987); Atkinson, *Dynamic Dominion*, p. 248.

35. Atkinson, *Dynamic Dominion*, pp. 249–250.

36. Ibid., pp. 385, 388.

37. On North Carolina politics, see Key, *Southern Politics*, pp. 205–228; Julian M. Pleasants and Augustus M. Burns III, *Frank Porter Graham and the 1950 Senate Race in North Carolina* (Chapel Hill: University of North Carolina Press, 1990); Paul R. Clancy, *Just a Country Lawyer: A Biography of Senator Sam Ervin* (Bloomington: Indiana University Press, 1974); Dick Dabney, *A Good Man: The Life of Sam J. Ervin* (Boston: Houghton Mifflin, 1976); Ben F. Bulla, *Textiles and Politics: The Life of B. Everett Jordan* (Durham, N.C.: Carolina Academic Press, 1992); Jack D. Fleer, *North Carolina Politics* (Chapel Hill: University of North Carolina Press, 1968); Preston W. Edsall and J. Oliver Williams, "North Carolina: Bipartisan Paradox," in Havard, *Changing Politics of the South*, pp. 366–423; Thad Beyle and Merle Black, eds., *Politics and Policy in North Carolina* (New York: MSS, 1975); Bass and DeVries, *Transformation*, pp. 218–247; Jack D. Fleer, Roger C. Lowery, and Charles L. Prysby, "Political Change in North Carolina," in Swansbrough and Brodsky, *South's New Politics*, pp. 94–111; Paul Luebke, *Tar Heel Politics* (Chapel Hill: University of North Carolina Press, 1990); idem, *Tar Heel Politics 2000* (Chapel Hill: University of North Carolina Press, 1998); and Thomas A. Kazee, "North Carolina: Conservatism, Traditionalism, and the GOP," in Bullock and Rozell, *New Politics of the Old South*, pp. 141–165.

38. Bulla, *Textiles and Politics*, p. 309.

39. *Washington Post*, October 5, 1990; Ernest B. Furgurson, *Hard Right: The Rise of Jesse Helms* (New York: Norton, 1986), pp. 90, 95, 97; William D. Snider, *Helms and Hunt: The North Carolina Senate Race, 1984* (Chapel Hill: University of North Carolina Press, 1985); and Luebke, *Tar Heel Politics*, pp. 124–155.

40. *Washington Post*, August 20, 1973; Peter Applebome, "Pit Bull Politician," *New York Times Magazine*, October 28, 1990.

41. Applebome, "Pit Bull Politician."

42. *Washington Post*, October 5, 1990; Applebome, "Pit Bull Politician."

43. Luebke, *Tar Heel Politics 2000*, pp. 161–188.

44. *Washington Post*, October 5, 1990; *Raleigh News and Observer*, September 10, 1984.

45. *St. Petersburg Times*, October 22, 1990; Applebome, "Pit Bull Politician"; *Washington Post*, November 4, 1990.

46. *San Diego Union-Tribune*, June 6, 1990; *USA Today*, June 6, 1990.

47. Applebome, "Pit Bull Politician"; *Washington Post*, October 5, 1990.

48. *New York Times*, November 8, 1990; *Washington Post*, October 5, 1990; *St. Petersburg Times*, October 22, 1990.

49. *Washington Post*, November 1, 1990.

50. *New York Times*, November 8, 1990.

51. Ibid.; *Boston Globe*, November 8, 1990.

52. *Washington Post*, October 5, 1990.

53. *New York Times*, November 8, 1990.

54. *Raleigh Spectator*, March 12, 1981.

55. Key, *Southern Politics*, pp. 183–204; Randall Bennett Woods, *Fulbright* (Cambridge: Cambridge University Press, 1995); Richard E. Yates, "Arkansas: Independent and Unpredictable," in Havard, *Changing Politics of the South*, pp. 233–293; Bass and DeVries, *Transformation*, pp. 87–106; Diane D. Blair and Robert L. Savage, "The Appearances of Realignment and Dealignment in Arkansas," in Swansbrough and Brodsky, *South's New Politics*, pp. 126–140); Diane D. Blair, *Arkansas Politics and Government* (Lincoln: University of Nebraska Press, 1988); and Gary D. Wekkin, "Arkansas: Electoral Competition in the 1990s," in Bullock and Rozell, *New Politics of the Old South*, pp. 185–203.

4. THE IMPENETRABLE DEEP SOUTH

1. Jack Bass and Marilyn W. Thompson, *Ol' Strom* (Atlanta: Longstreet, 1998), p. 3. On South Carolina politics, see David Robertson, *Sly and Able: A Political Biography of James F. Byrnes* (New York: Norton, 1994); V. O. Key Jr., *Southern Politics in State and Nation* (New York: Knopf, 1949), pp. 130–155; Chester W. Bain, "South Carolina: Partisan Prelude," in *The Changing Politics of the South*, ed. William C. Havard (Baton Rouge: Louisiana State University Press, 1972), pp. 588–636; Jack Bass and Walter DeVries, *The Transformation of Southern Politics* (New York: Basic Books, 1976), pp. 248–283; Cole Blease Graham Jr., "Partisan Change in South Carolina," in *The South's New Politics*, ed. Robert H. Swansbrough and David M. Brodsky (Columbia: University of South Carolina Press, 1988), pp. 158–174; Cole Blease Graham Jr. and William V. Moore, *South Carolina Government and Politics* (Lincoln: University of Nebraska Press, 1994); John C. Kuzenski, "South Carolina: The Heart of GOP Realignment in the South," in *The New Politics of the Old South*, ed. Charles S. Bullock III and Mark J. Rozell (Lanham, Md.: Rowman & Littlefield, 1998), pp. 25–47.

2. Nadine Cohodas, *Strom Thurmond and the Politics of Southern Change* (New York: Simon & Schuster, 1993), pp. 414–415.

3. Earl Black and Merle Black, *The Vital South: How Presidents Are Elected* (Cambridge, Mass.: Harvard University Press, 1992), p. 3.

4. Bass and Thompson, *Ol' Strom*, p. 3.

5. *Congressional Quarterly Weekly Report*, October 7, 1966, pp. 2379–80; see also Earl Black, *Southern Governors and Civil Rights* (Cambridge, Mass.: Harvard University Press, 1976), pp. 80–83.

6. *Washington Post*, May 30, 1978; October 10, 1978. For Mississippi party politics, see Key, *Southern Politics*, pp. 229–253; James W. Silver, *Mississippi: The Closed Society* (New York: Harcourt, Brace and World, 1966); Charles N. Fortenberry and F. Glenn Abney, "Mississippi: Unreconstructed and Unredeemed," in Havard, *Changing Politics of the South*, pp. 472–524; Stephen D. Shaffer, "Changing Party Politics in Mississippi," in Swansbrough and Brodsky,

South's New Politics, pp. 189–203; Dale Krane and Stephen Shaffer, eds., *Mississippi Government and Politics* (Lincoln: University of Nebraska Press, 1992); David A. Breaux, Don E. Slabach, and Daye Dearing, "Mississippi: A Synthesis of Race, Region, and Republicanism," in Bullock and Rozell, *New Politics of the Old South,* pp. 85–104.

7. Cohodas, *Thurmond,* p. 16; *Washington Post,* June 16, 1984.

8. *Washington Post,* June 16, 1984.

9. On Georgia politics, see Gilbert C. Fite, *Richard B. Russell, Jr., Senator from Georgia* (Chapel Hill: University of North Carolina Press, 1991); William Anderson, *The Wild Man from Sugar Creek* (Baton Rouge: Louisiana State University Press, 1975); Herman E. Talmadge with Mark Royden Winchell, *Talmadge* (Atlanta: Peachtree, 1987); Key, *Southern Politics,* pp. 106–129; Joseph N. Bernd, "Georgia: Static and Dynamic," in Havard, *Changing Politics of the South,* pp. 294–365; Bass and DeVries, *Transformation,* pp. 136–157; Numan V. Bartley, *From Thurmond to Wallace: Political Trends in Georgia* (Baltimore: Johns Hopkins Press, 1970); Michael B. Binford, "Georgia: Political Realignment or Partisan Evolution," in Swansbrough and Brodsky, *South's New Politics,* pp. 175–188; Charles S. Bullock III, "Georgia: Election Rules and Partisan Conflict," in Bullock and Rozell, *New Politics of the Old South,* pp. 49–65.

10. *Atlanta Journal,* October 29, 1972.

11. Ibid., November 5, 8, 1972.

12. Ibid., October 16, 1972.

13. Ibid., October 14, November 7, 1972; Black and Black, *Vital South,* p. 295.

14. Michael Barone and Grant Ujifusa, *The Almanac of American Politics 1984* (Washington, D.C.: National Journal, 1983), p. 275.

15. *New York Times,* August 27, 1980; Talmadge, *Talmadge,* p. 351.

16. *Washington Post,* November 18, 1980.

17. Ibid.

18. L. Marvin Overby, "Political Amateurism, Legislative Inexperience, and Incumbency Behavior: Southern Republican Senators, 1980–1986," *Polity* 3 (Spring 1993): 416; idem, "The Politics of Parochialism: Southern Senators and the Southern Democracy in the 1980s," paper delivered at the 1989 annual meeting of the American Political Science Association, Atlanta, Georgia, p. 11.

19. *New York Times,* October 1, 1986; *Los Angeles Times,* October 23, 1986; and *Washington Post,* November 6, 1986.

20. On Alabama politics, see William D. Barnard, *Dixiecrats and Democrats, Alabama Politics, 1942–1950* (University: University of Alabama Press, 1974); Virginia Van der Veer Hamilton, *Lister Hill* (Chapel Hill: University of North Carolina Press, 1987); Key, *Southern Politics,* pp. 36–57; Bass and DeVries, *Transformation,* pp. 57–86; Dan T. Carter, *The Politics of Rage: George Wallace, The Origins of the New Conservatism, and the Transformation of American Politics* (New York: Simon & Schuster, 1995); Patrick R. Cotter and James Glen Stovall, "Party

Identification and Political Change in Alabama," in Swansbrough and Brodsky, *South's New Politics,* pp. 142–157; Harold W. Stanley, "Alabama: Republicans Win the Heart of Dixie," in Bullock and Rozell, *New Politics of the Old South,* pp. 67–83.

21. Hamilton, *Lister Hill,* pp. 241–259; Numan V. Bartley and Hugh D. Graham, *Southern Politics and the Second Reconstruction* (Baltimore: Johns Hopkins University Press, 1975), pp. 98–99; Walter Dean Burnham, "The Alabama Senatorial Election of 1962: Return of Inter-Party Competition," *Journal of Politics* 26 (November 1964): 798–829.

22. Overby, "Political Amateurism," p. 416.

23. Ibid., pp. 419–420.

24. On Louisiana politics, see Robert Mann, *Legacy to Power: Senator Russell Long of Louisiana* (New York: Paragon, 1992); Thomas Becnel, *Senator Allen J. Ellender of Louisiana* (Baton Rouge: Louisiana State University Press, 1995); Key, *Southern Politics,* pp. 156–182; Perry H. Howard, "Louisiana: Resistance and Change," in Havard, *Changing Politics of the South,* pp. 525–587; Bass and DeVries, *Transformation,* pp. 158–185; Wayne Parent, "The Rise and Stall of Republican Ascendancy in Louisiana Politics," in Swansbrough and Brodsky, *South's New Politics,* pp. 204–217; Wayne Parent and Huey Perry, "Louisiana: African Americans, Republicans, and Party Competition," in Bullock and Rozell, *New Politics of the Old South,* pp. 105–120.

25. Douglas D. Rose, "Six Explanations in Search of Support: David Duke's U.S. Senate Campaign," in *The Emergence of David Duke and the Politics of Race,* ed. Douglas D. Rose (Chapel Hill: University of North Carolina Press, 1992), p. 157; John C. Kuzenski, Charles S. Bullock III, and Ronald Keith Gaddie, eds., *David Duke and the Politics of Racism in the South* (Nashville: Vanderbilt University Press, 1995); and Tyler Bridges, *The Rise of David Duke* (Jackson: University Press of Mississippi, 1994).

5. THE DEMOCRATIC SMOTHER

1. Richard H. Rovere, *The Goldwater Caper* (New York: Harcourt, Brace and World, 1965), pp. 141–142.

2. Earl Black and Merle Black, *The Vital South: How Presidents Are Elected* (Cambridge, Mass.: Harvard University Press, 1992), p. 147.

3. Rovere, *Goldwater Caper,* p. 141.

4. For a masterly analysis of the southern Democratic protest, see W. Wayne Shannon, "Revolt in Washington: The South in Congress," in *The Changing Politics of the South,* ed. William C. Havard (Baton Rouge: Louisiana State University Press, 1972), pp. 637–687. See also Steven K. Smith, "Southern Congressional Politics since the Great Society" (Ph.D. diss., University of South Carolina, 1983).

5. 376 U.S. 1.

6. *Congressional Quarterly Weekly Report*, October 7, 1966, p. 2351.

7. Ibid., October 9, 1964, p. 2348.

8. Black and Black, *Vital South*, pp. 141–175, 199–210, 298–303.

9. Dan T. Carter, *The Politics of Rage: George Wallace, the Origins of the New Conservatism, and the Transformation of American Politics* (New York: Simon & Schuster, 1995).

10. Black and Black, *Vital South*, p. 147.

11. Alexander Heard, *A Two-Party South?* (Chapel Hill: University of North Carolina Press, 1952), p. 103.

12. Richard F. Fenno Jr., *Congress at the Grassroots* (Chapel Hill: University of North Carolina Press, 2000), pp. 13–50.

13. Ibid., p. 40; *Congressional Quarterly Weekly Report*, October 7, 1966, p. 2357.

14. Fenno, *Congress at the Grassroots*, pp. 51–64.

15. Ibid., p. 63.

16. See Carl Elliott Sr. and Michael D'Orso, *The Cost of Courage* (New York: Doubleday, 1992), pp. 241–258.

17. *Congressional Quarterly Weekly Report*, October 7, 1972, p. 2496.

18. Ibid., October 7, 1966, p. 2362.

19. Ibid., December 8, 1961, p. 1942.

20. Quoted in Rovere, *Goldwater Caper*, p. 134.

21. *Congressional Quarterly Weekly Report*, December 8, 1961, p. 1942.

22. Ibid.; and December 22, 1961, p. 1973.

23. Ibid., December 22, 1961, p. 1973; and December 8, 1961, p. 1942.

24. Ibid., October 20, 1961, p. 1770; December 8, 1961, p. 1942; December 23, 1961, p. 1973.

25. See Merle Black, "Racial Composition of Congressional Districts and Support for Federal Voting Rights in the American South," *Social Science Quarterly* 59 (December 1978): 435–450.

6. THE DEMOCRATIC DOMINATION

1. See Earl Black and Merle Black, *Politics and Society in the South* (Cambridge, Mass.: Harvard University Press, 1987), pp. 138–144, 286–291, 312–316.

2. On the decline of conservative southern Democrats, see James M. Glaser, *Race, Campaign Politics, and the Realignment in the South* (New Haven: Yale University Press, 1996); Carol M. Swain, *Black Faces, Black Interests* (Cambridge, Mass.: Harvard University Press, 1993), esp. pp. 145–189; Nicol C. Rae, *Southern Democrats* (New York: Oxford University Press, 1994), pp. 65–110; Kenny J. Whitby, *The Color of Representation* (Ann Arbor: University of Michigan Press, 1997); Richard Fleisher, "Explaining the Change in Roll-Call Voting Behavior of Southern Democrats," *Journal of Politics* 55 (May 1993): 327–341; Charles S.

Bullock III, "Congressional Voting and the Mobilization of a Black Electorate in the South," ibid., 43 (1981): 662–682; Charles S. Bullock III, "Congressional Roll Call Voting in a Two-Party South," *Social Science Quarterly* 66 (December 1985): 789–804; Mary Alice Nye and Charles S. Bullock III, "Civil Rights Support: A Comparison of Southern and Border State Representatives," *Legislative Studies Quarterly* 17 (February 1992): 81–94; M. V. Hood III and Irwin L. Morris, "Boll Weevils and Roll-Call Voting: A Study in Time and Space," ibid., 23 (May 1998): 245–269.

3. See David W. Rohde, *Parties and Leaders in the Postreform House* (Chicago: University of Chicago Press, 1991); and idem, "'Something's Happening Here; What It Is Ain't Exactly Clear': Southern Democrats in the House of Representatives," in *Home Style and Washington Work*, ed. Morris P. Fiorina and David W. Rohde (Ann Arbor: University of Michigan Press, 1989), pp. 137–163.

4. Nick Kotz, *Let Them Eat Promises* (New York: Anchor, 1971), p. 80. See also pp. 79–97.

5. Michael Barone and Grant Ujifusa, *The Almanac of American Politics 1990* (Washington, D.C.: National Journal, 1989), p. 664.

6. On Wright's career, see John M. Barry, *The Ambition and the Power* (New York: Viking, 1989).

7. The Democratic advantage in open-seat special elections during the 1980s is carefully analyzed in Glaser, *Race, Campaign Politics, and Realignment*.

8. Richard F. Fenno Jr., *Congress at the Grassroots* (Chapel Hill: University of North Carolina Press, 2000).

7. REAGAN'S REALIGNMENT OF WHITE SOUTHERNERS

1. Martin P. Wattenberg, "The Building of a Republican Regional Base in the South," *Public Opinion Quarterly* 55 (Autumn 1991): 424–431.

2. Earl Black and Merle Black, *The Vital South: How Presidents Are Elected* (Cambridge, Mass.: Harvard University Press, 1992), pp. 94–99; 141–149. See also Kari Frederickson, *The Dixiecrat Revolt and the End of the Solid South, 1932–1968* (Chapel Hill: University of North Carolina Press, 2001).

3. Louis Harris, *Is There a Republican Majority?* (New York: Harper and Brothers, 1954), p. 67.

4. Numan V. Bartley, *The New South: 1945–1980* (Baton Rouge: Louisiana State University Press, 1995), pp. 101–102. See also Donald S. Strong, *The 1952 Presidential Election in the South* (University, Ala.: Bureau of Public Administration, 1955).

5. Numan V. Bartley and Hugh D. Graham, *Southern Politics and the Second Reconstruction* (Baltimore: Johns Hopkins University Press, 1975), p. 187; Black and Black, *Vital South,* pp. 149–158; Edward G. Carmines and James A. Stimson, *Issue Evolution* (Princeton: Princeton University Press, 1989); Jack Bass

and Walter DeVries, *The Transformation of Southern Politics* (New York: Basic Books, 1976), pp. 27–32; Louis M. Seagull, *Southern Republicanism* (Cambridge, Mass.: Schenkman, 1975); Donald S. Strong, *Urban Republicanism in the South* (University, Ala.: Bureau of Public Administration, 1960).

6. Kevin P. Phillips, *The Emerging Republican Majority* (Garden City, N.Y.: Anchor, 1970), pp. 187–289; Reg Murphy and Hal Gulliver, *The Southern Strategy* (New York: Scribner's, 1971); and Joseph A. Aistrup, *The Southern Strategy Revisited* (Lexington: University Press of Kentucky, 1996), pp. 18–64.

7. Dewey W. Grantham, *The South in Modern America* (New York: Harper-Collins, 1994), pp. 281–282.

8. Bartley, *New South*, p. 469; Charles W. Dunn and J. David Woodward, "Ideological Images for a Television Age: Ronald Reagan as Party Leader," in *The Reagan Presidency*, ed. Dilys M. Hill, Raymond A. Moore, and Phil Williams (London: Macmillan, 1990), pp. 118–119, 121; and Lou Cannon, *Reagan* (New York: Putnam, 1982), pp. 93–94.

9. Bartley, *New South*, pp. 455–456; *Washington Post*, November 4, 1980; September 14, 1980.

10. Bartley, *New South*, p. 455; *Washington Post*, October 30, 1980; November 4, 1980; *New York Times*, October 14, 1980.

11. *Washington Post*, October 28, 1980; *New York Times*, October 14, 1980; November 6, 1980.

12. *New York Times*, August 4, 1980; October 24, 1980; November 1, 1980; *Washington Post*, October 3, 1980; *Charlotte Observer*, November 6, 1980.

13. *Washington Post*, September 14, 1980.

14. John C. Green, Lyman A. Kellstedt, Corwin E. Smidt, and James L. Guth, "The Soul of the South: Religion and the New Electoral Order," in *The New Politics of the Old South*, ed. Charles S. Bullock III and Mark J. Rozell (Lanham, Md.: Rowman & Littlefield, 1998), p. 262; see also John C. Green, James L. Guth, Corwin E. Smidt, and Lyman A. Kellstedt, *Religion and the Culture Wars* (Lanham, Md.: Rowman & Littlefield, 1996); James L. Guth and John C. Green, eds., *The Bible and the Ballot* (Boulder: Westview, 1992); Mark J. Rozell and Clyde Wilcox, *God at the Grassroots* (Lanham, Md.: Rowman & Littlefield, 1995); Oran P. Smith, *The Rise of Baptist Republicanism* (New York: New York University Press, 1997); Samuel S. Hill, *Southern Churches in Crisis* (New York: Holt, Rinehart and Winston, 1966); Tod A. Baker, Robert P. Steed, and Laurence W. Moreland, eds., *Religion and Politics in the South* (New York: Praeger, 1983); C. Eric Lincoln and Lawrence H. Mamiya, *The Black Church in the African-American Experience* (Durham: Duke University Press, 1990); Ted G. Jelen, *The Political Mobilization of Religious Beliefs* (New York: Praeger, 1991); Duane M. Oldfield, *The Right and the Righteous: The Christian Right Confronts the Republican Party* (Lanham, Md.: Rowman & Littlefield, 1996); Clyde Wilcox, *"God's Warriors": The Christian Right in Twentieth-Century America* (Baltimore: Johns Hopkins University Press, 1992); and Paige Schneider, "The Impact of the

Christian Right on Republican Party Development in the South" (Ph.D. diss., Emory University, 2000).

15. Dunn and Woodward, "Ideological Images for a Television Age," p. 123.

16. *Washington Post,* October 4, 28, 1980; *New York Times,* November 6, 1980.

17. Quoted in Dan Balz and Ronald Brownstein, *Storming the Gates* (Boston: Little, Brown, 1996), p. 226.

18. Ronnie Dugger, *On Reagan* (New York: McGraw-Hill, 1983), p. 198; Richard Reeves, *The Reagan Detour* (New York: Simon & Schuster, 1985), p. 98; *Washington Post,* August 9, 1980.

19. Lou Cannon, *President Reagan* (New York: Simon & Schuster, 1991), p. 520; Lewis Chester, Godfrey Hodgson, and Bruce Page, *An American Melodrama* (New York: Viking, 1969), p. 438.

20. Dan T. Carter, *From George Wallace to Newt Gingrich* (Baton Rouge: Louisiana State University Press, 1996), p. 64.

21. *Washington Post,* August 4, 1980; *New York Times,* August 4, 1980; Cannon, *Reagan,* p. 270.

22. *Washington Post,* August 11, 1980.

23. Black and Black, *Vital South,* p. 295; Carter, *From George Wallace to Newt Gingrich,* p. 68; Dugger, *On Reagan,* p. 196.

24. *New York Times,* November 1, 1980.

25. Michael Dawson, *Behind the Mule: Race and Class in African-American Politics* (Princeton: Princeton University Press, 1994), p. 206; Carter, *From George Wallace to Newt Gingrich,* p. 68.

26. *New York Times,* November 6, 1980.

27. Grantham, *South in Modern America,* pp. 296–297; Dunn and Woodward, "Ideological Images for a Television Age," p. 123; Black and Black, *Vital South,* p. 295.

28. The evaluations of Reagan among southern whites are based upon our analyses of survey responses from the 1988 National Election Study; *Raleigh News and Observer,* October 23, 1980.

29. *Raleigh News and Observer,* October 23, 1980.

30. Alexander Heard, *A Two-Party South?* (Chapel Hill: University of North Carolina Press, 1952), p. 247.

31. Quoted in Grantham, *South in Modern America,* p. 296.

32. For previous analyses of the partisanship of conservative southern whites, see Earl Black and Merle Black, *Politics and Society in the South* (Cambridge, Mass.: Harvard University Press, 1987), pp. 249–256; Black and Black, *Vital South,* pp. 357–360; and Edward G. Carmines and Harold W. Stanley, "Ideological Realignment in the Contemporary South," in *The Disappearing South?,* ed. Robert P. Steed, Laurence W. Moreland, and Tod A. Baker (Tuscaloosa: University of Alabama Press, 1990), pp. 21–33.

33. Robert P. Steed, Laurence W. Moreland, and Tod A. Baker, "Searching for the Mind of the South in the Second Reconstruction," in Steed, Moreland,

and Baker, *Disappearing South?*, p. 129. See also Robert P. Steed, John A. Clark, Lewis Bowman, and Charles D. Hadley, eds., *Party Organization and Activism in the American South* (Tuscaloosa: University of Alabama Press, 1998).

34. Evaluations of the candidates were calculated from the relevant National Election Study surveys.

35. Unless otherwise noted, the survey questions analyzed in this chapter are from the 1996 National Election Study or the 1996 Voter News Service exit poll.

36. *Washington Times National Weekly Edition,* April 17–23, 1995.

37. Respondents were asked their preferences about racial integration in the spring of 1999 by the Southern Focus Poll, conducted by John Shelton Reed for the Institute for Research in Social Science of the University of North Carolina at Chapel Hill.

38. Glenn H. Utter and John W. Storey, *The Religious Right* (Santa Barbara: ABC-CLIO, 1995), pp. 83–84.

39. *Atlanta Constitution,* March 1, 1996.

40. Ibid.

41. Michael Barone and Grant Ujifusa, *The Almanac of American Politics 1996* (Washington, D.C.: National Journal, 1995), pp. xxxi–xxxiii, 371–375.

42. Michael Barone and Grant Ujifusa, *The Almanac of American Politics 1998* (Washington, D.C.: National Journal, 1997), p. 418; David Maraniss and Michael Weisskopf, *"Tell Newt to Shut Up!"* (New York: Simon & Schuster, 1996).

43. Richard F. Fenno Jr., *Learning to Govern* (Washington, D.C.: Brookings Institution, 1997).

44. Richard E. Neustadt, *Presidential Power* (New York: Mentor, 1964), p. 42.

45. Maraniss and Weisskopf, *"Tell Newt to Shut Up!"* p. 150; Larry Kudlow, *National Review Online,* March 14, 2000.

46. *Washington Post,* January 29, 1988.

47. Balz and Brownstein, *Storming the Gates,* p. 244.

48. Richard F. Fenno Jr., *Congress at the Grassroots* (Chapel Hill: University of North Carolina Press, 2000), p. 113.

8. A NEW PARTY SYSTEM IN THE SOUTH

1. Earl Black and Merle Black, *The Vital South: How Presidents Are Elected* (Cambridge, Mass.: Harvard University Press, 1992), pp. 19–28.

2. Numan V. Bartley and Hugh D. Graham, *Southern Politics and the Second Reconstruction* (Baltimore: Johns Hopkins University Press, 1975), pp. 199–200; V. O. Key Jr., *Southern Politics in State and Nation* (New York: Knopf, 1949), p. 5.

3. Key, *Southern Politics,* p. 307.

4. See Earl Black and Merle Black, *Politics and Society in the South* (Cambridge, Mass.: Harvard University Press, 1987), pp. 3–72.

5. *Washington Post,* January 29, 1988.

6. Michael C. Dawson, *Behind the Mule: Race and Class in African-American Politics* (Princeton: Princeton University Press, 1994), pp. 4–7, 204–205; see also Katherine Tate, *From Protest to Politics: The New Black Voters in American Elections* (Cambridge, Mass.: Harvard University Press, 1993); Diane Pinderhughes, *Race and Ethnicity in Chicago Politics* (Urbana: University of Illinois Press, 1987); Ronald W. Walters, *Black Presidential Politics in America* (Albany: State University of New York Press, 1988).

7. Dawson, *Behind the Mule*, p. 205.

8. Glenn H. Utter and John W. Storey, *The Religious Right* (Santa Barbara, Calif.: ABE-CLIO, 1995), pp. 83–84. For other works relevant to understanding the role of religion in southern politics, see Chapter 7, note 14.

9. *Washington Post*, May 12, 2000.

10. Ibid.

11. Southern Republican strength was even more pronounced among *native white men*, those males who had been raised in the South. Although we cannot explore the native-migrant distinction with the exit poll data because respondents were not asked where they were raised, a telephone poll conducted by the Institute for Research in Social Science by the University of North Carolina at Chapel Hill in the spring of 1999 suggests its importance: 62 percent of native white men in the region were core Republicans, while only 18 percent were core Democrats. The new Republican loyalties of native white men represent the partisan realignment of the primary social group that had once been the backbone of the Democratic party in the South. In 1999, 52 percent of them classified themselves as conservatives. By contrast, white men who had migrated into the region displayed a much smaller Republican advantage in 1999: 44 percent were core Republicans, and 31 percent were core Democrats. Native southern white men did stand out as more conservative than the other white males in the South on several important racial, social, and religious issues. Eighty-one percent of native white men believed that affirmative action on behalf of "women and minorities" discriminated against white men. Among this huge group, core Republicans led core Democrats by 70 to 16 percent. According to the 1996 National Election Study, 70 percent of white men native to the South opposed help to blacks. Fifty-one percent said that equal opportunity did not matter much to them, and 70 percent believed that society was pushing equal rights too much. Two-thirds were cold toward gays and lesbians, attitudes held by only 36 percent of the white male migrants. More than half of the native men took conservative positions on abortion compared to only 30 percent of the migrant men. Fundamentalist religion also separated southern white men by their origins. Fifty percent of the native white men believed that the Bible was the literal word of God, a view shared by only 10 percent of the migrant males. Majorities of white native men were warmly disposed toward fundamentalists and the Christian Coalition, groups that attracted similar warmth from few migrants.

12. Quoted in Alexander Heard, *A Two-Party South?* (Chapel Hill: University of North Carolina Press, 1952), p. 48.

13. Ibid., pp. 153, 247. See also Bruce J. Schulman, *From Cotton Belt to Sunbelt* (New York: Oxford University Press, 1991); and Kari Frederickson, *The Dixiecrat Revolt and the End of the Solid South, 1932–1968* (Chapel Hill: University of North Carolina Press, 2001), pp. 11–66.

14. Heard, *Two-Party South?*, p. 155.

15. Louis Harris, *Is There a Republican Majority?* (New York: Harper and Brothers, 1954), p. 69.

16. Numan V. Bartley, *The New South: 1945–1980* (Baton Rouge: Louisiana State University Press, 1995), pp. 449–450.

17. Leonard Reissman, "Social Development and the American South," *Journal of Social Issues* 22 (January 1966): 106.

18. Heard, *Two-Party South?*, p. 295; Harris, *Republican Majority?*, pp. 135–136.

19. Robert Emil Botsch, *We Shall Not Overcome* (Chapel Hill: University of North Carolina Press, 1980), p. 157.

20. Heard, *Two-Party South?*, pp. 248–249.

21. See also Joseph A. Aistrup, *The Southern Strategy Revisited* (Lexington: University Press of Kentucky, 1996), pp. 211–242.

9. THE PERIPHERAL SOUTH BREAKTHROUGH

1. *Memphis Commercial Appeal*, September 28, November 5, 1994.

2. Ibid., November 5, 1994.

3. *Washington Post*, October 13, 1992.

4. *Roll Call*, October 12, 26, 2000; *Memphis Commercial Appeal*, October 29, 1992.

5. *USA Today*, June 3, 1993.

6. *Guardian*, June 7, 1993; *Washington Post*, May 2, June 6, 1993.

7. Philip Ashford and Richard Locker, "Tennessee: A Partisan Big Bang amid Quiet Accommodation," in *Southern Politics in the 1990s*, ed. Alexander P. Lamis (Baton Rouge: Louisiana State University Press, 1999), pp. 211–212.

8. *Knoxville News-Sentinel*, November 6, 1994; Ashford and Locker, "Tennessee," pp. 212–213.

9. *Memphis Commercial Appeal*, November 5, 1994; *Knoxville News-Sentinel*, November 10, 1994.

10. *Washington Post*, November 9, 1994.

11. Ashford and Locker, "Tennessee," p. 220.

12. *Memphis Commercial Appeal*, November 9, 1994; Ashford and Locker, "Tennessee," p. 210.

13. *Memphis Commercial Appeal*, November 5, 1994.

14. Ibid., September 7, October 18, November 3, 1994.

15. *Knoxville News-Sentinel,* November 10, 1994.

16. Michael Barone and Grant Ujifusa, *The Almanac of American Politics 2000* (Washington, D.C.: National Journal, 1999), p. 1634.

17. *Washington Times,* December 6, 30, 1996.

18. *Chattanooga Free Press,* October 27, 1996; *Arkansas Democrat-Gazette,* November 7, 1996; *Washington Times,* November 8, 1996.

19. *Chattanooga Free Press,* October 27, November 4, 1996; *Arkansas Democratic Gazette,* November 1, 1996.

20. *Arkansas Democrat Gazette,* November 1, 6, 1996.

21. Ibid., November 7, 10, 1996; *Memphis Commercial Appeal,* November 6, 1996; *Washington Times,* December 30, 1996.

22. *Virginian-Pilot,* November 3, 1996.

23. Margaret Edds and Thomas R. Morris, "Virginia: Republicans Surge in the Competitive Dominion," in Lamis, *Southern Politics in the 1990s,* p. 155; *Washington Post,* November 4, 1996.

24. *Washington Post,* November 6, 1996.

25. *Greensboro News and Record,* November 4, 1998; *Raleigh News and Observer,* November 2, 1998.

26. *New York Times,* October 25, 1998; *Raleigh News and Observer,* November 2–4, 1998.

27. Barone and Ujifusa, *Almanac of American Politics 2000,* p. 140.

10. THE DEEP SOUTH CHALLENGE

1. *Atlanta Constitution,* November 19, 1992.

2. *Washington Post,* October 31, 1992; *New York Times,* October 30, 1992.

3. *New York Times,* October 30, 1992.

4. Richard F. Fenno Jr., *Senators on the Campaign Trail* (Norman: University of Oklahoma Press, 1996), pp. 163–164, 172–175, 186.

5. Ibid., pp. 173, 181.

6. Ibid., pp. 177–178, 187.

7. *Atlanta Journal and Constitution,* November 28, 1992.

8. *Washington Post,* November 18, 1992; *Atlanta Constitution,* November 26, 1992.

9. *Washington Post,* November 18, 1992; *Atlanta Constitution,* November 6, 1992.

10. *Atlanta Constitution,* November 12, 19, 1992.

11. Ibid., November 19, 1992.

12. Ibid.; *Washington Post,* November 18, 1992.

13. *Washington Post,* November 25, 1992.

14. *Atlanta Constitution,* November 26, 29, 1992.

15. *Time,* November 21, 1988; *Washington Post,* November 1, 1988; *New York Times,* October 21, 1988.

16. Philip D. Duncan and Christine C. Lawrence, *Congressional Quarterly's Politics in America 1996* (Washington, D.C., 1995), p. 722.

17. Michael Barone and Grant Ujifusa, *The Almanac of American Politics 1998* (Washington, D.C.: National Journal, 1997), p. 804.

18. *New York Times,* November 18, 1997.

19. *Roll Call,* November 10, 1994; *Boston Globe,* January 20, 1995.

20. *Birmingham News,* September 10, 1995.

21. Barone and Ujifusa, *Almanac of American Politics 2000,* p. 900.

22. *Washington Post,* October 11, 1996.

23. Ibid.; *The Times* (London), October 11, 1996; *Atlanta Constitution,* October 13, 1996.

24. *Washington Post,* October 11, 1996.

25. *Atlanta Constitution,* October 13, 1996; *Houston Chronicle,* October 22, 1996; *St. Petersburg Times,* October 23, 1996; *New York Times,* October 24, 1996.

26. *Washington Post,* October 11, 1996; *New York Times,* October 24, 1996.

27. *Atlanta Journal Constitution,* November 6, 1996; *New York Times,* October 24, 1996.

28. *Washington Post,* August 26, 1996; *Chattanooga Free Press,* October 9, 1996.

29. *Chattanooga Free Press,* October 9, 1996; *Washington Times,* October 14, 1996.

30. *Washington Post,* August 26, 1996; *Washington Times,* October 14, 1996.

31. *Washington Post,* August 26, 1996; *Washington Times,* October 14, 1996.

32. *Atlanta Constitution,* October 27, 1996; *Washington Post,* October 18, 1996.

33. *Atlanta Constitution,* August 7, 1996; *Chattanooga Times,* August 7, 1996; Paige Schneider, "The Impact of the Christian Right on Republican Party Development in the South" (Ph.D. diss., Emory University, 2000).

34. *Atlanta Constitution,* August 7, 11, 1996; *Washington Post,* October 18, 1996.

35. *Atlanta Constitution,* September 15, 1996.

36. *Washington Post,* October 18, 1996.

37. *Florida Times-Union,* September 29, 1996.

38. *New Orleans Times-Picayune,* November 5, 1996; *Baton Rouge Advocate,* November 6, 1996.

39. *Baton Rouge Advocate,* November 3, 1996.

40. Ibid., October 25 and November 3, 15, 1996.

41. For an analysis of the Landrieu-Jenkins election, see Edward F. Renwick, T. Wayne Parent, and Jack Wardlow, "Louisiana: Still *Sui Generis* like Huey," in *Southern Politics in the 1990s,* ed. Alexander P. Lamis (Baton Rouge: Louisiana State University Press, 1999), pp. 296–300.

42. *Atlanta Constitution,* November 4, 1998.

43. *The Hill,* September 24, 1997; *Montgomery Advertiser,* March 11, 1998; *Huntsville Times,* June 23, 1998.

44. *Atlanta Constitution,* November 10, 1994; *Roll Call,* October 12, 1998.

45. *Atlanta Constitution,* October 24, 1998.

46. *De Kalb* (Ga.) *Neighbor,* May 28, 1997; and April 29, 1998.

47. *Washington Post,* August 30, 1998; *Atlanta Constitution,* October 24, 1998.

48. *Washington Post,* August 30, 1998.

49. *Washington Times,* September 11, 1998; *Raleigh News and Observer,* October 31, 1998.

50. *Roll Call,* October 28, 1998; *The Hill,* October 28, 1998.

51. *The Hill,* October 28, 1998; *Roll Call,* October 22, 1998.

52. *Raleigh News and Observer,* October 31, 1998; *Roll Call,* October 22, 1998; *Charleston Post and Courier,* October 21, 1998.

53. *Charleston Post and Courier,* October 25, 1998; *The Hill,* October 28, 1998; *Roll Call,* October 28, 1998.

54. *Charleston Post and Courier,* October 21, 1998.

55. Robert Sherrill, *Gothic Politics in the Deep South* (New York: Grossman, 1968), p. 212.

56. *Memphis Commercial Appeal,* November 10, 1994.

11. THE REPUBLICAN SURGE

1. *Wall Street Journal,* September 2, 1986.

2. Earl Black and Merle Black, *The Vital South: How Presidents Are Elected* (Cambridge, Mass.: Harvard University Press, 1992), p. 295.

3. There is an extensive literature on reapportionment and redistricting. See esp. Kimball Brace, Bernard Grofman, and Lisa Handley, "Does Redistricting Aimed to Help Blacks Necessarily Help Republicans?" *Journal of Politics* 49 (1987): 169–185; Bernard Grofman, ed., *Race and Redistricting in the 1990s* (New York: Agathon, 1998); David Lublin, *The Paradox of Representation* (Princeton: Princeton University Press, 1997); Chandler Davidson and Bernard Grofman, eds., *Quiet Revolution in the South* (Princeton: Princeton University Press, 1994); Carol M. Swain, *Black Faces, Black Interests* (Cambridge, Mass.: Harvard University Press, 1993); Kenny J. Whitby, *The Color of Representation* (Ann Arbor: University of Michigan Press, 1997); David T. Canon, *Race, Redistricting, and Representation* (Chicago: University of Chicago Press, 1999); J. Morgan Kousser, *Colorblind Injustice* (Chapel Hill: University of North Carolina Press, 1999); Charles S. Bullock III, "The Impact of Changing the Racial Composition of Congressional Districts on Legislators' Roll Call Behavior," *American Politics Quarterly* 23 (April 1995): 141–158; John R. Petrocik and Scott W. Desposato, "The Partisan Consequences of Majority-Minority Redistricting in the South, 1992 and 1994," *Journal of Politics* 60 (August 1998): 613–633; Kevin A. Hill,

"Does the Creation of Majority Black Districts Aid Republicans? An Analysis of the 1992 Congressional Elections in Eight Southern States," ibid., 57 (May 1995): 384–401; L. Marvin Overby and Kenneth M. Cosgrove, "Unintended Consequences? Racial Redistricting and the Representation of Minority Interests," ibid., 58 (May 1996): 540–550.

4. Reported in Michael Barone and Grant Ujifusa, *The Almanac of American Politics 1994* (Washington, D.C.: National Journal, 1993).

5. See Black and Black, *Vital South*, pp. 315–325.

6. Barone and Ujifusa, *Almanac of American Politics 1994*, p. 1209.

7. *Congressional Quarterly's Politics in America 1998* (Washington, D.C., 1997), pp. 1381, 1384; Michael Barone and Grant Ujifusa, *The Almanac of American Politics 1998* (Washington, D.C.: National Journal, 1997), p. 1389.

8. *Congressional Quarterly's Politics in America 1996* (Washington, D.C., 1995), p. 1388.

9. *U.S. News & World Report*, November 21, 1994.

10. *Congressional Quarterly Weekly Report*, April 23, 1994, pp. 951, 953.

11. *USA Today*, September 26, 1996; *Wall Street Journal*, September 2, 1986.

12. *USA Today*, September 26, 1996.

13. Ibid.

14. Barone and Ujifusa, *Almanac of American Politics 1994*, p. 339; *Congressional Quarterly Weekly Report*, October 22, 1994; and Richard F. Fenno Jr., *Congress at the Grassroots* (Chapel Hill: University of North Carolina Press, 2000), pp. 89–146.

12. COMPETITIVE SOUTH, COMPETITIVE AMERICA

1. Earl Black and Merle Black, *Politics and Society in the South* (Cambridge, Mass.: Harvard University Press, 1987); Numan V. Bartley, *The New South: 1945–1980* (Baton Rouge: Louisiana State University Press, 1995); Dewey W. Grantham, *The Life and Death of the Solid South* (Lexington: University Press of Kentucky, 1988); idem, *The South in Modern America* (New York: HarperCollins, 1994).

2. V. O. Key Jr., *Southern Politics in State and Nation* (New York: Knopf, 1949), p. 665.

3. See David R. Mayhew, *Party Loyalty among Congressmen* (Cambridge, Mass.: Harvard University Press, 1966).

4. W. Wayne Shannon, "Revolt in Washington: The South in Congress," in *The Changing Politics of the South*, ed. William C. Havard (Baton Rouge: Louisiana State University Press, 1972), pp. 637–687.

5. James M. Glaser analyzes Democratic efforts to build biracial coalitions in congressional elections in *Race, Campaign Politics, and the Realignment in the South* (New Haven: Yale University Press, 1996).

6. See Earl Black, "The Newest Southern Politics," *Journal of Politics* 60 (August 1998): 591–612.

7. See Edward R. Tufte's *Envisioning Information* (Cheshire, Conn.: Graphics Press, 1990) and *Visual Explanations* (Cheshire, Conn.: Graphics Press, 1997).

8. Richard F. Fenno Jr., *Home Style: House Members in Their Districts* (Boston: Little, Brown, 1978), pp. 8–18.

9. David W. Rohde, *Parties and Leaders in the Postreform House* (Chicago: University of Chicago Press, 1991).

10. James L. Sundquist, *Dynamics of the Party System,* rev. ed. (Washington, D.C.: Brookings Institution, 1983), pp. 262–268.

11. Rohde, *Parties and Leaders,* pp. 40–119.

12. David E. Price, *The Congressional Experience* (Boulder: Westview, 1992), p. 86.

13. See Shannon, "Revolt in Washington."

14. See William F. Connelly Jr. and John J. Pitney Jr., *Congress' Permanent Minority?* (Lanham, Md.: Rowman & Littlefield, 1994).

15. See Richard F. Fenno Jr., *Learning to Govern* (Washington, D.C.: Brookings Institution, 1997).

16. Price, *Congressional Experience,* p. 86.

17. These calculations are based on the results of the 2000 Census reported in the *Atlanta Journal-Constitution,* December 28, 2000.

INDEX

Abbitt, Watkins, 170, 195
Adams, Hoover, 104
Adamson, William, 50
Aderholt, Robert, 197
Affluent voters, 256–259
Alabama, 126–129, 296, 304–305, 308–309, 314–315
Alexander, Bill, 184
Alexander, Lamar, 327
Alger, Bruce, 65, 69
Allen, George, 99, 102, 292
Allen, Jim, 82, 127
Almanac of American Politics (Barone and Ujifusa), 345–346
Andrews, Glen, 147
Andrews, Mike, 184
Apple, R. W., Jr., 125
Applebome, Peter, 6, 104–106, 108–110
Archer, Bill, 192, 346
Arkansas, 111–112, 285–287, 291–292
Armey, Dick, 5–6, 8, 38, 186, 337–338, 388, 394–395
Arrington, Ted, 109
Ashford, Philip, 281, 282–283
Atkinson, Frank, 65, 101–102
Atwater, Lee, 73, 213
Ayres, Whit, 299, 302, 316

Bachus, Spencer, 197, 336, 355
Bailey, Josiah W., 32, 53
Baker, Howard H., 3, 64, 72, 93–94, 113, 281
Baker, Richard, 351
Baker, Tod, 224
Balz, Dan, 4–6, 239
Bandy, Lee, 319
Barden, Graham, 51
Barkley, Alben, 50
Barnes, Roy, 295, 320
Barone, Michael, 23–24, 305, 345–346
Barr, Bob, 356
Barth, Jay, 286–287
Bartley, Numan V., 127, 209, 211–212, 244, 257
Barton, Joe, 185
Bass, Hal, 285
Bass, Jack, 33, 115–116
Bass, Ross, 77, 93
Battlefield sectionalism, 14–20, 399–404
Bedford, Roger, 308–309
Bennett, Charles, 184
Bensel, Richard Franklin, 19
Bentsen, Lloyd, 26, 82, 92–93, 123, 136, 269, 280
Bevill, Tom, 184, 197
Beyle, Thad, 107
Bilbo, Theodore J., 46

Biracial districts, 146; New South, 143–144, 191, 194–195, 199–200; Old South, 143–144, 191, 195–196, 200–201

Bishop, Sanford, 334, 360, 389

Blackburn, Ben, 147, 161

Black contributions, 384–389

Blacks: as voters, 28–30, 82–83, 171, 244–249, 273–274, 370; and Senate elections, 98, 104, 115–118, 122–123; and biracial coalitions, 134; and House elections, 147, 374–382; as politicians, 331–332, 334, 389. *See also* Biracial districts; Racial divisions

Blakely, William, 90

Blanton, Ray, 94

Boggs, Hale, 161–162, 199

Boggs, Lindy, 199

Bond, Julian, 122

Bonier, David, 395

Bonilla, Henry, 365

Bonner, Herbert, 196

Booth, William, 311

Boozman, Fay, 291–292

Botsch, Robert, 264

Boucher, Rick, 194

Brady, John, 73

Breaux, John, 129, 136, 296, 314, 321

Brinkley, Jack, 175

Bryant, Winston, 285–286

Brock, Bill, 72, 94–96, 132, 146–147, 282

Broder, David, 215, 222, 277

Brooks, Overton, 165

Browder, Glen, 184, 353

Brown, Corrine, 334

Brown, George, 56–57

Brown, Herman, 56

Brownstein, Ronald, 5–6, 239

Broyhill, James, 146

Broyhill, Joel, 65, 69, 146

Broyhill, William, 111

Bryant, John, 184

Buchanan, John, 147–148

Buchanan, Pat, 233

Bullock, Charles, 310

Bumpers, Dale, 82–83, 112, 276, 291

Burke, Herbert, 146

Burleson, Omar, 180

Bush, George H. W., 27–28, 97, 328; 1988 presidential vote, 26, 330, 336, 339, 344–345, 347–348, 352–353, 356, 361, 370; 1970 Senate defeat, 92; congressional district, 147, 192, 202; and Reagan, 206, 218, 220–222; and moderates, 230

Bush, George W., 234, 399

Byrd, Harry F., 45, 51, 54, 98

Byrd, Harry F., Jr., 98–99, 271–272

Byrne, Leslie, 348

Byrnes, James R., 53

Calloway, Howard, 147

Campbell, Carroll, 213, 296–297, 355

Cannon, Lou, 211, 216–217

Caro, Robert A., 55, 57

Carr, Waggoner, 90

Carter, Dan T., 216–217

Carter, Jimmy, 94–95, 120, 211–214, 218–219, 230

Cavanaugh, John, 317

Chapman, Jim, 196

Cheney, Richard, 9

Chester, Lewis, 216

Chiles, Lawton, 82, 97–98

Cisneros, Henry, 212

Civil Rights Act, 75–77, 215

Clayton, Eva, 196, 334, 349

Cleland, Max, 123, 309–312, 321, 323

Clement, Frank, 93

Clements, William, 214

Clinton, Bill, 287; 1992 presidential campaign, 27, 220, 347; and health care reform, 28; and conservatives, 224, 231; and moderates, 230; and Gingrich, 232–234, 338, 398; senatorial attitudes toward, 290, 319; as Democratic liability, 284, 329–330, 354, 356, 361

Clinton, Hillary, 253

Close, Elliott Springs, 306–307

Clyburn, James, 199, 334

Cochran, Thad, 72, 130, 136, 295; and Lott, 7, 303–304; and Republican realignment, 34; and Senate campaigns, 118–119; 1996 election, 305

Cohodas, Nadine, 115–116

Coleman, Marshall, 284
Coleman, William C., 66
Coles, Michael, 315–316
Collins, James, 146
Collins, LeRoy, 96
Collins, Mac, 200, 240, 336, 356
Colmer, William, 157, 163, 176
Combest, Larry, 186, 192
Congress at the Grassroots (Fenno), 200
Connally, Tom, 51
Conservative Democrats, 67; decline of, 34–36, 326; advantages of, 81–82, 138, 142, 156–160, 162, 164–167, 377; in 1980s, 184–185
Conservative Republicans, 4, 36, 137, 224–229
Conservative white voters, 221–229
Cooley, Howard, 147
Cooper, Jim, 281–282
Core white Democrats, 241–247, 254–259, 261–263, 265–266, 274–275, 373
Core white Republicans, 241–247, 250–259, 261–263, 265–267, 274–275, 373
Coverdell, Paul, 126, 269–270, 294–295, 297, 299–302, 314–317
Cox, Eugene, 46, 51
Cramer, Bud, 197, 359
Cramer, William, 65, 97, 146–147
Crisp, Charles, 50

Daniel, Dan, 175
Daniel, Robert, 170, 195
Darden, Buddy, 184, 356
Daschle, Tom, 308
Davis, Dick, 99
Davis, Jim, 58–59
Davis, John W., 161
Davis, Tom, 348
Dawson, Michael, 218, 247–249
Deal, Nathan, 199
Deep South, 17; Senate campaigns in, 114–115, 130, 294–295, 320–323; 1960s and 1970s House elections in, 143–151, 159–168, 170–171; 1980s and 1990s House elections in, 196–201, 350–360
DeLay, Tom, 5–6, 8, 38, 346, 394–395

Dellums, Ron, 200
Democratic juggernaut, 40–41, 46–49, 52–57, 70–73, 78, 403
Demography of House districts, 143–148, 186, 331–335, 380–382
Denton, Jeremiah, 127–128, 130, 136
Derrick, Butler, 177, 179–180, 184
Deutsch, Peter, 192
Dewar, Helen, 300, 308
Dewey, Thomas, 207, 256
Diaz-Balart, Lincoln, 336
Dickenson, William, 147–148
Dirksen, Everett, 75
Doggett, Lloyd, 91–92
Dole, Robert, 7, 220, 224, 230, 233, 303
Donelan, Jim, 314
Dorn, William Jennings Bryan, 176
Douglas, Paul H., 50–51, 54
Dowdy, John, 303
Dowdy, Wayne, 119
Dukakis, Michael, 27, 220, 330
Duke, David, 129
Dulles, John Foster, 42
Duncan, John, 146–147
Dunn, Charles W., 211–212, 214

East, John, 111, 290
Eastland, Jim, 34, 51, 81, 117–118, 326
Eaves, John, Jr., 354
Eckhardt, Bob, 170
Economic class divisions, 5, 242, 244–250, 254–256, 373. *See also* Affluent voters; Middle-class voters; Working-class voters
Eddings, Jerelyn, 349
Edds, Margaret, 289
Edsall, Thomas, 104–108, 110, 237, 251–252, 280
Edwards, Jack, 147–148
Edwards, John, 111, 270, 290–291
Eisenhower, Dwight, 24–25, 61–66, 69–70, 165, 207–209, 257
Elections, 86–87, 130–137; with Democratic incumbents, 48–49, 66–67, 155–162, 181–185; open-seat, 48–49, 67–69, 84–85, 162–167, 185–186; with Repub-

Elections (*continued*)
lican incumbents, 69, 85–87, 167–171, 186–189
Ellender, Allen, 81, 129
Elliott, Carl, 161
English, Art, 285
Erdreich, Ben, 197, 336, 355
Ervin, Sam, 102, 110
Eskind, Jane, 94, 282
Espy, Mike, 186, 200, 332
Evans, Randy, 316
Evans, Rowland W., 51, 54, 97

Faircloth, Lauch, 111, 269, 276–280, 290–291
Falwell, Jerry, 215
Fascell, Dante, 192
Federal intervention on race relations, 28–29, 74–77, 81–83, 148–149, 171–172
Fenno, Richard F., Jr., 74, 86, 153–155, 200, 298–299, 385, 395
Fields, Cleo, 334
Fields, Jack, 170, 336
Filibuster, 74–76
Fisher, Richard, 281
Fite, Gilbert, 78
Flippo, Ronnie, 197
Florida, 96–98, 281, 292–293
Flynt, Jack, 58, 153–155, 200
Foley, Tom, 8, 398
Ford, Harold, 170, 332
Foskett, Ken, 310
Fowler, Wyche, 83, 125–126, 136, 269, 294, 296–302, 315
Franklin, Webb, 186–187
Frisby, Michael K., 109
Frist, Bill, 95, 268, 283–284, 292
Frost, Martin, 184, 194
Fulbright, J. William, 112
Furgurson, Ernest, 103

Galifanakis, Nick, 102–103
Gambrell, David, 120
Gantt, Harvey, 105–110, 287
Gardner, James, 147
Garner, John Nance, 49–50, 53, 55–56
Gaylord, Joseph, 353

Geiger, Kim, 55
Gender divisions, 5, 242, 251–256, 373. *See also* Women
Georgia, 6–7, 120–126, 294, 297–302, 309–312, 315–317
Gephardt, Richard, 8, 395
Gerald, J. Bates, 59
Gilliam, Dorothy, 215
Gingrich, Newt: and Republican House leadership, 5–9, 30–32, 38, 231–233, 315–316, 329, 337–338, 388, 394–398; and congressional races, 154–155, 171, 200, 351–352; and 1992 district, 197; and conservative whites, 224–225; and moderates, 230; and blacks, 248; and religious right, 250; and white men, 252, 259; and white women, 253, 259; and middle class, 261–262; and working class, 263; and Democratic attacks, 286, 308–309; and Republican successes, 302; and black contribution, 384–385
Goldwater, Barry: and black voters, 4, 25, 28–29; and white southerners, 33, 127; and civil rights, 76–77; and Democratic attacks, 92–93; 1964 campaign, 149–150; 1964 southern white vote, 205, 209–210; and Reagan, 217; ideology of, 225
Goldwater Republicanism: and race, 25, 28–29, 138–140, 171, 173, 209, 367; and Wallace, 149–150
Goode, Virgil, 13, 343, 357–359
Gordon, Bart, 338, 357
Gordon, Houston, 288
Gore, Al, 27, 94, 134, 136, 184, 221, 234, 270
Gore, Albert, 77, 93–94, 96
Graham, Bob, 83, 97–98, 136, 276, 290
Graham, Hugh D., 127, 209, 244
Graham, Lindsay, 180
Gramm, Phil, 72, 113, 136, 184, 269, 276; career of, 91–92; switch in parties, 185; support for, 287–288; and Coverdell, 315
Granger, Kay, 180
Grantham, Dewey W., 210–211, 219

Gray, William, 8
Great Depression, 12, 15, 19, 41–42, 56, 369, 400–402
Great White Switches, 4, 205–207
Green, John C., 214
Greenhaw, Wayne, 42
Griffin, Marvin, 120
Gugliotta, Guy, 282, 305–306
Gurney, Edward, 72, 96–98, 147
Guth, James L., 214

Hagan, Elliott, 161
Halberstam, David, 94–95
Hall, Ralph, 185, 338, 357
Hall, Sam, 196
Hammerschmidt, John Paul, 146
Hance, Kent, 192
Harris, Art, 123–124
Harris, Louis, 260–261
Harrison, Pat, 50
Hartnett, Tommy, 117, 296–297
Hastert, Dennis, 329, 398
Hastings, Alcee, 334
Hawkins, Paula, 97–99, 136
Hayes, Robin, 367
Heard, Alexander, 43, 58, 60–61, 153, 256–257, 260, 262, 264
Hebert, Edward, 176
Heflin, Howard, 128, 136, 308
Heflin, Tom, 46
Hefner, Bill, 184, 343, 367
Heineman, Fred, 346
Helms, Jesse, 72, 103–111, 113, 136, 269, 276–277, 287, 290–291
Hemphill, Robert, 160–161
Herlong, Sydney, 66
Hill, Lister, 126–127
Hilliard, Earl, 199, 334
Hispanic voters, 244–245, 249–250, 254
Hodgson, Godfrey, 216
Holland, Spessard, 81, 96–98
Hollings, Ernest, 81–82, 117, 296–297, 314, 317–319, 321
Holloway, Clyde, 186–187, 351
Hoover, Herbert, 15, 41–42, 127
House Democrats, 396–398
House party system, 374–379

House Republicans, 396–399
Huckabee, Mike, 225, 285–286
Humphrey, Hubert, 75–76, 210
Humphrey, Tom, 282
Hunt, Jim, 105
Hutchinson, Tim, 111–112, 270, 285–287
Hutchison, Kay Bailey, 93, 269, 280–281, 292
Hutto, Earl, 185, 347

Inglis, Bob, 117, 317–319, 355
Inner Club, 54
Isakson, Johnny, 310, 315

Jackson, Jesse, 226, 233
Jefferson, William, 199, 332
Jeffords, James, 9–11
Jenerett, John, 184
Jenkins, Bill, 194
Jenkins, Ed, 197, 199
Jenkins, Woody, 129–130, 312–314, 323
Jennings, Pat, 194
Jetton, Susan, 109
Johnson, Don, 356
Johnson, Eddie Bernice, 334
Johnson, LeRoy, 122
Johnson, Loch, 125
Johnson, Lyndon, 3, 72, 88, 142, 179, 268; career of, 51; and Senate Democrats, 54; and New Deal policies, 56–57; and civil rights, 75–77, 141, 209–210, 374; and Texas politics, 90, 92
Johnston, J. Bennett, 81–82, 123, 129–130, 312
Johnston, Olin D., 33, 115, 117
Jonas, Charles R., 65, 147, 195
Jones, G. Paul, Jr., 153–154
Jones, Jesse, 256
Jones, Robert, 161–162, 197
Jones, Walter, 196, 348
Jones, Walter, Jr., 348–349
Jordan, Everett, 102

Katznelson, Ira, 55
Kefauver, Estes, 93, 96
Kellstedt, Lyman A., 214
Kemp, Jack, 301

Kennedy, Edward, 129, 233, 308
Kennedy, John F., 72, 141
Key, V.O., Jr., 3, 17, 43, 58, 60, 244–245, 375
King, Martin Luther, Jr., 217
Kingston, Jack, 352
Krueger, Bob, 91, 280
Kryder, Daniel, 55
Kudlow, Larry, 233
Kuykendall, Dan, 146–147, 170

Labor unions, 55–56, 264–265
Lake, Celinda, 251–252
Lancaster, Martin, 349
Landrieu, Mary, 129, 312–314, 321, 323
Landrum, Phil, 161, 199
Lehman, William, 203
Leland, Mickey, 184
Lewinsky, Monica, 319
Lewis, John, 184, 232, 332, 384–385
Liberal Democrats, 4, 67, 159
Lincoln, Abraham, 13–14, 41
Lincoln, Blanche, 112, 291–292
Lincoln strategy, 13–16, 400–402
Livingston, Robert, 203, 329
Locker, Richard, 281–283
Long, Gillis, 161, 186
Long, Russell, 82–83, 129
Long, Speedy O., 161
Lott, Trent, 130, 295; and Republican House leadership, 7, 38, 119, 171, 285; and Democratic South, 40; and congressional races, 136; switch to Republican party, 163, 186, 269; and Reagan, 216; and 1994 Senate race, 302–304, 319–320
Louisiana, 129–130, 295–296, 312–314
Lubell, Samuel, 260
Lyons, Charlton, 165–166

Mack, Connie, 7, 97–98, 113, 276, 281, 292–293
MacKay, Buddy, 97, 186
Mackay, James, 161
Maddox, Lester, 120, 161
Mahon, George, 176–177, 192

Mann, Robert, 76
Maraniss, David, 232–233
Martin, James D., 126–127, 147, 195
Martin, Thomas, 50
Mathews, Harlan, 281
Matthews, Donald R., 42
Mattingly, Mack, 72, 123–126, 136, 295, 298, 320
McClellan, John, 81–82, 112
McCollum, Bill, 98, 293
McCormick, John, 162
McCrery, Jim, 186, 336
McDonald, Larry, 175
McGovern, George, 25, 103, 120, 211, 233
McKinney, Cynthia, 334
McMaster, Henry, 296
McMillan, Alex, 195
McMillan, John, 51, 176
McWherter, Ned, 281
Meek, Carrie, 194, 334
Metropolitan districts, 146, 192, 194–195, 236–237, 266
Michael, Robert, 230–231, 398
Middle-class voters, 5–7, 259–263
Milford, Dale, 194
Miller, Andrew, 101–102
Miller, Zell, 123, 126, 295, 310, 316, 320–321
Millner, Guy, 310–312, 323
Mills, Wilber, 157, 176
Minor, Bill, 352–353
Mississippi, 117–120, 302–305
Mitchell, George, 8, 95
Moderate Democrats, 4, 67, 159, 160–162, 172–184, 201–202
Moderate white voters, 229–237
Mondale, Walter, 26, 105, 219–220
Montgomery, Sonny, 164, 175, 200, 353
Moore, Henson, 129
Moore, Herman, 352
Morales, Victor, 288
Moreland, Laurence, 224
Morgan, John, 328
Morgan, Robert, 82, 110–111
Morial, Marc, 313

Morris, Thomas R., 289
Morrison, Jimmy, 161
Mowry, George W., 53
Myrick, Sue, 195

Nelson, Bill, 98, 185, 293
New Deal, 12
Nichols, Bill, 147–148, 175
Nixon, Richard: southern strategy of, 25, 120, 210–211, 217, 222; and Helms election, 103; and presidential votes, 122, 150, 165, 209; ideology of, 225; and moderates, 230, 233
North, Oliver, 99, 102, 284
North Carolina, 102–111, 276–280, 287, 290–291
Northern Democrats, 176–177, 391–395
Northern Republicans, 391–392, 394–395
Norwood, Charlie, 356
Novak, Robert, 51, 54, 97
Nunn, Sam, 81–82, 120–123, 298

Obenshain, Richard, 101
O'Neill, Tip, 396–398
Overby, Marvin, 124–125, 127

Page, Bruce, 216
Parker, Mike, 360, 365
Patman, Wright, 176, 196
Patterson, Liz, 355
Pepper, Claude, 96, 186
Perdue, Tom, 299
Peripheral South, 17; Senate campaigns in, 87–88, 112–113, 275–276, 293; 1960s and 1970s House elections in, 143–152, 159, 162–164, 168–170; 1980s and 1990s House elections in, 191–196, 343–350
Perot, Ross, 27, 220, 230, 233
Pickering, Chip, 200, 353–354
Pickett, Owen, 184, 357
Poage, Bob, 176
Poff, Richard, 63, 65, 146
Pogue, William, 157
Politics in America (*Congressional Quarterly*), 345–346
Potter, David, 52

Powell, Colin, 226
Presidential Republicanism, 24–28, 60–64, 174, 202–205, 207–211, 328–331, 335–339
Price, David, 184, 346, 393, 396
Price, Robert, 146
Pritchard, Jeter, 59
Prothro, James W., 42
Pryor, David, 8, 82–83, 112, 285

Quillen, Jimmy, 146–147, 194–196
Quinn, Richard, 237

Racial divisions, 3, 4–5, 28–30, 242–250, 254–256, 373, 374–391; demography of, 16–23, 143–148; and civil rights legislation, 52–55, 75–77, 83, 215–217; and Helms-Gantt race, 107–110; and white racial conservatism, 148–152, 172; and House redistricting, 204, 331–337. *See also* Biracial districts; Black voters
Rankin, John, 46
Rarick, John, 161
Ray, Richard, 336, 356
Rayburn, Sam, 41–42, 46, 50, 53–54, 70, 156, 179, 377
Reagan, Ronald: impact on South, 4, 25–26, 28–31, 39, 173–174, 367, 370; and southern congressional candidates, 91, 99, 105, 139, 202; popularity in South, 211–221, 230, 328, 330, 344, 361; ideology of, 225, 233, 393; and religious right, 266
Reagan realignment: significance of, 25–27, 205–207, 237–238, 370–373; and conservative whites, 36, 39, 211–224; impact on Senate elections, 320–321, 327; impact on House elections, 360–368
Reconstruction, 11
Reece, B. Carroll, 64, 196
Reed, Clarke, 84
Reeves, Richard, 215
Reid, T. R., 36
Religious divisions, 5, 227–229, 242, 250–251, 253–256, 373

Religious right, 8–9, 36–37, 214–215, 227–229, 250–251, 262, 265

Richards, Ann, 280

Riley, Robert, 353

Rivers, Mendel, 157, 176

Robb, Charles, 99, 102, 136, 284, 292

Robertson, Pat, 233

Robertson, Willis, 98–99

Robinson, Joseph, 50

Rodham, Hugh, 281

Roemer, Buddy, 186

Roman, Nancy E., 285, 309

Roosevelt, Franklin, 15, 50, 56, 207, 211, 256

Rose, Douglas D., 129

Rosen, James, 317

Ros-Lehtinen, Ileana, 186–187, 336

Rovere, Richard, 139–140

Rural districts, 17–18, 23, 236–237

Rural voters, 266–267

Russell, Richard, 50–51, 53, 75–76, 78–79, 81–82, 120, 122–123

Rutherford, Skip, 285

Sack, Kevin, 290, 307

Sanders, Barefoot, 91

Sanders, Carl, 120

Sandlin, Max, 196

Sanford, Terry, 83, 111, 136, 269, 276–280

Sasser, Jim, 8, 83, 95–96, 268–269, 282–284

Schneider, Paige, 310

Schram, Martin, 213

Schrock, Edward, 357

Scott, Robert, 334

Scott, William, 72, 101, 147

Sectionalism, 2, 8–9, 13–20, 391–399

Sellers, Richard, 296

Senate party system, 323–327

Sessions, Jeff, 128, 270, 308–309

Shelby, Richard, 136, 175, 269; career of, 128; switch to Republican party, 270, 304–305, 320, 326; 1992 reelection, 296; 1998 election, 314–315

Sherman, Mark, 294, 300

Shipp, Bill, 315–316

Shows, Ronnie, 360, 365

Shribman, David, 304, 328

Shuler, Marsha, 313

Sikes, Robert, 157

Simpson, Alan, 7, 119, 303

Sisisky, Norman, 170, 184, 195

Smathers, George, 96, 98

Smidt, Corwin, 214

Smith, Ellison D., 42–43, 46

Smith, Howard, 51, 99, 147

Snider, Charles, 218

Solid Democratic South, 11–12, 15, 42–49, 69–70, 369

South Carolina, 1–2, 115–117, 296–297, 305–308, 317–319

"Southern beginnings," 382–384

Southern congressional delegation, 11–13, 34–36, 382–390

Southern Democrats: as House leaders, 7–8, 50; as Senate leaders, 8, 50–51, 268; support for white supremacy, 32, 40–46, 52–53; impact on nation, 49–57, 176, 270–272, 329, 369, 403–404; and northern Democrats, 52–55, 176–177, 391, 393–394; use of filibusters, 52–55, 74–77; strength in 1950s, 66–70; ideology in 1950s, 67–70; assets in Senate elections, 78–83, 134–137; assets in 1960s and 1970s House elections, 138–143, 152–160, 162–167, 171–173; assets in 1980s House elections, 174–176, 180–185, 201–202; biracial strategy of, 210; as competitive minority party, 242; changing ideology of, 390–394

Southern demographic anatomy, 20–24

"Southern endings," 388–390

"Southern racial landscape," 384–388

Southern Republicans: impact on nation, 2–4, 37–38, 270–273, 329–330, 369–370, 399–404; as House leaders, 5–9, 30–32, 37–38, 394–398; as Senate leaders, 7, 269; need for white majorities, 28–30; weakness through 1950s, 57–60; 1950s congressional campaigns, 64–71; liabilities in Senate elections, 73–74, 83–87, 114–115, 133–137; and structure of Senate elections, 130–134, 321–323; liabilities in 1960s and 1970s House

Southern Republicans (*continued*)
elections, 138–141, 167–168, 171–173;
liabilities in 1980s House elections,
174–175, 180–181, 201–202; and structure of House elections, 187–189, 340–
343; party development strategy of,
206–207; white target of, 210; as competitive minority party, 237–240, 242;
ideology of, 238–240, 394–396; and
presidential landslide districts, 339;
promising situations for, 341, 345, 351,
364–368; less promising situations for,
341–343, 365–367; unpromising situa-
tions for, 343, 345, 351, 367; 1990s
congressional surge of, 370–373
Sparkman, John, 62, 82, 126, 128
Spence, Floyd, 148, 164, 199–200, 336
Spong, William, 99–101, 132
Spratt, John, 184, 200–201, 360, 364,
384–385
Stearns, Cliff, 186–187
Steed, Robert, 224
Stenholm, Charles, 177, 179–180, 184
Stennis, John, 51, 82–83, 117–119
Stephens, Robert, 161
Stevenson, Adlai, 62
Stone, Richard, 82, 97–98
Storey, John W., 227
Stuckey, W. S., 161
Suburbs, 6–7
Sundquist, James L., 58
Swing voters, 241–244

Taft, Robert A., 54
Tallon, Robin, 184
Talmadge, Herman, 49, 82, 120, 122–125,
130
Tanner, John, 184
Taylor, Charles, 187
Taylor, Gene, 359
Teague, Olin, 157, 176
Tennessee, 93–96, 268–269, 281–284,
288, 292
Texas, 23–24, 88–93, 280, 287–288, 292,
344–345
Thomas, Clarence, 298, 301
Thomas, Lindsay, 352

Thompkins, Warren, 215
Thompson, Bennie, 200
Thompson, Fletcher, 120–122, 147
Thompson, Fred, 94, 269–270, 281–282,
287–288
Thompson, Marilyn W., 33, 115–116
Thurmond, Strom: 1996 election, 1–2,
305–308; career of, 32–34, 72, 115–117,
136; and Republican Party, 86, 269,
295, 320; and Helms, 103–104; and
Cochran, 118; and Nixon, 150; and
Reagan, 216
Tillman, Benjamin Ryan, 44–45
Tower, John, 64, 72, 88–91, 113, 271
Trible, Paul, 99
Trimble, James, 146
Truman, Harry S, 46, 53, 207
Tufte, Edward, 384
Tuten, J. Russell, 161

Ujifusa, Grant, 23–24, 305, 345–346
Underwood, Oscar, 50
Urban districts. *See* Metropolitan districts
Utter, Glenn H., 227

Vandergriff, Tom, 186
Vandiver, Ernest, 120
Vinson, Carl, 160–161
Virginia, 98–102, 284, 288–289, 292
Von Drehle, David, 302
Voting Rights Act, 73, 76–77, 82–83, 98–
99, 104, 149; 1982 extension of, 34,
175–176; and southern Democrats,
142, 164; 1975 extension of, 172

Waggonner, Joe, 165–167
Walker, Prentiss, 81, 147, 164
Wallace, George C.: and protégés, 81,
122, 147; legacy of, 95, 106, 126; 1968
campaign, 149–151, 210; and Reagan,
217–218
Wampler, William, 64–65, 69, 146, 194
Wardlow, Jack, 312
Warner, John, 72, 269; career of, 101–102;
and incumbency, 113, 136, 276, 287;
and North, 284; Warner-Warner race,
288–289

Warner, Mark, 288–289

Warren, Earl, 65

Washington, Craig, 332

Watson, Albert, 147–148, 164, 199

Watt, Mel, 106–107, 334

Weisskopf, Michael, 232–233

Weltner, Charles, 161

West, John, 115

White districts, 144–146; New South, 143–144, 189–193, 197; Old South, 143–144, 189–191, 193–194, 197–199

White shares, 385–388

White voters, 24–25, 28–30, 83, 251–253, 273–275, 370–373; middle-class, 5–7, 261–262; affluent, 256–259; working-class, 263–265; metropolitan, 266; rural, 267

Whitten, Jamie, 157, 177–179, 180, 184, 197, 352–353

Wicker, Roger, 180, 353

Williams, Dick, 299

Willis, Edwin, 161

Winter, William, 119

Women: in black electorate, 248–249; in white electorate, 251, 253–254, 262, 265; and Georgia voters, 311–312. *See also* Gender divisions

Woodward, J. David, 211–212, 214

Wooten, Jim, 300

Working-class voters, 263–266

Worley, David, 352

Wright, Jim, 7, 159, 177, 179–180, 398

Yarborough, Ralph, 76–77, 92–93

Young, Andrew, 217, 334